Endangered Rivers and the Conservation Movement

Also by Tim Palmer:

Rivers of Pennsylvania
Stanislaus: The Struggle for a River
Youghiogheny: Appalachian River

Endangered Rivers and the Conservation Movement

Tim Palmer

QH
76
P35
1986

UNIVERSITY OF CALIFORNIA PRESS
Berkeley · Los Angeles · London

Photographs by Tim Palmer.

University of California Press
Berkeley and Los Angeles, California

University of California Press, Ltd.
London, England

© 1986 by
The Regents of the University of California

Library of Congress Cataloging-in-Publication Data

Palmer, Tim.
    Endangered rivers and the conservation movement.

    Includes index.
    1. Stream conservation—United States.   I. Title.
QH76.P35   1986   333.91′6216′0973   85-24710
ISBN 0-520-05714-7 (alk. paper)
ISBN 0-520-05715-5 (pbk. : alk. paper)

Printed in the United States of America

1 2 3 4 5 6 7 8 9

A project of the
River Conservation Fund,
Washington, D.C.

*To Bob McCullough, working to save his
rivers, and helping me at the start*

Contents

Preface

Walk the easy way, downhill, and sooner or later you will probably come to a river. Then look around at the high country. All of it drains to that low, wet divider of the valley. The river is the center of the land, the place where the waters, and much more, come together. Here is the home of wildlife, the route of explorers, and a recreation paradise. The word *river* is so symbolic that it is used in the titles of scores of novels having nothing to do with water flowing toward the sea.

To many people, rivers are the most extraordinary part of the land. Only fragments of our inheritance remain unexploited, but these streams are more valuable than ever.

People have worked to protect the rivers—to leave some of them the way they are—and this book is the story of those efforts.

Acknowledgments

All across the country there are people who enjoy rivers and work to protect their special streamside places. I want to thank these people for what they have done, and for sharing their experiences, their homes, their boats, and their scrapbooks with me.

Sometimes friends give encouragement that makes a difference a decade or two later, and for this I want to thank Peter Fletcher, Jim McClure, and Bob Butler. Without their enthusiasm for the Appalachian streams of Pennsylvania, I may never have looked so closely at rivers. Ernest Callenbach of the University of California Press supported the book in crucial ways, and Barbara Ras, Mary Anne Stewart, and Anne Canright of the Press made many improvements. Ronnie James typed the manuscript and noticed dozens of places in need of correcting. Printer Ed Grady, another rivers enthusiast, loaned me the use of his copy machines when he heard what this story was about.

Endangered Rivers is a project of the River Conservation Fund, a nonprofit group dedicated to the promotion of education, information, and research. The interest of Mason Walsh and George Taber led to a Richard King Mellon Foundation grant that made my work economically possible. Robert Scrivner's interest led to a grant from Laurance Rockefeller, who paid for the printing of the color photographs.

The entire manuscript was reviewed by Samuel Hays, Jerry Meral, Jeffrey Stine, and Brent Blackwelder, each drawing on a wealth of experience in conservation history, water development, and river protection. In

addition to excellent comments about content, Jerry Meral noted many
improvements to the wording of the text. Kathy Garrett read the final draft
and shared her encouragement throughout my writing of the book. Arthur
Davis reviewed and sharpened my original proposal, and read several chapters. Stanford Young read Chapter 6 and offered insight that comes only
from twenty years of river protection experience. His excellent report,
Stream Protection in the United States, includes the wild and scenic rivers
list that I used.

The staff of the American Rivers Conservation Council contributed
much information, and also their files, newsletters, address books, and
telephones. Special thanks go to Howard Brown, one of the first people
who agreed that I should write the book in 1976. He offered valuable
knowledge and sound advice on people to see. Pat Munoz, Christopher
Brown, Ron Vlaskamp, and Bill Painter (the first director) of the council all
shared their experience. Jeffrey Stine, a historian under contract to the
Army Corps of Engineers, offered information, fine perspectives, and a
valuable list of sources. Barbara Lekisch, the Sierra Club's librarian in San
Francisco, was very helpful. Martin Reuss, a historian at the chief of the
Army Corps of Engineers' office, provided reports found nowhere else and
agreed to let me use draft manuscripts from an informative series of publications that he is editing.

Endangered Rivers leans heavily on more than a hundred people who
took the time to talk to me. Most of these are listed as sources, and I want
to thank each individual. For various reasons, some people asked that their
names not be printed, and I have respected this request. I appreciated
important meetings and talks with former secretary of the interior Stewart
Udall, Congressman Robert Edgar, and wildlife biologist John Craighead.
Also Brent Blackwelder of the Environmental Policy Center; Chuck Hoffman of the River Conservation Fund; Ted Schad, who held several important jobs; John Kauffmann and Ted Swem, formerly of the National Park
Service; Richard Leonard of the Sierra Club; Robert Herbst and Guy Martin, formerly of the Carter administration; Gaylord Nelson of the Senate
and the Wilderness Society; Bob Teeters of the Army Corps of Engineers;
and Robert Broadbent, commissioner of the Bureau of Reclamation. Before I started the book, it was a privilege to discuss river protection with
Governor Tom McCall of Oregon and Congressman John Saylor of Pennsylvania.

The book draws from articles in magazines and newspapers, from government reports, and from books about conservation and water development. The major works are listed at the end of the book under Sources.

Excellent accounts of certain aspects of river conservation have been written by William Amos, Paul Brooks, David Brower, Bruce Brown, John Cassidy, John Graves, Verne Huser, John Kauffmann, George Laycock, Luna Leopold, James Nathan Miller, Roderick Nash, Anthony Netboy, Fred Powledge, Marc Reisner, Elmo Richardson, Richard Roos-Collins, Wallace Stegner, T. H. Watkins, and Gilbert White.

For places to stay while I worked on parts of the book, I want to thank Ray and Elaine Crissman, Art and Neen Davis, Randy and Marcia Hester, Ronnie James, Jim and Lois Palmer, André Pessis, Denny Piper, and Jim Prothero.

CHAPTER ONE

Rivers and Dams

Settlers drained swamps at Jamestown, Virginia, and ever since, the waters of America have been changed for people's use and economic gain. Projects grew from small reservoirs and ditches to dams taller than seventy-story skyscrapers and canals hundreds of miles long delivering water to desert cities. Fifty thousand large dams in the United States affect every major river outside Alaska but two — the Salmon and the Yellowstone.

Reservoirs have flooded the oldest known settlement in North America, the second-deepest canyon, the second most popular whitewater, the habitat of endangered species, one of the first national parks, tens of thousands of homes, rich farmland, desert canyons, and virgin forests. In building dams we have blocked the best runs of salmon and broken the oldest Indian treaty — one that George Washington signed.

For generations, the manipulation of flowing water seemed useful and good. Through water development, the West was settled. California farmland is irrigated to grow nearly one-quarter of the nation's food on what used to be drylands. The Ohio River is fitted with locks to serve more commerce than the Panama Canal. Twenty-six thousand miles of waterways are channeled for shipping, fifty-eight million acres are irrigated, thirty million kilowatts of hydroelectricity can be generated, and four hundred large dams lower the levels of floods. Our society, as we know it, cannot function without some of these water projects. People say that the places buried by reservoirs are simply one of the costs to be paid.

For other people, the damming of a river means landscape consumption worse than paved-over farms or strip-mined mountains. Flooding by a reservoir is seen as complete and permanent, the ultimate in change, leaving nothing of the past. When a dam is proposed, some people may gain but others will lose: landowners, the homes; farmers, the fields; fishermen, the pools and riffles hiding trout; canoeists, the rapids and water trails; wildlife watchers and hunters, the animals; historians, the sites and reminders of old importance. And the dams cause secondary effects that nobody wants: they block the migration of fish to spawning beds; they trap nutrients in a way that damages the streams, the estuaries, and even the commercial fisheries at sea; they pose safety risks. Dams are usually paid for by the taxpayers but sometimes benefit few people. So rivers have become a battleground for those who want to keep certain parts of the land the way they are, against those who want more water development.

River protection began in the first decade of this century and gained momentum, and important places were spared. In the 1960s, full-page advertisements in the *New York Times* warned the nation that the Grand Canyon needed saving from dams. The Oklawaha River and its swamps were partly dammed and dredged for a canal, but the project was halted to prevent the loss of Florida's groundwater. At the Delaware, conservationists and landowners stopped Tocks Island Dam, and Congress designated a national wild and scenic river instead. Dozens of waterways still flow free because thousands of people worked to save special places.

New proposals threaten other sites — hundreds of them — but developers face high costs and dubious gains in blocking the remaining sections of rivers. In Oklahoma, 70 percent of the benefits of a proposed federal project would go to one catfish farmer. Auburn Dam would cost $2.5 billion and flood forty-three miles of canyons to deliver subsidized water to farmers who are not yet using existing supplies. The most expensive project of all is the Tennessee-Tombigbee Waterway, requiring $4 billion to serve barges already floating on other rivers and to move goods already moved by railroads. The Garrison Diversion in North Dakota will take 220,000 acres out of agricultural production to irrigate 250,000.

Government water projects were originally meant to entice family farmers to the unsettled West, but many of the benefits now go to absentee agribusinesses and urban developers. Through taxes, easterners from economically depressed areas help to pay for federal projects that lure settlers to the booming Sun Belt. Billions will be spent on the Central Arizona Project serving Phoenix, and corporate farmers, including oil companies, enjoy subsidies of millions every year.

Dams become unsafe without maintenance, and even with it, reservoirs fill with silt that settles to the bottom of the lakes. Some have become brown quagmires after thirty years. Most reservoirs are designed for only a hundred years. What will become of the dams when they are white elephants? Who will pay the costs or live with the safety risks then?

Underlying many aspects of water development is a myth: the myth that we must always have more. Meeting needs is one thing, but recklessly subsidizing waste is another. For generations we have used water as though it were free: we wash sidewalks with it, grow rice in the desert, spend millions so that ocean-going vessels can reach Idaho, Oklahoma, and Minnesota. A toilet (invented in Shakespeare's time) uses four gallons per flush when one gallon would do. Up to four thousand gallons of water is used to put one pound of beef on the table. The nation's tallest fountain, three hundred feet high, decorates an Arizona subdivision within view of Yavapai Indians who were asked and pushed to give up the Verde River so that Phoenix could sprawl farther (the Indians did not yield).

Back when we were getting by on less Will Rogers said, "Everybody can get along on half of what they think they can." Vast amounts of water can be saved and today's supplies can be stretched far into the future. Eighty-one percent of the water consumed in America is for irrigation, and the General Accounting Office reported that 50 percent of irrigation supplies were wasted. New York City reduced its water use by 150 million gallons a day in 1980 through public information only. Marin County, California, cut its use by 75 percent. Ten-cent flow-reducers curb shower consumption — one of the big water spenders in the home — by one-third.

Other approaches that do not depend on costly dams have been mostly ignored. Floodplain management — reserving lowlands for uses, such as farming and parks, that do not incur heavy damage — can be cheaper than building dams to catch floodwater. The Army Corps of Engineers recommended an economic nonstructural approach — buying the floodplain — for the South Fork of the Platte River in Colorado. Billions are spent on barge canals without consideration for total transportation planning, and expanded locks and channelization in the Mississippi may lead to bankrupt railroads that could require subsidies from the same government that built the competing barge route. Free river recreation is eliminated at great cost by dams that are justified in the name of flatwater recreation.

Changes in water policies have been proposed to embrace traditional values: cut waste, build only economic projects, require people who benefit to pay the costs, recognize the value of natural rivers as homelands and as places for escape and recreation. Federal agencies attempted to reform water policies under President Carter. The Reagan administration continued some of the reforms but dropped river protection programs.

While budgets for other domestic agencies were cut to the bone, a 25

percent increase was handed to the Bureau of Reclamation—the largest
dam builder in the West. More than 450 new projects are authorized for
construction by the Army Corps of Engineers. Private hydroelectric developers are encouraged by the Public Utility Regulatory Policies Act of 1978,
causing permit applications for new hydropower facilities to jump from 18
in 1978 to 1,859 in 1981. By 1983, more than six thousand applications for
dams were on file. In California alone, six hundred applications were filed
between 1978 and 1983, including a proposal to dam the Tuolumne—the
river where protection efforts began eighty years ago when John Muir tried
to save Hetch Hetchy Valley.

Except for Chapter 3, *Endangered Rivers* is about people protecting rivers.
Readers who want to learn more about water development face no difficult
search. Dozens of books accept the wisdom of "harnessing the rivers" and
tell about the Tennessee Valley Authority "working wonders" in Appalachia, the Bureau of Reclamation creating "gardens in the desert," and the
Army Corps of Engineers "taming the raging floods." Other books acclaim
the wildlife, beauty, and recreation along rivers but do not cover the threats
from development. Whereas many excellent articles and a few books relate
the stories of certain streams, the larger story of river protection has not
been told. Much of *Endangered Rivers* focuses on the fights against dams,
because they completely destroy their sections of rivers and valleys. I have
stressed the changing attitudes about rivers. The control of water pollution
and the management of recreation and riverfront land deserve entire vol-
umes of their own.

PORTRAITS

There is a certain feeling and knowledge that comes only from seeing a
place—only from being there—but pictures may be the best substitute.
River photographs in the illustration section following page 16 appear in
roughly the order the rivers are discussed in the book. A few of the scenes
have recently been dammed and will never be seen again. Several others
show places where river conservationists won important struggles, at least
for now. Many of the pictures are of rivers that remain threatened.

CHAPTER TWO

A Delicate Balance

Three and a half million miles of rivers and streams have penetrated every part of the country, and they affect the lives of people in countless ways. The water shapes the land. The topography in a place like West Virginia seems chaotic but is the result of a simple rule — water runs downhill and carries soil with it. Because of this, the landscape drops an average of one foot in ten thousand years, and some places erode much faster.

The rivers and land share a partnership: mountains and landforms determine the routes of rivers, then the rivers further mold the land. Flooding shows this give-and-take. With rain and runoff, streams swell until the banks are full. In canyons, rivers carve deeper because they cannot spread out, but most valleys have floodplains — flat areas just above the banks. Here the river overflows, and silt in the muddy water settles to the ground to build terraces that grow higher — sometimes two inches — during each flood. In this way rivers fertilize the fields by bringing rich soil from many square miles and concentrating it at one workable place. Floodplains are temporary storage reservoirs, lowering downstream floods. While ponded, water soaks through the soil to underground reservoirs that can be pumped out later or that seep slowly back to the river and add to its flow during dry seasons.

Wet, fertile, and next to the water, floodplains are ideal for wildlife, for trees, and for some kinds of farming. In most ways, the plains are ideal for towns, roads, and railroads — the land is flat and next to the river, which was often a transportation artery. But when people build along the river, they compete directly with it, and sooner or later they are hit with high water.

The soil that is added to the floodplain comes from up above. It washes loose with sheet erosion from places without plants, such as strip mines or plowed fields. Other soil comes from riverbanks where the current cuts on the outside of bends. Forty-foot widths of floodplain have vanished in one night, sliced like butter by the Mississippi or the Yukon.

Water is always working, reorganizing the land. Rivers follow paths of least resistance, cutting first through soft rock. If there isn't any, the water carves slowly like a sculptor, creating smooth, rounded forms. Even in flat valleys without hills or bedrock to guide the flow, the river veers back and forth, rarely flowing straight for more than ten times its width.[1] Abandoned channels where the current used to run can be seen in swales behind banks, in swamps, and in oxbow lakes along flatland streams. If left alone, the river will someday return to these old channels, each time wearing a deeper path. Eroded soil eventually reaches the ocean and forms a delta. Forty tons of soil per hour are delivered to the delta of the Mississippi.

Three kinds of rapids form in the river: Outcrops of bedrock block the flow, holding back water before it drops over the ledges. At landslides, boulders clog the channel and make whitewater. But the most common rapid is where water runs over gravel bars, often at the mouths of streams. Where tributaries meet the river, their speed is checked, and rocks that had been washed down from the mountains pile up and form bars. Young rivers are full of these ledges, boulders, and bars that cause steep drops, then pools, then steep drops again. The rocks causing the rapids eventually wear away, leaving the steady gradient of ancient streams.

Steep pitches of a river are rocky because the fast water rolls smaller and lighter stones away. As the current slows down it sorts the rocks by dropping the largest first and smallest last. Rocks as big as watermelons might lie in a riffle at the upstream end of an island. Farther down, the river drops cobbles, gravel, pebbles, sand, and fine silt at the lowest point, where channels from either side of the island meet and eddy into a quiet pool.

Gradient causes the river to churn, to hiss onto sandy beaches, to boil into holes, and to pile up in haystack waves. During floods the river clatters, rolling stones down its bed, and it rattles the brush. The river pounds over falls, then as a gentle force it is almost unheard.

LIVING WITH THE RIVER

Entire communities of plants and animals depend on the streams. Floodplain forests need water and alluvial soil that is washed in. Stands of silver maple in the East, cypress in the South, cottonwood on the Plains, and cedar in the Northwest grow at the water's edge. Hemlocks throw shade over Appalachian trout pools, blocking summer heat.

The sycamore is tailored to the riverfront. Roots of most other trees die if soaked in water for more than a few days, but the sycamore thrives, shading the stream while miles of roots tie the loose-knit soil together and hold it. Other trees suffocate if dirt is piled around their trunks, but the sycamore keeps growing even with three feet of fresh flood-deposited gravel. After a century, when a sycamore finally dies, its usefulness is not over. The wood resists rot and lies as a "sweeper" — shelter that lasts for many generations of fish. Wild rice, cattails, arrowhead, and hundreds of plants grow as forage. Royal ferns in the Appalachians have a special adaptation: their fronds are on foot-long stalks reaching above the high-water surges of summertime.

The water's edge is the most important place for wildlife. Raccoons eat crayfish, and grizzly bears eat salmon. The river is the only home for many animals. Otters are fast swimmers and are playful, sliding down mud banks, wrestling, and balancing stones on their noses. Some fishermen shoot the furbearers, thinking that they kill trout, but research shows them eating suckers, mudminnows, sticklebacks, and other slow forage fish. Before 1800, otters lived in rivers all over the country except in the Southwest, but because of shooting, trapping, pollution, habitat loss, channelization, and dams they survive only in wild pockets of their old range.

More than half of the American bird species nest near waterways. Sandpipers and yellowlegs eat insects just above the waterline. The water ouzel or dipper walks underwater to catch insects at rapids. Flaps seal each nostril from the water, a nictitating membrane or specialized eyelid works like a windshield wiper, and a preen gland secreting waterproof oil is ten times the size found in other perching birds. The heron has stilt legs so that it can wade in the shallows and spear minnows, frogs, salamanders, and snakes. The kingfisher snatches minnows and rattles its call as it flies to another limb over the water. With sticks, the osprey builds a nest that grows larger each year in the top of a dead tree. This hawk dives from a hundred feet to catch fish with its inch-long talons. Thirty-four kinds of American ducks live on freshwater. Mallards, wood ducks, pintails, and teals are dabblers, usually swimming near shore and poking their heads underwater to snap up food. Some other ducks are divers: the sleek merganser swims underwater for fish, frogs, insects, and crayfish. Mergansers are so bad tasting that hunters ignore them.

The streams teem with life, including thousands of species of insects. Five hundred kinds of mayflies are a favorite feed of trout. Riffles are high in oxygen needed by the caddisfly, whose larva covers itself with sand, glued together as armor against the current. The water scorpion breathes through snorkels, the water boatman rows with legs like oars, the water strider walks on water, its legs covered with waxy hairs. Warm shallows house minnows, frogs, and turtles. Deep pools hide trout and large fish.[2]

Algae are basic to the chain of life. Brown and slimy on rocks or green like seaweed, these plants collect nutrients and are later broken down by bacteria and fungi. Insects and clams are primary consumers that sift out algae and organic particles and convert plants to animal tissue. Secondary consumers are dragonflies, hellgrammites, and minnows. They eat smaller creatures, then are eaten by larger ones. Mature fish hunt higher on the food chain, and on top are the animals eaten by no one: the kingfisher, merganser, osprey, otter, and people.

Fish are divided into warm-water and cold-water species. Trout, salmon, pike, and muskellunge live in the cold water of the north and the mountains. If water temperatures climb above seventy-seven degrees Fahrenheit for more than a few days, trout die. Bass, sunfish, and perch live in the warm water of southern streams. Some warm-water fish can flourish where nutrients are high from silt, farm waste, or sewage.[3] These are suckers, catfish, and carp, sometimes called trash fish. Carp can live with hundred-degree temperatures and are found even at the hot-water outlets of power plants.

It is a delicate balance that keeps the river creatures alive. Pesticides from farms flow into streams, where they are absorbed by insects, which are eaten by minnows. The eggs of many eagles and osprey were too weak for their young's survival because of DDT. Since DDT was banned from everyday use the osprey have begun to recover. Toxic wastes such as mercury contaminate fish that people eat. By volume, sediment is the largest pollutant; logging, plowing, and earth moving speed erosion far past the natural amount. The average cultivated acre in Pennsylvania loses twelve tons of soil a year. Raw sewage with coliform bacteria is consumed by microorganisms that use oxygen, leaving little for fish. Acid drainage from coal mines has killed the fish in eleven thousand miles of streams, and the poison discharges — often incorrectable — may last for hundreds of years. Acid rain from air pollution threatens streams and lakes of entire regions, especially in the Northeast.

When a stream is channelized it is straightened and dug to a uniform depth, causing water to run faster but destroying the habitat, increasing erosion, and aggravating downstream flooding. Levees protect local areas but cause worse floods downstream by speeding the flow and by eliminating the temporary reservoir of the floodplain.

But the most complete and permanent destruction of a river is by a dam. The rapids, streamside plants, and valley landscape are flooded. The current stops and the chemistry and temperature of the water change. Deep water blocks sunlight and stops the growth of bacteria and other building blocks in the food chain. Creatures needing the current to deliver food have nothing to eat.

Many fish need spawning beds of gravel that are washed and cleaned only by the current. Riffles are needed to bring fresh oxygen to fish eggs and to the larvae of mayflies, stoneflies, and other fish-feed, so all of these disappear. Nutrients may not hurt the river, but when the flow is stopped and the sun warms the reservoir's surface, eutrophication begins — an overfertilization when algae, including toxic blue-green species, bloom and stifle other life. Then the algae die and their rotting consumes oxygen and allows fungi, bacteria, sludge worms, and other anaerobic life to thrive. At reservoirs, cold-water and game fish are often replaced with warm-water species and carp. Eventually silt accumulates on the floor of the reservoir, suffocating life that might have survived until then. Few plants grow at the edge of the reservoir because the water level is constantly raised and lowered.[4]

As the buffalo were to the plains, salmon were to the Northwest. Indians, settlers, and wildlife lived on them. They made a cash economy unnecessary. To spawn, seven species of salmon plus steelhead trout, shad, blueback herring, and other anadromous fishes migrate from the seas up the rivers, sometimes twelve hundred miles. Now dams block their paths. Salmon are eliminated from almost every river in the Northeast, and two-thirds of the spawning grounds in the Columbia basin are plugged. Fish ladders allow some salmon and steelhead to climb over some dams, but many fish die. Those that survive the hazards reach the headwaters and spawn, but when the young run back to sea, up to 80 percent are lost in fields — dead ends of unscreened irrigation ditches. Nitrogen gas, concentrated from the air as water falls over the spillways of dams, dissolves into a supersaturation and blinds, cripples, or kills fish by the millions on the Columbia and Snake rivers.[5] Spillway deflectors that change the way the water flows over the dams have reduced the nitrogen problem at some sites.[6] As they descend the river, 15 percent of the fish may be killed at each large dam.[7]

Today's salmon are only a token from past runs. On hundreds of streams above dams without ladders, no anadromous fish can return, and on other rivers, including the Salmon in Idaho, fish and game officials had to outlaw sport fishing for salmon because the runs shrank dangerously toward extinction. Now we are dependent on the costly plumbing of hatcheries, which often hurt the surviving wild salmon. In 1979 the Department of the Interior began studies to determine if the Columbia River salmon — once the world's most plentiful — should be added to the threatened or endangered species list. The Reagan administration dropped the effort, a spokesman saying that "enough conservation programs already exist."[8]

Estuaries depend on rivers. Chesapeake Bay, fed mainly by the Susquehanna River, once teemed with oysters, crabs, fish, and waterfowl. In the early 1900s hydroelectric dams on the lower river blocked the force of high water and the flow of spring ice that had scoured out the upper bay. Biologists think that this allowed an accumulation of silt that chokes water plants needed by ducks and geese, which survive only in a fraction of their earlier numbers.

Even the oceans are fed and fertilized by rivers. Silt and organic detritus carried to the sea by streams are the food of plankton, which produce up to 80 percent of the earth's oxygen. Commercial fisheries thrive on nutrients entering the ocean's Japanese Current from the rivers of the West Coast. When these are dammed, the silt and nutrients settle to the bottom of the reservoirs instead of flowing out to sea.[9]

MORE THAN RECREATION

Waterfronts are used for recreation more than any other part of the land. People find relief from urban pressures along the Chattahoochee in Atlanta, the Susquehanna in Harrisburg, and the American in Sacramento. Nature refreshes and replenishes, and nowhere can this be seen better than along a river, where rain and snow are always sending new water. To float in a canoe or raft is to be part of the river. The rivers are an alternative way to travel — a way to see a different part of the land.

Whitewater paddlers on the Youghiogheny in Pennsylvania increased from 5,000 in 1968 to 150,000 in 1983.[10] The rapids of California's South Fork American drew almost as many people. In Missouri 250,000 canoeists travel the Jacks Fork and Current rivers each year. Ohio's Mohican and California's Russian are jammed with canoes on weekends. The upper Delaware lures New Yorkers and Philadelphians to clear water and green shores. People look for escape and excitement; they want to be participants instead of spectators, and to return to nature. They find all of these things in river travel: in the challenge of paddling whitewater or in the peace of drifting on a quiet stream and camping on its shore.

People spend five hundred million days a year swimming in rivers, lakes, and oceans. Forty million people fish for sport,[11] spending three hundred million days a year. In a recent five-year period, canoe manufacturing increased fivefold. More than a million are in use. And much of the river activity goes beyond the idea of recreation as sport. To some people, rivers are a way of life, a source of food, a place to live. The two-car garage is one American dream, and Huck Finn is another. Fishing poles, campfires, and leaky rowboats have been replaced by television and video games for many, but who does not regret the loss of youth and wilderness on islands and riverbanks?

A CULTURE OF RIVERS

Rivers were highways and gardens for whole Indian nations. In 1854 Suquamish Chief Seattle said: "The rivers are our brothers. They quench our thirst. The rivers carry our canoes, and feed our children. If we sell you our land, you must remember, and teach your children, that the rivers are our brothers, and yours, and you must henceforth give the rivers the kindness you would give any brother."

The explorers followed river routes: Cartier up the St. Lawrence; La Salle, Marquette, and Joliet down the Mississippi; Brulé on the Susquehanna; John Wesley Powell through the Colorado's canyons. We can read books or visit museums, but by traveling the water routes we can see and do the same things that the explorers did. One hundred and fifty miles of Montana's upper Missouri River remain mostly untouched since the journey of Lewis and Clark.

River stories are as old as the nation: Thoreau's Merrimack, James Fenimore Cooper's Hudson, Mark Twain's Mississippi, Hemingway's Big Two Hearted, Steinbeck's Salinas, and Wendell Berry's Kentucky. The Platte is the setting of Michener's *Centennial,* the Kennebec of Kenneth Roberts's *Arundel,* the Missouri of A. B. Guthrie's *Big Sky,* the Skagit of Tom Robbins's *Another Roadside Attraction,* and the Yukon of John McPhee's *Coming into the Country.*

Since Cro-Magnon Man, people have loved riverfronts as places to live. Here they found food, drinking water, transportation, and fields for crops. Farmers still plow fertile plains along Virginia's Jackson and James, and along hundreds of other rivers. Ranchland along the upper Yellowstone deserves its name: Paradise Valley. The waterfront is still a community center at Millersburg, Pennsylvania, where the Susquehanna ferryboat docks. People celebrate river festivals in dozens of towns.

Lacking Europe's centuries of cities, generations of artists, and landmarks of architecture, much of the American culture was shaped by the powerful presence of nature. But when the land and the rivers are changed or disappear, what happens to the national character? When children need tickets to swim and when older people have no place to fish, has something of value been lost?

From the Susitna River in Alaska to the Flint in Georgia, dozens of rivers have distinct personalities but share one thing in common—proposed dams. Many of the free-flowing rivers could be converted to reservoirs for hydroelectricity, irrigation, or other uses, in the same ways that rivers have been developed since European settlers first stepped off the boat.

CHAPTER THREE

Changing the Flow of Water

The story of water development is not only an important volume in the environmental journal of America, but also a small-scale version of the history of the United States itself. Take away the manipulation of rivers, and someone would have to rewrite the books about this nation. Take away the canals, dams, and ditches, and the westward movement — that bustling, bloody, promising pilgrimage that continues even today — would be more like the rush to Siberia. The story of what we did to rivers is the story of migration, of meeting a growing nation's needs, of ingenuity in squeezing wealth from the land, of technology, of politics, of governmental growth, of disregard for the natural world, and of homogenization on the land — giving everyplace the promises and the looks of anyplace else.

At first clinging to the lush Atlantic Coast, settlers did not need much development of water, but the farther west they went, the greater the call for canals or dams. Routes to the frontier were by water, and the Army Corps of Engineers' first job on rivers was to clear trees and sandbars from the paths of the Ohio River steamboats in 1824. The Bureau of Reclamation was created to populate the West by selling subsidized water for whatever price farmers could afford. The frontier outlook was that the land should be settled and subdued at all costs, and this dictum applied equally to rivers. The waterways were thought to exist for people — for turning the desert green and establishing a civilization like that of the rainy East.

Water projects served growth of many kinds. Hydropower by Yankee go-getters brought the Industrial Revolution to New England. Dams reduced floods in low-lying towns after 1936. Without diversions from

SELECTED EVENTS IN CHAPTER 3

300 B.C. Hohokam Indians dug irrigation canals.

1623 Piscataqua River dammed.

1717 Levees built at New Orleans.

1718 Missionaries dug irrigation canals at San Antonio, Texas.

1750 First municipal water system built in Philadelphia.

1776 Vineyards irrigated at Mission San Diego de Alcala.

1789 Hadley Falls Dam built on Connecticut River.

1799 Army Corps of Engineers organized.

1823 Corps authorized to study Presque Isle Harbor.

1824 Congress appropriated money for the corps to work on Ohio River.

1829 Erie Canal built.

1832 Arkansas River used for irrigation in Colorado.

1834 Pennsylvania Canal built.

1837 Columbia River used for irrigation.

1838 Kennebec River dammed, salmon eliminated.

1842 Croton River dammed, water delivered to New York City.

1847 City Creek diverted for irrigation at Salt Lake City.

1850 Corps of Engineers authorized to study Mississippi flood control.

1862 Homestead Act passed.

1869 John Wesley Powell led first trip down Colorado River.

1878 Powell published *Report on the Lands of the Arid Region of the United States.*

1879 Mississippi River Commission formed.

1882 First hydroelectric plant built, on Fox River.

1884 Big Bear Valley dammed for water supply in southern California.

1893 California Debris Commission formed.

1896 First major hydroelectric plant built, at Niagara Falls.

1902 Newlands Reclamation Act passed.

1903 Reclamation Service built Theodore Roosevelt Dam.

1904 Imperial Valley flooded by faulty irrigation system.

1907 Los Angeles passed bond issue to build Owens Valley Aqueduct.

1908 Pittsburgh completed flood control plan. Inland Waterways Commission called for integrated water development.

1911 Reclamation Service built Jackson Lake Dam.

1912 Elwah River dammed.

1915 Miami Conservancy District formed.

1917 Flood Control Act authorized Corps of Engineers to study flood control and hydropower.

1922 Colorado River Basin Compact established.

1923 Reclamation Service changed to Bureau of Reclamation.

1925 Senate Document 308 authorized Corps of Engineers to study most large rivers.

1928 Boulder Canyon Project Act passed. Metropolitan Water District created for southern California.

1929 First Ohio River navigation system completed.

1932 Rock Island Dam was built on Columbia River.

1933 Tennessee Valley Authority created.

1935 Corps's first large dam authorized, for Tygart River.

1936 First major flood control act passed.

1938 Bonneville Dam built.

1939 Reclamation Project Act expanded Bureau of Reclamation responsibilities.

1941 Hoover (Boulder) Dam built. Colorado River Aqueduct built. Grand Coulee Dam built.

1944 Shasta Dam built by Bureau of Reclamation.

1956 Recreation authorized as reason to build dams.

1958 Corps's Southeast Basins Study expanded dam purposes.

1964 Glen Canyon Dam built.

1965 Water Resources Planning Act strengthened state roles and created Water Resources Council.

1966 Corps's international program announced.

1978 Public Utility Regulatory Policies Act encouraged small hydroelectric projects.

1983 Interior Secretary James Watt disbanded Water Resources Council.

distant basins, Los Angeles, Denver, and other cities could not have sprawled across so much land. With irrigation water, property values in parts of California soared 1,400 percent, and statewide, dams and ditches nurtured more than $12 billion worth of farm products in 1982.

Engineers achieved impressive feats of technology. Three times the yearly runoff of the Colorado River is trapped in two dams, each higher than seven hundred feet. Through dark tunnels bored beneath the Continental Divide, water streams to Denver. For southern California, the Feather River is dammed six hundred miles away and pumped over a mountain range three thousand feet high.

The government paid for much of the water development, and the costs were great. By 1971, $200 billion in 1958 dollars had been spent.[1] In the early 1980s the Army Corps of Engineers and the Bureau of Reclamation spent about $4 billion yearly. In 1983, a single dam in California is proposed at a cost of $2.2 billion.

The rearrangement of waterways grew in dimensions that are still expanding. More than twenty-six thousand miles of streams were dredged or dammed for barges. Thousands more miles were channelized to speed runoff, while four hundred large dams and thousands of small ones were built to slow runoff and control floods. Tens of thousands of miles of streams are flooded to make twelve million acres of reservoirs—about the size of New Hampshire and Vermont. Fifty interstate compacts or international treaties allocate water to competing users, sometimes leaving dry riverbeds and nothing for fish, wildlife, recreation, and Mexico.

The development of water broke down differences between places. It reduced high water from valleys infamous for floods, it opened access to wilderness, it allowed cities and farms to grow in the lands of roadrunners and rattlesnakes. Drylands in California were flooded for rice paddies as in Louisiana. Semiarid valleys were dotted with Holsteins as in Wisconsin. Instead of adapting to the environment, people bent the environment to meet the needs of a society in which one of the few absolutely understood goals was to make money. The Southwest that housed Indians, miners, and scattered cattlemen boomed with homes and industries in developments that could be carbon copies of suburban Atlanta. Golf courses, swimming pools, and sprawling subdivisions were fed by dams. Water—once an unequalizer between regions—was imported, allowing for a future that many people thought was unlimited.

THE FIRST CHANGES

Hohokam Indians along Arizona's Salt and Gila rivers dug canals to irrigate thousands of acres around 300 B.C.[2] Small dams were also built in New

Mexico's Rio Grande basin, but by the year 1400 the Hohokam were gone. Maybe salt accumulated in the irrigated soil, or maybe a thirty-year-long drought drove people away.[3] Through the rest of North America, Indians accepted the rivers for what they were — rich providers of life. They were not to be changed, and to the extent that rivers were problems, people adjusted their lives to fit: they got off the floodplain when the water came up.

For European emigrants, tampering with the flow of water became a cultural obsession, essential to what was planned. They started soon after landing. At Jamestown men dug ditches to drain runoff from their swampy, mosquito-infested site — one of the first places where the European conquest of America began. Wanting lumber for houses, pioneers built a log dam in 1623 on Maine's Piscataqua River to power a sawmill,[4] and in 1717 the first levee was built to save New Orleans from the Mississippi. A year later, Spanish missionaries at San Antonio, Texas, dug irrigation canals to water crops, and in 1776 they used Indian labor to lay ditches through San Diego vineyards.[5] A dam built by the Spanish at Santa Barbara, California, is the oldest standing dam in the country. In 1789, Hadley Falls Dam on the Connecticut River blocked three hundred miles of waterway from the spawning of salmon and shad.[6] In defiance of state law, developers built a dam in 1838 at Augusta, Maine, eliminating salmon from the entire Kennebec River basin.[7]

Most people were oblivious to the values of a free-flowing stream. Rivers were to be *used*. Around 1850 a writer praised the Hudson, but only for its commerce: "It would outrage one's sense of justice if that broad stream were to roll down to the ocean in mere idle majesty and beauty."[8]

TO TURN THE TAP

In 1750 America's first municipal water system delivered Schuylkill River supplies to Philadelphia, then the nation's largest city. Some of those wooden pipes are still used. Street washing was intended to curb yellow fever epidemics that had sent thousands fleeing to the country. People had taken water freely from wells or the river, and a Philadelphian predicted, "It will be some time before the citizens will be reconciled to *buy* their water." The first year's receipts were only $537, but in thirty years, New Orleans, Richmond, and St. Louis also had public supplies.[9] When Pittsburgh's system was built in 1827, homeowners dumped trash in wells, now the targets of urban archaeologists.

New Yorkers bought water by the pail from vendors pushing carts, but

Tuolumne River above Hetch Hetchy Reservoir, Yosemite National Park, California, now protected as a national wild and scenic river.

North Fork Flathead River below Polebridge, Montana, at the proposed Glacier View Reservoir site, now protected as a national wild and scenic river.

North Fork Flathead River below Camas Bridge, Montana, at the proposed Smoky Range Dam site, now protected as a national wild and scenic river.

Colorado River in the Grand Canyon, Arizona, below Bright Angel
Creek, near the proposed Bridge Canyon Reservoir site.

Green River at Echo Park, Dinosaur National Monument, Colorado,
where the Echo Park Reservoir was proposed.

Great Egret, Withlacoochee River, near the proposed Cross Florida Barge Canal.

Silver River, just above its confluence with the Oklawaha River, site of the proposed Cross Florida Barge Canal.

Canoeist on the Delaware River at Namanock Island, Pennsylvania and New Jersey, at the proposed Tocks Island Reservoir site, now protected as a national wild and scenic river.

Delaware River below Milford, Pennsylvania, at the proposed Tocks Island Reservoir site, now protected as a national wild and scenic river.

Verde River below Route 87, Arizona, at the proposed Orme
Reservoir site.

North Fork American River below Iowa Hill Bridge, California, at
the proposed Auburn Reservoir site.

Little Tennessee River above the Tellico River, Tennessee, photo taken in 1978. The site is now flooded by Tellico Dam.

Tuolumne River below the Clavey River, California, site of the
proposed Clavey—Wards Ferry dams project. The Tuolumne is now
protected as a national wild and scenic river.

Stanislaus River, the jumping rocks below Mother
Rapid, photo taken in 1980, now flooded by New
Melones Dam.

Stanislaus River below Grapevine Gulch, California, photo taken
in 1979. The site is now flooded by New Melones Dam.

Savannah River above Route 184, South Carolina and Georgia, photo taken in 1978 above Russell Dam, where construction is now completed.

Applegate River, Oregon, photo taken in 1977. The site is now flooded by Applegate Dam.

Middle Fork Flathead River above Route 2, Montana, at the proposed Spruce Park Dam site, now protected as a national wild and scenic river.

Selway River below Paradise, Idaho, a national wild and scenic river.

Youghiogheny River, recommended for national wild and scenic
river protection. Alders and ferns along the shoreline are upstream
of Ohiopyle, Pennsylvania.

North Fork Flathead River, Montana, a national wild and scenic river.

Salmon River, Idaho, a national wild and scenic river.

Middle Fork Eel River above the proposed Dos Rios Dam site, California, now protected as a national wild and scenic river.

South Fork American River, temporarily protected by state law
below Coloma, California, site of a proposed reservoir.

North Fork Stanislaus River near Utica Reservoir, California, photo
taken in 1980. The site is to be flooded by the North Fork Stanislaus
hydroelectric project.

Piney River above Piney Lake, Colorado, site of a proposed dam and diversion.

Dolores River below the town of Dolores, Colorado, photo taken in 1978. This section of river is now flooded by McPhee Dam, and lower sections are threatened by diversions for irrigation.

Atchafalaya River, Louisiana, site of proposed channelization
projects.

Yellowstone River in Paradise Valley, Montana, site of the proposed
Allenspur Reservoir.

Niobrara River below Valentine, Nebraska, site of the proposed
Norden Reservoir.

Kootenai River at Kootenai Falls, Montana, site of a proposed
hydroelectric dam.

Roy Breuklander, a rancher along the
Niobrara River, Nebraska, fighting the proposed
Norden Dam.

Trinity River below Livingston Dam, Texas, site of the proposed
Trinity River Barge Canal.

Whiterocks River, Utah, site of a proposed Whiterocks River dam,
a part of the Central Utah Project.

Cedar and fir trees along Big Beaver Creek, a Skagit River tributary, threatened in the 1970s by the proposed High Ross Dam, Washington.

Kickapoo River above Rockton, Wisconsin, at the
proposed LaFarge Reservoir site.

Middle Fork Snoqualmie River at a proposed Snoqualmie River
reservoir site, Washington.

Blackwater River in Canaan Valley, West Virginia, site of the
proposed Davis hydroelectric dam.

Clarks Fork (of the Yellowstone) River, above Route 292, Wyoming.
An irrigation dam is proposed at the bottom of the canyon, though
the river is recommended as a national wild and scenic river.

Gauley River, West Virginia, site of a proposed hydroelectric diversion.

after cholera epidemics in 1832 and 1834, and after firemen had to battle uncontrolled blazes with dynamite because water was so short, the city built a fifty-foot-high dam on the Croton River thirty miles away and in 1842 imported water through America's first large city aqueduct. Tadpoles were swept through the pipes, and New Yorkers had "dreadful apprehensions of breeding bullfrogs inwardly."[10]

Setting a pattern that lasts to this day, public water was wasted even when it was a novel luxury. In 1853 the Boston Water Board estimated that people squandered two-thirds of their supply in livery stables and in urinals and commodes that never quit flushing. People opened taps wide to prevent freezing in winter. Only seven years old, city reservoirs were almost dry, and inspectors sneaked around houses at night listening for running water, then warned people that their supplies would be cut off. But the main solution was to develop new sources that seemed unlimited.

Some of the Catskill Mountain streams ran to the Delaware River and on to Philadelphia, but New York officials dug new routes, diverting the water to their Hudson. They reduced the Neversink River to a trickle.[11] Called by author Marc Reisner "the most magnificent water system the world has ever seen," the New York City network included eighteen dams, three aqueducts, and a siphon tunnel built in 1912 deep beneath the Hudson River.

In the West, one of the first dams for city water was built in 1884 at Big Bear Valley to serve Redlands in southern California. Los Angeles developed local streams and groundwater sources that were adequate only through the 1800s.

FLOATING TO THE HEARTLAND

Canals may be the best known and most romanticized of early water developments.[12] From 1829 to 1889 the Erie Canal lay as a thoroughfare from New York to the Great Lakes and the Midwest, the only east-west water route south of the St. Lawrence. Freight costs from the lakes to the coast plummeted from $100 to $5 a ton, and the canal helped transform New York City from a second-class seaport to the dominant American city. In 1834 the Pennsylvania Canal was the first to cross the Appalachians, boats being portaged by railroad locomotives from the Juniata River and over the eastern continental divide. The Illinois Canal launched Chicago's growth in the mid-1800s. Four thousand miles of canals were built between 1815 and 1860. Eighty percent of the investments were paid off, but some routes were dismal failures. Before the Chesapeake and Ohio Canal was finished along the Potomac River from Washington to Cumberland, Maryland, the Baltimore and Ohio Railroad carried freight cheaper and faster. Today the canal's greatest use is by hikers, runners, and bicyclists.

On larger rivers with gentle gradients, flatboats and keelboats floated people and everything they owned. Pioneers trekked on the National Road across Pennsylvania's Appalachians, then drifted down the Monongahela River to the Ohio at Pittsburgh, then to the Mississippi. Steam power revolutionized river travel through the interior; Morgan Neville wrote with considerable hype about the steamboat in 1829: "The art of printing scarcely surpassed it in its beneficial consequences."[13] Private companies developed some rivers, such as the Monongahela where eight-foot-high dams were built in 1844. These were uneconomic and were destroyed during floods. By 1860 steamboats cruised the Ohio, Mississippi, Missouri, Arkansas, Red, Rio Grande, and Columbia rivers. Gold miners were later hauled up the Yukon on boats powered by cordwood.

GRINDSTONES AND TURBINES

While cities diverted streams for drinking water and navigation companies dug canals, easterners built dams to tap rivers that powered the Industrial Revolution. Through the use of falling water, Lowell, Massachusetts, and Patterson, New Jersey, became two of the first manufacturing towns in the early 1800s.

Most of the work involved in hydropower is done by the sun as it evaporates ocean water into water vapor that is then carried by wind to mountains where the air cools and drops rain or snow. All the power broker needed to do was to catch the water as it came falling home toward the sea, and divert the flow through a channel where waterwheels were geared to grindstones, sawblades, or other hardware. Storage dams were needed to yield a regular flow so that power could be delivered at people's whims, not nature's, and to create a "head" with a sudden drop where water fell with force.

In 1882 Thomas Edison built the world's first electric generating station in the heart of Manhattan, and only twenty-six days later, on the Fox River in Appleton, Wisconsin, the first hydroelectric plant was built to power 250 lightbulbs. At Niagara Falls, Westinghouse constructed the first major hydroelectric plant in 1896.

The basic hydroelectric system involves a reservoir for storage and a pipe to carry water from the top of the dam to its bottom, where it turns turbine blades. These turn a rotor — the moving part of an electric generator —

where coils of wire sweep past a stationary coil and make electricity. In large projects, engineers embellished the formula: they dug tunnels through mountains to dump one river into another, and they arranged whole groups of reservoirs to store and release water to canals, pipes, and turbines. In a sense, rivers were dismantled and then reassembled by pipe fitters. By 1900, 57 percent of the nation's electricity came from hydroelectric power, dropping to one-third through most of the first half of the twentieth century, when fossil fuels were used. Many of New England's eleven thousand existing dams are relics of the hydropower era at the turn of the century.

Hydroelectric dams on the lower Susquehanna, the Connecticut, and New England streams generated power for eastern cities but destroyed salmon, shad, and eels having high commercial value. When the salmon disappeared from the rivers of Maine, 433 laws about fisheries were on the books, but few were enforced. Having learned from the East, where salmon were almost extinct, the first legislature of the state of Washington required fish ladders with any dam, but in 1912 on the Elwah River, a power company illegally constructed an eighty-foot-high dam without ladders, and the law was changed to allow the building of hatcheries — many of them ineffective — instead of ladders. Seven more dams in Washington followed shortly after. The Columbia River, larger than all United States rivers except the Mississippi and the St. Lawrence, was blocked in 1932 when the Puget Sound Power and Light Company built Rock Island Dam.[14] Devastating impacts on the salmon came later with huge Columbia dams built in the 1940s.

RELIGIOUS COLONIES AND BROKEN DREAMS

Spanish priests watered grapes at the Mission San Diego de Alcalá in 1776, and other Spaniards diverted the streams of the Sierra Madre in southern California. In 1832 ditches carried water from Colorado's Arkansas River, and in 1837 Marcus Whitman took water from creeks to irrigate mission gardens near the Columbia. Mormons herded mules carrying barrels of irrigation water across the Utah desert,[15] and these industrious settlers wasted no time in pioneering irrigation on a large scale by diverting City Creek in 1847 to grow potatoes at Salt Lake City. By 1865 they had built a thousand miles of canals to water 1.5 million acres.[16]

The Homestead Act of 1862 lured droves of easterners to the West. Myth and fantasy were mustered against the great American desert beyond Kansas. Speculators and real estate sharks promised that rain would follow the farmers because of evaporation from plowed soil. Rain would follow the train because smoke particles would give water vapor something to cling to. Even Ferdinand V. Hayden, director of the federal government's Geological and Geographical Survey of the Territories, in 1867 stated, "The planting of ten or fifteen acres of forest-trees on each quarter-section will have a most important effect on the climate, equalizing and increasing the moisture and adding greatly to the fertility of the soil."[17] If only because God was on the settlers' side, rain would fall. Those who were lucky enough to claim stream frontage dug ditches and sometimes controlled the flow of water and the lives of later settlers in a system more like vassalage than rugged independence. Homesteaders plowed the plains and destroyed a wealth of rangeland, described by Conrad Richter in *The Sea of Grass*. In dry seasons the exposed soil blew away. Two out of three homesteaders failed for the simple reason that they were trying to settle a desert and a semiarid steppe. A hostile environment was blamed for the suffering and disappointment of the miserable program, despite the warnings of John Wesley Powell.

A legendary figure of the West, the one-armed Powell had led the first river trip down the Colorado River in 1869. His scientific expedition — the last great exploration within the continental United States — started with four boats and nine men and ended a thousand miles and three months later with two boats and five men.[18] Powell was the second director of the U.S. Geological Survey, and warned against indiscriminate settling of the dry-lands: "I think it would be almost a criminal act to go on as we are doing now, and allow thousands and hundreds of thousands of people to establish homes where they cannot maintain themselves."

In 1878 Powell published his *Report on the Lands of the Arid Region of the United States,* proposing that the government reserve dam sites from settlement and that irrigation districts be organized by people who would draw up a plan and apply for a federal survey. His gospel was simply that settlement should be planned. Otherwise, lack of water, homestead failures, and water monopolies would cripple the growth of the West. At an irrigation convention in 1893 Powell angrily said, "I wish to make it clear to you, there is not sufficient water to irrigate all the lands which could be irrigated, and only a small portion can be irrigated. . . . I tell you, gentlemen, you are piling up a heritage of conflict!"

Under Powell's direction, federal surveyors located sites for water projects, but speculators trailed the surveyors and filed for lands before they could be reserved. To save the program, the General Land Office temporarily closed public lands from claiming, but western congressmen fought any curb in the federal giveaway and killed the irrigation survey in 1890.[19] Powell quit four years later, but in 1902 many of his recommendations became law in the Newlands Reclamation Act.

Powell is curiously a hero of both dam builders and river runners. The Bureau of Reclamation credits him for their dam-building heritage; the reservoir behind Glen Canyon Dam is named Lake Powell. Whitewater boaters who hate Lake Powell regard the man with awe because he was the first to run the Colorado River. Yet Powell was set on damming and irrigating the West. He wrote that the flooding rivers were "wasting into the sea."[20] He championed federal involvement, but in a limited way. Regarding the building of projects, he cautioned, "I say to the Government: Hands off: Furnish the people with institutions of justice, and let them do the work for themselves."

The California Gold Rush spurred irrigation as farmers supplied mining camps with food. By 1890, 3.7 million acres in the West were watered,[21] but at the turn of the century 90 percent of private irrigation companies were in or near bankruptcy because their projects were uneconomic.[22] William F. Cody, alias Buffalo Bill, invested in one of these doomed schemes, later completed as the Shoshone Project by the federal government, which did not have to worry whether irrigation was economic or not.

In the bungling of private irrigation, the California Development Company stands in a class by itself. The company intended to profit from a rare geographical twist: the Colorado River, through silt deposited during floods, had formed a forty-foot-high dike between it and southern California's Imperial Valley, which lay below sea level. Gravity flow from the Colorado could water new farms in the valley if a canal were sliced through the natural dike, though, like an inland Holland, the valley sat precariously below the level of the river. The canal was dug, and when an intake channel silted up in 1904, the directors waited for more cash before fixing it. The Colorado burst through a malfunctioning gate, washed out the new farms, and created the Salton Sea, which is still there. The investors' solution was to declare bankruptcy. This fiasco and others fueled the support for federal water development.

In 1887 California had passed the Wright Act, allowing county groups to form water districts with governmental power to dam rivers. Plagued with corruption, most districts failed until the 1920s, when many small- and medium-sized projects were built.[23]

The same year that Powell resigned, the Carey Act offered one million acres of federal land to any state that would irrigate it, but eight years later only 7,640 acres were patented. The states did not want to pay for water development. Western cities, however, were different. They needed water and reached far from home to dam and divert the rivers.

INFANT EMPIRES

In the 1890s Los Angeles had already tapped its local supplies, which were dependent on fifteen inches of yearly rain (Boston has forty-three and Jacksonville fifty-three). After the 1903 and 1904 droughts, the city water chief, William Mulholland, saw that new sources must be captured if the city was to grow. He took a buckboard ride to the distant Owens Valley in 1904 and devised a plan to drain the eastern Sierra runoff to the city. Los Angeles agents secretly bought land and water rights, and a bond issue was passed in 1907 to fund a 238-mile-long aqueduct to divert the water south.[24]

This marked one of the largest municipal water projects, the introduction of complex schemes to bring water to western cities, and one of the most intense conflicts between local people and distant water users. During the same years, San Francisco planned to import water 150 miles from Yosemite National Park, sparking America's first great environmental debate.

The development of water had grown and accelerated since the pioneering settlers, but all of this was only preparatory; private developers lacked the capital, the authority, and the political solidarity to accomplish truly enormous changes on the land. The massive changes in the flow of rivers were caused by federal agencies, beginning with the army.

THE CORPS

With no visions of dams or canals, the Continental Congress, on June 16, 1775, authorized the hiring of a chief engineer and two assistants for General Washington's army of revolutionaries. Washington appointed Colonel Richard Gridley, who directed the building of fortifications at Bunker Hill, where he was wounded on his first day at work. This was the beginning of the Army Corps of Engineers, formally organized in 1799, reconstituted in 1802 to start West Point, and now the world's largest engineering organization.

The primary mission of the corps was to support the military, but its civil responsibilities shaped American life and landscapes. The corps administered Yellowstone Park before the National Park Service was formed, built the Alaskan Highway, and helped to develop the atomic bomb.[25] The maintenance and improvement of waterways for navigation became a corps job with an 1823 survey of Lake Erie's Presque Isle Harbor and with studies the next year to determine "the routes of such roads and canals . . . of national importance, in a commercial or military point of view." A role with rivers began in 1824, when Congress appropriated $74,000 for the corps to dig up sandbars in the Ohio River and tow dead trees away so steamboats would not crash as often.

The maintenance job soon included the Mississippi, and construction work began in 1830 with locks to bypass the Falls of the Ohio (a rapid) at Louisville. Between 1910 and 1929, forty-six dams and locks blocked every inch of the 981-mile-long Ohio, and ninety-one dams were built on tributaries. To store water for higher flows needed by barges during dry months, the corps's first large dam was authorized in 1935 for West Virginia's Tygart River.[26] After World War II, the Ohio and Mississippi channels were deepened, and locks and dams were enlarged in a process that still continues. By 1973 the Ohio River Project was consolidated to twenty-six dams. Strings of barges a thousand feet long can fit through many of the locks and travel the Ohio's length in less than a week.

Twenty-six thousand miles of commercially navigable waterways and locks at 265 sites (not counting the Great Lakes) have been developed, most of them by the corps, at a federal cost of over $10 billion. Main routes are the Mississippi, Ohio, Illinois, Missouri, Arkansas, Tennessee, Hudson, St. Lawrence, and Columbia. Navigation improvements dominated corps activities until the late 1930s, when flood control reservoirs became the main program, but in 1965 navigation again received the largest share of the budget.[27] Nine percent of domestic freight travels on inland waterways, including the Great Lakes' St. Lawrence Seaway. Oil and coal products account for 61.4 percent of goods; grains are the second-largest group.

IMPROVING THE ODDS AGAINST FLOODS

The corps's work in flood control began in 1850, when Congress authorized a survey of the Mississippi. Recognizing that some flood problems were too complex for single states, the federal government formed the Mississippi River Commission in 1879. For two decades, federal funds, often matched by local communities, were spent for levees. With the California Debris Commission in 1893 the corps developed plans to control silt that had resulted from hydraulic gold mining and that aggravated flooding. In 1917 a flood control act was passed authorizing further work on the Sacramento and Mississippi, but these jobs were not large, and they diverted little of the corps's attention from navigation.

The first plans for flood control dams were drawn by local groups. In 1908 the city of Pittsburgh wrote the pioneering American plan for trapping high water, then releasing it slowly to reduce downstream flooding. But the city's Flood Commission and its president, H. J. Heinz, sought federal help without success, and none of the dams was built.[28]

In 1913 the Miami River in Ohio flooded, killing 360 people, and two years later the Miami Conservancy District was formed to help in rebuilding the damaged towns. This led to a second group, the Miami Valley Flood Prevention Association, and it did not wait for federal aid. The association collected $2 million from twenty-three thousand subscribers to build five dams and to clear the river's channel through the cities. Landowners were assessed, bonds were sold, and the dams were built. As proof of the project's success, the association later refunded many of the contributions.

The Miami program is significant because it was privately organized and financed by direct beneficiaries, not taxpayers. It was also a milestone in hydrologic planning. Similar plans were followed on Colorado's Arkansas River at Pueblo and on New Mexico's Rio Grande near Albuquerque. But along the Muskingum in Ohio, local initiative and funding evaporated in the 1930s after the federal government stepped in. This, rather than the Miami experience, became the model for the future. In *The Flood Control Controversy,* Luna Leopold and Thomas Maddock concluded, "Where the damage is great and the benefits are real and recognizable, as in the case of the Miami Conservancy District, local communities can and will contribute a large portion of the cost of flood control facilities for their protection. If there is a federal subsidy, as shown in the Muskingum example, they will not."

Following a large flood on the Mississippi, the first major federal role in flood control began in 1928 when the corps expanded its program of levee construction. The corps argued against reservoirs, believing them to be too costly and of dubious value, but when levees failed and were overtopped, dam building began to gain acceptance anyway. During the Depression, work relief projects by the corps included Fort Peck Dam on the Missouri River, Conchas Dam in New Mexico, Winooski River dams in Vermont, and Muskingum River dams in Ohio, all for flood control, and all establishing a growing federal role.

In 1936, severe floods in the Ohio basin and the East moved Congress to pass the first major flood control act. Comparable in importance to the reclamation law of 1902, the Flood Control Act of 1936 set a policy of dam building that clinched the fate of hundreds of rivers. Declaring flood control to be a nationwide responsibility of the corps, the law stated, "It is hereby recognized that destructive floods upon the rivers of the United States, upsetting orderly processes and causing loss of life and property . . . constitute a menace to national welfare; that it is the sense of Congress that flood control on navigable waters or their tributaries is a proper activity of the Federal Government." With the hardships of the Depression outdone only by those of high water, nothing could have been more popular than the corps spending millions to hire men, move earth, and stop floods. The corps was regarded as a savior, and riding this wave of popularity, the agency built dams not even authorized by Congress. One unauthorized "project modification" relocated a dam a hundred miles to another river and another state — from the West Fork in West Virginia to the Youghiogheny in Pennsylvania.[29] Now that advanced technology made huge dams possible, the flood control act and the hydroelectric dam authorizations during the Depression started the big-dam era.

About four hundred large flood control dams have been built by the corps. The Tennessee Valley Authority and the Bureau of Reclamation also built dams, and the Soil Conservation Service constructed hundreds of small flood control dams. Including private power dams managed partly for flood control, eight thousand dams help to reduce downstream floods, though the corps inspected half of these and in 1979 reported that one-third — mostly in private ownership — were unsafe with the potential of causing more harm than good. The corps built more than 9,000 miles of levees and 7,500 miles of channels intended to contain floods, and about a thousand flood control projects all together.

The corps has estimated that its flood control investments have returned $3.50 per dollar spent. Construction peaked in the 1950s and 1960s and has used 28 percent of all the corps's funds, compared to 23 percent for navigation.[30]

By 1980 flood control expenses by all federal agencies exceeded $13 billion and projects had prevented $40 billion in damages; yet destruction grows worse, both because flood control does not keep up with new floodplain development[31] and because projects entice people to build on lowlands that are not protected from the worst floods. Support for flood control waned in the 1970s owing to the completion of important projects, citizen opposition, and federal policies encouraging floodplain management, but it seemed that damming for hydroelectricity would grow.

WIRING THE RIVERS

The corps bought a dam with a hydroelectric plant on Michigan's St. Mary's River in 1909, and in 1918 it built a small dam with generators on the Tennessee River, but the agency's first large hydroelectric project was on the Columbia, which carries ten times the flow of the Colorado. Bonneville Dam was a New Deal jobs project employing five thousand workers. When a 518-megawatt power plant was installed in 1938, *U.S. News and World Report* wrote that with hydropower industrialists believed that the Northwest "could rival the productive abilities of the North Atlantic and Great Lakes regions." Fishermen saw that the country's richest runs of salmon would be destroyed and wondered why anyone would want to turn the Cascades into another Appalachia, but they had no influence. More Columbia dams built by the corps and by the Bureau of Reclamation brought cheap electricity, and the region captured one-third of the nation's aluminum production. The corps generated power at Grand Coulee Dam, built by the Bureau of Reclamation on the Columbia in 1941. Producing 3,492 megawatts, this has been the world's largest single source of electricity.[32] With a height of 550 feet and a reservoir 150 miles long, Grand Coulee was the first structure in the world with more volume than the Great Pyramid of Cheops.[33] It also eliminated a thousand miles of salmon-spawning streams, but this was overlooked in the hype of dam building. Even youth got the message: *Scholastic* magazine, a high school weekly, reported, "A giant river is being harnessed to make the life of our people more secure."[34] John Day Dam, also on the Columbia, is the country's second largest for hydropower. It and The Dalles Dam each produces two times the electricity of the largest nuclear plant. In the late 1960s, 78 percent of the Northwest's electricity came from dams.[35]

The corps generates more hydropower than any other producer. Sixty-five projects are capable of 15,600 megawatts, or 4.4 percent of United States electricity and 27 percent of its hydroelectricity. About two-thirds of corps-generated power comes from the Columbia.

All hydroelectricity in the United States accounts for 12 percent of the electrical supply, having grown from 7,800 megawatts in 1930 to 69,000 megawatts at 1,400 plants in 1978.[36] Dams in the Columbia and Tennessee basins produce half of the nation's hydropower.

THE CORPS'S ACCOMPLISHMENTS

The corps lists its responsibilities as constructing and operating navigation projects, flood control, major drainage, shore and beach restoration and protection, hurricane flood protection, hydroelectric power production, water supply, water quality control, fish and wildlife conservation and enhancement, outdoor recreation, emergency relief, protection and preservation of navigable water, emergency flood control and shore protection, and other jobs.

The agency was running out of economic projects in the United States when worldwide markets for dams opened up. President Johnson introduced a "Water for Peace" program calling for corps dams in undeveloped countries. Announcing the program at the corps's Summersville Dam dedication at West Virginia's Gauley River in 1966, the president said, "We are in a race with disaster. Either the world's water needs will be met, or the inevitable result will be mass starvation. . . . If we fail, I can assure you today that not even America's unprecedented military might will be able to preserve the peace for very long."[37] The president reasoned that sending the army corps to Third World countries was better than sending the army itself.

In 1981 the corps's civil works division employed thirty-two thousand civilians and three hundred officers working out of thirty-eight district offices. More than four thousand civil works projects of all types were built. Most require continuing maintenance. The corps is responsible for 538 dams, not counting ones built by other agencies but managed by the corps. At four hundred large reservoirs the corps counts 350 million recreation visits a year — more than the national parks. One hundred and fifty corps projects supply water to towns or industries.[38]

Excluding the Mississippi River, 284 projects were under construction by the corps in 1982. More than 450 others were authorized, though 271 of these were approved long ago and are now inactive. Another 323 studies were under way. The 1983 corps budget was $3.3 billion, but in 1984 the budget was cut to $2.7 billion.

THE BUREAU AND THE WEST

Homesteaders had tried to settle the West, but, as John Wesley Powell warned, they found that land was worthless without water. The Riparian Doctrine was used in the East: people owning stream frontage held the rights to the water. No one needed to irrigate, so conflicts were rare. In the West, many farmers and ranchers without stream frontage needed water, so after a period of gunfighting and dynamited dams, the Wyoming Doctrine was devised, granting water rights based on applications, preference going to the first person who applied. A continuing right was dependent on the person's using the water for a "beneficial" purpose. That usually meant raising cattle or crops. A few private dams were built, but most of the people with water were ranchers who simply dug ditches from streams. The success of further settlement depended on dams to store the water.

The land and the rivers would change with President Theodore Roosevelt, who had been a cowboy in the Dakotas and had traveled through the West. In his autobiography he wrote that the "first work I took up when I became President was the work of reclamation." This did not mean the reclaiming of anything, but the damming of rivers to irrigate and cultivate arid lands for the first time. Roosevelt's objective was not to cash in on crops but to lure families west. He said, "Successful homemaking is but another name for the upbuilding of the nation." Asking for passage of the reclamation act, he stated, "If we could save the waters running now to waste, the western part of the country could sustain a population greater than even the legendary Major Powell dreamed."[39]

The Army Corps of Engineers, already active for more than a hundred years, fought the creation of a competing agency, but the Newlands Reclamation Act was passed in 1902 and created the Reclamation Service to dam rivers in the seventeen western states. (In 1923 the agency's name was changed to the Bureau of Reclamation. In 1976 it was changed to the Water and Power Resources Service, but in 1980 it was changed back to the Bureau of Reclamation.) The government's costs were to be recovered through water sales. According to the bureau, these "reimbursable" costs constitute more than 86 percent of total investments,[40] but repayment rates are based on the farmers' abilities to pay, and no interest on the investments is charged, resulting in a substantial subsidy. Roosevelt and lawmakers saw how this could yield enormous profits to businessmen instead of benefiting family farmers, so a provision prohibited the sale of water to farmers owning more than 160 acres. This was later interpreted to mean 320 acres for a farmer and his wife, but the limit was often overlooked and argued about, and new, generous limits were set in 1982.

Starting in 1903, the Salt River Project's 280-foot-high Theodore Roosevelt Dam formed the largest of the early reservoirs, and it remains the highest rock masonry dam in the world. This was the government's first combined irrigation and hydroelectric effort, serving farms and eventually real estate development near Phoenix.[41]

In 1904 the bureau began the Lower Yellowstone Project in Montana, digging 75 miles of canals and 250 miles of ditches with manual labor and horses, and building a small 9$\frac{1}{2}$-foot-high diversion dam. Without this dam, the Yellowstone would be the longest undammed river in the forty-eight contiguous states. Other early projects were on the Snake River, where Jackson Lake Dam flooded a spectacular valley at the foot of the Grand Tetons in 1911. Lake Tahoe Dam in 1913 raised the level of that natural lake; Elephant Butte Dam was built in 1916 on New Mexico's Rio Grande; and nineteen other projects were authorized in 1907.[42] Some of these were large dams, but it was the bureau's work on the Colorado River that really brought multiple-use reservoirs to the forefront of western development.

DAMMING THE COLORADO

The Colorado begins as free as a river can flow in alpine meadows of Rocky Mountain National Park, but only 7.6 miles from its source the North Fork is diverted into the Red Top Ditch, dug for ranchers in 1910. Other parts of the river are diverted through tunnels beneath the Continental Divide to irrigate east-slope farms, though most of the river plunges down the western side of the Rockies, through red-wall canyons of Utah, and through the Grand Canyon, which the river created. After 1,440 miles the Colorado meets the Pacific Ocean at Mexico's Gulf of California. The basin averages only fifteen inches of precipitation a year, and the river's volume annually varies as much as 600 percent. Though it has only the flow of the Delaware River and less than Indiana's Wabash or Florida's Apalachicola, the Colorado drains one-twelfth of the nation and is the Southwest's only major river.

The desolate beauty of the river is unbroken by large cities. Urban Colorado is east of the Rockies; in Utah the river runs safely southeast of Salt Lake City; in Arizona its canyons lie hundreds of miles from Phoenix; and, bordering California, the river flows no closer than 250 miles from Los Angeles. So Denver tapped the South Platte, which runs through town; Salt Lake City drained local streams; Phoenix pumped groundwater; and Los Angeles captured the Owens Valley. These supplies, however, were not enough for those four promising empires, so the cities each turned to the Colorado, eventually diverting it to serve half of the population of the West, in the process calling in presidents, the Supreme Court, and the National Guard. The question of dividing the waters of this river became one of extensive legal debate, moral conscience, and political muscle.

The Colorado River Basin Compact of 1922 cut the river in two, and because of this division one of the finest desert canyons would be dammed. The compact allocated the water equally to an upper basin of Colorado, Wyoming, Utah, and New Mexico and a lower basin of Arizona, Nevada, and California. Upper states held nearly all of the river's source, but they guaranteed 7.5 million acre-feet a year to the lower basin. The upper states expected to receive the same amount plus surplus flows.

All of this was based on a mistake that may become one of the most consequential errors in American hydrologic planning. In 1922 engineers estimated that the river carried 16.8 million acre-feet (maf) of water per year. With 1.5 maf guaranteed to Mexico in 1944, a total of 16.5 maf was allocated.[43] But a dry cycle began in 1924, and the flows from 1922 to 1976 averaged only 13.9 maf. There is not enough water in the river to give all states and Mexico their legal shares. In 1980 85 percent of the river was used. No plan exists to solve the problem.

In the 1920s, southern California developers predicted one of their many growth booms and were not about to let a shortage of water interfere. They needed the Colorado, and they found an unlikely ally in Herbert Hoover. He had normally championed private utilities and opposed government dams, but he was also an engineer who could not resist the challenge of the Colorado, and he pursued its damming with an enthusiasm not shared for other pressing social and economic problems.

Congress passed the Boulder Canyon Project Act in 1928, authorizing the Bureau of Reclamation to build a 726-foot-high dam, the world's tallest at the time and America's largest single-site public works project ever. Contractors poured enough concrete for a sixteen-foot-wide highway from San Francisco to New York. Boulder Dam, later renamed Hoover Dam, was the prototype of a large multiple-use project,[44] incorporating irrigation, hydropower (nearly one-third of it for pumping water to California), flood control, cities, and industry. The reservoir — Lake Mead — could hold the entire flow of the river for two years and was large enough to flood Pennsylvania one foot deep.

Also in 1928, the California legislature created the Metropolitan Water District, an agency that became the largest water agency in the country, supplying one-half of all water to southern California cities and suburbs.[45] To move the water from Hoover Dam to the customers, the district built the Colorado River Aqueduct, stretching 242 miles from the river to Riverside, including a 1,617-foot pumped lift carrying one billion gallons a day. Arizona did not agree that California should take so much water, and when work began in 1934 on Parker Dam to divert water into the aqueduct, the governor of Arizona dispatched the National Guard to prevent contractors funded by the Metropolitan Water District from landing on the Arizona shore. Just before the militia reached the site, the secretary of the interior ordered a temporary halt to the work. In 1941 the aqueduct was finished, but court battles between the two states continued until 1963, and animosity persists to this day.

Though California had only 1.6 percent of the 243,000-square-mile Colorado basin, state negotiators secured more than one-fourth of the water — 4.4 million acre-feet a year. California had a tight grip on the other states, and agribusiness had the grip on California: whereas 3.85 million acre-feet went to big farms, only 0.55 million acre-feet went for urban use. Although this was a large addition to Los Angeles's Owens River supply, it was not enough. The other six states were not ready to use their full shares of the Colorado, so the Bureau of Reclamation agreed to a California plan to divert one million acre-feet of surplus water until Arizona could use it. Many cities grew on borrowed money, but southern California grew on borrowed water. Alternate supplies could be considered later. California hoped to gain permanent title to the water simply by using it, but this plan failed.

Hoover Dam was planned in the ambitious years of the 1920s, built during the Depression, and finished in 1941, when people saw it as a marvel of technology meeting real needs. Tourists stand awestruck at the face of the dam as at an Egyptian pyramid. The next big Colorado River project — Glen Canyon Dam — was different. It created Lake Powell, drowning one of the most sublime of all desert canyons. Completed by the Bureau of Reclamation in 1964, the dam became a symbol of wild river and wilderness destruction. Lakes Powell and Mead are the two largest reservoirs in the country, and with its total of fourteen major dams, the Colorado River has more consumptive use and more interbasin transfers of water than any other river.[46]

Another part of the bureau's work on the Colorado is the Central Arizona Project, with a three-hundred-mile-long canal and a two-thousand-foot lift from Parker Dam to the Phoenix-Tucson area, where groundwater is overdrawn while urban growth booms — Phoenix expanding from one hundred thousand to eight hundred thousand people in thirty years.[47] The project was authorized in 1968 only after resolution of the forty-year-long feud between California and Arizona over allocations. The new supply will initially be 1.2 million acre-feet, but whereas the urban area is expected to double during the next fifty years, Colorado River supplies will sharply decrease when upper-basin states finally take their share of the river. This bleak future does not even consider reductions that will be needed because of the overestimated volume of the river. People may someday regard Phoenix as a geographical blunder the likes of which built San Francisco on the fault and New Orleans on the floodplain, but none of these problems is taken seriously as long as the engineering fix is available.

The Bureau of Reclamation describes Arizona's problem as the "relative inefficiency of nature in producing precipitation at the times and places where it can be better utilized for man's benefit,"[48] and in an effort to improve the situation, the agency seeds clouds over the Colorado mountains to increase snowfall and runoff. With the bureau "stealing" the moisture from downwind regions, a quagmire of court cases will probably be heard over the ownership of no less than the clouds in the sky. Another way Arizona could meet its urban demands is simple but expensive: cities could acquire agricultural land now using 89 percent of the water.

Indian water rights could supersede many others in the allocation of the Colorado and water throughout the West. Under the Winters Doctrine, the Supreme Court ruled that Indians on reservations may claim all the water that they can use. But in 1973 the National Water Commission stated that developments were built "with little or no regard for Indian water rights." On the Gila and Papago reservations in Arizona, upstream diversions and wells outside the reservations depleted Indian supplies without compensation.[49] Sprawling 25,000 square miles, the Navaho reservation has enough irrigable land to use most of the Colorado River, and claims are unresolved. Indians are girding themselves with legal and scientific expertise to gain title to many water sources.

Demands for water in the Southwest seem to be increasing so irreversibly that the pressure to import water from rivers in Oregon and Washington could overcome the opposing votes of the sparsely populated north. At the insistence of Senator Henry Jackson from Washington, Congress agreed to a temporary moratorium outlawing the discussion of northwestern water transfers.

WATERBOY OF THE WEST

The Central Valley Project (CVP) in California is the Bureau of Reclamation's largest piece of work, comparable to what the Tennessee Valley Authority did in size and complexity. Beginning with Shasta, Friant, and Keswick dams in the late 1930s and early 1940s, the project grew to include seventeen other dams. Investments costing $6 billion were designed to deliver 6.5 million acre-feet of water a year from the north and the Sierra Nevada to Central Valley farmers and to cities. The 560-foot-high Shasta Dam stores water that is released to the Sacramento River and then to the dry but fertile south. The Interior Department's Office of Audit found that in spite of repayments required under the reclamation law, the CVP is operating at a deficit projected at $10 billion by the year 2038 if water prices do not radically change.[50]

Another important part of most bureau dams is hydroelectricity — the strong leg that the agency leans on to subsidize uneconomic irrigation. The original agricultural emphasis of bureau projects was broadened with the Reclamation Project Act of 1939 to include flood control, navigation, and municipal and industrial supplies. The bureau now describes its goals as "multipurpose water development to meet the diverse water needs of a maturing economy and an expanding population." Project purposes are municipal and industrial water service; hydroelectric power generation, transmission, and marketing; irrigation water service; water quality improvement; fish and wildlife enhancement; outdoor recreation; flood control; navigation; river regulation and control; and related uses.

Dams proposed by the bureau at Echo Park, Glen Canyon, the Grand Canyon, the Stanislaus River, and elsewhere led to intense environmental struggles. Even more than the corps, the bureau would be criticized for the flooding of irreplaceable resources, for faulty benefit-cost analysis, and for misuse of government subsidies. In 1982 when the corps dropped consideration of construction of Big Sandy Lake in Texas because of its poor economics, the bureau adopted the study. Whereas the corps used reformed rules for project evaluation, the bureau pushed for elimination of the criteria, and in 1983 Interior Secretary James Watt — in charge of the bureau — rescinded the rules.

The Bureau of Reclamation built 329 storage reservoirs, with enough water to flood New England three feet deep and 346 diversion dams. Distributing the water are 15,545 miles of canals, 239 miles of tunnels, and 196 pumping plants of more than one thousand horsepower each. More than 16,000 miles of drains channel wastewater, and fifty power plants make electricity. In 1980, twenty-seven million acre-feet of reclamation water irrigated all or part of 148,000 farms and 10.2 million acres growing $7.4 billion worth of crops, enough to feed thirty-nine million people.[51] Each year 620 billion gallons of bureau water are delivered to sixteen million people in cities and towns. Flood control savings are listed at $1.2 billion, and annual hydropower output at forty billion kilowatt hours — enough to supply New York City, Washington, D.C., Dallas, Chicago, and San Francisco. The bureau counts sixty million annual visitor days at 251 recreation sites. More than $11 billion have been spent, and construction continues at about seventy-five projects;[52] some of them, such as the Central Valley Project and the Central Arizona Project, embrace many dams. Ninety projects were in planning but not authorized in 1981, when the bureau employed 9,075 people with a budget of nearly $800 million. Under President Reagan the bureau saw budget increases of a larger percentage than those of the defense department. In the last quarter century, bureau engineers exported dam-building technology to sixty-two countries by working through the Agency for International Development, the Department of State, the World Bank, and the United Nations.

Total irrigation by all groups and agencies in the United States covers fifty-eight million acres, one-fourth of it in California, one-eighth in Texas, and one-fifteenth in the East, where Florida irrigates more than all other eastern states combined. Nationwide, irrigation takes 47 percent of all water withdrawn and 81 percent of all water withdrawn and not returned to a stream.[53]

A CORPORATION WITHIN THE GOVERNMENT

Theodore Roosevelt vetoed a bill to license a private hydroelectric dam at Muscle Shoals on the Tennessee River, opening the door to government development of this site. Bills for a federal dam were passed in 1928 and 1931 but vetoed by President Coolidge, who did not believe that the government should act as an electric utility company, and by Hoover, who was called "the great engineer" but said that the Muscle Shoals Project would "break down the initiative and enterprise of the American people" and was "the negation of the ideal upon which our civilization has been based." Henry Ford proposed to build the power plant, but he wanted the government to build the dam.[54]

Franklin D. Roosevelt endorsed the Muscle Shoals site in his 1932 campaign. During his famous One Hundred Days, when fifteen major laws were passed in 1933, the Tennessee Valley Authority (TVA) was created. The Muscle Shoals proposal was the start of the nation's largest plan for regional development. The president called the TVA "a corporation clothed with the power of government, but possessed with the flexibility and initiative of a private enterprise."

Few regions of the country had more people on relief or earning less money than along the Tennessee, 650 miles long and draining parts of seven states. The TVA's first chairman, Arthur E. Morgan, wrote, "Three fortunes had been taken off that country — forests, oil and gas. . . . The wreckage of the rugged individualism has been handed to us with a request that we try to do something about it." The agency, promoting navigation, flood control, reforestation, agricultural and industrial development, and defense, became America's largest electric utility.

New dams were at the cutting edge of the TVA, and the national attitude about rivers was reflected and shaped by the agency. Senator George W. Norris, who sponsored TVA legislation, spoke of "the dawning of that day when every rippling stream that flows down the mountain side and winds its way through the meadows to the sea shall be harnessed and made to work for the welfare and comfort of man."[55] Even in 1963, when Stewart Udall wrote *The Quiet Crisis* — a history of conservation — the free-flowing Tennessee was not called a great river of the East, but "a final piece of mockery," because it "had a score of superior hydro-power sites and yet its silt-swollen waters rushed unharnessed and unchecked through counties and states where very few farmers had electricity."

The damming began and continued with speed and painstaking thoroughness unmatched in the history of water development. Wilson Dam at Muscle Shoals was completed, and Cove Creek Dam on the Clinch River was built and renamed Norris Dam. In ten years, more than seven hundred miles of streams were channeled or dammed for barges. In twelve years, sixteen of the TVA's twenty-three major dams were built. Programs for soil conservation, tree planting, recreation, and fertilizer production were begun. Critics complained of socialism, but others called the TVA "the greatest peace-time achievement of Twentieth Century America." It became the "exemplar" of multiple use of resources for social change and the "resource conservancy project" most visited by leaders from other countries. Although President Truman asked that similar authorities for the Missouri and Columbia rivers be created, Congress did not approve.[56] Nine major dams were eventually built on the Tennessee River and forty-two on tributaries, costing $1.47 billion and flooding 635,400 acres of river channels and land. More flatwater shoreline was created than encircles the Great Lakes. Forty-nine TVA hydroelectric plants with one corps plant can produce 4,600 megawatts of electricity.

Not all the analysis is so flattering. In *The Myth of TVA*, William Chandler of the Environmental Policy Institute reported in 1984 that the agency used 1930 costs against 1980 benefits to make investments appear sound, and even at a low 2 percent interest rate on investments, the TVA navigation system was barely breaking even. Ten percent of the valley's best farmland was sacrificed for the reservoirs.[57] Eighty-five percent of flood control benefits are enjoyed by one city — Chattanooga — yet a single dam required the relocation of 3,500 families. Chandler found that without

TVA's help, the per capita income of comparable areas in Georgia, Alabama, and Mississippi improved as fast or faster than the Tennessee Valley.

By 1945 water power was not keeping up with demands for electricity,
so the TVA began building coal-fired and nuclear plants. With only 12
percent of its electricity coming from dams in the late 1970s, the TVA
burned more coal—much of it coming from strip mines—than any other
electric system in the United States and caused 16 percent of the nation's
sulphur dioxide pollution.[58] While building Tellico Dam on the Little
Tennessee River the TVA became mired in debate, and a court injunction
halted the project because it threatened an endangered fish. The reservoir
was eventually filled.

Appointed by President Carter in 1978, S. David Freeman served as TVA
board chairman until 1981, stressing energy conservation and aid for solar
water heating, attic insulation, wood stoves, and industry powered by
waste heat from nuclear power plants. Freeman said, "The dam building era
is over. Now we have a more complex job." Yet the TVA went ahead with
plans to build controversial dams on the Duck River.

FROM SAVING SOIL TO DAMMING STREAMS

Poor land management led to massive topsoil losses in the 1930s; eastern
farms became wastelands of gullies, and Dust Bowl winds literally blew
midwestern soil into the halls of Congress. The Soil Conservation Service
(SCS) was created as another Depression program and was given the goal of
reducing erosion.

Spreading the word about saving the soil, the "district conservationist"
of the SCS became a household figure in thousands of rural areas. Steeped
in science but at home in the fields, he was a friend to farmers and advised
them to contour plow, to grow grass on drainageways, to reduce numbers
of cattle in overgrazed pastures, to plant windbreaks, and to grow trees on
idle land. The agency also sought to reduce stormwater runoff from unprotected lands (studies of strip mines show that water runs off six times as fast
as on nonstripped land). By decreasing the amount of suspended soil in the
water, the volume of floodwater is also decreased, and the silt deposits that
reduce a stream's capacity are avoided. "Watershed management" was the
name given to techniques intended to improve runoff patterns for steadier
and cleaner flows. The SCS and its county conservation districts—citizen
groups affiliated with the agency—became the leaders in planning and
caring for small watersheds.

Good land management resulted in flood control, which gradually became a goal in itself. The SCS later realized that its techniques reduced flood crests after small storms but did little to hold back floods after large storms had saturated even protected soil. So in 1944 the agency started building small dams in the Washita Valley of Oklahoma. After World War II, engineers replaced agronomists and range specialists in SCS policy posts, more structural solutions were proposed, and in the mid-1950s Congress granted a blanket authorization for the construction of small dams averaging fifty feet high with pools of fifty acres.

The SCS fought the Army Corps of Engineers in one of the major water resource debates of the 1950s.[59] The corps recognized that the SCS dams cut the benefits and economic justifications claimed for the large dams, and argued that its own dams offered more protection. Conservationists, opposed to the flooding of large rivers, sided with the SCS. But in the 1960s conservationists began to oppose certain SCS dams, and in the 1970s lawsuits were filed on streams such as Broadhead Creek in Pennsylvania, where Trout Unlimited saved an excellent fishery.

The SCS has built more than 4,000 dams. Another 1,224 were approved and an additional 6,000 planned when the program was reevaluated and scaled back in the late 1970s.

Other work of the SCS drew even more criticism than the dams: 9,200 miles of streams were channelized to speed runoff and drain lowlands, and another 11,600 miles of ditches were planned. By 1968 state fish and game agencies and fishermen fought some of these projects, and by 1970 the program drew intense fire from new environmental groups. This "conservation service" was sued, and magazines and newspapers published pictures of SCS draglines and bulldozers digging up streams. Sensitive about its conservation heritage, the agency temporarily halted channelization in 1971 and stopped many proposals. But in the early 1980s some of these were reintroduced, and most of the money in the small-watersheds program is still for dams and channelization—not for erosion control.

THE NONFEDERAL MULTITUDE

Most large water projects were built by federal agencies, but 88 percent of all dams belong to other levels of government or to private owners. Large city projects include dams on the upper Delaware by New York, on the Tuolumne by San Francisco, on the South Fork of the Platte by Denver, on the Owens by Los Angeles, and on the Skagit by Seattle. Thousands of dams, most of them small, were built by fifty thousand public and private utilities nationwide.[60]

In the 1930s California hoped to build a Central Valley Project, but when the state was unable to sell $170 million worth of bonds during the Depression, the CVP was picked up by the Bureau of Reclamation, ever ready to adopt someone else's project. The idea of a state-owned development was later revived, and in the 1960s the State Water Project became the largest of any nonfederal water system. At Oroville on the Feather River, the nation's tallest dam was built to deliver water to distant southern California. To pump the water requires almost as much electricity as all of the people in Los Angeles use.[61]

The New York State Barge Canal is a nonfederal navigation project, but this kind of state project is rare. Most states did not have the competence, money, or need to develop large projects. Most states were not even able to review federal proposals, and plans by the corps or bureau were rubber stamped. This pattern changed when the Water Resources Planning Act of 1965 strengthened state agencies. Dissent began to rise as states became involved. In 1972 Governor Jimmy Carter withdrew support for Spewrell Bluff Dam in Georgia. After economic studies showed that a Kickapoo River dam would benefit few landowners, Wisconsin governor Patrick Lucey stopped construction. In California, the State Water Resources Control Board fought one federal plan to fill New Melones Dam and another plan to divert American River water from its channel through Sacramento.

Most states, however, supported all the federal dam building they could get. When states finally had the money to write their own water plans, many reflected nothing more than the conventional view: build more dams. In the mid-1970s, Pennsylvania still called for Tocks Island Dam on the Delaware and Rowlesburg Dam on the Cheat. The state water plan projected large new demands for irrigation in the wet Susquehanna basin (but it also called for wild and scenic river designations).

With tighter restrictions on federal money in the 1980s, some western states increased their dam-building programs. Utah authorized $25 million for water projects, Wyoming collected $4.5 million for water development from a coal severance tax in 1979, and Alaska budgeted oil revenues for Susitna River dams costing billions of dollars. The Texas Water Plan called for dams and Mississippi River diversions to be funded with state oil and gas revenues but was defeated.

Though overshadowed by federal projects since the New Deal, private construction of dams continued, especially for hydropower. In the early 1980s, private dams generated one-half of the United States's hydroelectricity. To entice more developers, the 1978 Public Utility Regulatory

Policies Act created incentives for alternate energy such as wind, solar, and water by requiring utilities to buy power from any supplier and to pay "avoided cost"—the cost of alternate generation, usually oil. This requirement seemed to guarantee profits to the renovators of existing dams and to the builders of new ones. The hydro rush of the 1980s was like the Gold Rush of 1849, and applicants raced to the Federal Energy Regulatory Commission (FERC) office to stake claims for permits that gave exclusive rights to study a site for three years, after which developers could apply for construction licenses. The FERC received 1,859 applications in 1981 (compared to 18 in 1978), the heaviest hit areas being California, New England, Pennsylvania, Oregon, and Washington. In 1982 utility companies contested the avoided-cost provision, and the rate of applications decreased, yet private development of hydropower remained the largest reason for new dams.

North America's largest hydroelectric project sprawls across Quebec, where, after long court battles, Cree Indians who had sustained an ancient hunting culture were forced to give up 5,400 square miles of land. Three dams on the La Grande River produce 5,300 megawatts, and 13,700 megawatts (the equivalent of more than ten nuclear power plants) were planned by the year 2000, when an area two times the size of New England will be flooded.[62]

COMPETITION

That the streams would be dammed was rarely questioned until the 1950s, and so utility companies and bureaucracies battled each other in cutthroat competition. If San Francisco had not applied to dam the Hetch Hetchy Valley, the Pacific Gas and Electric Company probably would have. Private power companies derided the Tennessee Valley Authority as socialism. In the 1930s utilities hired movie stars to campaign against a vote regarding public power in the state of Washington. In retaliation, the Roosevelt-created Bonneville Power Administration hired Woody Guthrie as a "research assistant" and "public relations" consultant. Guthrie hitchhiked to Portland and in less than a month wrote twenty-six ballads touting public power, which easily won.

The corps and the bureau fought each other to spend tax dollars and realize imperial ambitions. Captain H. M. Chittenden of the corps fought the creation of the Reclamation Service, saying that the army could do the job. Franklin D. Roosevelt's powerful interior secretary, Harold Ickes, failed to draw the corps into a proposed department of conservation and said that "the two most powerful intra-governmental lobbies in Washington are the Forest Service and the Army Engineers" and that the corps was "above the law."

The corps and bureau argued over the 2,775-mile-long Missouri River (the Mississippi is only 2,300 miles long). Under the Pick plan, the corps would build five dams for flood control and navigation, but the bureau's Sloan plan called for upstream dams for irrigation and hydropower. Inspired by the TVA, politicians finally proposed a Missouri Valley Authority. Realizing that neither agency might get the work, the corps and bureau endorsed a combined Pick-Sloan plan approving nearly all the projects.

Six major dams now flood six hundred miles of the Missouri; Oahe Dam forms the country's third-largest reservoir. In North Dakota alone, five hundred thousand acres were taken. The Missouri Basin Project proposed 112 dams; 81 are built or under construction.[63]

In 1945 both the corps and bureau were authorized to dam California's Kings River at Pine Flat.[64] After seven years of jockeying for the job, the corps won. On California's American and Stanislaus rivers, differences were settled by allowing the corps to build Folsom and New Melones dams, and the bureau to operate them. Affecting water policy nationwide, the large-versus-small-dam contests between the corps and the SCS preempted attention from other water issues through the 1940s and 1950s.[65]

Twenty-five government agencies now spend $10 billion a year on water, but they do not work in unison. The Department of Agriculture drains wetlands while the Fish and Wildlife Service in the Department of the Interior tries to preserve them. The Bureau of Reclamation in the Department of the Interior irrigates new farmland while the Department of Agriculture pays farmers to leave the land idle. The Fish and Wildlife Service tries to halt channelization while the Federal Emergency Management Administration pays for bulldozers to plow through streams in attempts to push gravel away after floods.

The Water Resources Planning Act of 1965 created the Federal Water Resources Council to coordinate development and encourage a rational, balanced program. It provided, for the first time since the 1940s, a way for representatives of many governments and agencies to talk and plan together and for an agency that was not building the projects to review them. Under President Reagan, Interior Secretary James Watt disbanded the council in 1983.

The uses of dams have also been in competition. Early dams served single purposes, such as navigation, drinking water, or hydropower, but not mixtures of purposes. For water supply, reservoirs are kept as full as possible with reserve for droughts. But for flood control, an empty reservoir is best, so that the deluge can be caught whenever it comes. Swimmers and boaters need a large reservoir in the summer to cover mud flats. At multipurpose dams the uses compete: once water is drained for thirsty cities or hydropower in the summer, the water is not there for recreation; if reservoirs are emptied in the fall for flood control but no high water comes, then there may not be enough water for irrigation the next summer. Juggling uses is complicated by fish and water quality goals; for example, salmon on some rivers need large flows in the spring to wash smolts to sea and in the fall so adults can swim up the rivers, but these releases may clash with irrigation or hydropower needs.

Yet dams were destined to become multiple purpose. In 1908 the federal Inland Waterways Commission called for integrated development, with hydropower revenues paying for the dams.[66] The Flood Control Act of 1917 included Congress's first mandate that floods and hydropower be considered with navigation. In 1925, Senate Document 308 authorized the corps to study most large rivers, marking the government's initial effort to appraise problems of whole watersheds.

The Great Depression brought an awareness of limits and of the needs for planning. Both concepts led to river preservation in later years, but in the 1930s and 1940s they led only to wholesale damming in the name of resource management. The corps built dams mostly for flood control and navigation, whereas the Bureau of Reclamation built for irrigation and hydroelectric power.

To overcome the conflicts of multiple use, reservoirs were simply built larger, storing water for several uses, expanding economic justifications, and broadening political favor. With Hoover Dam in 1941 the benefits of multiple use were fully realized. The corps's Southeast Basins Study in 1958 called for a further expansion of dam purposes to include navigation, flood control, hydropower, irrigation, municipal supply, waste disposal, industrial supply, recreation, wildlife conservation, low-flow regulation, and soil conservation. This is the so-called bananas list: cynics proclaimed that it included enough categories that a banana plantation in West Virginia could surely be justified. "Framework" studies were written by the corps in the 1960s, each generation of plans recognizing broader goals, more reasons to build dams, further integration of uses, and expanding concerns for social, economic, and environmental impacts.

Multiple use became customary, but multiple means, including solutions other than dams, did not. Floodplain management, water conservation, and other ways of avoiding the need for dams were the last things on the developers' minds. In 1965 President Johnson issued an executive order calling for multiple means toward flood control, and in 1979 President Carter issued policy reforms stressing nonstructural alternatives, but even then, the dam builders enjoyed their largest budgets ever.

Along with competing agencies and conflicting users, neighboring regions fought for rivers. Drier areas diverted water from neighboring basins that were regarded as resource colonies. New York City redirected the Croton River and Catskill streams. Los Angeles took Owens River water, and San Francisco piped the Tuolumne from Yosemite National Park.

In 1931 Supreme Court Justice Oliver Wendell Holmes declared that "a river is more than an amenity; it is a treasure." For this reason, he ruled that the Delaware's water should be divided among states on a basis of need, rather than on the length of stream within each state. Holmes essentially meant that a river is an economic treasure. New York diverted 490 million gallons a day,[67] causing low flows damaging to the Delaware. Holmes's quotation has often been used out of context by river enthusiasts.

In 1963 the Bureau of Reclamation's Pacific Southwest Water Plan stated, "As water becomes more critical in the West, river basin boundaries will become even less rigid in water and land resource development."[68] The bureau proposed to divert northern California rivers to the south and to study Columbia diversions to the Southwest. To export water from Oregon's Rogue River, a pipeline in the ocean was considered. In 1983, one out of five residents in the West depended on water from a source that was more than a hundred miles away[69] — from rivers and lands never seen by many of the people turning the taps.

THE MANY FACES OF WATER
DEVELOPMENT

In different regions, distinctive kinds of water development dominated. In the Northeast, old hydropower dams can be found as often as villages. Flood control reservoirs flood steep-sloped valleys through the Appalachians and the East. Sprawling, shallow reservoirs for flood control and recreation dot the Midwest, and low dams have converted the big river arteries of the heartland into steps for barges. In the Southwest and California, dams for irrigation and for cities plug narrow canyons. In the Northwest, hydroelectric dams block scores of rivers, producing 80 percent of Washington's electricity in 1980.

And in different eras, the types of water development changed. Navigation projects were among the first to be built: large eastern and midwestern rivers were dredged, then blocked by low dams. While cities grew in the 1800s, reservoirs were constructed for urban water and hydropower. Flood control levees lined the Mississippi in the 1920s, and then the 1930s marked a dramatic turn. Income redistribution through public works became a national economic strategy. The big era of hydropower began with dams on the Tennessee and Columbia. After 1936, flood control reservoirs proliferated. Dams became the most visible symbols of FDR's resource philosophy, and extravagant spending on water projects became a way of politics. River development in the 1930s marked a convergence of the concepts of multiple use, river basin planning, regional development, and government authority.

In the 1940s dams were synonymous with progress, and the rivers were to be conquered with the fervor of a pioneer wielding an axe. When Shasta Dam blocked the Sacramento River in 1944, construction boss Francis Trenholm Crowe said, "That meant we had the river licked. Pinned down, shoulders right on the mat. Hell, that's what we came up here for."[70]

The 1950s and 1960s saw headlong growth in dam construction as projects planned in the 1930s and 1940s were built. Ted Schad, who worked for the Bureau of the Budget, said, "If ever there was an age of dam building, the 40s and 50s were it. In 2,000 years historians will look at these structures the way they look at the pyramids today, and they'll call us 'the dam builders.' " Remote sections of the Rockies, northern California, and parts of the Northwest were among few areas not touched by the developers. In 1956 Congress authorized recreation as a new reason to build dams. Water supply became a priority after an eastern drought in the 1960s when Congress authorized the corps's Northeastern United States Water Supply Study; however, little construction resulted. By the mid-1960s, conservationists' challenges began to slow the big water projects.

With rising environmental and economic concerns in the 1970s and with awareness of nonstructural alternatives, it seemed that dam construction would nearly stop, but then energy costs soared, and hydropower developers returned to rivers that were passed over before.

THE RESULTS

By 1980 all agencies and private developers had built about fifty thousand dams of twenty-five or more feet in height, each holding at least fifty acre-feet (about sixteen million gallons).[71] Oroville Dam in California rises 770 feet, and the breast of Watkins Dam in Utah stretches for 14.5 miles.

Oahe Reservoir on the Missouri River in South Dakota is 250 miles long. Another 1.8 million small reservoirs were built. The Connecticut was changed from a free-flowing river to a staircase of reservoirs. In 1979, 783 federal water projects, including dams and other developments, were under construction and would require $20 billion to finish.

For the future, another 497 projects are authorized. The corps's National Waterways Study in 1981 proposed fifty-eight new or renovated locks and other navigation projects to cost $22.2 billion in 1977 dollars.[72] Two thousand more miles of barge canals were under study, with construction costs projected at $2.5 million a mile. The corps inventoried 1,700 potential new hydroelectric sites. Bureau of Reclamation plans called for more dams, including the unfinished giant of the think-big mentality: Auburn Dam would rise seven hundred feet above California's American River. Hundreds of small dams or channelization projects were planned by the Soil Conservation Service. Several thousand dams or turbine additions were proposed by private developers. The Texas Water Plan included about seventy new reservoirs.

Energy needs — the main reason for dam proposals in the 1980s — could be eclipsed by urban water supply needs in the coming years. If growth in the Southwest continues with current water-consumption rates, supplies will not last, and the water seekers may go farther and farther from home. Consider recent proposals: In the late 1960s southern California's grasp tightened on the Eel River, six hundred miles away, where Dos Rios Dam was planned. Texans hoped for nothing less than to divert the Mississippi. Denver owned water rights to a dozen western Colorado streams and planned to bring them home through ditches across the Eagle's Nest Wilderness and through tunnels beneath the Continental Divide. Arizonans longed for the electricity that Grand Canyon dams could yield. To prime the economic pump of the new state Alaska, boosters and the corps wanted to build Rampart Dam. Like spilled ink, its reservoir would have darkened a waterfowl wilderness the size of Lake Erie. For vanishing wealth in water, the future could bring a relentless search. Where will it end?

The transformation of rivers went mostly unnoticed in a society that supported water development and, for that matter, almost any kind of development, wherever possible. Unconsumed rivers were regarded as wasted. Unused rivers were to be harnessed by those who were strong enough, clever enough, and — in curious discord to the rugged and independent West — by those who could get the government to do the harnessing for them.

The history of water development has been one of progress but also one of destruction. Like the river's building of a floodplain with soil that was eroded from lands upstream, any building is a partner with the tearing down of something else. Historian Daniel Boorstin wrote, "The first charm and virgin promise of America were that it was so different a place. But the fulfillment of modern America would be its power to level times and places, to erase differences between here and there, between now and then. And finally the uniqueness of America would prove to be its ability to erase uniqueness." On the Snake River alone, seventeen dams were built, flooding a valley at the foot of the Grand Tetons, the Marmes Rockshelter — where the oldest human bones in North America had been found, and the second-deepest canyon on the continent.

New river development proposals caused some people to reconsider. Goals that once seemed to be useful had grown to appear extravagant, in what René Dubos called "the absurd development of characteristics that were highly desirable when they first emerged." Where in the statistics of water development does the qualitative support the quantitative? And where is the view of people who stood to lose through the development of rivers?

Why would Congress labor for years over the fate of a river, when only two decades before, the Army Corps of Engineers built dams without so much as an authorization? Why would a secretary of the interior fight for Grand Canyon dams one year and for the preservation of rivers the next? Why would an aqueduct be bombed by angry citizens and a dam in Idaho be blasted into chunks of rubble by a governor?

CHAPTER FOUR

The Beginnings of River Protection

Unwanted side effects came with the dams and the canals. Migrations of fish were stopped, entire ecosystems eliminated, and unique landscapes flooded. Poorly constructed dams were dangerous; a failure at Johnstown, Pennsylvania, killed two thousand people in 1889. Yet even when the early water projects caused problems, there is little record that people knew, cared, or objected. There was no serious protest or nationwide opposition to a dam until a spectacular landscape was to be flooded in a national park.

HETCH HETCHY: FROM BARREN ROCKS TO CATHEDRAL

More than anyone else, John Muir made the wilderness popular; he praised its spiritual value and encouraged its preservation. Having seen Yosemite Valley under state mismanagement, including the damming of Mirror Lake, he successfully lobbied for the creation of Yosemite National Park in 1890. In 1892, one year after the National Irrigation Congress was formed to support new dams, Muir and twenty-six other people founded the Sierra Club, which would later lead efforts to save rivers.

In the northern part of Yosemite Park, the Tuolumne (too-OL-uh-mee) River crashed over granite, then wound through the untouched meadows of Hetch Hetchy Valley. Glaciated walls decorated by waterfalls surrounded a garden of deep grass, girthy oaks, and evergreens.

During his wanderings in the Sierra Nevada, Muir visited Hetch Hetchy and became committed to its protection, writing, "I have always called it the 'Tuolumne Yosemite,' for it is a wonderfully exact counterpart of the

Merced Yosemite, not only in its sublime rocks and waterfalls but in the gardens, groves and meadows of its flowery park-like floor." Albert Bierstadt painted the valley, assuring its recognition as a classic American landscape, and the director of the California Geological Survey said, "If there were no Yosemite, the Hetch Hetchy would be fairly entitled to world-wide fame."

One hundred and fifty miles away, and with vastly different motives, San Francisco officials had their own interest in Hetch Hetchy. The city filed a claim for the Tuolumne in 1901, proposing to dam the valley for water supply and hydroelectricity. Because the site was in a national park, no private owners controlled the land or water rights, so none had to be bought. But for the city to tap the public domain, a permit was required from the secretary of the interior, and Congress needed to approve. The stage was set for the first great dam fight and for what historian Roderick Nash called "the first great conservation controversy in American history."[1]

Theodore Roosevelt's first secretary of the interior, E. A. Hitchcock, refused to allow the dam because it would violate the mandate of protecting Yosemite Park as a natural landscape, but the 1906 San Francisco earthquake and fire brought public sympathy as only a natural disaster can deliver, and the city's plea for water assumed humanitarian appeal.

In 1903 Muir had met President Theodore Roosevelt when the two camped out in four inches of fresh snow at Yosemite, and the president said, "This has been the greatest day of my life." In 1907 Muir wrote to Roosevelt, asking him to spare Hetch Hetchy.

The case widened a rift between the "preservationists" and the "utilitarianists" that had already begun in the young conservation community. Muir and his supporters argued that the natural landscape had intrinsic worth and that some places should be preserved. This was the national park and wilderness idea, and underlying it was the concept that the earth — at least certain places on it — has values beyond those of hardware and profits. In addition to minerals for industry, trees for houses, and water for cities, the land holds spiritual qualities that people need. Certain places ought to be left alone, especially when Congress had already decided to leave them alone by creating a national park.

Gifford Pinchot — the nation's chief forester, a friend of Roosevelt's, and the man who popularized the term *conservation* — believed that resources should be managed. His view of the public domain as an efficient workshop represented reform from the cut-and-run mentality that had allowed public resources to be depleted for the profits of a few powerful

SELECTED EVENTS IN CHAPTER 4

1890 Yosemite National Park designated.
1892 Sierra Club organized.
1901 San Francisco representatives filed claim for Tuolumne River.
1905 Wisconsin stopped dams on Brule River.
1906 General Dam Act passed.
1908 Permit issued to dam Hetch Hetchy Valley.
President Roosevelt stopped dam on Rainy River.
1909 President Roosevelt withdrew 16 rivers from dam permit eligibility.
1913 Raker Act passed to dam Hetch Hetchy Valley.
Owens River aqueduct finished.
1916 National Parks Act passed.
1920 Federal Power Act passed.
Three dams proposed in Yellowstone National Park.
1921 Jones-Esch Act passed.
International commission recommended dam in Glacier National Park.
1922 Izaak Walton League organized.
1923 Permits for Kings River dams denied.
1924 Owens Valley residents bombed aqueduct.
1926 Saint Francis Dam built.
1927 Bechler Meadows Dam proposed in Yellowstone National Park.
1928 Hydroelectric plant proposed for Cumberland Falls.
Saint Francis Dam failed.
1934 Fish and Wildlife Coordination Act passed.
1936 Kinzua Dam authorized.
National Wildlife Federation organized.
1940 Potomac River dams proposed.
1941 Tennessee residents fought Douglas Dam.
Santee-Cooper rivers project built.
1942 Corps dropped Clarion River dam proposal.
1943 Bureau of Reclamation proposed Echo Park dams.
1946 Residents fought Land Between the Lakes project.
1947 Grand Canyon dams proposed.
1948 Glacier View Dam proposed.
Indians lost fight against Garrison Dam.
Wilderness Society opposed Wilson Dam.

1949 Washington state passed Dam Sanctuary Act.
1950 Higley Mountain and Moose River dams in Adirondack Park prohibited.
1952 Namakagon River power project stopped.
Diversion of Trinity River fought.
1953 Dam in Blue Valley started.
1956 Echo Park dams stopped.
President Eisenhower vetoed water projects.
Smoky Range Dam proposed.
Glen Canyon Dam approved, along with Flaming Gorge, Curecanti, and Navajo dams.
1957 Effort started to save Buffalo River.
1958 Dworshak Dam authorized.
1959 Corps proposed Rampart Dam.
Seneca Indians lost fight against Kinzua Dam.
1961 Interior Secretary Udall intervened to try to save Clearwater River.
1962 Supreme Court ruled in favor of Mayfield Dam.
1963 Glen Canyon flooded.
Sierra Club published *The Place No One Knew*.
National Park Service recommended national river status for Buffalo River.
Trinity River dam proposal at the Hoopa Reservation stopped.
Corps proposed Potomac River dams.
1965 Interior Secretary Udall dropped support for Grand Canyon dam.
Kings Canyon National Park expanded to stop dams.
1967 Rampart Dam stopped.
1968 Central Arizona Project passed without Grand Canyon dams.
Corps dropped plans for dam at Cumberland Falls.
1970 Second Owens Valley aqueduct built.
Clarion River dam proposal stopped.
1972 Buffalo River named national river.
1973 Lawsuit to save Rainbow Bridge lost.
1976 Flathead River designated national river.

men, but when in doubt, Pinchot favored development: "Conservation demands the welfare of this generation first, and afterward the welfare of generations to follow."

Muir disagreed: "Much is said on questions of this kind about the greatest good for the greatest number . . . but the greatest number is too often found to be number one." For most lands, the preservationists did not disagree with Pinchot's view of management; they simply wanted a few places, such as the national parks, to be left alone.

Pinchot wrote, "Conservation stands emphatically for the development and use of water-power now, without delay." Against Muir he argued, "As to my attitude regarding the proposed use of Hetch Hetchy . . . I am fully persuaded that . . . the injury . . . by substituting a lake for the present swampy floor of the valley . . . is altogether unimportant compared with the benefits to be derived from its use as a reservoir." Disagreement over the two views of conservation had been building, and a showdown would come at Hetch Hetchy.

An advisory board of army engineers discovered four excellent alternatives but stated, "The necessity of preserving all available water in the Valley of California will sooner or later make the demand for the use of Hetch Hetchy as a reservoir practically irresistible." The board reported that Hetch Hetchy was San Francisco's least expensive and only practical solution, though the city of Oakland would tap a cheaper Sierra source, other cities found alternatives in the Sierra, and dams were later built on the Tuolumne below Hetch Hetchy. San Francisco's engineers claimed that the best alternative to the $77 million Hetch Hetchy site would cost $20 million more.

Roosevelt appointed James Garfield, a friend of Gifford Pinchot, as the new interior secretary, and Pinchot advised the dam promoters to renew their permit request.[2] In 1908 the permit was issued, though Roosevelt later wrote to Robert Underwood Johnson, an ally of John Muir's and editor of *Century* magazine, that Hetch Hetchy was "one of those cases where I was extremely doubtful." Now the fate of the valley went to Congress.

Muir and his supporters appealed to the people and started the first great movement to save a landscape from being dammed (though in 1912 the seventy-four-year-old Muir took time out to explore the Amazon). With the help of magazine and newspaper editors, the Hetch Hetchy question was delivered to the public. Many people gave up on saving the valley, but Muir argued fervently, attacking San Francisco by calling it "the Prince of the powers of Darkness" and "Satan and Company." In the conclusion of *The Yosemite,* Muir thundered,

These temple destroyers, devotees of ravaging commercialism, seem to have a
perfect contempt for Nature, and, instead of lifting their eyes to the God of the
mountains, lift them to the Almighty Dollar.

Dam Hetch Hetchy! As well dam for water-tanks the people's cathedrals and
churches, for no holier temple has ever been consecrated by the heart of man.

The preservationists' plea was that national parks should not be sacrificed
for special interests and that alternate sites lay outside the park.

While the *New York Times* opposed the dam, the *San Francisco Chron-
icle* named Muir and the preservationists "hoggish and mushy esthetes."
The city argued that people's needs should come first and that the reservoir
would enhance the valley, to which Congressman Holvor Steenerson of
Minnesota challenged, "You may as well improve upon the lily of the field
by handpainting it."

Sponsoring the bill to allow the dam, California congressman John
Raker said that the "old barren rocks" had a "cash value" of less than
$300,000 but a reservoir was worth millions. Representative Finly Gray
from Indiana said, "I admire the beauties of nature and deplore the dese-
cration of God's Creation, yet when the two considerations come in conflict the conservation of nature should yield to the conservation of human
welfare, health, and life."

Outlook Magazine countered, "While the Yosemite National Park
might very properly be sacrificed to save the lives and health of the citizens
of San Francisco, it ought not to be sacrificed to save their dollars."

To protect people from private power monopolies, a "progressive" view
that San Francisco would deliver publicly owned power was touted by
some congressmen. One of these was William Kent from Marin County,
north of San Francisco, who had bought Muir Woods to save it from
logging and then persuaded President Roosevelt to designate it a national
monument in 1908 to save it from a local water company that planned to
condemn the woods for a reservoir.[3] The progressives said that Hetch
Hetchy would make citizens "forever free from any danger of being held up
in the interest of private profit."[4] Kent and others made certain that the bill
allowing the dam prohibited power sales to private utility companies.

Woodrow Wilson appointed Franklin Lane as secretary of the interior in
1913. He had been a lawyer for San Francisco when the city planned the
dam. In September, after hearings at which the park supporters were
scarcely represented because of short notice, the House passed the Raker
Act, 183–43. No western congressman opposed the dam. Having lost in
the House, Robert Underwood Johnson called for a plan to "flood the
Senate with letters from influential people." One member received an

estimated five thousand letters against the dam. The *New York Times* and hundreds of newspapers nationwide printed editorials against the dam. But San Francisco lobbied quietly and with precision in Washington.

Some senators could not understand why people opposed a dam appearing to promise only public good. On the sixth day of debate, Missouri's James Reed said,

> The Senate of the United States has devoted a full week of time to discussing the disposition of about two square miles of land, located at a point remote from civilization, in the heart of the Sierra Nevada mountains, and possessing an intrinsic value of probably not to exceed four or five hundred dollars. . . . It is merely proposed to put water on these two square miles. Over this trivial matter, the business of the country is halted, the Senate goes into profound debate, the country is thrown into a condition of hysteria, and one would imagine that chaos and old night were about to descend upon the land.

On the morning of the vote a "Special Washington Edition" of the *San Francisco Examiner* greeted congressmen at their desks. Drawings showed idyllic recreation scenes with vacationing families at the reservoir. Late that night senators voted 43 – 25 to allow the dam. President Woodrow Wilson signed the bill, and the fight was over. As a part of the plan, a second dam, Eleanor, would flood Eleanor Creek, a spectacular Tuolumne tributary also in the park. Because the dam had received so much attention, John Muir said, "The conscience of the whole country has been aroused from sleep," though this was poor satisfaction. Muir died one year later.

John Muir and his supporters did not come close to winning: Presidents Roosevelt and Wilson supported the dam, Interior Secretaries Garfield and Lane approved it, the House committee voted unanimously for it, and the full House and Senate cleared the bill by wide margins. But for the first time, people read articles and editorials pleading to save a landscape, thousands of people wrote to congressmen, and some politicians argued eloquently for preservation.

In *Wilderness and the American Mind,* Roderick Nash wrote,

> Indeed the most significant thing about the controversy over the valley was that it occurred at all. . . . Traditional American assumptions about the use of undeveloped country did not include reserving it in national parks for its recreational, aesthetic, and inspirational values. The emphasis was all the other way — on civilizing it in the name of progress. What had formerly been the subject of national celebration was made to appear a national tragedy.

The Hetch Hetchy struggle proved that people would become motivated and committed to save a special piece of land. With dam proposals that would cause an absolute loss of tangible property, the stakes were utterly clear. "When a dam is proposed," said Jerry Meral, deputy director of the Department of Water Resources for California in 1982, "it's easy to see what is at stake. All that people have to do is go to the river and look. It's not like a bottle bill for recycling where you can always try again next year."

Construction of O'Shaughnessy Dam in Hetch Hetchy Valley began, though the dam was not completed until 1934. In spite of legal requirements that the hydroelectric power be sold only by public agencies, San Francisco sold it to the Pacific Gas and Electric Company, which owned the transmission lines.

Other river activists would share John Muir's setbacks: technical reports supporting dams; grass roots campaigns beaten by quiet but powerful lobbying of the developers with support of local newspapers; western congressmen voting together for dams; a lack of interest in alternatives; and government officials' and congressmen's refusal to accept the view that the natural river held more than a frivolous recreational value. These same problems would be seen in 1980 during the Stanislaus River debate near John Muir's old battleground.

Public attitudes had a long way to go before the values of a free-flowing river would be widely recognized. If the threat to Yosemite National Park had been logging or commercialization or almost anything but a water project, it might have been stopped. As Ludwik and Eileen Teclaff put it, "Nonuse of wilderness was an accepted (if precariously established) principle by the end of the nineteenth century: nonuse of water was not."[5]

Even with Muir and the preservationists, the struggle was not so much to save a river as to save a national park. Before the Hetch Hetchy proposal, other dams were built on the nearby Stanislaus River at Upper and Lower Strawberry, Utica, Union, Spicer Meadow, and Relief—all flooding outstanding scenic areas but drawing little if any opposition. And at Hetch Hetchy, the river was secondary; it happened to flow through the wilderness valley that looked like Yosemite. The name *Tuolumne* was seldom even used in the dam fighters' rhetoric. Among the preservationists, the land was the main issue. Rivers for their own values would not receive much attention for many years.

A struggle of Hetch Hetchy's scale would not be repeated for nearly half a century. Few people objected to dams when rivers seemed to be worthless—the continent had no scarcity of running water. In the 1930s dams were one solution to unemployment. World War II and the economic boom immediately following the war spawned few challengers of "progress." Gifford Pinchot's idea of conservation prevailed: the utilitarian view overwhelmed preservation, perhaps more with water management than with other resources. Teddy Roosevelt championed the protection of forests but launched the federal damming of the West with his Bull Moose enthusiasm. Historian Samuel Hays said, "The building of dams and the development of water—especially for irrigation—was regarded as 'conservation.'"[6]

Hetch Hetchy was not a turning point but a cry of dissent in a culture poised for massive river development, a culture that was nearly oblivious to environmental costs. In the name of conservation, the 1902 reclamation act was passed to dam the rivers of the West. The year Hetch Hetchy was lost, Frederick Haynes Newell, an architect of the reclamation program, wrote,

> The achievement of the national government in conserving flood or waste waters and in converting parts of the desert into prosperous farms is both proof and prophecy of what can and should be done on a larger scale. . . . There is every incentive, therefore, for the young man of the present day to seriously and persistently study these matters and to identify himself with the great forward movement which must necessarily take place along these lines.[7]

W. J. McGee, Roosevelt's chief advisor on water programs, wrote that the "Conquest of Water" was "the single step remaining to be taken before Man becomes master over Nature."[8]

Yet after the Census Bureau announced in 1890 that the frontier was closed, some people sensed that the country had lost its youth and that a reminder of the frontier could survive in wild refuges. The Progressive Movement of 1900–1917 gave the government a role that included not only public development of rivers but also the regulation of private water development, and with this came an unrealized boost to river protection. In the Teddy Roosevelt years, scientific management of resources was started, initially justifying development but preparing the way for studies that would address secondary effects of damming rivers. The developers embraced science to support their cause, not realizing the self-destructive element that they had thereby introduced.

It would be half a century after Hetch Hetchy that a consensus, even then vague, would form for the saving of rivers, yet from 1913 to 1965 the seeds of a movement were planted in many places.

PRIVATE POWER AND PUBLIC PARKS

Unlike the dominant American attitude that private ownership of land should be unhampered by government controls, public rights to water and rivers have had long-standing recognition. Although the idea of "public rights" was always slanted toward development — not preservation — nevertheless the use of water could be planned, where we never had the chance with private land. Common rights to large rivers had been established for navigation in the 1800s, and the first decade of the twentieth century brought federal controls on hydroelectricity.

The General Dam Act of 1906 established federal authority to prohibit certain private power dams. Teddy Roosevelt vetoed a dam on Minnesota's Rainy River in 1908. He stated, "The present policy pursued in making these grants is unwise in giving away the property of the people in the flowing waters to individuals or organizations practically unknown, and granting in perpetuity these valuable privileges."[9] Roosevelt later stopped dam builders on Missouri's James River.

At the 1908 White House Conference of Governors on Conservation, New York's Charles Evans Hughes opposed permits for the Morgan and duPont companies to dam the St. Lawrence and other rivers. He said that the sites "should be preserved and held for the benefit of all the people and should not be surrendered to private interest."[10] In his final act to protect natural resources, Roosevelt withdrew sixteen western rivers from permit eligibility in 1909.

The concern of Roosevelt and the governors was not that rivers be protected as free-flowing streams, but that the public receive the best bargain on the hydroelectricity to be produced and that private utilities not gain a monopoly. Realizing the coming importance of electric power, the Inland Waterways Commission called for better public regulation and warned that power costs could control "the daily life of our people to an unprecedented degree."[11] Between 1909 and 1913 President Taft disapproved a dam on Alabama's Coosa River and reserved 135 other rivers until there were controls to protect the public from higher prices and until regulations assured proper planning within the Pinchot concept of efficiency. Many of the permit denials simply saved the rivers so that the government could dam them later.

In sharp contrast, the state of Wisconsin recognized natural river values and passed a law in 1905 stopping dams on the Brule River and another in 1908 to save the Flambeau,[12] but such concern was the exception during that era. Even the limited public rights championed by Roosevelt faced intense opposition by power companies, and the controls would later be compromised by business-oriented administrations.

The Federal Power Act of 1920, born of the Progressive Movement, required dam builders to apply for Federal Power Commission (FPC) permits granting fifty-year leases and offering limited protection of public rights. The FPC, however, was charged with fostering construction and did not consider alternatives. The commission could also allow dams in national parks, and this provision led to the next episode in the protection of rivers.

In 1916 the National Parks Act had stated that "the fundamental purpose of the . . . parks . . . is to conserve the scenery and the natural historic objects and the wildlife therein, and to provide for the enjoyment of the same in such manner and by such means as will leave them unimpaired for the enjoyment of future generations." Several years later the National Parks Association (NPA) was started by Robert Sterling Yard, a friend of park service director Stephen Mather, as a lobby for protection. One of the first tests of the park service and the NPA was to stop the licensing of hydroelectric dams.

In 1921 the parks supporters were successful, and President Wilson signed the Jones-Esch Act banning FPC permits from existing parks but not from future parks. Eventually the act was changed to prohibit licenses in all national parks or monuments, but this simply redirected the dam builders' lobbyists from the FPC office to Congress, where protection could be overridden.

In 1920 Idaho irrigation districts proposed three dams in the Falls River basin of Yellowstone Park. The NPA argued, maybe with too much alarm, that "the granting of even one irrigation privilege in any national park will mark the beginning of a swift end; within five years thereafter all our national parks will be controlled by local irrigationists, and complete commercialization inevitably will follow."[13] The bill allowing the dams passed the Senate but was beaten on the House floor. Taking a slightly different tack, dam supporters proposed to delete the Falls River basin from park boundaries, but this also failed. The case never received the attention given to Hetch Hetchy eight years earlier, but the Yellowstone debate was probably the first successful opposition to a major dam proposal, and it reversed the Hetch Hetchy precedent of allowing a dam in a national park (a distinction often given to the Echo Park case, which came thirty-five years later).

Another proposal was introduced by the Yellowstone Irrigation Association to build a six-foot-high dam at Yellowstone Lake's outlet near Fishing Bridge. Business groups in Livingston, Montana, tried to sidestep opposition by calling the structure a "weir" instead of a "dam," by claiming that the higher level of the lake would make the park more beautiful, and by saying that navigation would be improved on the distant Missouri River. Labeling the scheme a "war on the national parks," the NPA claimed the support of five million members from groups including the American Civic Association, the Boone and Crockett clubs, the Audubon Society, the Sierra Club, the Civic Club of Philadelphia, the American Automobile Association, the Massachusetts Forestry Association, and the National Institute of Architects. This diversity is enough to make modern coalition builders envious. America's most famous landscape architect, Frederick Law Olmsted, spoke out to stop the dam.

With rhetoric equaled by James Watt sixty years later, Interior Secretary Albert Fall in 1922 called the national park defenders "meddlers interfering with the sworn duty of the Secretary of the Interior" and said that the Yellowstone dam was "being taken into politics" and would be built.[14] The same year, Fall received $404,000 from two oil companies in the Teapot Dome Scandal. He was eventually convicted and became the first cabinet officer ever imprisoned for a serious crime committed while in office. Much of President Harding's bad reputation was ascribed to Fall.[15]

Four bills were introduced for the Fishing Bridge Dam, and to fight them, the NPA built on the Hetch Hetchy experience in grass roots organizing. In Montana, opposition to the dam grew, especially from women's clubs, and the sponsoring congressman lost the 1922 election by a 2–1 margin to an antidam candidate, ending the threat.

In 1927 another bill would have allowed Bechler Meadows Dam in Yellowstone. Park superintendent Horace M. Albright, who later became a distinguished National Park Service director, described the basin as one of the park's most interesting primitive areas. The NPA called for the dam's defeat and fought to avoid the "nationally depreciated desolation" of Jackson Lake Reservoir, which had been built by the Reclamation Service on the Snake River at the Grand Tetons. Dozens of groups opposed the Bechler Meadows proposal, and it was killed.

Through all of these debates, it was still parks, not rivers, that were the main issue. About the Yellowstone Lake dam the NPA's Robert Yard said, "Of course we all want this water used in some proper way. One way would be to dam the high fifty-mile Yellowstone Valley north of the Park boundary. But the schemers do not want to do the trick that way, for they would have to purchase the land."[16] In an NPA article about Bechler Meadows Dam, Henry van Dyke wrote, "Let the dam be built, if it is needed. But build it outside the park, lower down, where it will spoil nothing," as if the river outside the park was "nothing." Robert Yard's alternative — Allenspur Dam — would be proposed and fought in later years, and may again become a threat.

Other parks were endangered. In 1921 a joint international commission had recommended an irrigation dam that would turn Glacier National Park's Upper and Lower St. Mary's lakes — jewels of the northern Rockies — into one reservoir, impounding water ten miles into the park. In 1922 copper miners applied for a Grand Canyon dam at Diamond Creek.

In the southern Sierra, John Muir had drawn his recommended boundaries for a national park, but dam proposals by Los Angeles thwarted protection efforts for decades. Kings Canyon National Park was formed in the late 1920s, but it excluded the dam sites of Tehipite Valley, shadowed by a granite dome 3,500 feet high, and of Cedar Grove, now a campground. Robert Yard wrote about these sites: "They are both deeper, more rugged, more romantic and in the writer's opinion, far more beautiful than the Hetch Hetchy Valley. . . . The Tehipite Valley is nothing short of the most inspiring chasm in the Sierra. It ranks in its own way with the greatest American spectacles!" With an average depth of 5,700 feet, Kings Canyon is the deepest canyon in the country, exceeding even Hells Canyon of the Snake, the Salmon River canyon, and the Grand Canyon.

The NPA lobbied for a "power proof park," and the San Joaquin Power Company was willing to withdraw applications for dams on Kings River tributaries at Roaring River and Bubbs Creek to allow passage of a park expansion bill in 1922, but the Los Angeles Bureau of Power and Light blocked the additions. Though farmers proposed Kings Canyon dams of their own, Central Valley cities fought the "monstrous and selfish schemes" of Los Angeles and called it "the dictator of central California."[17]

In a rare ruling favoring wild rivers, the FPC denied the permits in 1923, stating that "all said developments are located in whole or in part within the proposed extension of the Sequoia National Park." The FPC also rejected Los Angeles's proposals for the nearby San Joaquin and Kaweah rivers. Still, the park expansions remained unapproved, and Los Angeles waited for the opportune time to push its plan.

WHOSE RIVER IN THE OWENS VALLEY?

Whereas antidam efforts in the early 1900s were mostly aimed at national parks, violence broke out in the Owens Valley of California over the diversion of water from farms and ranches. With plans to channel Sierra Nevada runoff south, Los Angeles agents had secretly bought land and water rights before Owens Valley residents knew what was happening, and the Reclamation Service, which had supported local irrigation from the Owens River, reversed its stance to favor Los Angeles. After President Theodore Roosevelt's approval of the city's project, expanses of sagebrush were declared a forest reserve to block settlement of lands needed for the city's water system. The aqueduct was finished in 1913.

Southern California businessmen involved in the project knew that it would yield four times the needed amount of water. They bought land in the San Fernando Valley and later collected rich profits from subdivisions when the Owens supply arrived. To store the water, Saint Francis Dam was hurriedly built in 1926, but two years later it broke, killing four hundred people.

Where seven hundred thousand cattle and sheep had grazed in the Owens Valley during the 1870s, the farms and ranches were now scorched. Few people questioned the city's legal claim to the water, but the moral right to turn the farmers' homeland into a desert was another matter.[18]

Armed residents took control of an irrigation canal that was to be closed for the aqueduct, and they pushed the city's grading equipment into the water. At 1:00 A.M. on May 21, 1924, dynamite blasted an aqueduct spillway, and water poured onto the desert. Forty people from Inyo County scattered from the site, and the Owens Valley war began. Dead cats were thrown into the city's water; when more than twelve holes were blasted in the aqueduct, Los Angeles officials stationed armed guards with orders to kill. Legal battles were fought, and the city eventually passed a $12 million bond issue to buy more land. When only 1 percent of the property remained in private ownership, the fighting ceased.

This is one of few water projects that bred violence, and it should not be confused with river protection. The residents' interest was not in saving the river. The questions were, Who would enjoy the wealth and livelihoods delivered by the water? And, How much would the local people be paid?

Having dried up the river, Los Angeles began pumping groundwater during a 1929 drought. After completion of a second aqueduct in 1970, pumping increased. The seventy-five-square-mile Owens Lake became a dust pit. New fights over the eastern Sierra water began, and the aqueduct was bombed again during a drought in 1976. Statewide concern focused on the evaporation of Mono Lake, a unique refuge for wildlife, as Los Angeles intercepted the water that had filled the landlocked lake near Yosemite.

SAVING THE SPECTACULAR

Another episode during the 1920s, although scarcely publicized, marked an important success for river protection and a milestone of private investment. In Kentucky, the Cumberland River plunges over the East's largest waterfall except Niagara. Cumberland Falls's moonbow — the only one in the world known to regularly appear — is a white "rainbow" during clear nights. In 1928 private developers proposed to divert the water around the falls for hydroelectric power. Robert Blair, a local businessman, organized the Cumberland Falls Preservation Association and persuaded T. Coleman duPont to buy the falls and surrounding land for $400,000 and deed it to the state with strings attached: "Said property shall not be used . . . for the production of hydroelectric energy." The purchase is one of the outstanding examples of private money being used to save a river. In the 1950s another hydroelectric plan was announced by the Army Corps of Engineers, but Blair reactivated his association, and in 1968 the corps dropped the project.[19] With the Cumberland, river protection expanded beyond national parks to include this spectacular falls.

RIVERS FOR FISH

The saving of Cumberland Falls was exceptional during the Harding and Hoover eras, which were otherwise flush for private hydroelectric developers. Support for government dams was also growing indomitably. Dams were viewed as a progressive part of responsible government, economic advancement, and resource management. Through the 1920s and 1930s, magazines, including *Scientific American,* published articles full of technological hype about dams but without thought to the land that was flooded, the changes in the environment, or other effects.

Yet river protection slowly spread from concern for national parks to broader interests in fish and wildlife. Outdoor reporter Miller Freeman wrote about power dams in the July 16, 1925, *Seattle Star:* "We all remember when the railroads were very nearly the government of this country. This has been in a measure corrected, but a new evil has arisen overnight. . . . The Federal Power Commission is a creature of the power interests. . . . Would it not be well for the public to slow up a bit in its insistence on development of natural resources so far in advance of our needs?"[20]

Founded in 1922, the Izaak Walton League was the first conservation group to attract a large membership and to campaign for protection of rivers and fish. When the league declined in the late 1940s, the National Wildlife Federation, formed in 1936, took over this role.

In the 1930s and 1940s, leaders of young conservation groups objected to the eradication of salmon on the Columbia River. With more success, Oregon fishermen fought dams proposed for the Rogue and McKenzie rivers. In North Carolina, the U.S. Biological Survey, the Izaak Walton League, and the Audubon Society argued for protection of aquatic habitat and fought a corps project for reservoirs and diversions of South Carolina's Santee River to the Cooper River, which was nevertheless built in 1941.[21]

The Izaak Walton League tried to save the Upper Mississippi River Wildlife and Bird Refuge from the corps's dredging of a nine-foot-deep channel with dams and locks for 564 miles to Minneapolis. Although the conservationists failed to stop the dams, they won some concessions to protect habitat during construction.

The Fish and Wildlife Coordination Act of 1934 required federal dam builders to consult with the Fish and Wildlife Service in the Department of the Interior, the first major law to protect wildlife from water projects. Another act in 1958 reinforced this role.

River conservation in the first two decades of the century had been to save parks, and now in the 1930s and 1940s it recognized few values beyond fish and wildlife. Most of this concern was further limited to fishing and hunting. For example, the lower Colorado was a poor sport fishing river, so Kenneth A. Reid, director of the Izaak Walton League, supported Hoover Dam, calling the river "too thin to plow and too thick to drink."

STATE PARK RIVERS

Opposition to dams expanded to state parks at Pennsylvania's Clarion River in 1940. Proposed as the eighth flood control reservoir in an Army Corps of Engineers system to protect Pittsburgh, Mill Creek Dam would have flooded 103 acres of rare virgin hemlock in Cook Forest State Park.

After local conservationists fought the dam, the National Resources Planning Board — created by Franklin D. Roosevelt to strive for water policy reform — hired Bernard Frank, a specialist in watershed management, to study the corps's proposal. He reported that with reservoir flooding and resulting wind damage to remaining trees, 85 percent of the virgin forest would die within ten years, and he recommended two smaller dams outside the park. The Pennsylvania Federation of Sportsmen's Clubs joined to save the park, and even the mayor of Pittsburgh wrote to the Bureau of the Budget that "this monument of nature" had "social and aesthetic values which would justify a modest increase in expense." In 1942 the chief of engineers ordered that alternate plans be drawn, but these were not economic.[22] The corps returned to the Clarion in 1970 to propose a larger dam at St. Petersburg, but this was also stopped.

AT HOME IN THE VALLEY

In the 1940s dam builders faced a different kind of opposition, so basic to the American way of life. People began fighting to save their homes and farms. Along the French Broad River, residents fought the Tennessee Valley Authority (TVA) over Douglas Dam, though most of the publicity was given to the loss of potential marble mines.[23] As with other dam proposals of the early 1940s, government officials said that the project was needed for the war effort, and it was built. In the media, including the popular film *Wild River,* local people were characterized as backward hillbillies with no understanding of progress, yet in 1941 the Tennessee Farm Bureau presidents wrote, "Could not . . . other power sites [be] found that would not result in such profound economic and social disturbance and maladjustments to people resident in the reservoir areas . . . ? There is no price that can compensate people for these values in a home and a farm."[24]

In 1946 people along the Cumberland River below Nashville fought a proposed TVA dam and supported two smaller Army Corps of Engineers dams. The Lower Cumberland Association stated that the farmland to be flooded was seven times more valuable than the power to be produced, but the TVA built the project anyway and much of the homeowners' property is now a part of the Land Between the Lakes recreation area[25] (dubbed "Land Under the Lakes" by critics). As of the late 1940s, TVA reported that 13,638 families had been moved for reservoirs and that 593,651 acres would be flooded. Landowners, however, were unorganized, the dam-building momentum continued, and most people remained oblivious to the values of free-flowing rivers. TVA director David Lilienthal wrote in 1953, "For the first time in the history of the nation, the resources of a river were not only to be 'envisioned in their entirety'; they were to be developed in that unity which nature herself regards her resources."[26]

The landowners' view was shown in a painting by Lowell Hayes titled *A TVA Commonplace,* shown at the Smithsonian Institution in 1982. One side of an eight-by-eight-foot panel showed homes, barns, fences, children playing, cows grazing, boys fishing, and other details of rural life. The opposite side of the panel showed a landless sea with the caption "In the greater Tennessee Valley the TVA has done much to eradicate rural poverty."

Mountain people did not want to be evicted, but neither did they fight with force or believe that they could stop the government. Elsie Spurgeon, one of three hundred residents who was forced to move in the late 1930s for Youghiogheny Dam in Pennsylvania said, "People just didn't think they had any say in the matter."

But in the 1940s, residents of Kansas's Blue Valley organized against a dam, marking a new determination to save homes and farms. Tuttle Creek Dam had been authorized for corps construction and would flood fifty thousand acres of farmland and nine villages housing four thousand people. Residents delayed the proposal for a decade, but after a flood in 1951,

Kansas City lobbied for construction. By this time some planners were arguing for small headwaters dams instead of large downriver dams;[27] Blue Valley gave national publicity to the debate. *Reader's Digest* published an article by Elmer T. Peterson called "Big-Dam Foolishness," and the same title was later used for one of the first books opposing dams. *Farm Journal* called Blue Valley "one of the richest valleys in Kansas."[28] Unlike most other angry but despairing landowners, the Kansas people testified at hearings where they asked why their lands should be sacrificed for more industry on Kansas City's floodplain. The corps answered that to defer would be "dangerous" because levees that the corps had constructed downstream would be "deathtraps" without the dam.[29] With an election campaign then unequaled in dam fights, local people ran a candidate for Congress against a fourth-term Republican incumbent, and even against the momentum of Eisenhower's victory, the dam fighters won, electing the district's first Democrat in a century. But it was too late. In 1952 Harry Truman said, "Nobody can save the valley." Campaigning for president, Dwight Eisenhower said, "I sympathize with citizens who object to Federal encroachment in their affairs," but he did not stop construction, which began in 1953.

The next year, Kansans fought another dam at Glen Elder, where the local newspaper editor wrote, "The people are against it, but it seems there's nothing we can do about it, because the higher-ups have ordained that the dam must be built." Landowners were speaking out against government projects, but a sense of hopelessness still prevailed. On Montana's South Fork of the Flathead, Hungry Horse Dam went unopposed, a local resident saying, "Everybody just figured it would go through. You didn't hear anything about it." In Missouri, the Ozark Protective Association delayed dams on the Current River until preservation programs succeeded in the mid-1960s, but this was exceptional, and landowners would not consistently win until the 1970s.

A BROADER APPEAL

The Potomac River attracted a larger base of opposition to river destruction in the 1940s when the corps identified twenty-five dam sites within the basin. Seneca Dam would flood thirty-five miles between Washington and Harpers Ferry. Three dams would block gorges within the Washington area, and others would impound the Shenandoah River. The main purpose was to dilute pollution and improve the city's water supply.

Fishing groups, including the Izaak Walton League and the League of

Maryland Sportsmen, fought the plan and were joined by the National Capitol Park and Planning Commission and other groups. Frederick Law Olmsted, Jr., argued for protection of the Chesapeake and Ohio Canal, historic sites, gorges, islands, and forests, making the Potomac one of the first cases in which historic sites and the more commonplace features of the natural environment were emphasized as reasons to save a river. Farmers and landowners joined, 1,200 of them crowding angrily to a meeting called by the corps. Railroads fought the plan because their tracks would be eliminated. Few cases had attracted such solid opposition, and probably none had drawn such diverse opponents. The corps settled back and waited for a better time to reintroduce the plan.[30]

STILL NOT SACRED

In spite of the preservation precedent set at Yellowstone and Kings Canyon, proposals for dams in national parks did not die easily. Expansion of Kings Canyon Park in 1940 again left important dam sites unprotected. Facing its postwar population boom in 1949, Los Angeles renewed an FPC application for six Kings Canyon dams: Zumwalt Meadows, Sentinel, Paradise Valley, Tehipite Valley, Cedar Grove, and the Middle Fork–South Fork confluence, all with magnificent scenery. Park superintendent E. T. Scoyen wrote, "No proposal ever made relative to any national park ever carried the seeds of such vast destruction as is now faced by Kings Canyon."[31] Martin Litton opposed the dams in a *Los Angeles Times* article, writing that with an average depth of 5,700 feet, Kings Canyon is "easily the deepest canyon of the Western Hemisphere if not the entire globe. . . . For many Californians it would be hard to believe that another Hetch Hetchy can ever happen." By this time Central Valley farmers had bought water from another dam on the Kings River, and fearing that the hydroelectric plan would jeopardize irrigation, they joined the park supporters in fighting Los Angeles.

Several sites were in the national park and could not be dammed without congressional approval. After alternatives were studied, the dam plans were withdrawn, and in 1965 Tehipite Valley and Cedar Grove were finally added to the park, ending forty-five years of threats to the upper Kings River.

Other parks were also threatened. The National Parks Association had testified in 1937 against the Big Thompson Aqueduct to be tunneled under Rocky Mountain National Park, but Interior Secretary Ickes reluctantly approved it.[32] In 1949 the Mining City Dam on Kentucky's Green River at

Mammoth Cave National Park was proposed to flood the Echo, Styx, and Roaring rivers — unique underground streams and habitat of blind fish — but was stopped.

In Montana, conservationists faced the Army Corps of Engineers' first major threat to a national park river. As one unit of a seven-reservoir plan for the upper Columbia basin, Glacier View Dam, proposed in 1948, would flood 19,460 acres in Glacier National Park and twenty-five miles of the North Fork of the Flathead for flood control and power. Promoters argued that with the dam, industry could move inland from the coast and not be so vulnerable to enemy attack.[33] The project was opposed by the Sierra Club in their largest dam fight since Hetch Hetchy, by the National Parks Association, and by the Wilderness Society.

Newton B. Drury, National Park Service director, had been praised for saving the parks from wholesale development in the name of national security during World War II, and about Glacier View he said, "Eight thousand acres of virgin forest would be flooded, including one of the finest ponderosa pine stands in North America. . . . Threatened with permanent destruction . . . is an extraordinarily fine sample of original America."[34] The Sierra Club's David Brower, not one to support dams, called for development of an alternate site on Montana's Clark Fork River at Knowles, "because adequate development there could end the threat of upstream dams that would encroach on a national park, on a wilderness area, and on lands of high scenic and resource values that should be dedicated." The sites at Glacier View, Knowles, and Paradise (another Clark Fork proposal) were not developed, but Hungry Horse Dam, near Glacier National Park on the South Fork of the Flathead, destroyed a wild river that local people said was the best in a region of stunning streams.

In 1956 the corps proposed Smoky Range Dam on the North Fork of the Flathead as an alternate to Glacier View. Opposition culminated in national wild and scenic river designation for the Flathead in 1976, ending three decades of dam proposals on this crystal-clear river, one of the nation's finest for whitewater canoeing and camping. In 1984 Canadian logging and coal mining threatened the Flathead's remarkable water quality.

WILDERNESS, WEST AND EAST

Though not receiving congressional protection until 1964, some of the finest untouched areas of the West had been set aside as wilderness and primitive areas by the Forest Service. Dams were proposed in some of these, and river conservationists expanded their influence beyond the parks. In 1948 the Wilderness Society's Howard Zahniser testified against Wilson Dam, planned for flood control on the North Fork of the Sun River in Montana's Bob Marshall Wilderness: "We desperately need a national inventory of outdoor recreation needs, carried on with a determination to plan all our resource development programs in the light of the data from such an inventory."[35] The dam was not built, and the inventory eventually led to a nationwide recreation study and recommendations for a national rivers system. Other dams were proposed but not built in wild sections of Utah's Uinta Mountains and in Colorado's Flat Tops Wilderness.

The largest protected wilderness in the East became the target of dam builders in 1945. In the Adirondack Park, "forever wild" by order of the New York state constitution, the state Water Resources Commission proposed Higley Mountain Dam to flood the Moose River and the Adirondacks' best deer yarding area. The project was one of the first dam controversies to appear on billboards, on television, and in the Supreme Court. Statewide, voters finally killed the dam by plugging a loophole in the constitution. The commission proposed another Moose River site to flood four thousand acres at Panther Mountain. This was also voted down, and in 1950 the governor signed a bill banning the dam.

With fears that New York City's water supply would run short, threats to Adirondack rivers increased in the 1950s. Gooley Dam would have flooded sixteen thousand acres of the park and a reach of the Hudson River that John Kauffmann in *Flow East* called the "grandest of all whitewater runs in the East." The Adirondack Hudson River Association promoted alternatives for New York City, including water metering to cut waste. A bill was eventually passed unanimously and signed by the governor banning any dam on the upper Hudson.

In the Adirondacks and in national parks, it was for water development more than land development that the laws protecting the parks were challenged. Whereas the damming of the Hudson was plausible, the strip-mining of the Adirondacks' Mt. Marcy would have been anathema. But through public debate, the rivers were gaining status earlier given only to special lands. Describing the importance of the Hudson, an Adirondack ranger said that the river was "part of the soul of the Adirondacks. To dam it up and destroy it would be like bulldozing off the high peaks." The conventional wisdom was gradually accepting that, like mountains, rivers were worth saving. Widespread recognition of the value of deserts and wetlands later followed the same pattern.

A GREATER SENSE OF LOSS

Opposition to dams through the 1940s was sporadic and based mainly on the saving of outstanding valleys, but a new consciousness about rivers and dams was taking hold. In April 1952, Dr. Julian A. Steyermark wrote in *Scientific Monthly* about the destruction of "valuable scientific records" by corps projects; for example, Bull Shoals Dam on Missouri's White River eliminated a rare species of mulberry from the state. An article in *Science* stated that four hundred archaeological sites were buried by Bull Shoals. In a 1949 *Harper's* magazine, Robert deRoos and Arthur A. Maas wrote one of the first powerful exposés against the corps: "The Lobby That Can't Be Licked." in 1952 an *American Forests* article criticized the corps's damming of the Angelina River in Texas, where two hundred thousand acres of productive forests were lost, and the flooding of twenty-two thousand acres of timber along the South Fork of the Flathead.

Criticism against dams expanded from specific cases to generic issues, though the criticism did not hit hard and make much difference until the 1970s. In 1950, Bernard Frank and Anthony Netboy wrote in *Water, Land, and People,* "Finally, despite the expenditure of hundreds of millions of dollars annually for damming, dredging, cleansing, and otherwise stabilizing and normalizing our major rivers, we do not seem perceptibly to be reducing floods, siltation, or contamination." In March 1951, E. Laurence Palmer wrote in *Nature* magazine,

> Dams are not undisguised blessings. . . . We must frankly admit that we as a group support the building of a given dam for a specific purpose, and are willing to sacrifice certain other things when we do this. In spite of what the politicians tell us, we cannot build a power dam that will be of maximum use for flood control, for irrigation and also provide superior facilities for recreation and for wildlife.

A 1954 *Audubon* article reported that with desalting plants and atomic power, "scientific progress" may make big dams obsolete.

In 1950 the President's Water Resources Policy Commission addressed the irreversible effects of dams, stating, "There is a sobering finality in the construction of a river basin development, and it behooves us to be sure we are right before we go ahead."[36] Under a contract to write history for the corps, Michael C. Robinson stated that by the 1950s, "Dams came to be regarded as despoilers of immense expanses of beautiful landscape, valuable forests and plant habitat, as well as historic and archaeological sites." But, Robinson added, "The Corps was in a position to shrug off a few setbacks at the hands of conservationists and other critics. Due to its huge inventory of authorized projects, resources and emphasis could be shifted elsewhere and plans kept on the shelf until the political climate was more favorable."

THE EISENHOWER SLOWDOWN

Eisenhower reversed the New Deal philosophy of government spending and public hydroelectric power. He referred to the TVA as "creeping socialism." The Bureau of the Budget sent the president a memo stating that big dams had been "spectacular but exceedingly costly" and that reclamation projects had been authorized to meet "political demands."[37] Eisenhower vetoed two rivers and harbors authorization bills. Ted Schad, who drafted the veto messages while working for the Bureau of the Budget, said, "Many of the projects had no reports prepared, and we wanted to see cost sharing. Federal money was being given for levees on the lower Mississippi with no local cost sharing at all; it was one of the biggest ripoffs I can think of, and it drained wetlands too."[38] Congress sustained the two vetoes, then passed a bill in 1958 excluding most of the uneconomic projects. Pointing out that executive policies change like the wind, Schad added, "Through the following years all the bad projects were added back in."

Eisenhower stressed a federal "partnership" with state and private-developer building projects but maintained a "no new starts" policy for the corps and Bureau of Reclamation (with several major exceptions, including Echo Park and Kinzua dams). Schad said, "None of this was in the sense of preserving rivers—it was promoting private investment."

For Hells Canyon of the Snake River, the Eisenhower administration turned its back on corps and Bureau of Reclamation plans and approved three Idaho Power Company dams—Brownlee, Oxbow, and Hells Canyon—flooding the best rapids of the country's second-deepest canyon, hundreds of miles of salmon habitat, and a whitewater run that outfitter Martin Litton said "was comparable in many ways to the Grand Canyon itself." Some conservationists supported the dams as alternatives to an even more destructive Bureau of Reclamation proposal at the Nez Perce site that would have blocked both the Salmon and the Snake rivers.

In retaliation against Eisenhower's "no new starts" policy, the Senate formed a select committee to press for business as usual. Ted Schad was chosen to write the committee's report. "I approached it as a professional job," Schad said, "but some senators were like dogs at my heels saying, 'When are you going to get to the need for new projects?'" The report found pollution — not Eisenhower's austerity — to be the largest water resource problem.

ECHO PARK

The national attention brought by Hetch Hetchy was not repeated until Echo Park was to be flooded. In northern Colorado near the Utah border, the Green and Yampa rivers meet in red sandstone canyons. Just below the confluence is an oasis of cottonwoods, called Echo Park because cliffs echo voices perfectly. Steamboat Rock rises two thousand feet straight from the water. Just below lies Whirlpool Canyon; above is Ladore Canyon of the Green and a wilderness reach of the Yampa. The Green River is larger than the Colorado, where the two later meet, and the Yampa is the Colorado basin's only large undammed river.

Because of dinosaur skeletons trapped in sediment, Woodrow Wilson designated eighty acres as Dinosaur National Monument in 1915. A national monument is protected like a national park, the main difference being that Congress designates a park, whereas a president designates a monument. Franklin Roosevelt enlarged the monument in 1938 to protect about one hundred miles of the Green and Yampa canyons.

As part of the Upper Colorado River Storage Project calling for nine dams, the Bureau of Reclamation in 1943 proposed two reservoirs to flood most of the monument's canyons so that upper-basin states could withdraw irrigation water and still deliver a prescribed amount to California, Nevada, and Arizona. Echo Park Dam, 525 feet high, was proposed as the upstream version of Hoover Dam, with revenues from hydroelectricity to pay for irrigation.

National Park Service director Newton Drury opposed the dams. When Interior Secretary Oscar Chapman said that he supported the sites because of their low evaporation rates, Drury asked, "How about the evaporation rate of the national parks and monuments?" In 1950 Chapman approved Echo Park Dam in a memorandum to the Bureau of Reclamation and the park service. In the style of Pinchot, Chapman stated that his choice was "in the interest of the greatest public good."[39] Drury resigned. Chapman also supported using the Everglades as a bombing range — a proposal that even the Defense Department rejected. In *Echo Park Controversy*, Owen Stratton and Phillip Sirotkin suggested that western democratic congressmen, expecting to lose their elections if the dam were stopped, spoke to President Truman. The president said, "It has always been my opinion that food for coming generations is much more important than bones of the Mesozoic period."[40] (The dinosaurs were not even in the threatened area.) Spectacular wild canyons were about to be lost, and most people did not even know that the place existed.

The debate became the conservation issue of the 1950s, bringing the question of national parks and wild rivers to the attention of more people than any earlier case. Devereux Butcher, director of the National Parks Association, wrote about the threat and gained allies. Authors Bernard DeVoto and Wallace Stegner brought an unprecedented quality of journalism to the cause of river protection. Ulysses S. Grant III, a retired army engineer and president of the American Planning and Civic Association, argued against the dams. The Wilderness Society's Howard Zahniser made some of his strongest pleas for wildlands protection, and David Brower—the first full-time director of the Sierra Club—built his rising career on the saving of this place.

Born in 1912, two years before John Muir died, Brower grew up in Berkeley, California, and became an avid mountaineer. While hiking on Pilot Knob in 1933 he met photographer Ansel Adams, who later proposed to his fellow Sierra Club board members that Brower be hired as executive secretary, but the board declined. In World War II Brower taught climbing to soldiers and served as an intelligence officer, earning three battle stars and a Bronze Star. He returned to California and worked as an editor for the University of California Press. In 1952, climbing partner Richard Leonard proposed Brower as the first full-time executive director of the Sierra Club. This time the board approved.[41]

The commitments of most conservation leaders began with outdoor activities. For Brower these were hiking and climbing. His river traveling was limited to a few desert canyons, but fighting dams is what built Brower's reputation and started an important part of the environmental movement.

As Sierra Club executive director, Brower's first major effort was to save Echo Park, which presented a new challenge requiring opposition to the Department of the Interior. The old club leadership was inclined to accept the dams, but influenced by Brower, the board now decided to fight. Brower became known for his adamant views on park protection, leading an activist element of the club that thrived on conflict and sought publicity in national campaigns. In *Voices for the Wilderness*, Brower wrote, "Polite conservationists leave no mark except the scars on the land," and, "When a living heritage is being put to death—perpetual, eternal, permanent death—there is no fairness in giving the attacker and the savior equal time."

The club did not object to the Upper Colorado River Storage Project because such opposition would alienate many congressmen, but it sought an amendment to eliminate the Echo Park dams. As Elmo Richardson wrote in *Dams, Parks and Politics,* "The burden of these polemics was tactfully more pro-park than it was anti-dam." Brower wrote, "The Club does not oppose a sound upper Colorado project that does not adversely affect Parks, Monuments, or Dedicated Wilderness."[42] The conservationists encouraged alternatives to Echo Park — one of these they would later deeply regret.

Dam opponents again thought that they were fighting for the entire park system; if a dam were built in Dinosaur, the precedent would support old proposals at Glacier, Kings Canyon, and the Grand Canyon. The original upper Colorado basin plan plotted projects in a dozen parks, but Echo Park was the most serious and imminent threat to the system since Hetch Hetchy. Congressman Wayne Aspinall verified the conservationists' concern when he said, "If we let them knock out Echo Park Dam, we'll hand them a tool they'll use for the next hundred years."[43]

Ted Schad, working on Echo Park Dam as a budget analyst for the Bureau of Reclamation, denied the importance of the precedent: "The bureau was not trying to eliminate the parks. It was just a good power project, and the bureau had an old water reservation for the dam."

In the *Saturday Evening Post,* Bernard DeVoto alerted the nation and said that Dinosaur was important "as wilderness that is preserved intact."[44] DeVoto blasted the dam many times in his column in *Harper's.*[45] In *Speaking for Nature,* Paul Brooks wrote that DeVoto "may well have been the most potent one-man force for the conservation of nature in the mid-twentieth century."

Wyoming Senator Joseph C. O'Mahoney argued for the dam in *Collier's:* "Water, precious and priceless water, actually is being wasted. It is being allowed to flow on down the Colorado River, over the wonder-working Hoover Dam and finally into the Gulf of California." He stressed that the upper-basin congressmen favored the dam and that the opposition had "an incidental and sentimental reason." He wrote that many dinosaurs may have "died in uncontrolled floods" and that the river's "dangerous rapids" would be "eliminated." He added, "The basic issue here is between the sentimental and aesthetic feelings of some people, mostly outside the area, and the welfare of the several hundred thousand who live there."[46]

The *Denver Post* charged that the entire preservationist attitude was unwestern, but Utah-born DeVoto advised westerners not to criticize easterners "too loudly or too obnoxiously. You might make them so mad that they would stop paying for your water developments." He added, "Massachusetts will pay a larger part of the cost of any dam in the project than Colorado will."[47]

In *Collier's,* Ulysses S. Grant III called for substitute measures that would allow the upper Colorado project to be completed without Echo Park Dam, writing that it would be a tragedy to give up the canyons for "a few acre-feet of water and a few kilowatt hours." His alternatives included Flaming Gorge Dam on the Green (later built) and Cross Mountain on the Yampa (opposed by conservationists in 1982).

In 1955 the *Salt Lake Tribune* wrote, "Echo Dam would turn a hidden wilderness area into a great Scenic Resource." The paper printed an illustration of the proposed reservoir, and editors asked. "What has been obliterated? Between 200 and 300 feet of talus at the base of cliffs rising 2,000 feet and higher—adding much and detracting nothing from the scenery." The Mormons' *Deseret News* called the conservationists' view "romantic tripe."[48]

To generate public support, and to record "what once was" if the dam were built, Wallace Stegner edited *This Is Dinosaur: Echo Park Country and Its Magic Rivers,* writing, "It will not be only the buffalo and the trumpeter swan who need sanctuaries. Our own species is going to need them too. It needs them now." Publisher Alfred Knopf sent copies of the book to all congressmen.

Collier's stressed that this was no local project: "One third, for example, would be paid by the taxpayers of New York, Ohio, Pennsylvania, Illinois and Michigan." *Newsweek's* column about the dam was titled "Pork, Unlimited."[49]

A defense plant, once given as a reason for the dam, was planned for the Ohio River instead. Interior Secretary Chapman reversed his earlier decision, now stating that the dam was "absolutely not necessary." The election of 1952, however, brought Eisenhower's Douglas McKay, a Chevrolet dealer from Salem, Oregon, as secretary of the interior, and contrary to the president's "no new starts" policy, McKay renewed the dam's approval and called the conservationists "long-haired punks."[50] Dam supporters calling themselves the "Aqualantes" campaigned with a Bureau of Reclamation film and a brochure titled "Echo Park—Tomorrow's Playground for Millions of Americans."

David Brower and Howard Zahniser organized support and publicity. Zahniser persuaded a St. Louis chemical manufacturer to fund the cause.[51] Conservationists printed a pamphlet titled "Will You DAM the Scenic Wild Canyons of Our National Park System?" and produced a film that was shown nationwide. In one of the first cases in which river traveling was used to gain political support, the conservationists offered raft trips to show people that the canyons were worth saving, and the number of people floating at Dinosaur grew from 47 in 1950 to 912 in 1954.

The Hoover Commission Task Force on Water and Power reported that the upper Colorado project was a glaring example of subsidies, poor planning, and dubious management. Conservationists took a new attack aimed at costs, which embarrassed Republicans and angered easterners. Even Governor J. Bracken Lee of Utah was hesitant to support the dams because they would add to the "terrific" federal deficit.[52]

At congressional hearings, David Brower held up photographs of Hetch Hetchy before and after it was dammed and said, "If we heed the lesson learned from the tragedy of the misplaced dam in Hetch Hetchy, we can prevent a far more disastrous stumble in Dinosaur National Monument."[53] The conservationists were almost alone because National Park Service employees and Geological Survey scientists, being in the same department as the Bureau of Reclamation, were not allowed to testify.

Southern California was the conservationists' paradoxical ally. Not only would upper Colorado dams cut flows, causing less hydroelectric generation at Hoover Dam, but delays in upstream impounding would also give California more time to use its extra share of the Colorado. However, help from the West Coast was not worth much; dam supporters were quick to associate the environmental groups with the hated California interests that for years had competed with other states for water, and animosity burned hotter.

Echo Park Dam bills passed interior committees of both houses, but mail ran 80 – 1 against the project and editorials in many papers attacked the dam. Floor action was postponed, giving Brower and the others time to rally.

Hearings in 1955 brought bureau officials, governors, congressmen, water users, utilities, and chambers of commerce touting the dam. Navaho Indians supported the dam after they were promised a tribal irrigation project to be built at Navajo Dam on the San Juan River. Fighting Echo Park Dam were conservationists, eastern congressmen, and educational groups. Minnesota canoeist and author Sigurd Olson asked if "we might not destroy the very things that have made life in America worth cherishing and defending?"

Without belaboring the issues of parks and aesthetics, David Brower exposed a Bureau of Reclamation error in arithmetic about reservoir evaporation and proved that more water would be lost than was reported and that alternate sites would lose less. He said that it "would be making a great mistake to rely upon the figures presented by the Bureau of Reclamation when they cannot add, subtract, multiply, or divide."[54] The bureau had called evaporation the "fundamental issue" for favoring Echo Park, but after Brower's testimony, the evaporation figures were twice revised downward.

In April 1955, Oregon senator Richard Neuberger, in a courageous step for a westerner, offered an amendment to delete Echo Park Dam. Senator Hubert Humphrey supported him, gaining more mileage out of John Muir's defeat by saying, "Where once there was the beautiful Hetch Hetchy Valley . . . there is now the stark, drab reservoir of O'Shaughnessy Dam."[55] The amendment failed, but in the House, Pennsylvania's John Saylor— "Big John" —led the way toward defeat of the dam.

Saylor was one of the first and strongest modern conservationists in the House, later sponsoring the Wilderness Act and the Wild and Scenic Rivers acts. Saylor opposed pork barrel because it could not be justified. Unlike many of his Republican contemporaries, he favored spending for social needs such as education. Help came when Governor Johnson of Colorado called the dam atrocious.

Facing Saylor's insurmountable objections, and fearing that nothing would be passed if the dam were included, the House Committee on Interior and Insular Affairs endorsed the project without Echo Park Dam. For future insurance, the conservationists had lawmakers add a phrase in the Colorado River Storage Project Act of April 11, 1956: "It is the intention of Congress that no dam or reservoir constructed under this Act shall be within any national park or monument." Seventeen years later, at Echo Park's alternate site, David Brower would sue the Bureau of Reclamation over this provision.

With Echo Park the dam fighters proved that they could master the political process and mobilize support. Although David Brower went on to a long and remarkable career, Frank Graham, Jr., wrote in *Audubon* that Echo Park was Brower's "most spectacular success." Some people even say that Echo Park was the birth of the environmental movement or, as John McPhee wrote, "the turning point at which conservation became something more than contour plowing."[56] Roderick Nash wrote that at Echo Park "the American wilderness movement had its finest hour to that date."

Unlike the Hetch Hetchy debate, many more organizations and supporters were available to save Echo Park (the coalition included thirty groups), river supporters raised technical arguments, and congressional leadership was strong. No newspapers campaigned as effectively as had the San Francisco papers for Hetch Hetchy, and Senator Neuberger and Governor Johnson broke the western bloc for the dam.

As with Hetch Hetchy, the point was still to save a park. Few people fought the philosophy of big water development or the loss of wild rivers outside the national park system. This view had served conservationists well, but its limitations were soon to be seen. The irony of saving Echo Park was that Glen Canyon would be dammed.

FIGHTING FOR A FISHERY

Even though Washington state law required fish ladders or hatcheries with new dams, Tacoma City Light built five dams with neither ladders nor hatcheries, while offering the lowest residential electricity rates in the nation and selling even cheaper power to Kaiser Aluminum, Boise-Cascade, and other industries. In the early 1950s, Tacoma proposed Mayfield Dam on the Cowlitz River.

Fishermen objected, but sports columnist Elliot Metcalf of the *Tacoma News Tribune* answered with the boosterism of that era. "Forget your worry, sportsmen . . . rise to move Tacoma ahead to better things industrially and economically. . . . It is inevitable as death that the power productive Cowlitz will be harnessed for the good of all, not set aside for the minority, or few."[57]

Residents near the site joined sport and commercial fishermen, and state agencies attempted to enforce the Dam Sanctuary Act of 1949, which banned dams in Washington's lower Columbia basin. The license was denied by an FPC examiner, who found that the project was not adapted to "beneficial uses," including recreation, and that the need to preserve fish outweighed the need for power. But the FPC granted the license anyway. The state director of fisheries sued and for eight years won court victories ending at the U.S. Supreme Court in 1958, where after a poor presentation by the state attorney general, who had supported the dam before his election, earlier decisions were reversed. Tacoma began building the dam while fishermen appealed to voters statewide in an antidam initiative. They won, but in 1962 the state supreme court ruled that the vote could not stop construction.

Mayfield Dam was finished, but the state required Tacoma City Light to build a hatchery costing $20 million — more than the cost of the turbines and generators. Plagued with diseases, fish required treatment three times to keep them alive to spawn, and the hatchery failed to meet its goals 75 percent of the time.

Even though the Cowlitz was lost, the episode heightened awareness about salmon. A commitment grew through the 1960s, but not as fast as the dams. Fishermen again lost in California, where they fought a Bureau of

Reclamation dam and diversion on the Trinity River in 1952, but on the Namakagon River, Wisconsin convinced the FPC to stop a hydroelectric dam because of fisheries, scenic beauty, and recreational values.[58]

THE KINZUA MUD

While park supporters and fishermen fought dams in the West and Midwest, the Seneca Nation of the Iroquois Confederacy tried to save the last Indian lands in Pennsylvania.

In 1794 President George Washington signed the Pickering Treaty — the oldest Indian treaty — granting the Seneca under Chief Cornplanter 30,189 acres along the Allegheny River, including the village of Kinzua (meaning "fish on spear"), and stating that the Indians' land "shall remain theirs, until they choose to sell the same to the people of the United States, who have the right to purchase." The Senecas did not trust the government and refused to sign until the Society of Friends (the Quakers) guaranteed the president's word.

In 1936 Congress authorized the Army Corps of Engineers to build Kinzua Dam on Seneca lands so that floods could be controlled at Pittsburgh, two hundred miles downstream. Indians objected. One sent a Christmas card to Herbert Vogel, district engineer of the corps, wishing him all the blessings of the new year to which "he might be rightfully entitled." Having fourteen other dams in their upper Ohio basin plan (which was similar to the Pittsburgh Flood Commission plan written in 1908), the corps procrastinated on the troublesome Kinzua.

But civic leaders in Pittsburgh campaigned for the dam in 1955, and support grew a year later after a flood caused $2 million of damage at Warren, eight miles below the prospective dam site. When the corps recommended funding for the project, Congressman John Saylor said, "Apparently you have become so calloused and so crass that the breaking of the oldest treaty in the United States is a matter of little concern to you,"[59] but the local congressman wanted the dam, and Eisenhower approved funding. The condemnation of Seneca lands and the relocation of several hundred Indians was scheduled to begin.

Backing their word from 160 years before, the Quakers tried to save the reservation. They recommended that the Seneca hire Dr. Arthur E. Morgan to study alternatives. Morgan had designed the Miami River Project — America's first comprehensive flood control project and a landmark of hydrologic planning — and served as the first chairman of the Tennessee Valley Authority. In 1956 Indian president Cornelius Seneca met with

Morgan, who agreed to help but advised acceptance of the dam if no alternative could be found.

With Barton Jones, former TVA chief design engineer, Morgan identified several options that would divert flood water to a glacial depression in the nearby Conewango basin. Morgan reported that more water could be stored and that low-flow augmentation would be improved through the Conewango plan, costing less than Kinzua Dam.

The corps hired the "independent" engineering firm of Tippetts-Abbett-McCarthy-Stratton to review the alternative. Morgan objected because the firm's founder was a former corps engineer, three of four partners had worked for the corps, and for twenty years the corps had been the firm's major client.[60] The consultants reported that the alternative was feasible but would cost $91 million more than Kinzua, would flood more land, and require relocation of more people. Morgan was not allowed to review the appraisal and said that his plans were misrepresented. He was so enraged by ridicule from congressmen and the corps that he wrote *Dams and Other Disasters*—a book criticizing the corps—as the last major project of his career.

The Seneca had filed suit, and sympathy for them grew during the next two years. A song called "Cornplanter, Can You Swim?"—about the flooding of the chief's grave—was broadcast. But editors of the *Pittsburgh Press* wrote that the Indians deserved no more consideration than 2,500 white people who had been moved for the nearby Conemaugh Dam. The editors had no sympathy for the view that "Indians were so poorly treated by white men that we shouldn't take their lands now—even to save ourselves from flood disaster." In 1957 the district court ruled that Congress had been informed of the treaty and had intended to take the lands regardless. In 1959 the Supreme Court denied an injunction request.

The 180-foot-high dam was finished in 1965, flooding the Allegheny River and the Indian villages of Jennesadaga and Kinzua. The Seneca were moved from riverfront homes to southern New York, where each family could buy subdivided plots of one to three acres. On these, ranch houses were built. The graves of Cornplanter and three thousand other Indians were relocated.

Public opinion changed later. Concern for Indian rights grew in the 1960s and 1970s as some people heeded a Seneca leader's advice: "Why feel guilty about what happened in the nineteenth century? Pay closer attention to what you are still doing to us." Folk singer Buffy Saint Marie sang of the "liberty bell, as it rang with a thud over Kinzua mud." Pittsburgh's largest newspaper no longer referred to people concerned about America's oldest treaty as "bleeding hearts." A few years later, more arguments would have been added to the Indians' case. The Allegheny had been a magnificent Appalachian river, clean, undeveloped, and full of fish, but to save it for its river qualities had not been a part of the fight against the dam.

The Allegheny battle was outstanding, but the history of dam building is littered with projects that took the last shreds of Indian homelands. Authorized in 1944 as part of the Pick-Sloan plan for the Missouri River, Garrison Dam in North Dakota displaced 1,544 Indians. The business council of three tribes opposed the dam, but seeing that it would be built, the Indians asked for access to electric power, for pasture along the reservoir, for the use of timber from the reservoir area, and for a bridge so that neighbors could see each other without traveling hundreds of miles around the impoundment. Angered by a splinter group of Indians fighting the plan, General Pick of the corps withdrew from negotiations. The Indians were required to move out of the protected and fertile river valley and were relocated on the high plains, where there were no usable water supplies. They received few of the compromise benefits they had requested. A 1948 photograph shows the Indian chairman weeping as Interior Secretary J. A. Krug signs the contract for the land.[61]

By the 1960s, dam proposals on Indian lands were fought and won. A Bureau of Reclamation proposal to dam California's Trinity River on the Hoopa Reservation was stopped in 1963. On the Middle Fork of the Eel in California, Dos Rios Dam was halted, in part because it would flood the Round Valley Reservation. With changing attitudes and the melding of Indian rights and resource issues, Orme Dam in Arizona and Copper Creek Dam in Washington were stopped in the late 1970s.

THE POTOMAC AGAIN

In 1963 the corps revitalized their Potomac River plan and called for sixteen dams (and also, in an unusual move, for preservation of the Cacapon River). Fighting with vigor until now reserved for places like Yellowstone and Kings Canyon, the National Parks Association published *Analysis of the Potomac River Basin Report,* one of the first places in which Supreme Court Justice William O. Douglas spoke against dams. He led a hike on the historic Chesapeake and Ohio Canal, argued for pollution control instead of dilution, and called the dams' thirty-nine thousand kilowatts of power "trivial." A federal task force finally recommended small dams instead. Only one large dam was built. The defeat of the dams led to the restoration of the Chesapeake and Ohio Canal and to President Johnson's proposal for a Potomac national river with open space, trails, and pollution abatement, but the proposal was defeated because of landowner opposition.[62]

THE WEST'S LARGEST MISTAKE

Glen Canyon was called "incomparably beautiful" (Richard C. Bradley), "extraordinarily majestic" (Wiley and Gottlieb), and "a place of haunting beauty" (William Wyant). Wallace Stegner wrote that the canyon was "almost absolutely serene. . . . Its walls are the monolithic Navajo sandstone . . . fantastically eroded by silt side canyons, alcoves, grottos green with redbud and maiden-hair and with springs of sweet water."[63] Above all, Glen Canyon was "The Place No One Knew," and with a river awareness rarely expressed in the early dam fights, photographer Eliot Porter wrote, "The architect, the life-giver, and the moderator of Glen Canyon is the Colorado River." The dam site was in Arizona, upstream from Grand Canyon.

In 1916 the first survey of the Colorado had identified a Glen Canyon dam site, but its Navajo Sandstone — the red showpiece of southwestern national parks — is porous and absorptive. In 1954 the interior secretary stated that "the poorly cemented and relatively weak condition" of Glen Canyon rock caused "some concern" that foundations could not support a dam higher than seven hundred feet. The Bureau of Reclamation opposed Echo Park alternatives, but this view changed as politics required. In 1955 — the year before Congress banned Echo Park Dam — an Interior Department geologist stated that Glen Canyon was an excellent site for a dam.

When arguing against Echo Park Dam, David Brower had said, "If the river disappeared in its course through Dinosaur, or was somehow unavailable, a sound upper Colorado storage project could be developed elsewhere." Glen Canyon was the Bureau of Reclamation's "elsewhere," and because it was not a national park or monument, the dam was scarcely opposed.

When the authorization reached Congress in 1956, Florida Congressman James Haley argued that the site was unsafe. He dropped a piece of canyon shale into a glass of water, and Congress watched the rock disintegrate. Supporting the dam, Arizona's Stewart Udall dropped his own shale in a glass and said that he would drink the water when he finished his speech.[64] The Bureau of Reclamation later estimated seepage losses of 15 percent at the reservoir.

Some senators wanted conservationists to fight the entire Upper Colorado River Storage Project, but the act faced no firm opposition, and it passed in 1956. The bureau was authorized to build Glen Canyon Dam,

Flaming Gorge Dam in Wyoming, Curecanti Dam in Colorado, and Navajo Dam in New Mexico.

Soon after Congress's vote, the Interior Department's Geological Survey stated that the Colorado River could be regulated by thirty million acre-feet of storage, already held by existing dams (mostly by Hoover Dam). Glen Canyon would increase the total to nearly twice the needed amount. The Geological Survey's report stated that the gain in regulation would be largely offset by a corresponding increase in evaporation and that "storage development may be approaching, if not exceeding, the useful limit."[65] Other proposals by the bureau would bring total storage to eighty-six million acre-feet — nearly three times the needed amount, causing evaporation of 13 percent of the river's supply. The storage needs of the dam could have been met by amending the Colorado compact to allow for upper basin storage credits at Hoover Dam, but the hydroelectric plant at Glen Canyon was to be the upper basin's "cash register," with revenue from nine hundred thousand kilowatts to fund irrigation in the headwater states.

Started in 1956, the dam rose 710 feet, its five million cubic yards of concrete exceeding those of Hoover Dam. In 1963 the gates were closed to fill Lake Powell, eventually flooding 180 miles of Colorado River canyons and scores of tributaries, including the Escalante River and small canyons named Twilight, Mystery, Cathedral, and Music Temple. A Bureau of Reclamation brochure named the reservoir the "Jewel of the Colorado" and stated,

> To have a deep blue lake
> Where no lake was before
> Seems to bring man
> A little closer to God.

"We didn't know how much devastation would occur," said river outfitter Martin Litton in 1983. "With a national park, there was a constituency that we didn't have with Glen Canyon. We weren't thinking of potential parks. Looking back, I'd say Echo Park was less valuable than Glen Canyon. We tried to fight the dam, but we were tired. We didn't know our own strength. We didn't realize the snowball we had started at Echo Park."[66]

In 1983 Stewart Udall said, "The Sierra Club fought for the middle-sized fish and let the big one get away. If I could switch it, I'd have Glen Canyon be the national park and build the dam at Echo Park." Floating through Glen Canyon just before its flooding is one of the experiences that changed Udall's goals to include river conservation as well as development.

Never having seen what was at stake, David Brower also rafted through

Glen Canyon before its flooding, and he later called this canyon the greatest loss of wilderness in his lifetime. In a 1982 *Audubon* interview Brower said, "My failure to act still haunts me. It was the greatest sin I have ever committed." In *The Place No One Knew,* Brower wrote, "Glen Canyon died in 1963. . . . Neither you nor I, nor anyone else, knew it well enough to insist that at all costs it should endure." This book of Eliot Porter photographs was a milestone celebrating a lost place and documenting a remarkable, extinct landscape. With its powerful message that a place must be known to be saved, it created an entire movement for wilderness awareness and publicity. Other award-winning Sierra Club books designed by Brower followed, showing threatened landscapes and pressing people into action at the Redwoods, the North Cascades, and the Grand Canyon.

Richard Leonard, honorary president of the Sierra Club in 1984, said, "Dave Brower and Martin Litton feel that it was wrong to let Glen Canyon be built. But I think we were right at the time. We couldn't stop Dinosaur and Glen Canyon both. If we hadn't fought at Dinosaur we would have lost the National Park system. If we would have fought at Glen Canyon people would have been fed up with conservationists stopping everything."[67]

Edward Abbey wrote of Glen Canyon in *Desert Solitaire:* "To grasp the nature of the crime that was committed imagine the Taj Mahal or Chartres Cathedral buried in mud until only the spires remain visible. With this difference; those man-made celebrations of human aspiration could conceivably be reconstructed while Glen Canyon was a living thing, irreplaceable, which can never be recovered through any human agency."

Attitudes about rivers and dams had been slowly changing, and Glen Canyon polarized two views. In *Encounters with the Archdruid* by John McPhee, Commissioner of Reclamation Floyd Dominy was quoted as saying, "The unregulated Colorado was a son of a bitch. It wasn't any good. It was in flood or in trickle"; of the reservoir he said, "It is the most beautiful lake in the world." About the same lake, Edward Abbey wrote in *The Monkey Wrench Gang:* "Instead of a river he looked down on a motionless body of murky green effluent, dead, stagnant, dull, a scum of oil floating on the surface. On the canyon was a coating of dried silt and mineral salts, like a bathtub ring, recorded high-water mark. Lake Powell: storage pond, silt trap, evaporation tank and lagoon." In the memory and mythology of western river people, there are the three greatest losses: Hetch Hetchy, Glen Canyon, and the Stanislaus, flooded in 1982.

The Glen Canyon loss gave David Brower and the conservationists the determination to stop the Bureau of Reclamation's next proposal — dams in the Grand Canyon. And with utter clarity, Glen Canyon showed that rivers in addition to those flowing through national parks deserved protection.

REGARDLESS OF THE LAW

Rainbow Bridge is a 160-acre national monument in the upper recesses of Glen Canyon. The largest-known natural bridge on earth, this sandstone arch could cover the Capitol dome in Washington. In defeating Echo Park Dam, conservationists made certain that the law prohibited the flooding of any national park or monument, but a full Lake Powell would be forty-eight feet deep beneath the bridge, possibly undermining its foundation.[68] The Bureau of Reclamation proposed a $25 million barrier dam to hold back the reservoir, but despite Interior Secretary Udall's urging, Congress funded other water projects instead.

In 1970 a suit was filed by Friends of the Earth (an organization formed by David Brower when he was ousted from the Sierra Club after disagreements over his opposition to a nuclear power plant), the Wasatch Mountain Club, and river outfitter Ken Sleight to prevent the flooding of Rainbow Bridge. In 1973 District Court Judge Willis Ritter ordered the government "to take forthwith such actions as were necessary to prevent any waters of Lake Powell and the Glen Canyon unit from entering within the boundaries of Rainbow Bridge National Monument." He added, "It was pretty sneaky of Congress to pass a law and then ignore it completely."[69]

To keep Rainbow Bridge dry, Lake Powell's depth would need to be reduced one hundred feet, cutting storage capacity in half and losing annual hydroelectric revenues of several million dollars. The lower level would also save two hundred miles of canyons from inundation, including parts of the Colorado's Cataract Canyon and the proposed Escalante Wilderness. This was perhaps the first time a serious effort was made to stop the filling of a reservoir behind a dam that was already built.

Conservationists held that the upper basin's lost storage capacity could be acquired in a paper transaction amending the basin compact so that some of Lake Mead's water would be shared, and that evaporative losses would be cut with a smaller reservoir. But a water resource attorney remarked that "pigs will fly" before Congress would tamper with the compact that had divided the basin in two.

The Supreme Court ruled that congressional action in denying funds for the barrier dam took precedence over the Upper Colorado River Storage

Project Act, which prohibited Rainbow Bridge's flooding. Lake Powell would be filled to the brim.

THE ULTIMATE SITE

Glen Canyon was unknown, but millions had seen the Colorado in the Grand Canyon. In a legendary journey, John Wesley Powell led the first known boating expedition through the canyon, and he wrote, "The glories and the beauties of form, color and sound unite in the Grand Canyon. . . . It is a region more difficult to traverse than the Alps or the Himalayas, but if strength and courage are sufficient for the task, by a year's toil a concept of sublimity can be obtained never again to be equalled on the hither side of Paradise."

The canyon became a symbol of scenery and wilderness; in 1874 Congress approved $10,000 to buy a Thomas Moran painting of the canyon for the Senate lobby. To protect the canyon was a goal of John Muir's, and Teddy Roosevelt had stood at the rim and said, "Leave it as it is. You cannot improve on it. The ages have been at work on it, and man can only mar it." In 1908 Roosevelt declared part of the canyon a national monument. More than three million people a year visited there in the 1970s, and during each season fourteen thousand people float the river that Powell had so perilously explored.

Part of the 280-mile-long canyon became a national park in 1919, but not before Arizona congressman Carl Hyden deleted large areas for grazing and mining. Water interests also tried to allow dams. The bill from which the 1919 act was derived had been reported from committee with provisions that the Reclamation Service could use the park for a reservoir, but on the Senate floor in 1918, a condition was added that dams must be "consistent with the primary purposes of the said park."[70]

As a part of the Central Arizona Project (CAP), in 1947 the Bureau of Reclamation proposed two Grand Canyon dams to generate 2.1 million kilowatts of power needed to lift water from the Colorado River to Arizona cities. A Bridge Canyon site would impound ninety-three miles of the river, including twenty-seven miles beside Grand Canyon National Monument and thirteen miles in the national park. The Marble Canyon site would flood the upper reaches of the canyon. Only about one-third of the Colorado in the Grand Canyon would remain free flowing, with no access to the river between the dams. Lava Falls, regarded by some people as the most exciting rapid in the country, would be under 214 feet of water, and Havasu Creek — a paradise to many — would be eighty-five feet under.

In 1947 the Sierra Club directors approved of the Bridge Canyon Dam, providing certain changes were made, but the leadership voted the next year against any dam in the national monument or park. Some conservationists thought that the only way to prevent Bridge Canyon Dam was to allow Marble Canyon Dam outside the park, but under David Brower the club abandoned the earlier prejudice of protecting only national park rivers, and it opposed both dams when the bureau reintroduced them in the 1960s.

The arguments against Echo Park Dam were repeated with new fervor. The dam fighters said that all parks could be commercialized if the Grand Canyon were dammed, and in fact, threats to the parks had proliferated: a Buffalo River dam in Grand Teton Park, the Wawona Project in Yosemite, Rio Grande dams in Big Bend Park, and Moab Dam in Arches National Monument.

Conservationists brought more analysis to the Grand Canyon case than any earlier dam fight. From the two reservoirs, two hundred thousand acre-feet of water — almost enough to supply Detroit — would evaporate, leaving bicarbonates, chlorides, and sulfates of sodium, calcium, and magnesium in an already-saline river. The Geological Survey reported that the reservoirs would result in "no significant gain in net regulation."[71] Using government data, the Sierra Club calculated that the dams would be full of silt in 60 to 160 years, and uneconomic much sooner. The bureau listed a life of 163 years for Bridge Canyon Reservoir if sediment-catching dams were not built on tributaries, 250 years with the catchment dams.

Because the dams would serve urban growth at Phoenix, John Saylor, ranking Republican on the House Interior and Insular Affairs Committee, said,

> The Federal reclamation program was begun over half a century ago for the basic purpose of reclaiming the arid, barren lands of the West in order to make them more productive. In the ensuing decades, and particularly in the past few years, the policies and programs of the bureaucrats in the Bureau of Reclamation have wandered so far afield from this basic goal that it seems reclamation has become of only incidental importance. . . . A reclamation program is needed to reclaim the Bureau of Reclamation for its original purpose before it is too late.[72]

The Sierra Club argued that cheaper power could be generated at coal-fired or nuclear plants and stated, "The day may be near when atomic energy will begin to produce really inexpensive electricity," and, "Coal-fired generation plants would use a fuel that is plentiful in the region and would leave Grand Canyon National Park inviolate."[73] Later recognizing the narrowness of this view, David Brower said, "We thought that strip mines were not of scenic importance to the Grand Canyon."

The dams' approval hinged partly on Secretary of the Interior Stewart Udall, the great-grandson of John D. Lee, for whom Lee's Ferry just below Glen Canyon was named. Udall was the son of a judge, and after becoming a lawyer and congressman he was appointed by President Kennedy to the interior job. At the suggestion of author Wallace Stegner, Udall wrote *The Quiet Crisis* early in his term. The book carried a strong conservation message but reflected the view still prevalent in 1961 that water development was a positive part of conservation. About the New Deal dam-building programs Udall wrote, "This is a new kind of American empire building; its goal was the common good . . . and its most visible symbols were the huge dams that began to rise from the bedrock of such rivers as the Colorado, the Tennessee, and the Sacramento." Udall's term as interior secretary ran eight years, exceeded only by that of Harold Ickes, who served nearly thirteen years under Roosevelt and Truman. The Grand Canyon dams presented a dilemma for Udall and his brother, Morris, who succeeded to Stewart's seat in Congress. Both believed in conservation, yet both were Arizonans knowing that water development takes political priority.

Speaking to the Senate Subcommittee on Irrigation and Reclamation, Stewart Udall recognized the need to protect parks but said, "It should be noted that such a reservoir invasion would be a peripheral one which would occur in the most remote and inaccessible area of the park. It should be further noted that 98 percent of the land area in the park would remain in its natural condition."[74] He argued that "the pristine natural condition of the river has already been permanently altered by the construction of upstream dams which regulate the flow of the river." This prodam argument that the river was regulated and therefore not worth saving was not accepted by Congress or by policy makers of the national rivers system. Udall told the Senate, "A fresh water lake could provide boat-type access to a region . . . that would otherwise be available for only the most limited use." His opponents argued that the Grand Canyon reservoirs would be like bathtubs with mud rings, vertical shorelines, and cliffs magnifying motorboat noise. The National Park Service under Stewart Udall took no strong stands against the dams.

Led by David Brower and the Sierra Club, the conservationists mounted the largest campaign yet to protect wild lands. They produced brochures, bulletins, films, news releases, and a book of color photographs with a narrative by François Leydet about a Grand Canyon journey and the dams.

In an unprecedented move among conservation groups, Brower spent $15,000 for a full-page advertisement in the *New York Times* and also bought a page in the *San Francisco Chronicle*. Addressing Udall's argument that more people would see the canyon from motorboats, the ads stated, "Should we also flood the Sistine Chapel so tourists can get nearer the ceiling?" After these ads, the Internal Revenue Service revoked the club's tax-exempt status, but club membership doubled in a surge of growth not exceeded until environmentalists rallied in outrage against Interior Secretary James Watt in 1981.

The conservationists did not oppose the whole Central Arizona Project, only the Grand Canyon dams. Yet broader questions indicated growing concerns related to water: Should Phoenix become another Los Angeles? Are artificial rivers for the development of arid lands the most economic use of national resources? Would the money benefit the people more if it were invested elsewhere?

Two utilities in Arizona and one in Los Angeles favored coal-burning power plants as alternatives to dams, and Stewart Udall's Indian policy supported a power plant on the Navaho reservation. In 1965 Udall dropped his support for one of the dams, and in 1967 he proposed that the coal plants be built instead of either dam.

What changed Udall's mind? "Taking the trip down the river," he answered in 1983. "There was a lot of pressure from my Arizona constituents and my brother and so forth — we had to have a dam. But when I came off the river, I knew we were going to abandon the dams." Udall had become involved in other river-saving efforts and in a proposal for a national system of protected waterways. He said, "How could I be for scenic rivers and build a dam in the Grand Canyon?"[75]

Central Arizona Project supporters decided to drop the controversial dams in order to save the rest of the project. In September 1968, President Johnson signed the CAP law without the Grand Canyon dams. Conservationists, concerned with pollution, later fought coal-fired power plants, running another full-page newspaper advertisement stating that strip mining on the Navaho's Black Mesa was "Like Ripping Apart St. Peter's in Order to Sell the Marble." But the coal was mined, and the pollution from the Four Corners power plants is one of the few man-made features visible from outer space.

In saving the Colorado in the Grand Canyon, the conservationists gained new strength and confirmed that they were a political force. The debate led to broader concerns about energy, coal and nuclear power, air pollution, and urban sprawl, and at the end of the Grand Canyon effort the environmental community was at the brink of a nationwide movement, poised to plunge into issues encompassing the totality of life in America. After the CAP fight, Morris Udall became a leader in environmental legislation, and in 1972 he wrote, "There was little to tell us in 1963 that the great ecology-environment movement would take center stage by the end of the decade. In retrospect, it is clear that the battle of the Grand Canyon dams was a central, symbolic event which played a major role in awakening environmental awareness in America.[76]

At a 1977 conference about river recreation, historian Roderick Nash stated that Boulder Dam's

completion in 1935 was a reason for universal jubilation in the United States. A wild river had been tamed. The engineers were heros, and as Lake Mead began to fill, a proud nation proclaimed Boulder Dam the eighth wonder of the civilized world.

Thirty years later the tables were almost totally turned. Again engineers proposed a dam on the Colorado River—upstream from Hoover Dam in the Grand Canyon. But this time the engineers did not seem to be the agents of progress that they had in the 1930s. For a great many Americans the Colorado River in the Grand Canyon was not a monster to be shackled and put to work for the economy but something valuable in its own right and already working to enhance the quality of American life. . . . In 1968 the cheers that forty years before greeted the authorization of Boulder Dam now sounded in support of the defeat of the Grand Canyon dam projects.

Yet, looking at other rivers being dammed, it still seemed that, beyond the national parks, not much was really sacred. In *Goodbye to a River* John Graves wrote about his final canoe journey on Texas's Brazos River before it was dammed: "Maybe you save a Dinosaur Monument from time to time, but in between such salvations you lose ten Brazoses." Dozens of wild and scenic rivers were still being destroyed: the Kootenai in Montana, the upper Rogue in Oregon, the Feather in California, the Gauley in West Virginia, the Allegheny in Pennsylvania, and the Coosawattee in Georgia (which inspired *Deliverance,* though the movie was filmed on the Chattooga). Dam builders thrived in a refuge from would-be opponents who never knew that these places existed.

But conservation leaders made the Grand Canyon a nationwide issue, and the Colorado River was supported more than any river so far. Not only the park but also the rapids and the water-based geological process were reasons to fight dams. As free-flowing streams became scarce, the river protection movement was on the verge of a giant step. Values were to be recognized in many rivers, in all regions.

In 1975 Congress extended national park boundaries to include most of the Grand Canyon, but in 1982 Arizona congressman Eldon Rudd introduced a new bill for dams. Brandt Calkin of the Sierra Club said, "I'm not concerned for this year or next, but I'm still concerned. I've seen too many of these things come back. It seems like all of our victories are temporary, all our defeats permanent."

The Grand Canyon victory has remained solid. Other decisions for permanence in river protection would spring from the loss of a spectacular wild river in Idaho.

THE SEEDS OF PERMANENCE

Forty-nine new dams were proposed for the Columbia basin in the 1950s. Libby Dam on the Kootenai River was stalled by Canada, railroads, and local conservationists but was later built, and it flooded ninety-eight miles of river stretching into British Columbia. John Day Dam on the Columbia was delayed by private versus public power disputes but built. In the incredibly wild and beautiful Clearwater basin of Idaho, Penny Cliffs Dam was proposed to flood the Clearwater, Selway, and Lochsa rivers, but first Bruce's Eddy Dam (now called Dworshak) was planned as one of America's tallest dams, on the Clearwater's North Fork.

Fishing and conservation groups fought Bruce's Eddy Dam, which would destroy forty-eight miles of excellent steelhead and salmon habitat and one of the state's most important elk ranges. The dam had been delayed by Eisenhower's rivers and harbors veto in 1956, but in spite of opposition by the Idaho Fish and Game Department, the dam was authorized in 1958 at the insistence of Senator Henry C. Dworshak, who argued that Idaho never received its share of corps spending.

In 1961 dam opponents asked Interior Secretary Stewart Udall to intervene. With the Grand Canyon dams, Udall was "caught in the politics" of his own state and of his own agency — the Bureau of Reclamation — which would do the building. But Bruce's Eddy was an Army Corps of Engineers dam, and the Interior Department had nothing to lose.

Udall was impressed by the fishermen's arguments and by the wildness of the place, but it was too late. The most he could do was work with congressmen who added an amendment — stricken before the vote — to prohibit additional Clearwater dams. However, the Clearwater case led Udall to reconsider nothing less than the philosophy of dam building, and he suddenly became committed to balancing the federal water program.

The Clearwater case alerted Udall and others that one dam could cause enormous losses of fish and wildlife, significant to the entire northern Rockies region. But in Alaska, a dam was proposed that would have continental effects by destroying a river that supported more waterfowl breeding than all national wildlife refuges combined.

THE SIZE OF LAKE ERIE

The Yukon River was without national park status and without the household recognition of a Grand Canyon, yet it became a nationwide environmental issue because of Rampart Dam. Hetch Hetchy had been the first great conservation battle in the nation; Rampart was the first in Alaska.

Echo Park had exemplified the threat dams posed to national parks — the first reason to save rivers. The second main reason was wildlife protection, and Rampart represented the ultimate in wildlife destruction. The debate over the proposed dam was thus a culmination of wildlife protection efforts.

The two-thousand-mile-long Yukon is the fourth-largest river in North America, penetrating wild mountains, dark forests of spruce, and subarctic plains grazed by caribou and ranged by wolves. The Yukon Flats are a maze of sloughs and thirty-six thousand lakes, where the river and its islands are eighty miles wide. River travelers must use a compass to find their way through.

Below the 180-mile-long Flats are the Ramparts — a deep canyon where the Army Corps of Engineers proposed the dam in 1959. Five hundred and thirty feet high and 4,700 feet wide, the dam would form the largest reservoir ever built, 280 miles long and flooding 10,200 square miles — larger than Lake Erie or New Jersey. With a patriotic flare, Harold L. Moats of the corps's Alaska office said to the Alaska Rural Electric Cooperative Association, "Rampart Canyon, the big one, is Alaska's most valuable resource, and as it is developed, Alaska will take her rightful place in the family of states contributing richly to the economy of the nation and to the welfare of the whole free world."[77]

Alaska's economy had suffered after a 1950s military boom collapsed. Taxes threatened to strangle the new state, and the corps's $3 billion for Rampart looked like a solution. Rampart would be the country's costliest dam ever, having as its sole purpose the generation of five thousand megawatts of electricity. Promoters hoped that the aluminum industry, which needed vast amounts of electricity, would move north. Senator Ernest Gruening boosted the project: "Alaska is confronted with the task of catching up after years of federal neglect." His staff called the area worthless, containing "not more than ten flush toilets. [In fact it had none.] Search the whole world and it would be difficult to find an equivalent area with so little to be lost through flooding."[78]

Native groups did not agree. About 1,500 Athapascan Indians and a few hundred white people lived in the reservoir area, and twice that number lived along the river below the dam site. The natives' *Tundra Times* reported that all but one village from the head of the reservoir to the Bering Sea were against the dam. The livelihood of other natives in Alaska and 3,500 in the Yukon Territory would be affected or eliminated by the loss of salmon.

The corps was required to ask for comments from federal agencies, including the Fish and Wildlife Service in the Department of the Interior, where biologists reported, "Nowhere in the history of water development in North America have the fish and wildlife losses anticipated to result from a single project been so overwhelming." They projected elimination of 1.6 percent of all North American ducks; 12,800 geese; 10,000 cranes; 20,000 grebes; a total destruction of the salmon run for thousands of miles of rivers and streams above the dam; and a loss of furbearers that accounted for 7 percent of the total state harvest. Altogether, 1.5 million waterfowl migrated south from the Flats—more than the annual production of all other national wildlife refuges in 1964. Wildlife losses would extend 750 miles to the Bering Sea because of lack of seasonal flooding, which maintains the wetlands, renourishes the soil, and rejuvenates the willows—food for twelve thousand moose.

Alerted by the Fish and Wildlife Service studies and by a few lonely Alaskans fighting the dam, conservationists and duck hunters argued not only that the wildlife should be saved but also that the power would be too expensive and would be thirty times the amount used in the state. Devil's Canyon on the Susitna River was supported by some conservationists as an alternative—a site that was threatened in 1984.

Rampart supporters asked, "Who ever heard of a duck drowning?" and because the reservoir would require twenty years to fill, they said, "The ducks and animals have twenty years to move out of the area." State politicians who opposed the dam lost elections. After a University of Alaska faculty member questioned the building of the dam, a member of the state House of Representatives suggested cutting university appropriations.

At the North American Wildlife and Natural Resources Conference in 1963, Dr. Ira N. Gabrielson of the Wildlife Management Institute warned that Rampart was about to be rushed through Congress and that the dam "is synonymous with resources destruction." Fifteen organizations in the

Natural Resources Council of America pooled $25,000 for a study docu-
menting the case against Rampart; this move showed the growing role of
scientists in fighting dams.[79]

In 1967 Interior Secretary Udall released a report on Rampart. Beyond
the impacts on wildlife, the Interior Department stated that the power
would not be used and that the timber industry would lose the equivalent
of three years of total Alaska production. Udall's recommendation that the
dam not be built was a setback to the corps. Alaska Governor Walter
Hickel, who had backed the dam, was appointed as interior secretary under
Richard Nixon, but when oil was discovered on the North Slope in 1968,
the development interests turned all their attention to the Trans-Alaska
Pipeline. Under President Carter, the 8.5-million-acre Yukon Flats National Wildlife Refuge was designated, ending all planning for the dam.

The argument that rivers should be saved for fish and wildlife had failed
on the Mississippi, Cowlitz, Trinity, Santee, and Clearwater rivers, but here
on the faraway Yukon, conservationists won. Effects of the project were
simply too ruinous to be dismissed as "frivolous" concerns about fish.

Along with the park savers, landowners, and fish and wildlife supporters,
one more group of river activists came together in the 1960s, not in the
mile-deep canyons of the West or the howling wilderness of the north, but
in the gentle hills of Arkansas.

THE RIVER PEOPLE

In northern Arkansas there are wild lands, rocky cliffs, clean water, quick
rapids, smallmouth bass, and bubbling springs that attracted people who
were aware of the many complex values of a river. The Buffalo River
supporters were canoeists, and the very nature of their interest led to
concerns that crossed boundaries and combined issues. Because they traveled on nearly the whole river, they were interested in the entire length, not
just farms and not just fish. The free flow of the river was not just compati-
ble, it was essential to what they did. They used both the water and the
shores. After paddling the river from top to bottom, it was easier to see the
ecological and philosophical concepts of the river as one lively unit, like an
organism with all parts connected.

Newspaper reporter George Wells wrote in the *Pine Bluff Commercial,*
"It was largely due to the availability of these canoes that more people were
exposed closeup to the beauty of the Buffalo and joined the crusade to
'save' it from the dam."[80] Wells's writing includes one of the first references
to "river people."

Harold Alexander, who worked for the Arkansas Fish and Game Department and expanded an interest in fisheries to encompass many river values, wrote, "A stream is a living thing. It moves, dances and shimmers in the sun. It furnishes opportunities for enjoyment and its beauty moves men's souls. Like the condor, the whooping crane and the wolf, the streams of America are on the road to oblivion." In 1957 Alexander wrote an Arkansas Audubon Society resolution against the corps's Gilbert Dam, which would flood forty-seven miles of the Buffalo. The next year, Alexander asked for help from Paul Bruce Dowling of the Nature Conservancy, who recommended that the National Park Service consider federal protection for the river. Citizen leader Dr. Neil Compton asked Senator Fulbright to persuade the park service to do a study, which was started with a $7,000 budget.

Compton tried to enlist nationwide support for the Buffalo. He traveled to California to meet with David Brower of the Sierra Club in 1962, but that was during the Grand Canyon debate, and Compton reported, "It was my belief that we would not be able to generate enough interest under this label or with the high annual dues levied by the Sierra Club." Instead, Compton and others formed the Ozark Society, bringing national attention to the Buffalo in 1962 when William O. Douglas joined them on a canoe trip and called the Buffalo "a national treasure too beautiful to die." Park service planners recommended national river status in 1963, following the model of the Current River, which they had studied several years earlier (see Chapter 6).

The Buffalo is one of few cases in which a river controversy broke into violence. Canoeists were shot at after being stopped by trees that had been cut to block their path. Barbed wire was strung across the stream. A fight at a local basketball game was blamed on the Buffalo River issue. When a student chapter of the Ozark Society advertised a "coeducational float," a local sheriff saw a chance to discredit the Ozark group, and he staged a raid to expose his idea of immorality. But instead of finding the canoeists' camp, he stumbled onto an outing of the Landsman's Society — a group of local lawyers and realtors, who were fined for possession of untaxed whiskey.[81]

Governor Orval Faubus opposed the dam in 1965, temporarily ending the threat. Senator Fulbright introduced a national river bill, but in spite of opposition to the dam by the next two governors the bill languished because the representative from the local district still backed the dam. In the spirit of *This Is Dinosaur,* a book of photographs by Kenneth Smith titled *Buffalo River Country* was published in 1967 as a call for preservation. In 1972 the dam was finally banned when Congress designated the Buffalo as a national river.

Canoeists had become one of the important groups in river protection.

Led by Randy Carter — author of whitewater guidebooks — they stopped
the corps's Salem Church Dam on the Rappahannock River in Virginia. In
the nationwide movement to save rivers in the 1970s, river runners were a
prime force in creating the American Rivers Conservation Council and in
fighting dams on the St. John and Stanislaus, where they brought awareness
of river values to a new peak.

THE BURDEN OF PROOF

A different view of rivers and water development had grown from Hetch
Hetchy to include other national park rivers: the Yellowstone, Kings, Flathead, Green, Yampa, and Colorado. The new view expanded to state parks
and wilderness areas along the Clarion, Hudson, and Sun rivers. With
mixed success and failure, fishermen worked to protect their best streams:
the Rogue, Cowlitz, Namakagon, and Clearwater. The commitment to
build dams was attacked by landowners in Kansas's Blue Valley and by
Indians along the Allegheny. For the Potomac, diverse interests joined to
protect the river. The Yukon was saved for wildlife; the Buffalo was saved
by canoeists. To justify dams, the burden of proof was shifting from the
conservationists to the developers. Sydney Howe of the Conservation
Foundation wrote, "Few, if any of our institutions face a greater crisis of
confidence than does the public works establishment."

Beyond the political thicket, the smallest seeds were planted for a spiritual outlook toward the rivers. The phrase "reverence for life" occurred to
Albert Schweitzer as he stood on the deck of a steamer going up Africa's
Ogovve River. The land ethic described by Aldo Leopold began to gain
acceptance and would be expanded to waters. In the years to come, some
people felt a spiritual importance in the rivers and tried to describe this in a
society not anxious to listen.

By the mid-1960s the four main groups of river conservationists — park
supporters, fishermen, landowners, and canoeists — were growing in
power, and their concerns were reaching more people. The reasons to
protect rivers were growing, overlapping, and attracting supporters, and
through the bitter losses and the precedent-setting successes, a movement
was born to save the rivers that were left.

CHAPTER FIVE

The Movement to Save Rivers

A revolution in attitudes about rivers moved through the country and touched every stream. The late 1960s and early 1970s brought powerful ingredients for change: a growing sense of scarcity, the environmental movement, activism by conservationists and landowners, applications of science and economics coupled with publicity, recreational use, and tight money — all contributing to a national movement to save threatened rivers.

The sense of scarcity came when people realized that thousands of dams had been built but free-flowing rivers were rare. All of the Columbia was dammed except for a fifty-mile section, inaccessible because of the Hanford nuclear power reservation, and even there Ben Franklin Dam was proposed. In California, 1,300 dams blocked every major river but one, and huge second-generation dams such as New Melones and New Don Pedro were planned to flood out the old dams. Still foreseeing scarcities, the water developers searched with the zeal of the desperate. Cities fearing shortages sent their engineers hundreds of miles away to claim new supplies.

The environmental movement galvanized support for river protection, it expanded awareness, and it brought new expertise. The message of Earth Day, April 22, 1970, reached almost everyone. An easy place to see the problem was at a dam site where one action, often funded by the taxpayers themselves, caused destruction that was immediate, obvious, and vulnerable to citizen outrage. New laws, especially the National Environmental Policy Act, gave citizens unprecedented influence.

Patriotism, fear, and hopelessness were no longer reasons to accept plans of the Army Corps of Engineers or other builders. Antigovernment activism became accepted. The type of landowners who had trembled before the

SELECTED EVENTS IN CHAPTER 5

1964   Construction started on Cross Florida Barge Canal.
Delaware Valley Conservation Association fought Sunfish Pond power project.

1967   Conservationists and William O. Douglas protested Red River Dam.
Environmental Defense Fund organized.
Supreme Court ruled on Hells Canyon dams.

1969   National Environmental Policy Act passed Congress.

1970   Environmental Defense Fund sued to stop Gillham Dam.
Earth Day held on April 22.
Natural Resources Defense Council organized.
Save the Delaware Coalition opposed Tocks Island Dam.

1971   Cross Florida Barge Canal halted.
Environmental Defense Fund sued to stop Oakley Dam.

1972   Environmental Policy Center organized.
Environmental Defense Fund sued to delay Tellico Dam.

1973   Governor Jimmy Carter halted work on Sprewrell Bluff Dam.
Friends of the River sponsored state-wide initiative against New Melones Dam.
Snail darter discovered in Little Tennessee River.
Environmental Policy Center published *Disasters in Water Development*.

1974   License issued for New River dams.
Natural Resources Defense Council sued to delay Auburn Dam.
Friends of the St. John organized.

1975   Oakley Dam halted.
Governor Wendell Ford opposed Red River Dam.
Hells Canyon National Recreation Area stopped dam proposals.
Delaware River Basin Commission recommended deauthorization of Tocks Island Dam.
Earthquake reached 5.9 on Richter scale near Auburn Dam site.

1976   New River designated national river.
Teton Dam ruptured.
Irrigation districts and San Francisco applied for permits to dam Tuolumne River.
First national conference for river conservation held.

1977   Corps recommended that Cross Florida Barge Canal be terminated.

1978   National Parks and Recreation Act passed.
Supreme Court ruled to stop Tellico Dam.

1979   Interior Secretary Andrus announced that Auburn Dam would need to be reauthorized.
Congress approved Tellico Dam.
Friends of the River opposed filling of reservoir at New Melones Dam.

1980   Dickey-Lincoln dams deauthorized.

1981   Orme Dam stopped.
Tuolumne River Preservation Trust organized.

1982   Reservoir at New Melones Dam filled.

1984   Tuolumne River designated a national river.

agencies condemning land now fought back. Even small dam proposals stirred up people willing to battle a bureaucracy and the local chamber of commerce.

Scientists proved that water projects were wreaking havoc and upsetting entire ecosystems. Economists calculated enormous costs in dollars and cents. Journalists got the word out. The issues of river protection made headlines in magazines, in newspapers, and on television. National publicity, begun by John Muir in *Century* magazine, was resumed in *Harper's, Collier's,* the *Atlantic,* the *New Yorker, Reader's Digest, American Forests, Outdoor Life,* and other magazines after the mid-1950s, peaking in the 1970s. Some of this attention responded to public interest, and some created interest.

Support for development was shaken by a proliferation of dam fiascos hurting dozens of communities, and people's protests were like ripples overlapping in a pool. Instead of gaining popular support with new dams, the builders were losing it. Many people saw exorbitant costs, unsafe construction, exterminated wildlife, and the relocation of families pushed from their homes by a force that seemed like war. A consensus was building in a group including millions more people than the park supporters and fishermen of the first dam fights.

In the 1970s, use of rivers boomed with canoeists, kayakers, and rafters. Even beer and cigar commercials featured whitewater boaters. Tourism took many Americans to the scenic rivers of the mountains, and people saw what was at stake. Once they experienced a wild river—any wild river— people could understand conservationists wanting to save a similar place. Paddlers and river guides became activists, and like the hikers and climbers of the 1950s who matured into the wilderness preservationists of the 1960s, these river runners forced their way into the political process.

The growing strength of the river conservationists was met by waning strength among dam builders. By the 1970s most of the economic projects were finished, and the water developers were left with proposals difficult to justify.

The river protection movement grew in tangled relationships of issues, places, and people. Two main directions evolved: the fighting of dams described in this chapter, and the start of a national wild and scenic rivers system. National river designation, which prohibits the construction of more dams, is covered in Chapter 6.

THE NEW LAW AND THE CASSATOT

More than anything else, the National Environmental Policy Act (NEPA) of 1969 changed the way federal actions affecting the environment were decided, and the Cassatot in Arkansas was the first case in which people used the new law to try to save a river.

The National Environmental Policy Act requires that an environmental impact statement be written before a federal agency can build, license, or participate in a project likely to harm the environment. For dams, canals, highways, and other developments, the statement describes the project, the impacts, and the alternatives. The law does not demand that the destruction be stopped, only that the statement be prepared. Yet the act's sponsors reasoned that if agencies were required to think about problems, publicize them, and be held accountable, then projects would improve. The new law set the nation on a course painful to those who had been profiting from the status quo but hopeful to people seeking change. Under a contract from the Army Corps of Engineers, historian Jeffrey Stine wrote, "The Corps was now faced with dealing with an environmental community with much more power."[1] To advise the president and coordinate federal programs, the NEPA created the Council on Environmental Quality, which also helped to stop some water projects. The dam-building agencies, however, would have bypassed the new law if citizen groups had let them.

The Environmental Defense Fund (EDF) was organized in 1967 to fight environmental destruction through the courts. Cofounder Victor Yannacone said that the worst environmental problems were from "allegedly public-interest agencies such as the U.S. Department of Agriculture, the U.S. Army Corps of Engineers and many state and regional development agencies."[2] The group's first major victory was the banning of DDT—a cause that signified to many people the beginnings of the environmental movement itself. Scores of times nationwide, EDF sued the government for inadequate environmental impact statements. The Natural Resources Defense Council, formed in 1970, worked in similar ways to protect the environment through the courts.

Gillham Dam on the Cassatot had been authorized in 1958 mainly for hydropower, but this use was dropped and flood control inserted. After completion of other dams, flood control could not be justified, so the corps credited 70 percent of benefits to water supply, though the Interior Department found that Gillham and several other ongoing projects could meet four times the region's needs in the year 2080. For this, the 13.8-mile-long reservoir would destroy the last large stream in the Ouachita Mountains.

In 1970 the EDF and other groups filed suit against the dam. With the land acquired, access roads built, and spillway finished, construction was one-third complete, yet the 160-foot-high dam itself was not yet built. The corps argued that an impact statement was not needed because construction was started, but a district court judge disagreed, ruling in 1971 that

NEPA compliance was mandatory no matter when the project was begun. Addressing an aspect of planning that had for years been regarded as deficient by policy analysts, the judge ruled that NEPA required consideration of alternatives to the dam, and he stated, "The most glaring deficiency in this respect is the failure to set forth and fully describe the alternative of leaving the Cassatot alone. . . . Then, if the decision-makers choose to ignore such factors, they will be doing so with their eyes wide open." Environmental Defense Fund attorneys called the case a landmark because it was the first final order under the NEPA to stop a dam.

After the corps released a twelve-pound impact statement in 1972, a federal court ended the injunction. The dam was finished, but the National Environmental Policy Act stood as a threat to other projects.

For river conservation, a new turning point was in sight. The NEPA had been passed because of a broadening view of environmental protection; it then in turn forced agencies to consider the environment, broadening the view further. With the availability of new analytic tools and a more sophisticated awareness of ecology, the dam fights of the future would be organized less around the philosophical and romantic views of wilderness, parks, and rivers and more around scientific studies showing ecological damage, quantifiable impacts, social injustice, and financial costs.

RIVERS AS ECOSYSTEMS: THE OKLAWAHA

In 1875 poet Sidney Lanier called Florida's Oklawaha River "the sweetest water-lane in the world." With a sandy bottom, the tea-colored river twists through a mile-wide valley of hydric hammock ecosystems and forest homes of panthers, black bears, otters, and bobcats. Herons, ducks, and shorebirds feed along the river's edge. Alligators and turtles sun themselves. The Silver River, an Oklawaha tributary, runs full of fish and crystal clear from Florida's largest spring—a $200 million-a-year tourist attraction where *Cross Creek* was filmed. The Oklawaha is one of Florida's two wild rivers and was recommended for national protection by the Interior Department in its first national wild and scenic rivers proposal of 1963.

In 1825 Congress considered a canal to cut across Florida so that shippers could avoid West Indies pirates. Later studies to connect the Atlantic and Gulf coasts through the Oklawaha basin appeared in 1913 and 1924, but high costs led the corps to recommend against construction. Franklin D. Roosevelt proposed a canal to make jobs, but not until World War II and fears of German submarines did Congress authorize the Cross Florida Barge Canal, to run 107 miles up the Oklawaha and across Florida's central hump to the Gulf of Mexico near the mouth of another outstanding river—the Withlacoochee. The canal would be dug 150 feet wide and 12 feet deep, draining the river and slicing into the Ocala dome—a ground-water reservoir forming the largest single water storage basin in the nation. Rodman and Eureka dams would flood 27,350 acres of wild swamp. Forty-five miles of the Oklawaha would be eliminated by dams, ditching, or draining.[3]

John F. Kennedy was convinced that his support for the canal would win Florida votes, and in 1960 he said, "If elected, I will cooperate in making this project a reality." The corps revised the benefit-cost ratio by adding benefits and slashing 12 percent from costs, even though five bridges were added and even though the national index for construction had risen 15 percent since 1958. But on paper the canal looked good with a new ratio of 1.17–1, and Congress approved it in 1964.

Unlike earlier dam fights to save national parks or wildlife, this struggle was launched to save the river itself. Marjorie Carr of Florida Defenders of the Environment (FDE) said, "The environmental threat of the Cross Flor-ida Barge Canal that first caught our attention was the destruction of the Oklawaha River." The FDE tried to get the canal rerouted away from the Oklawaha, but Lyndon Johnson turned the first spade of earth in 1964 and contractors dug a six-mile-long ditch through the lower river. Rodman Dam was built in 1968 to flood sixteen miles of river. In 1968 the FDE approached the Environmental Defense Fund, and while the canal was delayed in court, other events were changing an entire attitude, nationwide.

Earth Day came in 1970, and *Time* magazine named the environment the issue of the year. A Gallup poll found that environmental problems were regarded as the second most important issue of the decade (the Vietnam war was first). But also in 1970, Lieutenant General F. J. Clarke, chief of the Army Corps of Engineers, said, "With our country growing the way it is, we cannot simply sit back and let nature take its course."

The conservationists were moving beyond ideology and developing po-litical savvy, following the advice of James Nathan Miller, who wrote, "Conservationists must band their presently fractionalized forces into tough and demanding legislative lobbies. By properly mobilizing their enor-mous potential power, they can force our state and national lawmakers to treat the land not merely as a machine to be made more efficient, but also as a place for ourselves, and even our grandchildren, to live in." Miller brought professional journalism to the cause of river protection, continu-ing a tradition set by Wallace Stegner and Bernard DeVoto in the mid-1950s, but reaching many more people because he wrote for *Reader's Digest*.

At the same time, scientists were becoming involved in environmental causes nationwide, changing the whole complexion of conservation toward greater professionalism.[4] In the case of the Oklawaha, the FDE sponsored environmental and economic studies of the Cross Florida Canal, enlisting the aid of dozens of volunteer scientists, who stressed ecology more than in any dam fight so far. The case reflected the environmental movement by recognizing the entire ecosystem and the effects of a project on the web of life, including support systems such as water supplies of entire cities and regions.

Economists with the FDE charged that the corps's claims for barge traffic were overestimated: for oil products the corps projected an increase of 80 percent per capita, when in fact consumption would decrease. Five million dollars were claimed as benefits from two shippers that would not use the canal. Twenty-four percent of the benefits counted for recreation were for lakes that would be weed filled. Without this padding of numbers, the ratio would not have allowed construction.[5]

The western section of the canal — sometimes ninety feet deep — would fill with groundwater. Hydrologists found that ocean salt and pollution from boats would mix with underground supplies, perhaps contaminating the drinking water of many towns. Fluctuating levels in canal locks would be reflected in nearby springs (the canal would pass only five miles from Silver Spring). The conservationists gained broad support when people saw that more than wildlife was affected. Real estate developers and city officials — earlier anticipating an economic boom from the canal — agreed that groundwater was more important. As Marjorie Carr said, "The canal was in competition with new growth." The FDE's 150-page analysis, signed by 150 scientists, was used in the EDF lawsuit and helped to influence Interior Secretary Walter Hickel to call for a moratorium on construction in January 1970. (Like Dworshak and Rampart dams, this is another example of a corps project being fair game to the Interior Department, whereas Bureau of Reclamation dams such as Teton Dam went unchecked.)

The conservationists won when a federal judge halted the $210-million project, one-third completed in January 1971. Bob Teeters, the corps's representative on an Oklawaha task force, said, "The canal fight showed the Army Corps that NEPA was for real. The decision shocked a lot of people in the corps, and led to better analysis in the 'statement of findings' that the corps did after the Rivers and Harbors Act of 1970. There's nothing like writing down the balance to realize what's happening." [6] With a recommendation from his Council on Environmental Quality, President Nixon signed an executive order to stop construction. He called the Oklawaha "a national treasure" and sought to "prevent a past mistake from causing permanent damage."

The Canal Authority — a local promotion group — called the president's action unconstitutional. In February 1974, a federal judge agreed that the president could not by himself halt the canal, but stated that construction should not proceed until a new environmental impact statement was written. In 1976, pressured by Florida conservationists and influenced by studies by state agencies, the governor and state cabinet voted 6–1 for deauthorization. Governor Reubin Askew later said, "I favor restoring the Oklawaha."

In February 1977, in a landmark decision to stop a project, Chief of Engineers J. W. Morris recommended that the canal be "terminated" due to "marginal" economic justification and "adverse environmental impacts."

The canal is important as a case in which river development was halted after construction had begun and in which a dam was built but its reservoir remained unfilled. The FDE estimated that the Rodman Dam section could be restored for the cost of reservoir weed control through only a five-year period. Without restoration, operation of locks, dams, and a six-mile-long canal for motorboats would require $250,000 a year. Without dissent, federal and state agencies agreed to the largest restoration ever considered for a river. They would drain Rodman, restore sixteen miles of river channel, remove the unfilled Eureka Dam, and repair the western end of the canal. In May 1977, President Carter called for legislation to deauthorize the canal, to begin a national river study of the Oklawaha, and to restore the damaged sections.

Only a few years before, saving a river had been a new concept, but on the Oklawaha, officials, including the president, were recommending that dams be dismantled and rivers be reclaimed. A federal task force in 1978 recommended $25 million for restoration; the money was not approved, however, and the dams remain in place.

Water development had been slowed in the 1960s, and now it was almost stopped in the 1970s. A few large projects would still be built, but only after costly fights that further sapped the momentum of development.

JIMMY CARTER'S RIVER: THE FLINT

Few people start out with an interest in rivers. They start with one river — one place that they grow to know and care about, one that later leads them to other streams. Jimmy Carter's river was the Flint.

Georgia conservationists asked Carter to stop Spewrell Bluff Dam, authorized in 1963 for corps construction. The 211-foot-high dam would flood twenty-eight miles of the Flint as it wound through hill country south of Atlanta. Prized by fishermen, canoeists, and naturalists, the river was ranked the top resource of the state by the Georgia Natural Areas Council. This was the only river whose fall line — the rocky drop separating the piedmont and the coastal plain — remained undammed. With a technique started at Echo Park, river supporters promoted the Flint through raft and canoe trips, winning supporters by simply showing the place to people. In 1972 Carter decided to see for himself what was at stake, and after his canoe trip he said, "If we are going to destroy all this natural beauty, we better make sure that what we get in return is worth the price." [7] Carter told his staff to study the project. He received six thousand letters in support of the Flint and called them "enough to get any politician's attention."

Under corps policy, a governor's disapproval halts a project, and this is what Carter did. In October 1973 he stated,

> It became obvious to me that none of the [corps's] claims were true. The report was primarily promotional literature supporting construction. Population figures . . . had been strangely doubled. Flood control benefits had been increased by a factor of 287 percent since the initial estimates. In just a few months, the Corps more than quadrupled the economic benefits from recreation, and federal recreational advantages computed by the Corps were 1,650 percent more than those originally computed by the National Park Service.

The project had been justified for flood control, recreation, and hydropower, but Carter pointed out that only 12 percent of the flood control benefits were for existing development; the rest were for increased floodplain use. About $1 million of yearly benefits were for increased farm production in counties where $4 million was paid annually to farmers to keep fifty thousand acres idle. Electric power reserves were an adequate 16.9 percent without the dam. Eight underused recreational lakes sat within sixty miles. Nearly all state and federal recreation agencies opposed the dam, and a state survey showed a "gigantic present deficit" of recreational opportunities along streams.

The governor recommended that a river park be created and "that the apparent bias of the Corps of Engineers in favor of dam construction be assessed by the General Accounting Office, by the Congress, and by other responsible agencies — in this project, and other similar projects now planned or to be considered in the future. The construction of unwarranted dams and other projects at public expense should be prevented." [8]

Spewrell Bluff remained an inactive project but was reconsidered in a metropolitan Atlanta water supply study in 1981. The river still lacks long-term protection.

The Flint is one of the best examples of a dam stopped by a governor. The case molded Carter's commitment to river protection and led to reforms during his presidency, though he would find that changing federal policy and stopping dams in the West would be more difficult than saving the Flint.

SAVING A PARK AT THE SANGAMON

In Illinois conservationists combined the proven politics of saving parks with the economic analysis that became one of the most important requirements for river protection in the 1970s.

Oakley Dam was authorized in 1962 for flood control, water supply, and other uses. The proposal drew little attention until the corps enlarged plans in 1966 to flood part of Allerton Park — 1,500 acres registered as a national natural landmark, with virgin woodland given to the University of Illinois for research and public use as a nature reserve. The Committee to Save Allerton Park was formed one year later, and arguments and alternatives were developed with analysis by economists and scientists from the university. *Battle for the Sangamon,* a ninety-three-page booklet, was one of the most effective citizen reports against a dam. The committee argued that a 21,000-acre greenbelt would offer cheaper and better flood protection than the dam, that sewage should be treated instead of diluted, and that groundwater could be pumped economically.[9]

The EDF sued in 1971 to delay the corps because of an incomplete environmental statement, and in 1973 the Washington-based Environmental Policy Center included Oakley among thirteen proposals that would be the worst "disasters in water development."

After the cost climbed to four times the authorized level, the General Accounting Office in 1975 questioned the corps's claims, and the governor opposed the dam, temporarily ending the threat. John Marlin had worked to stop Oakley, emerging as a master of local political processes. Through the 1970s he organized landowners to halt other dams in the Midwest.

Michael Robinson, a historian under contract with the corps, wrote that the Sangamon case was one of the most outstanding in showing that environmentalists had "marshalled economic resources, professional expertise, and political skill."[10] As in earlier dam fights, the main cause first attracting

Sangamon supporters was the saving of a park, but with the Sangamon, technical and economic analyses of the project were paramount. River conservationists had refined their rationale for the protection of park lands, fish and wildlife, recreation, environmental quality, and now economic values. To this arsenal of arguments, landowners brought new power.

THE RED RIVER AND THE MOUNTAIN FARMERS

Conservationists wanting to save the natural environment and landowners wanting to save their homes combined efforts along the Red River in Kentucky. The North Fork, used by a million people a year for hiking, geological study, and canoeing, flows from Daniel Boone National Forest, where eighty-four rock arches were called a "geological art gallery." Below the gorge the river winds through a valley of Appalachian farms. Authorized by Congress in 1962, the 141-foot-high Red River Dam would flood 1,500 acres and fifteen miles of the North Fork, including fourteen rare or endangered plant species. The American Association for the Advancement of Science opposed the dam, stating that it would destroy "a unique natural area of geological, botanical, and zoological significance, valuable in research and instruction." With thirty-one archaeological sites, the area may hold more Indian petroglyphs than anywhere else in the East.

Residents and the Kentucky chapter of the Sierra Club held a protest hike in 1967, when Justice William O. Douglas led six hundred people through the gorge and urged them to write to congressmen. Douglas had already traveled to the Allagash to speak against Rankin Rapids Dam and to the Buffalo to fight Gilbert Dam. Through the late 1960s and the 1970s he became one of the best-known public figures speaking out against dams at the Sangamon, Sunfish Pond in New Jersey, and the Little Tennessee.

Dam opponents pushed for an alternate site five miles downstream. The corps agreed to this site in 1969 but also raised the height of the dam so that much of the gorge would still be flooded. The conservationists now fought the alternative, thinking that because they had won once, they could win again. With support from conservation groups in eighteen states, the Red River Gorge Legal Defense Fund sued and won time to turn the politics around.

Unlike the Green, Colorado, or Yukon, where the river was important to the entire nation and could be saved in spite of local politicians, the Red

River needed backing at home, so dam fighters organized in Kentucky and collected forty-four thousand signatures on a petition to the governor. One local couple — H. B. Farmer and his wife — wrote three hundred letters, and two thousand people protested at the state capitol. Organizer Chuck Hoffman said, "The Red River was the closest thing to a movement that Kentucky ever had." [11] The dam was impossible to ignore.

Opponents argued against flood control because only eighty-seven homes in Clay City, below the dam, had ever been damaged by floods. Ten of twelve cities to use the new water supply denied wanting it. The Environmental Protection Agency found that the water was too high in iron and manganese during some months, and questioned the water supply benefits. The corps counted flatwater recreation as a benefit, but existing river recreation was considered intangible and was not recorded among costs. [12]

In August 1975 the General Accounting Office stated that recreation and flood control figures were "overstated" and that water supply was "included without an adequate assessment." The GAO recommended that the corps recalculate benefits. The planning stopped when Governor Wendell Ford announced his opposition. The river was designated by Congress for a national wild and scenic river study in 1978, but has not been designated.

Red River supporters, seeing threats to other streams, in the mid-1970s formed the Kentucky Rivers Coalition, one of the strongest statewide river groups. They listed rivers worth protecting, then worked with other groups to save the most threatened. "There was a lack of experience in many of the out-of-the-way places," Chuck Hoffman said, "and the coalition was able to pool leadership so that there was enough to operate."

The Red River showed that landowners were no longer reluctant to fight the government. Residents were no longer dismissed as vested interests or as an uneducated minority against progress. The 1960s had brought growing awareness of folklore (especially in Appalachia), a rekindled interest in rural self-sufficiency, sympathy for the individual against the government, and a revitalized image of the landowner as a taxpayer. Whereas "outsiders" with the national conservation groups had led dam fights in the West, conservationists in the East would stand behind united landowners, effectively influencing local politics and capitalizing on the antigovernment sentiment of the late 1970s.

Most of the major dam fights of the 1970s were fought by local and statewide groups, but one site remained where the nationwide conservation community would rise powerfully again to save a dark canyon in one of the most isolated corners of the country.

THE SNAKE AND THE SECOND-DEEPEST CANYON

In the early 1830s Captain Benjamin L. E. Bonneville wrote of the Snake River's Hells Canyon: "Nothing we had ever gazed upon in any other region could for a moment compare in wild majesty and impressive sternness with the series of scenes which here at every turn astonished our senses and filled us with awe and delight." Since then the 1,038-mile-long Snake has been dammed eighteen times for hydropower and irrigation of Idaho drylands. Three dams blocked upper Hells Canyon, but below them a reach of nearly 100 miles remained as the continent's second-deepest canyon, averaging 5,500 feet from rim to river. (Some people contend that Hells Canyon is the deepest canyon.) Alpine peaks rise 8,000 feet above a cactus-spotted floor. The river was home to steelhead and ten-foot-long great white sturgeon—the largest freshwater fish in North America. A surrounding wilderness supported elk and bear. With two major rapids and many small ones, the canyon became popular as the largest river for white-water trips in the nation (at its mouth the Snake carries three times the flow of the Colorado). Luna Leopold of the University of California, who developed an intricate process for measuring the uniqueness of canyons, ranked Hells Canyon behind only the Grand Canyon.

When the Pacific Northwest Power Company applied to impound the remaining canyon of the Snake, the only question was which dam to build.[13] An eight-hundred-foot-high Nez Perce site was favored by the Federal Power Commission (FPC) because the dam would block both the Salmon and Snake rivers. This was later abandoned for the High Mountain Sheep site, just above the mouth of the Salmon, to spare that river's anadromous fish. A license was issued in 1964 for High Mountain Sheep and its fifty-eight-mile-long reservoir but was contested. In 1967 the Supreme Court ruled on the case of which dam should be built, and William O. Douglas wrote the decision. Not limiting himself to the question of alternate dams, Douglas stated, "The grant of authority . . . does not, of course, turn simply on whether the project will be beneficial to the licensee. . . . The test is whether the project will be in the public interest. . . . The Commission must hold more hearings on the subject of whether any dams should be built at all, not just on which one."[14] Douglas called for study of power needs, public interest in wild rivers, and fish and wildlife. The case was a landmark because it held the FPC accountable for more than power production, and it recognized the values of a wild river. Douglas did not stop the dam but cleared the way for someone who would.

Like David Brower, Brock Evans had not traveled much on rivers, but during one weekend he sat alongside the Snake at Lewiston below Hells Canyon and felt "the power, the feeling, the tugs and the murmurs, the enchantment. The river had a life of its own. Lower Granite Dam flooded that site soon after, but the Snake in Hells Canyon would become a big river in my life." [15] Evans had grown up in the Midwest, then worked as a lawyer in Seattle. After volunteering with the Sierra Club, he left his law office, which represented power companies building dams, and became the Sierra Club's Northwest representative. "Soon I was visited by an emissary out of darkest Idaho," Evans recalled. Floyd Harvey, a jet boat pilot on the Snake, asked Evans to fight for Hells Canyon. Douglas had created an opportunity and Evans jumped on it, filing an appeal against the FPC and mailing it twenty minutes before midnight on the due date.

Evans recalled, "At the hearing in Portland there were twenty-seven lawyers in a circle, and after two hours of testimony for the dam, the judge, up in his seat high above us, asked with the greatest contempt, 'Does the Sierra Club really want to add to this?' Well, we did, and three long bitter years of hearings followed, giving us precious delay. Before the fight was over, there was no more contempt, but respect. We forever changed the balance of power. While courts heard the appeal, conservationists formed the Hells Canyon Preservation Council with the ambitious goal of reversing the politics of water in three states whose modern existence depended on dams.

Cecil Andrus was elected governor of Idaho in 1970 and said that there would be no more dams in Hells Canyon "unless it's over my dead body." Wildlife biologist John Craighead rowed Interior Secretary Walter Hickel down the river. Brock Evans and river guide Verne Huser took freshman senator Bob Packwood through the canyon, and he introduced legislation to ban the dams.[16] Idaho senator Frank Church sponsored a preservation bill that passed, but John Saylor's companion bill failed in the House.

At more hearings in 1971 the power companies argued that Hells Canyon was one of the few remaining sites for large hydropower development in the Northwest and that their project would produce almost as much electricity as the whole TVA system. Conservationists argued for better use of existing dams: the Bonneville Power Administration had scheduled sixty new generators at federal dams and nine at private dams. Archaeologists said that two hundred important sites would be flooded. The Oregon Wildlife Commission opposed the dams because elk and deer needed the canyon for winter range. Craig Markham of the Central Cascades Conservation Council testified, "If we are incapable of surviving without hydroelectric power from Hells Canyon, then we are incapable of surviving."

National media covered the issue, additional conservation groups supported the river, and in 1973 all the senators from Idaho and Oregon, bordering the river, were ready to vote for protection. In 1975 the governors of Oregon, Idaho, and Washington all opposed the dam.

Cliff Merritt of the Wilderness Society, Brock Evans, and others discussed making the middle Snake a national wild river. "But why not do more?" Evans asked. They drew boundaries of surrounding wilderness in the Seven Devils Mountains in Idaho and the Wallawas in Oregon and lobbied for a bill reaching far beyond the river. In December 1975, President Ford signed legislation prohibiting the dam, adding the Snake and 28.5 miles of Idaho's Rapid River to the national wild and scenic rivers system, and creating a 662,000-acre Hells Canyon National Recreation Area "to assure that the natural beauty, historical and archaeological values of the Hells Canyon area and the 71-mile segment of the Snake River . . . are preserved for this and future generations."

Brock Evans wrote,

> Some day I want to return to Hells Canyon, to lie beside the river and listen to its music, to feel the breeze and watch the grand play of light and form, rock upon rock down the gorge, to watch eagles wheel and arc high above the rim. I may wander up one of the side valleys high into the alpine country far above the river and stroll among the flowers and quiet forests and great peaks. And I will remember, with great joy, that the canyon is safe now, safe forever, because enough people loved and cared enough to rush into the breach and turn a lost cause into a stunning victory. This new recreation area is one of the gifts we now leave to future generations. When more Americans come to know Hells Canyon, they will realize that it is one of the most beautiful victories environmentalists have ever enjoyed.[17]

Urgent threats to places like the Grand Canyon had awakened the nation and built the environmental movement in the 1960s, and the Hells Canyon debate followed the patterns of the big western dam fights. But after 1976 this kind of action was rare. With the rise of the environmental movement and conservation groups' involvement in air pollution, toxic wastes, nuclear power, and other issues, less time was spent on single places. It became the policy of national environmental leaders to choose one strategic route to accomplish as much as possible, and so some threatened places were passed over and controversial rivers were sometimes sacrificed. If a river was considered a political liability to a bill protecting a dozen areas, politicians dropped it. This happened with both the Stanislaus and Tuolumne rivers in California. In 1981 Sierra Club director Michael McCloskey said,

In the fifties and sixties things were so slow that programs were site-specific. But by the seventies we realized we couldn't work on one site at a time. We had to package areas by states and to work on generic effects. In Alaska, wilderness and wild rivers were packaged together. Maybe we'll return to rifle shooting at single places, but only if the political situation deteriorates so much that we have to.[18]

By the mid-1970s, then, river protection depended on the local and state levels, aided but not led by the national organizations. Whereas earlier, national groups had been important in drawing wider attention and in taking dam fights out of the local political arena, where dam supporters were the strongest, now the smaller groups had the determination, skills, and influence to achieve complex goals. Local organizations, aided by two new support groups in Washington — the American Rivers Conservation Council and the Environmental Policy Center — now filled much of the space left by the big national groups.

LEAVING THE OLDEST RIVER ALONE

Lacking the big-gorge grandeur of Hells Canyon, the New River is extraordinary in its Appalachian way: it is the oldest river in America; next to the Nile, it is the oldest in the world. Like the middle Snake, the New was threatened by a licensed power dam, and these rivers were the first cases in which national river status was granted in spite of power companies that were ready to build.

The Appalachian Power Company, a subsidiary of the American Electric Power Company, the nation's largest corporate utility, received an FPC license in 1974 for two dams to flood 44 river miles, 212 tributary miles, and forty-two thousand acres, displacing 2,800 people from the North and South forks of the New. Local people organized as they had done along the Red River. Five thousand attended a festival that followed a citizen organizers' rule — celebrate what you are trying to save (similar gatherings were later held to fight dams on the Little Tennessee, Stanislaus, Yampa, Ocoee, and Staunton). Partly because the power company sponsoring the dams was from Virginia, no elected official in North Carolina supported the project at the height of the campaign. The legislature added the New to the state's wild and scenic rivers system, but as in the Cowlitz case, courts found that the federal license overrode state law.

With heavy lobbying in Washington, river supporters and the state convinced Interior Secretary Thomas Kleppe to name twenty-six miles of the South Fork of the New in the national rivers system in 1976, but the power company appealed and the court ruled that only Congress could revoke the FPC permit. A bill to designate the New in the national rivers system was finally passed and signed by President Ford.[19]

The New is an example of state government working to save a river, of the need for national protection, and of teamwork between local people and the American Rivers Conservation Council (see Chapter 6). The New was also an indicator of changing times and attitudes. For North Carolina and the eastern mountains, the Appalachian Regional Commission had in 1964 touted recreational values from reservoirs while listing none from rivers. But in 1978 North Carolina advertised in national magazines: "Come see the state that kept the world's second oldest river from dying of unnatural causes. . . . Except for North Carolina, the prehistoric river would be just another man-made lake by now."

Saving the New was a landmark case, as conservationists stopped a utility company's dam even after land had been bought. But could river people halt a big federal project, one ready for construction, supported by four states, promoted by a river basin commission, and considered by some to be crucial to cities no less than Philadelphia and New York?

SERVING THE PEOPLE WITHOUT THE DAM: THE DELAWARE

After two hurricanes devastated parts of the Delaware basin in 1955, the corps studied the river under new guidelines, and Tocks Island Dam, sixty-two miles from New York City and seventy-five from Philadelphia, was proposed as a model of contemporary planning. Interior Secretary Stewart Udall pressed for Water Resources Council approval, calling Tocks Island the "Grand Coulee Dam" of the Delaware.[20] In 1962 Congress authorized the 160-foot-high dam and thirty-seven-mile-long reservoir, to stretch up to Port Jervis, New York.

The original authorization was mainly for flood control, but after the 1961–1965 drought, water supply benefits were increased, and during a ten-year delay due to lack of funds, the corps combated inflation by adding recreational benefits until these accounted for nearly half of the justification. The reservoir would be surrounded by the East's largest national recreation area under park service management.

In 1964 residents formed the Delaware Valley Conservation Association, and 604 landowners filed a class action suit to stop the dam, but the case was dismissed. In a seemingly unrelated effort, conservationists fought a power company's plan to pump Delaware water up Kittatinny Ridge for pumped storage power generation at Sunfish Pond (similar to a proposal that conservationists had recently beaten at Storm King above the Hudson). When the power company dropped the plan, the conservationists, inspired by their success, turned to Tocks Island. The Save the Delaware Coalition was started in 1970 as a union of landowners and conservationists.

The corps bought and reduced two-hundred-year-old stone farmhouses to rubble, enraging people who hadn't cared that much about ecology and recreation at the river. The coalition demanded protection under the Archaeological and Historic Preservation Act of 1974, which required agencies to identify and "mitigate" the loss of historic sites. The Historic Preservation Act of 1966 also called for federal agencies to protect sites named on the National Register of Historic Places. Action under these laws delayed, but did not stop, Tocks Island Dam, New Melones Dam, and other projects.[21] When squatters who had moved into homes that had been abandoned for the reservoir ignored orders to leave, armed U.S. marshals appeared without warning before dawn, gave the people five minutes to evacuate, then demolished the houses and everything in them with bulldozers.[22] The heavy-handed tactics turned more people against the project. Local people won an injunction to delay the razing of Zion Church because it was on the national register.

In a procedure that had become standard, the Environmental Defense Fund sued, saying that an eight-page impact statement for a $300 million project was incomplete. A longer statement was written. Freshman congressman Pete duPont of Delaware still tried to halt funds but wrote of the "frustration of trying to convince half of my 434 colleagues that a dam that had been under study for ten years needed further study."

Fighting duPont on the floor of Congress, Texan Jim Wright said, "We cannot keep people from intruding upon the earth. And the interests of people must come first. Nature sometimes, as in this case, needs the corrective surgery of intelligent man, under the injunction given to us in the book of Genesis, to subdue the earth and husband its resources." [23]

Appropriations passed the House in 1971, but in the Senate New Jersey's Clifford Case demanded study by independent scientists, leading to an interagency review. A crucial blow to the dam builders came in a report by the corps's consultants. Because of farm and poultry runoff and other pollution, eutrophication (overfertilization) would cause algae to grow, endangering water supplies and reservoir recreation (similar studies helped stop a Kickapoo River dam in Wisconsin). The President's Council on Environmental Quality called for a moratorium on construction until waste sources were controlled. Leo Eisel of the EDF developed nonstructural alternatives for flood control and proposed water conservation and the pumping of floodwaters to offstream reservoirs for storage. When other studies indicated that existing water supplies in New Jersey could be expanded at 20 percent less cost than the dam, the New Jersey governor abandoned Tocks, followed by the governors of New York and Delaware. Only Pennsylvania, arguing that Philadelphia needed the water, continued to back the dam. In a 3 – 1 vote, the Delaware River Basin Commission recommended deauthorization in 1975.

A debate had been staged between landscape architecture and recreation management students at Penn State University in 1970: to build the dam and national recreation area or not to. The National Park Service, army corps, and Save the Delaware Coalition participated. The winner was a splinter group opposing the dam but supporting the recreation area, and this is exactly what the park service did. Ten thousand acres that would have been flooded were added as recreation land. This was one of few times when river and flatwater recreation were given equal consideration in the assessment of people's needs.

Not satisfied that the dam's inactive status would last, Congressman Peter Kostmayer from Pennsylvania pushed to make the Delaware a national wild and scenic river, and the National Parks and Recreation Act of 1978 designated 110 miles for protection. To reactivate the dam now, Congress must override the national rivers system.

In 1980 the Pennsylvania Department of Environmental Resources estimated that Philadelphia would demand more water after the year 2000. The agency opposed the abandoning of Tocks Island Dam unless other alternatives were successful, including unlikely reductions in New York's diversions from Delaware headwaters and construction of at least four dams on smaller streams.

The gentle-flowing Delaware, with its fishing pools, canoeing reaches, and patchwork of fields and woods, is what motivated conservationists, but it was environmental impact statements and historic preservation requirements that enabled people to delay dam construction. The dam was finally beaten through technical studies of water quality and water supply alternatives, and protection gained through the national wild and scenic rivers system.

Because the proposed dam was close to large cities, the Tocks Island debate reached people who had never followed a river controversy, and the case heightened interest in alternatives to large dams. Pete duPont wrote, "After years of subsidizing inefficient water management projects, the Congress is beginning to scrutinize the value of these investments. . . .

The government must embrace new, flexible alternatives to the big dam."
Pointing out that New York City, with no residential water metering,
wastes more than one-half the amount supplied by all of its Delaware basin
reservoirs, the EDF urged the river basin commission to adopt a conservation plan. Finally in 1979 the commission called for a 15 percent reduction
in water use through leak detection and other measures. Yet the commission recommended reconsideration of Tocks Island after the year 2000.

THE INDIANS WIN

The Seneca Indians lost their lands along Pennsylvania's Allegheny River in
1965, but when Arizona politicians called for a dam on the Verde River, the
times had changed. Authorized in 1968 as part of the Central Arizona
Project (CAP), Orme Dam was to be built near Phoenix to store water
pumped from the Colorado River and to control floods. Twenty-five miles
of the Verde and Salt rivers would be flooded, including a section of the Salt
used for inner-tubing by thirty thousand people each week in summer, and
including 70 percent of the Yavapai's Fort McDowell Reservation.

In the late 1800s the Yavapai had been relocated and imprisoned, but
some of the Indians managed to return to ancestral lands, where a reservation was eventually established by executive order. After Roosevelt Dam
was built in 1911, valley farmers repeatedly tried to gain control of the
Indians' land and water, the greatest threat coming from the Orme Dam
proposal. Subdivisions in suburban Phoenix were built near river channels,
and when these subdivisions flooded in 1980, water lobbyists blamed the
Yavapai for delaying construction of the dam. An *Arizona Republic* editorial stated that with Orme the Indians could develop recreation facilities,
but the tribe voted 101–1 against the dam, one Indian saying, "If Phoenix
wants so much water, why don't they move to the ocean?" [24]

The Yavapai delayed the project with lawsuits while other opposition
grew. Environmental groups led by the Maricopa Audubon Society opposed destruction of some of the finest desert streamside in the Southwest,
including habitat for three pairs of endangered southern bald eagles, endangered Yuma clapper rails, zone-tailed hawks, and black-hawks. President Carter proposed elimination of Orme but later allowed funding provided alternatives were first studied.

In 1981 Interior Secretary Watt accepted recommendations from the
Bureau of Reclamation and the corps to build New Waddell Dam near
Phoenix and to reconstruct other dams instead of building Orme. The
Indians held new power and used it on other rivers, such as the Skagit in

Washington, where they blocked Copper Creek Dam because it would stop the migration of salmon, and the Kootenai in Montana, where they fought to protect a religious site from a hydroelectric project.[25]

DISASTER AT TETON

While many people remained oblivious to the problems of Indians and bald eagles at sites like Orme, another dam caught the attention of anybody who watched television.

Trout Unlimited and other conservation groups had sued to stop the Bureau of Reclamation from damming Idaho's Teton River, prized for cutthroat trout, west of Grand Teton National Park. Wildlife biologist Frank Craighead spoke out against Teton Dam, and it was rated by the Environmental Policy Center as one of the nation's thirteen worst water projects. As injunction delayed work, but the dam's political support in Idaho could not be eroded.

Construction had just been completed when two leaks, common to earth-filled dams, appeared downstream from the Teton site on June 3, 1976. The next day, a leak was found three hundred feet from the dam. Early in the morning on June 5, workers spotted two unquestionably dangerous leaks: one at the abutment and another at the foot of the dam, where water erupted at twenty-two thousand gallons a minute. At 10:00 A.M. the dam's right abutment ruptured. A hole grew rapidly, sucking fill from the embankment and washing it through the cavity. A hideous whirlpool drained water from the reservoir while on both sides of the dam men on bulldozers pushed dirt into the hole but accomplished nothing. The crews fled only minutes before their equipment was devoured and flushed through the whirlpool.

At 11:57 A.M. the dam burst. The newly filled, seventeen-mile-long reservoir descended as a twenty-foot-high wave upon the Teton River valley and killed eleven people, scoured one-hundred thousand acres of farmland, obliterated thousands of buildings, drowned sixteen thousand head of livestock, and washed away toxic chemicals that had been stored on the floodplain. The catastrophe caused $1 billion in damages and drove twenty-five thousand residents from their homes.

Scientists who had studied the site were not surprised. Geologists with the Department of the Interior's Geological Survey — the parent agency of the Bureau of Reclamation — had warned the bureau about earthquake faults and weak bedrock. David Schleicher of the Geological Survey had suggested that "we consider a series of strategically placed motion-picture cameras to document the process of catastrophic flooding." During the conservationists' court case, Shirley Pytlak, a former geologist for the Bureau of Reclamation, testified that the rhyolite bedrock was dangerously porous, but bureau officials assured that they would pump cement grouting into the cavities.[26] A memo alerting the Bureau of Reclamation to safety problems was delayed for six months, to be made "more objective," according to Harold Prostka of the Geological Survey.

This was one more case in which the power of the Bureau of Reclamation within the Interior Department was evident. The National Park Service, the Geological Survey, the Bureau of Land Management, the Fish and Wildlife Service, and the Bureau of Outdoor Recreation were all overpowered in dam fights, including those at Echo Park, Glen Canyon, Grand Canyon, Auburn, and the Stanislaus.

After the disaster the Bureau of Reclamation circulated a question-and-answer paper: "With the benefit of hindsight, is there anything that Reclamation might have done to prevent this disaster?" The answer was, "Nothing."

The Committee on Government Operations thought differently, stating in a September 23, 1976, report,

> Pressures to build Federal water resource projects have been so great in some cases that the Bureau of Reclamation officials have been blinded to dangers and hazards presented by some projects. In the case of the Teton Dam, great human and economic costs have been the price of succumbing to those pressures. . . . Once physical construction has commenced, the decision to halt construction is no longer an option available to the Bureau, and safety problems, regardless of their magnitude, are generally met with unquestioned reliance on the Bureau's ability to "engineer" workable solutions. The Teton Dam is a prime example of fulfilling the momentum to build at any cost.

The committee stated that the bureau had been "deficient in the geologic examination of the site" and "in resolving satisfactorily the warning of safety hazards," and it had "failed to comply with prescribed safety precautions during the course of the filling of the reservoir."

Not since 1928, when Los Angeles's Saint Francis Dam burst and killed four hundred people, had dam safety received so much attention. After Teton, dam fighters added safety to their bundle of arguments. While fighting a Snoqualmie River dam in Washington, opponents pointed out that the site's geology was the same as at Hansen Dam on Washington's Cedar River, where a weak foundation prevented complete filling.[27] Gathright Dam on Virginia's Jackson River was opposed in part because of porous bedrock. In 1977 President Carter ordered all federal dam-building agencies to review safety practices. With other dams proposed and under construction near large cities, nuclear power plants, and military bases, concerns for safety took a toll in the dam fights to come.

ONE DAM TOO FAR

Nowhere in the nation has the debate and conflict over water raged as much as in California. With two-thirds of California's water in the north and two-thirds of its people in the south, the politics of water are tense and volatile. Here are the most powerful water developers and the most active river protectors. The dams are among the largest and most costly, and the rivers among the most scenic and popular.

As a part of the Bureau of Reclamation's Central Valley Project, Auburn Dam was an engineer's dream: the world's largest double-curvature thin-arch dam, curved in width and height, something like the side of a teacup. The superior physics of this shape rather than its mass of earth or concrete was intended to hold back a six hundred-foot wall of water. The dam would have been the fifth tallest in the United States, by far the most expensive, and closer to a large city than any other high dam. It would plug the American River and flood forty-eight miles of the North and Middle forks — wild canyons thirty-two miles above Sacramento. Fifty-six percent of the alleged benefits were for irrigation, though the dam would add only one-fifth to existing Folsom Dam supplies, most of which remain undelivered thirty years after construction. At best, 25 percent of capital costs would be recovered from irrigators, the difference to be paid by electricity users and taxpayers.

In 1974 the Natural Resources Defense Council sued to delay the project because of an incomplete environmental statement. A judge halted canal construction but allowed work on the dam's foundation to continue. A citizens group formed, arguing that if 6 percent interest were charged, a $3.5 billion deficit would result in fifty years, and that the dam would provide for only 1 percent of California's water needs and 0.3 percent of its electricity. Local congressman Harold "Bizz" Johnson, however, had labored for the dam most of his life, and he chaired the House Public Works Committee; as another congressman said, "If Bizz says he wants the Auburn Dam built, it will be built."

In August 1975 the story was forever changed when the Sierra foothills, thought to be seismically quiet, lurched with an earthquake of 5.9 on the Richter scale, rattling windows for sixty miles around Oroville. The state had recently built Oroville Dam, a 770-foot pile of earth (some geologists think that the dam and its reservoir caused the earthquake). Oroville Dam was unharmed, but this side-of-a-teacup Auburn Dam could be different. Although $200 million had already been spent, work was stopped, making Auburn the nation's largest project to be halted after construction had begun. The Association of Engineering Geologists reported that the dam could "crack over thousands of feet horizontally and hundreds of feet vertically" and "would be unsafe even in a moderate earthquake." Bureau of Reclamation studies required by California stated that "complete failure" of the dam would flood 750,000 people, five military bases, and the state capital.[28]

Two months in office, President Carter called Auburn economically marginal and added it to a list of water projects to be scrapped. The Bureau of Reclamation defended the design, but when Teton Dam burst, the bureau's credibility went with it. At a 1977 hearing, members of Friends of the River, a California river protection group, released a Geological Survey memo identifying an active fault that had shifted three feet near the dam in the last seventy thousand years.

The Interior Department began the most extensive seismic studies ever done for a water project. After one hundred miles of trenching, geologists found that Auburn and seventy existing dams were near potentially damaging faults. Interior Secretary Andrus recommended a new design to withstand a foundation shift of five inches, though the Geological Survey had recommended three feet.

While technicians grappled with the safety issue, attitudes changed. New water policies of the president emphasized sound economics and discouraged the heavy subsidies epitomized by Auburn. Governor Brown's administration built the best water conservation program in the nation and defended wild rivers. The state Department of Water Resources compared capital costs of water from Auburn to the costs of other large dams: Shasta at $415 an acre-foot, Oroville at $901, and Auburn at $3,072. Auburn would preempt money from other projects; Assistant Interior Secretary Guy Martin wrote to Andrus: "If you decide to proceed with Auburn, it will completely dominate the water and power construction budget for the next ten years." He cautioned that the entire Auburn unit would cost more than all bureau funds spent in California since the 1930s and that the cost would be ten times that originally authorized by Congress. "Construction of Auburn would only drive the CVP account further into the red." [29]

The American River supported 14 percent of California's king salmon and five million user-days of recreation in Sacramento, but Auburn's Folsom South Canal would reduce the river to ankle depth to divert water to farms and other cities. A state official warned, "It's the same as Owens Valley — one part of California is trying to take water now used by other people."

Secretary Andrus stated that reauthorization was needed for work to resume, and the project receded under more studies. Replacing Andrus, James Watt called for fewer controls on federal irrigation water. To recommend Auburn, however, would have been absolute hypocrisy from an administration that cut domestic programs to the bone. The final decision rests with Congress, where Bizz Johnson's replacement, Eugene Chappie, said, "I intend to push for Auburn."

Realizing that the dam would not be dead if farmers still wanted its water, Friends of the River and the Brown administration promoted water conservation, citing federal reports that millions of acre-feet of irrigation water could be saved. Local groups supported a park system for the American River canyons, with their rapids, trails, and archaeological sites. Yet Michael Catino, acting regional director for the Bureau of Reclamation, said in 1981, "We would have a difficult time recommending deauthorization. Nearly $400 million will be sunk, which is a lot to write off as a poor investment." [30] Auburn may need only another politician with the disposition and power that Bizz Johnson had. Bureau staff offer tours of the site and wait for the politics to change. "You try to stay in readiness for the day you get green-lighted," Catino said. In 1983 reclamation commissioner Robert Broadbent said that the dam was not dead. "We're trying to find new sponsors for the project." [31] Bills were introduced in 1983 to reauthorize the dam at $2.2 billion.

A July 19, 1984, memorandum from Assistant Interior Secretary G. Ray Arnett cited the need to protect the fishery and recreational values of the American River below the Auburn site (a national river) as well as the fisheries of San Francisco Bay and the Sacramento Delta. Reserving water for these uses would make Auburn Dam even less feasible.

Auburn is unresolved, but it may have signaled a change in attitudes about technological wonders and a turning point in our reliance on engineering fixes. The size and intricate engineering of this dam were used as an argument, not for its construction, but against it. In this respect it was similar to the Supersonic Transport. The studies still go on, and the price goes up — $10 million a month when inflation was high — the dam's viability receding in a new era of limits.

At Auburn, the Bureau of Reclamation pushed the Central Valley Project one dam too far, into the economic wasteland of a dead investment. The Tennessee Valley Authority also fell prey to building too much, but unlike the bureau, it would be rescued by some of the most ludicrous lawmaking ever affecting a river.

THE FATE OF THE LITTLE TENNESSEE

The Tennessee Valley Authority had dammed the Tennessee and most of the Little Tennessee, but above the mouth of the Tellico River a thirty-three-mile section survived as one of the best trout rivers in the East and the only large, clean river in the state. Three hundred and forty farms populated the wide valley. William O. Douglas wrote that the Little Tennessee was "one of God's finest free-flowing rivers. . . . It is one of our best float streams because of its many islands for camping and because of its rainbow trout that run up to fifteen pounds." [32]

The valley was one of few sites known to be occupied continuously for ten thousand years, and a TVA study credited it with "world-wide significance." [33] The National Indian Youth Council wrote, "The Cherokee capital of Echota was located there. Echota was more than an old tribal town, it is the heart of what it means to be a Cherokee. It was called 'the mother town' or the 'beloved town.' . . . Echota, then, is a sacred place, the Cherokee Jerusalem. . . . The destruction of the Tellico Valley is to Indians as the flooding of the entire state of Israel would be to Christians." [34] Supporting the Indians, author Peter Matthiessen wrote, "Is there a human being who does not revere his homeland, even though he may not return?" [35] The valley also included the Indian town of Tennase, from which the state's name was derived. Toskeegee was a neighboring village where Sequoyah, the author of the Cherokee alphabet, was born in 1760.

In 1966 the TVA approved funding for Tellico Dam, to be built at the confluence of the Little Tennessee and Tellico rivers. Tennessee Valley Authority director Aubrey Wagner said that the dam would be one of the agency's best power projects. But it would produce only twenty-three megawatts — less than 0.1 percent of TVA's capacity. The dam would provide no flood control, and it did not even meet Department of the Interior standards for safety. Recreation was credited for 40 percent of the benefits, though twenty-four other large reservoirs are within sixty miles, and the Tennessee basin has more flatwater shoreline than the Great Lakes. Sixteen thousand acres of prime farmland were eliminated. Twenty percent of the claimed benefits were for real estate sales; much of the thirty-eight thousand acres bought (some of it through condemnation) from farmers would be sold to lakeside industrial developers at a TVA profit, leading

Michael Frome to write in *American Forests*, "It is not the business of the federal government to take the role of real estate developer." Fishermen and conservationists fought the dam in the late 1960s, and the EDF took the case to court in 1972 but only delayed construction.

While snorkeling in 1973 in the section of the river to be dammed, a University of Tennessee zoologist discovered a three-inch-long fish previously unknown. Named the snail darter because it eats snails, the fish was placed on the Department of the Interior's endangered species list in 1975, one year after the Endangered Species Act required federal protection of species near extinction. While $20 million was being spent to save another endangered creature — a vulture called the California condor — $103 million of government funds were being used for a land speculation project that could exterminate the snail darter; the TVA speeded construction with round-the-clock shifts.

National conservation groups considered fighting the dam but knew that it would be difficult to stop a project already under construction and having solid congressional support. Worst of all, they feared that the Endangered Species Act would be rescinded as an example of environmental extremism. But what they decided did not really matter, because Zygmunt Plater, a faculty member of the University of Tennessee law school, filed a lawsuit of his own.

The district court in Knoxville ruled against Plater, saying that Tellico was almost finished and the Congress's funding indicated its desire to complete the project (this was the same opinion given about Rainbow Bridge ten years earlier). Plater appealed, and Judge Anthony Celebrezze granted an injunction, stating, "Whether a dam is fifty percent or ninety percent completed is irrelevant in calculating the social and scientific costs attributable to the disappearance of a unique form of life." [36] In 1978 the Supreme Court agreed, ruling that the law required that the fish be saved but suggesting that Congress could change the law.

Politicians immediately assailed the environmental restriction. Senator William Scott from Virginia quoted from the Bible, saying that God gave humans dominion "over every creeping thing that creepeth upon the earth." Senator Jake Garn from Utah said that there was no justification for calling the acts of humans unnatural, because "beavers build dams too." Not wanting to sponsor legislation directly counter to the Endangered Species Act, Senator Howard Baker from Tennessee sponsored a bill creating a cabinet-level committee to review federal projects conflicting with the act. Congress empowered the committee to waive requirements if there were no reasonable alternatives or if the benefits of the project clearly outweighed those of alternatives. Environmentalists called this the "God committee."

The committee met in December 1978, and Charles Schultze, chairman of the President's Council of Economic Advisors, said that Tellico Dam's "costs clearly outweigh the benefits. It would be difficult to say there are no reasonable and prudent alternatives to this project. . . . Here is a project that is 95 percent complete, and if one takes just the cost of finishing it against the total project benefits, it doesn't pay, which says something about the original design."

Interior Secretary Cecil Andrus—a committee member—wrote to House Speaker Thomas P. O'Neill with the committee's arguments against finishing the dam: costs outweighed benefits, safety standards were not met, recreation benefits were inflated, hydropower would be insignificant, land uses other than a flooded valley would generate more income, and transplants of the snail darter to the Hiwassee River might not live. Tennessee Valley Authority chairman S. David Freeman agreed that use of the free-flowing river "has larger intangible benefits" and would provide more jobs than the dam.

Howard Baker responded with a bill to eliminate the committee that had been his own creation. When this failed, he sought to exempt Tellico Dam from the Endangered Species Act but lost again.

Few congressmen were on the floor on June 18, 1979, and most were Appropriations Committee members awaiting routine action on the energy and water development bill. House rules prohibit the use of an appropriations bill to change an existing law, so Congressman John Duncan, from the Tellico area, orchestrated an effort with fellow congressmen. He quietly placed an amendment in the hopper, then deftly stopped the clerk's reading of the measure just before the important paragraph. Another member interrupted, saying that the minority had reviewed the amendment and accepted it. Tom Bevill, chairman of the Appropriations Subcommittee on Energy and Water Development, stood and spoke for the Democratic majority: "We have no objection." Immediately, a voice vote was taken and the amendment passed. All of this required forty-two seconds. The *Congressional Record* printed the paragraph not read on the floor: the TVA would finish Tellico Dam and fill it notwithstanding the Endangered Species Act and "all other laws."

California's Paul McCloskey led an effort to rescind the amendment, McCloskey himself having been present but fooled by Duncan's scheme. The Senate voted 53–45 to remove the House amendment, but then the

House restored the Tellico approval. On September 10 the Senate debated the measure again. Baker called Tellico "an unfortunate symbol of environmental extremism." Dam opponents had the votes, but Baker walked the aisles, and in the last minute changed the votes of six senators. The dam won, 48–44.

Everyone expected President Carter to veto the uneconomic and destructive water developments he had opposed ever since Spewrell Bluff. Some White House staff members told environmentalists to lobby Congress to uphold a veto, but other White House staff needed political currency to trade for the Panama Canal Treaty and the creation of a department of education. The president signed the Tellico approval and said, "Even if I vetoed this bill, Tellico exemptions would be proposed repeatedly in the future." On the same day, Congressman Bevill had attached a Tellico rider on a funding bill that Carter would have had even more difficulty vetoing. Twelve hours after the president's signature, TVA bulldozers were finishing the dam. The gates were closed and the valley was flooded in December 1979.

Robert Cahn wrote in *Audubon:*

> More than a half-century ago, because of a congressional decision, conservationists lost a multi-year battle to stop the first dam's being built within a national park (Hetch Hetchy Dam in Yosemite). But a lesson was learned. No dam has been built since within any national park. Perhaps we can learn a similar lesson from the snail darter. Perhaps this will be the last time (as well as the first) that we consciously sacrifice a species or a habitat for political reasons.[37]

Conservation leaders who had steered clear of Tellico saw the final outcome as proof that the case was an unnecessary risk to the Endangered Species Act (since the debate the snail darter has been found in other rivers). Michael McCloskey of the Sierra Club was concerned that "river saving will be stigmatized as a loser issue."

But in 1983 Zygmunt Plater defended his work:

> It was not a mistake. We had the facts, the economic case, and the law on our side. If we had not pressed it, we would have been writing off the Endangered Species Act anyway—admitting that there was no way for rationality to run the system. Carter could have vetoed the bill. All he had to do was to take on Congressman Jim Wright in front of the American public and say that the issue was *not* that of a little fish. The media and the politicians sold the public a bill of goods about the snail darter. The real issue was that Tellico wasted money as a land speculation project.[38]

Tellico again proved a point known since the EDF tried to save the Cassatot: lawsuits must be part of a larger strategy and not an end in themselves. If the politics are not changed from prodam to proriver, Congress will simply pass whatever new laws are needed to build the dams. The Little Tennessee was a great loss, but in its wake came a great success.

THE NEW BREED

Without the more tangible goals of saving parks, homes, fish, or money, New Englanders working for the St. John River in Maine brought the river protection movement a long step closer to the simple goal of saving a river for the river's sake. This may be the best example so far in which the stream's specialties were the central issue. "Up there you had the river and that's all it took," said Bill Painter, director of the American Rivers Conservation Council.

Named by Samuel de Champlain in 1604 on the feast of John the Baptist, the river is more like a Canadian waterway than any other in the United States. Wild, clean, crowded by spruce, it is the habitat of moose, lynx, otter, marten, beaver, eagles, and osprey. From its source near Quebec, the St. John runs unblocked and undeveloped for more than 100 miles. Only three primitive bridges span the water. Most land is owned by lumber companies. The Appalachian Mountain Club's *New England Canoeing Guide* states that the upper 120 miles of the St. John have "no equal in the Eastern United States in the number and diversity of wilderness canoe trips which can be made." The region is considered one of the finest for brook trout in the country.

Canoeist, river activist, and lawyer Tom Arnold wrote,

> There is a magical moment on every St. John trip. When you push off from shore for the first time, you know that nothing lies ahead but paddling, floating, watching the sun and clouds, hearing the wind and river, and that each day your senses will open like flowers to the sun and absorb more of what is around you. The St. John is the only free-flowing river in New England that is long enough for this to happen.

For that matter, it is the longest undeveloped river in the East.

In the 1950s the Army Corps of Engineers proposed the Rankin Rapids hydroelectric dam to back water up the St. John and thirty-five miles up the Allagash River—a tributary and a favorite stream of river guides and fishermen. Fought by Maine conservationists, Senator Edmund Muskie, and Interior Secretary Stewart Udall, the dam was dropped. Udall recalled, "Senator Muskie was very astute on this; he was trying to balance things in Maine, so he moved the dam site upriver to Dickey, where the Allagash wouldn't be affected." [39] But the cost of saving the Allagash was that the St. John would be dammed farther upstream—a compromise that Muskie honored from his position as chairman of the Environmental and Public Works Committee. The senator's environmental record was otherwise excellent—he led efforts for the Clean Water Act of 1972—and so he was rankled by environmentalists' criticism of his support for Dickey-Lincoln. He believed that public hydroelectric power—never developed in a large New England project—would be good for Maine, and he echoed local boosters who hoped for construction jobs and an economic boom.

The dams had been authorized in 1966, but New England utilities lobbied successfully against funding until the 1973 oil embargo brought gasoline shortages and unexpected fuel price hikes. The dams were supported by twenty-two of twenty-five New England congressmen, including liberals who argued for public power in the same way that progressives such as William Kent had argued for the dam at Hetch Hetchy in 1913.

Dickey Dam would be the country's sixth largest, 340 feet high and 9,260 feet long. With a small dam downstream at Lincoln, the project would flood eighty-nine thousand acres, 55 miles of the St. John, 223 miles of tributaries, and thirty lakes and ponds. For peaking use, 830 megawatts of power would be generated for two and a half hours a day and exported to Boston and southern New England, 450 miles away. The dam would produce less power than a small coal-fired plant and would serve about 1.5 percent of New England's needs. [40]

Tom Arnold called New England conservationists together to organize Friends of the St. John in 1974. Within a month he collected a coalition of twenty groups and $3,000. By organizing people and lobbying in Washington, Arnold proved that one person can make a difference in saving rivers. "If you'd taken Tom Arnold out of that fight, I'm not sure what you would have had," said Bill Painter. And many other people worked for the river: thirty thousand brochures were mailed by the Natural Resources Council of Maine, and the L. L. Bean store in Freeport became an information center for the dam fighters.

Friends of the St. John argued that the wild river was worth saving, that the dams were not worth the cost (eventually estimated at $1 billion), and that energy conservation was cheaper. Flood control benefits were reduced when a new corps levee protected the town of Fort Kent. To operate the dams would employ only sixty-eight people, the jobs costing $15 million each if other benefits were not counted. Recreation on a pool with 6,000 acres of mudflats was branded absurd when Maine had three thousand natural lakes, many of them underused and nearly all of them closer to population centers. The corps assigned river recreation no value in the benefit-cost analysis, but as author Joel Garreau wrote of the St. John, "recreational wilderness is more scarce than Middle Eastern oil." [41] In a state economically dependent on logs, 110,000 acres of forests would be flooded. The New England Rivers Center — another group led by Arnold — found that new attic insulation would make available forty-three times the energy for the same price as the dams.

President Carter added Dickey-Lincoln to a list of water projects to be cut but then, influenced by Senator Muskie, deleted it. When the corps prepared an environmental statement, botanists discovered twenty rare plants along the river, including the Furbish lousewort and Josselyn sedge, which qualified for protection as endangered species.

It took five years of lobbying by Tom Arnold and others, but by 1979 most New England congressmen opposed the project as a waste of tax-payers' money. Congressmen Robert Edgar from Pennsylvania and James Cleveland from New Hampshire led an effort to deauthorize the dams and won a committee vote — the first time that the House Public Works Committee acted to stop a project on which substantial funds had been spent. After Edmund Muskie left the Senate to become secretary of state, the deauthorization bill passed in 1980. The corps began a new study of only the Lincoln Dam, which would flood eleven miles of the river in a lower section not as highly valued.

This was one of the first cases in which alternatives of energy conservation were publicized, dovetailing with the movements for nondestructive energy development, such as solar power. Other projects had been stopped even after earth moving had begun, but no other dam nearing construction had been deauthorized.

The St. John showed the growing strength of a new breed of river conservationists. They were people who traveled the rivers — canoeists, kayakers, and rafters — and the river was the center of their activity. The canoeists who saved the Buffalo marked a beginning of this movement in the 1960s, but with the Snake, New, Delaware, and now the St. John more than any other case so far, the river was recognized as valuable in its own right. People argued economics, but that was just political pragmatism. As Bill Painter said, "That's not the big issue in our hearts. We're not losing sleep because tax money is wasted but because it's used to destroy something we love. Dam fights always start with somebody who cares about that place." A spiritual side to river protection, not unlike John Muir's feeling for the wilderness, surfaced in the river protection movement, and nowhere was this dimension seen more vividly than on the Stanislaus River in California.

A HOLY PLACE

First authorized in 1944, New Melones Dam was to be built in the Sierra Nevada foothills north of Yosemite for flood control. In 1962, irrigation, hydropower, recreation, and fish and wildlife enhancement were added, and the proposal was enlarged to call for America's fourth-tallest dam. Twenty-six miles of the Stanislaus River would be buried; the upper nine miles were a wilderness and contained the deepest limestone canyon on the West Coast, with hundreds of archaeological and historic sites, thirty caves, rich wildlife habitat, and exciting rapids. By the mid-1970s the Stanislaus canyon was probably the second most boated whitewater in America, with forty-nine thousand floaters a year, including more handicapped people than any other river or wilderness. Here was a river having the finest of wild and recreational values, but the plans for its damming were drawn.

Whereas other people had written off the canyon to the army corps project, canoeist Jerry Meral paddled the river in 1967 and, like Tom Arnold on the St. John one year earlier, decided that the stream was worth saving. After futile attempts through the state resources secretary and a petition drive in which river supporters collected a hundred thousand signatures for President Nixon, Meral organized Friends of the River (FOR) in 1973 to campaign for a statewide initiative to stop the dam, already under construction. Other statewide votes had been taken to save rivers: the Cowlitz in Washington, which won but was dammed anyway, and the Hudson in New York, which won and was saved.

Many people saw New Melones as merely a local issue, but FOR propelled it to state and then national attention. Meral persuaded Mark Dubois, who had grown to know and love the Stanislaus while guiding raft trips, to work on the campaign. Helped by thousands of volunteers, the river people faced prodam advertising, funded by the contractors building the dam, that urged voters to "Save the River, Vote No on 17," which was a vote for the dam. Friends of the River narrowly lost, and a poll afterward found that 60 percent of the people intended to vote against the dam but were confused by the advertising.

Emerging from the campaign a charismatic leader, Mark Dubois led new efforts, all generating support and bringing the issues of river protection to more people, but failing to stop New Melones. Much of the campaign was funded by rafting outfitters, and some of the FOR leaders had discovered the river while working as guides. The group came within one committee vote of clearing a state wild and scenic river bill for legislative action.

Seeing no need to drown the whitewater until contracts were sold for irrigation supplies, the state Water Resources Control Board had blocked the filling of the reservoir even though the dam would be built. In a precedent-setting decision, the Supreme Court found that the state could dictate operations of a federal project provided that these conformed to Congress's authorization. But further court delays and district court decisions undercut the water board's decisions.

In the most dramatic case of direct action to save an American river, Mark Dubois chained himself to bedrock near the rising water's edge while the reservoir was filling in 1979. Search parties on foot and in boats and helicopters could not find Dubois. If the dam were filled much more, he would be drowned. In a letter to corps colonel Donald O'Shea, Dubois had stated, "Part of my spirit dies as the reservoir fills and floods the lower Stanislaus Canyon. . . . The life of the 9 million year old Stanislaus Canyon is far more significant than my short tenure on this planet."

Governor Jerry Brown sent a telegram to President Carter urging him to save Dubois and the river, and the corps released water to lower the level. Then FOR lobbyist Patricia Schifferle convinced Congressman Don Edwards to introduce legislation to name the Stanislaus a national river. With volunteer help from professional planners and a team of twelve people, FOR and the American Rivers Conservation Council completed the only citizen-prepared wild and scenic river study for a national river candidate. Economist and assistant resources secretary Guy Phillips prepared a study showing that the dam would yield a subsidy of $1 million to each of four hundred farmers over the next fifty years and that a partly filled reservoir sparing the upper canyon would fulfill most intended purposes and would be more economic than a full reservoir.

With a "row for the river" to San Francisco, a sixty-mile walk to Sacramento, political rallies, and river trips for scores of writers, newspeople, and politicians, FOR sought to make the Stanislaus the most publicized loss of wilderness in America, and they may have succeeded. Articles appeared in the *New York Times, Newsweek, American Forests, Audubon, Sports Afield,* a dozen other magazines, nearly all of the environmental publications, and California newspapers. Television brought the chaining incident to a nationwide audience, which for the first time saw that someone was willing to risk his life for a river. Again and again, FOR launched grass roots campaigns, and people wrote thousands of letters. On commercial river trips, guides stopped for breaks and customers wrote their congressmen. More than in any previous struggle to save a river, raft trips were used to publicize what was at stake and to promote protection.

Dam supporters derided the controversy as "recreation versus food," but with economic studies and growing sophistication, the river people stressed that the sacrifice of the canyon was not needed, did not pay, and violated the law. Water developers saw the Stanislaus as symbolic — since New Melones was already built, to leave the reservoir unfilled would shake the entire water development establishment.

An intense campaign for the national river designation fell two votes short of committee approval in 1980. When President Carter lost to Ronald Reagan, the last hope was gone. High runoff in 1982 and 1983 filled the reservoir, drowning a river that thousands of people had worked for years to save.

The Stanislaus case is filled with unequaled commitments and offers a whole chapter in the evolution of attitudes about rivers. The motivation of those fighting New Melones Dam went beyond the saving of parks and homes, beyond recreation, economics, and ecology. Like the St. John, the river was recognized as valuable for its own sake. Unlike the St. John, the Stanislaus was a people's river, known by millions through the media and known firsthand by hundreds of thousands of people who took raft trips. As Paul Brooks wrote, "It is obvious that we fight to preserve only what we have come to love and understand."

What was it that moved so many people? "It's not kilowatt hours or recreation days," Mark Dubois said. "It cannot be counted, but it is still a value that is important and real to many people. On trips I usually ask people to try to go and sit alone. They return with a glow on their faces. This canyon feeds people's spirits. They touch something that they haven't touched anywhere else."

Many people became involved who did not do that much with rivers — they had no particular concern. The river, alone, was enough. Jerry Meral said, "You had the anglers and the boaters and others, and then you had the people who just liked rivers. On the Stanislaus, they included many of the people who worked the hardest."

The Stanislaus was regarded as a thing of wonderful power, beauty, and life. Alexander Gaguine of FOR said, "This river has done a lot for people. Trying to keep up with the demand for more water or more power does not uplift people, but spending a day in the Stanislaus River canyon often does. The experience can raise people's spirits or bring out feelings of wonder and joy. The Stanislaus becomes a very real part of their home, whether people are there for three days or three months." The Stanislaus brought out feelings of reverence for the natural world, where rivers are a source of life and a center of attention. The river was a sacred and holy place. Gaguine said, "Europe has its great cathedrals, but in America it is our own great natural landscape which uplifts our spirits and souls as individuals and as a whole nation. What will inspire us when the holy places are gone? [42]

The reverence given to the Stanislaus could show a new regard for rivers. In many of the earlier dam fights, it was not so much the rivers as it was the parks, fish, and homes that people wanted to save. Then, with the environmentalism of the 1970s, people saw that the stream and ecological concerns were inseparable, and the movement came closer to that of saving rivers for themselves. With increased river travel by canoeists, rafters, and kayakers, a river culture was quietly born. People began to talk more about the joy, the wonder, and the spirituality brought by rivers. What they wanted to save would remain enigmatic and lost for words because it was so tied up in feelings and emotions condemned from public debate. Dubois, Gaguine, and others tried to describe the importance of their river, though they usually resorted to guiding people in rafts because the only thing that really worked was to experience the river personally. Why save a river? Because it is the unspoiled Eden, right here, available to all. Why save a river? Because it is a river.

One of the few North American precedents for this commitment to rivers lies in the Indians' ancient concept of holy and powerful places. Now, in a culture so responsive to economic gain and technology — in a society poorly prepared to face people who are spiritually committed to the earth — the rivers movement adopted the ideas of stewardship, responsibility, reverence for life, and spirituality in new ways that reached many people as they camped in canyons like the Stanislaus and as the fights against dams were dragged through Congress and publicized to the nation.

RETURN TO THE TUOLUMNE

Hetch Hetchy Valley of the Tuolumne was the site of the nation's first major dam fight, and in 1982 this river became the subject of the greatest controversy in river protection. On a section below Yosemite National Park, more remarkable natural and recreational values were threatened than anywhere else in the country. The twenty-seven-mile-long canyon between O'Shaughnessy Dam and New Don Pedro Reservoir includes some of the country's most challenging but regularly used whitewater.

Tuolumne raft trips offer the height of outdoor adventure along with the peace of canyon camping only four hours from San Francisco and eight hours from Los Angeles.

The canyon houses two hundred species of birds and animals, including the bobcat, black bear, and spotted owl. Yosemite Park's two largest deer herds winter in the canyon. Gold Rush relics and 250 archaeological sites from the Miwok Indians lie along the river. Many fishermen consider the Tuolumne the Sierra's best trout stream, and the state estimates that the river yields a thousand pounds of fish per acre, three times the amount of the best fishing reservoir in California. Congress designated the Tuolumne for a wild and scenic river study in 1975, and eighty-three miles were recommended for protection by the Carter administration.

In 1976 San Francisco and the Modesto and Turlock irrigation districts applied for federal permits to dam the lower canyon and to divert flows from the upper canyon for hydroelectricity. The $900-million project would destroy twenty-seven miles of the Tuolumne and seven miles of the Clavey River to produce 390 megawatts — less than 0.5 percent of California's projected electrical supplies in 1992. Additional plans called for dams on the South and Middle forks.

In 1978 Tuolumne County voters opposed the project by a two-thirds margin, and under Governor Jerry Brown the state supported wild and scenic river status. In 1981 the California Energy Commission reported that new reservoirs for power were fifth priority for meeting energy needs and that conservation, geothermal development, existing reservoirs, cogeneration, and interstate transfers of power could meet needs to 1992. Public Utilities Commission president John Bryson said, "The small increments of new supply that could be provided by additional damming of the Tuolumne are outweighed by the natural values associated with the protection of the remaining stretches of that beautiful canyon." The frail case for power production came from irrigation districts where electricity rates were among the lowest in the nation.[43] An economic analysis by Richard B. Norgaard of the University of California concluded that the project would cost more than it would earn.

In December 1982, editors of the *Los Angeles Times* wrote, "We think that a strong case has been made for permanent protection of one of the few relatively unspoiled rivers left in California. . . . California has nearly exhausted its supply of wild rivers to meet the water needs of its farms and cities."[44] On January 29, 1983, the *Los Angeles Times* stated, "The loss of one of the few remaining semi-free rivers within reach of millions of Californians is too high a price for the sake of lower power bills for a few thousand customers." San Francisco reversed its position and supported protection of the Tuolumne.

After the national river study moratorium expired in 1982, the Federal Energy Regulatory Commission issued permits for the planning of the dams. The sponsors spent $5 million on plans and hired Lee White — former chairman of the Federal Power Commission — to plead their case. In 1983 the irrigation districts spent $140,000 a month lobbying for their dams.

Realizing that the temporary protection would expire, Jerry Meral, who now headed the Planning and Conservation League of California, and others had formed the Tuolumne River Preservation Trust in 1981 and hired John Amodio to run the campaign to save the Tuolumne. Amodio had led the fight to expand Redwood National Park, and he brought political experience and a determination to gain broad-based support. "We needed to avoid polarization," he said. "We built our arguments on the concept of balanced use — *they* were the extremists, wanting to dedicate the river to hydroelectric power when it was already providing for many needs." The river's three dams already provided water for one of twelve homes in the state, for irrigation, and for hydroelectric power. Even the organization's name — a trust — was aimed at conservative people. The board of directors included some members who had even supported New Melones Dam. A $100-a-plate dinner at San Francisco's Meridian Hotel was attended by the political elite wearing tuxedos. The event, which earned $20,000, honored actor Richard Chamberlain, among others.

Chamberlain had rafted the river and met Don Briggs — a guide and longtime Friends of the River activist — who encouraged Chamberlain to become involved. He lobbied for two days in Washington and testified eloquently before congressional committees. "To my eyes, God seems to have lavished a special abundance of living gifts on this river. We have the power to destroy it. But never, never in our wildest imagination can we ever recreate it." To save the Tuolumne became the priority issue of the American Rivers Conservation Council, who hired lobbyist David Dickson — a river guide and former Friends of the River staff member.

Senator Alan Cranston had favored protection for years, and after Senator Pete Wilson received more mail about the Tuolumne than about any other issue, he supported national river status also. The trust and other groups gained wide support in the House, where the effort was led by Tuolumne area congressman Richard Lehman, John Siberling of Ohio, and Sala Burton of San Francisco, who took her husband Phillip's seat when he died in 1983. Fresno congressman Tony Coelho, in support of the dams, was isolated despite his powerful party position, which allowed him to control funding for Democratic campaigns.

National river status for the Tuolumne was attached to the California Wilderness Bill, which passed and was signed in September 1984. Capitalizing on the experience and support gathered during the Stanislaus battle, the river people won this extraordinary victory against great odds and again showed the strength of the river conservation movement by saving one of America's most valuable wild rivers.

THE CENTER OF THE MOVEMENT

In the 1970s the saving of rivers had grown from isolated dam fights to a major environmental issue. Certain problems were common to all the threatened rivers, and as awareness grew, people joined together. Conservationists became adept in science and economics, and a center for lobbying was established in Washington, D.C. Leading the way in much of this movement was Brent Blackwelder.

The son of a minister, Blackwelder was living in Washington and earning a doctorate in philosophy when he volunteered with Friends of the Earth in 1970. He had not been an avid canoeist or fisherman, but set out to stop the government from channelizing streams. Explaining his motivation, he said, "One picture of a channelization disaster was all it took." During the 1970 election campaign, Blackwelder worked for the League of Conservation Voters to defeat House Public Works Committee chairman Fallon. "That election showed me that if you know what you're doing, you can win," Blackwelder recalled with the optimism that would carry him through the dark tunnels of dozens of struggles to save rivers.

Blackwelder and others who had worked for Friends of the Earth formed the Environmental Policy Center (EPC) in 1972 specifically to lobby Congress, and ten years later the group employed more lobbyists than any other public interest organization in Washington. As the first lobbyist to work full time on river protection, Blackwelder fought Dickey-Lincoln dams, Tocks Island Dam, and many others. American Rivers Conservation Council (ARCC) director Bill Painter said, "Brent was the real genius at involving everybody whose ox was to be gored, and in gaining that broad base of opposition to water projects." He circulated information and told people along one river to talk to people along another river. Dam fighters who were flailing away on their own began to find each other and to form coalitions.

Why does Blackwelder do this work? He says simply that special places are being destroyed for no good reason, and at public expense. Bill Painter said, "Brent thinks that those water projects are wrong, just ethically and politically wrong. He's zealous, but you have to get outraged to fight what we're dealing with."

In 1973 the EPC, ARCC, and other groups published *Disasters in Water Development*, a booklet documenting the reasons why thirteen of the nation's worst water projects should not be built and calling people to action as no single publication had ever done. In 1976 the EPC and ARCC sponsored the first national conference for river conservationists in Washington. Just as the wilderness conferences that started in 1949 had drawn preservationists together and given them a forum, the "Dam Fighters Conference" brought river protectors together more than ever before. From the plains of Nebraska, the canyons of California, the valleys of Appalachia, law offices in Boston, universities in Florida, and Indian reservations in Arizona, two hundred people came, and they found that river protection was a common goal. Renamed the National Conference on Rivers, the meeting draws several hundred people every spring to hear the latest news, to join in workshops about political skills, and to testify at appropriations committee hearings. It is the event of the year for river activists.

With Peter Carlson at the EPC, Blackwelder helped to stop 140 dams, canals, and channelization projects by 1983, saving taxpayers $20 billion in the process. He said that the keys to success are

> strong local groups, good information, coalitions, connections to national organizations, and knowing how to influence congressmen. If all else fails, elect new representatives. The French Broad River in North Carolina is a case where the people organized and elected new local officials when the ones they had wouldn't fight the TVA dams that were proposed. Then the feds saw the handwriting on the wall and backed off. The media makes all the difference. We've built and built the coverage, and as our name became known, the reporters started coming here whenever some controversy came up.

Through all of these river conflicts, patterns had developed. Where conservationists started early enough, they almost always won. When the corps started a study for Keating Dam on the West Branch of the Susquehanna in Pennsylvania, environmental groups made a strong showing, and authorization was never recommended. No more authorizations slipped in ahead of the opposition. Coalitions of conservation groups were essential, and by the late 1970s, support from economic, business, labor, social, and education organizations was needed for the conservationists' political success.

Except for national parks and a few other special cases, river conservationists learned that all water politics is local. Organizations in Washington did much to help, but streams were won or lost in towns and counties where congressmen depended on votes.

Party politics was riddled with exceptions on the subject of river conservation and water development. Herbert Hoover, for example, fought the establishment of the TVA but fathered Hoover Dam. Dwight Eisenhower cut federal water project funding but supported Echo Park Dam and private dams in Hells Canyon. John F. Kennedy approved dams in the New Deal style of Democrats since Franklin Roosevelt, but he also encouraged conservation. Lyndon Johnson tipped this balance slightly toward conservation. With individuals who supported river development and others who supported river preservation, each party, particularly before 1970, has had enough champions to show any general analysis to be questionable. But a complex and imperfect pattern did evolve: Republican congressmen were less enthusiastic than Democrats about dams and public works projects, though they were under the same political pressures to bring money home from Washington and build dams with it. Republican administrations were more likely to cut funding for public works projects, though they were flatly unreceptive to river conservation as a positive initiative. Democrats faced a difficult dilemma. Steeped in the New Deal tradition of federal spending for public works and dependent on social welfare causes, they also sought the votes of conservationists. Though water developers and river savers were opposites, both represented "liberal" causes. What resulted was a remarkable effort to do everything—sometimes touted as balanced use—involving both continued destruction of rivers through federal projects and a newly popular saving of rivers, but only when conservationists launched powerful campaigns.

Another new pattern was that politicians' decisions were leveraged by technical studies. Although the Grand Canyon had been won by virtue of the place involved, it was a consultant's study of eutrophication that helped to kill Tocks Island Dam and a hydrologist's study of groundwater that helped to halt the Cross Florida Barge Canal. Use of the Environmental Policy Act and its requirement for environmental impact statements became a formula for delaying projects; seven hundred suits regarding all kinds of environmental issues were taken to court in five years.[45] Given time, the dam fighters turned the politics around by exposing hidden costs that had never been counted.

The late 1960s and early 1970s had seen a growing influence of science and economics, bringing hard data that were more convincing in a political forum than the old arguments for wilderness and national park ideals, wildlife, and philosophical views of nature. This shift was partly due to growing sophistication in the sciences, with new emphasis on the ability to apply scientific techniques and knowledge to everyday problems. Furthermore, scientists were now becoming personally involved in river protection; politicians were growing more receptive to stringent analysis when their decisions were placed in the public spotlight; and, perhaps most important, conservationists now saw that if they were to save more than the most sublime of natural wonders, they must oppose developers on the developers' terms — through economic arguments and through analysis that showed negative effects on the lives of average citizens.

Yet, curiously, the rationale to save rivers was also working in the opposite direction at the same time. People were becoming involved with rivers and supporting them for their own sake. Though the arguments put forth to Congress grew more analytical and scientific, the old river-saving rationale, which some have called "romantic," was growing — not shrinking — among the general public. More people were becoming more committed simply because they loved rivers.

Beyond the major river controversies, attitudes had changed. People had regarded the stream through the center of town as a storm sewer, but now they were cleaning it up and turning a cluttered riverfront into a park. Programs for pollution control and open space preservation improved waterways, and residents took new pride in their surroundings. Oregon's Willamette River, once a fetid dump for paper mills and cities, was reclaimed under Governor Tom McCall and became a community asset, a blue ribbon through the farmland. People had turned their backs on waterways since the demise of river navigation and since the first pollution killed the fish, but now, from the Potomac to the Sacramento, people flocked toward the water to bicycle, walk, swim, and paddle. Growing interest in protecting entire watersheds brought concern about logging, highway construction, and urban sprawl.

The aesthetics of water were changing. A corps brochure still stated, "The man-made lake behind a dam can often be an environmental enhancement. A lake not only offers an interesting change in scenery, but provides for recreation such as boating, swimming and water-skiing not found in many free-flowing rivers." But many people had come to see reservoirs as drowned rivers, mud ringed, monotonous, and lifeless in comparison to the streams, valleys, and canyons that had disappeared.

River protection had come from small groups of people striving to save a park or homeland to large groups fighting for many things. In addition to the controversies that drew national attention, people fought to protect scores of streams from small dams by the Soil Conservation Service, from channelization, and from land development. People were motivated not only by their individual interests in one river but also by a wider awareness of rivers as the best of nature, even as holy places with spiritual values earlier reserved for cathedrals.

These fights against dams and canals were only part of the movement to save rivers. Beginning in the 1950s, a few people had realized that instead of constant opposition to development, a positive approach was needed. Recognition of river values was crucial in making antidam decisions final. Otherwise the builders would simply return when the politics changed. Since 1824 Congress had passed laws to develop thousands of streams, and now a law was needed to save some of the best of what remained.

CHAPTER SIX

National Rivers

Even though they moved west after college, the Craighead brothers never escaped the outdoor memories of growing up along the Potomac River and in the Appalachians. "As kids we canoed and swam in the Potomac," John remembered. "Up at the Seneca Breaks we caught small-mouth bass and drank from the river. Bald eagles nested there." [1]

After studying wildlife biology, John and Frank Craighead settled in Montana and Wyoming, where they became the authorities on the grizzly bear, even seeking out the temperamental giants of the northern Rockies in their winter dens. Yet, part of the Potomac stayed with those two scientists: they were river lovers. They rafted upper Hells Canyon of the Snake, now dammed. Even in winter they ran Idaho's Salmon, called the River of No Return by Lewis and Clark in 1805. They traveled and made films on the Middle Fork of the Salmon, where they first publicized the term *wild river*. Then came an adventure that would change the course of river protection: they returned home.

"Years after we had moved west we went back and saw the Potomac. The water was polluted, it wasn't anything like what we had known," John said. A homeland — the place of growing up, good times, and first impressions — may be a universal love, and seeing the loss of that place has moved many people to act. "I realized that we still had wild rivers in the West, but we wouldn't for long if we didn't do something to save them."

Fighting the Army Corps of Engineers' Spruce Park Dam for the Middle Fork of the Flathead in Montana (an alternative to Glacier View Dam, stopped in the 1940s), John Craighead wrote that conservationists should have a rivers program of their own instead of always acting on the defensive. In a 1957 *Montana Wildlife* magazine he wrote about classifying rivers and protecting the least developed.[2] Adding to the wilderness preservation idea that had taken hold among conservationists since Aldo Leopold's work thirty years before, Craighead wrote, "Rivers and their watersheds are inseparable, and to maintain wild areas we must preserve the rivers that drain them." Wild rivers were a "species now close to extinction" and were needed "for recreation and education of future generations." With analysis of the rivers' potential for dams versus undeveloped use, Craighead believed that irreplaceable streams and landscapes could be saved while still meeting the needs for water.

At a Montana State University conference in 1957, John Craighead promoted his river protection idea, writing later in *Naturalist* magazine:

> Today it is still possible to challenge and to enjoy a wild river, but already they are a rarity. Only a few such rivers exist and these are threatened by an expanding, groping civilization, public indifference and bureaucratic sluggishness. In spite of the durability of rock-walled canyons and the surging power of cataracting water, the wild river is a fragile thing — the most fragile portion of wilderness country. A dam can still its turbulent flow, a road eternally change the river bank, and a logging operation completely alter the watershed.[3]

Craighead wrote that wild rivers are needed as "benchmarks" for comparison of environmental changes. In an earlier issue of *Naturalist*, Frank Craighead had described a system of river classification including wild rivers, semiwild rivers, semiharnessed rivers, and harnessed rivers. He reasoned that once rivers were categorized, people would see the scarcity of quality streams and realize the need to protect them.

"I had worked on the wilderness legislation with Olaus Murie, Howard Zahniser, Stewart Brandborg, and others," John Craighead recalled, "but they were not interested in rivers. They were most interested in specific areas of wilderness, many of them without rivers because the lands were at high altitudes. The more I became involved, the clearer it became that we needed a national river preservation system based on the wilderness system but separate from it."

STARTING WITH THE CURRENT

Like the Craighead brothers, Paul Bruce Dowling was a wildlife biologist and had spent part of his youth in the Appalachians of central Pennsylvania. He moved to Missouri, where fishing from flatboats had been a tradition for generations on the spring-fed Current and Jacks Fork rivers. Dam

SELECTED EVENTS IN CHAPTER 6

1905 Wisconsin protected Brule River.
1908 Wisconsin protected Flambeau River.
1915 Oregon protected certain streams and waterfalls.
1950 Missouri supported protection of Current River.
1956 National Park Service proposed national recreation area along Current and Eleven Point rivers.
1957 John Craighead wrote about wild river protection.
Paul Bruce Dowling introduced idea of national rivers.
1959 Craighead brothers testified for federally protected rivers system at Senate select committee hearing.
National Park Service studied protection of Missouri River.
1960 Interior Department supported protection of free-flowing streams.
Senate select committee supported system of protected rivers.
1961 Stewart Udall became secretary of the interior.
National Park Service recommended national recreation area for the Allagash River.
Outdoor Recreation Resources Review Commission supported protection of free-flowing rivers.
1963 Stewart Udall supported protection of Current River.
1964 National Park Service prepared potential list of national rivers.
First wild rivers bill drafted.
1965 Wisconsin passed first wild and scenic rivers act.
1966 Maine designated Allagash Wilderness Waterway.
1968 Tennessee, Ohio, and Maryland started state rivers systems.
National Wild and Scenic Rivers Act passed.
1972 Lower Saint Croix added to the national rivers system.
California designated state rivers for protection.

1973 American Rivers Conservation Council organized.
1974 North Carolina designated New River for protection.
Chattooga River added to national rivers system.
1975 Snake River in Hells Canyon designated national river.
Twenty-nine rivers designated for national river study.
Nationwide rivers inventory started.
1976 American Rivers Conservation Council fought to save New River.
Flathead, Obed, and Missouri rivers added to national rivers system.
1978 General Accounting Office criticized rivers program.
National Parks and Recreation Act passed, designating Delaware and six other rivers.
1979 President Carter issued directive to protect inventoried rivers on federal lands.
1980 Twenty-six Alaskan rivers added to national system.
Salmon River added to national system.
1981 Interior Secretary Andrus designated northern California rivers in national system.
1982 Development moratorium expired for eleven national study rivers.
1983 Federal judge determined designation of northern California rivers invalid.
Governor Brennan of Maine protected sixteen rivers in state system.
Bills introduced to delete national rivers.
1984 Appeals court restored national status to northern California rivers.
Tuolumne, Illinois, Owyhee, Verde, and Au Sable rivers added to the national system.

proposals at Blair Creek and Doniphan were temporarily beaten in the 1940s, and the state government — one of the most progressive in natural area preservation — supported protection of the two rivers in 1950. In one of the first cases in which the development of river recreation was promoted as an alternative to reservoirs, the Current River Protective Association proposed a river park with public ownership of recreation sites.

As secretary of the Missouri chapter of the Nature Conservancy in the mid-1950s, Bruce Dowling wrote to Senator Stuart Symington asking for a federal study of the Current and Jacks Fork. In 1983 Dowling remembered, "I had floated those rivers when I was a wildlife biologist with the state, and through a Nature Conservancy inventory we realized that many of the rare plant communities were along the streams of the Ozarks. Across the country we had national parks, and here I saw the potential for "national rivers"— maybe ten or twenty of the unique gems, free-flowing streams representing the different physiographic regions.[4]

In 1956 the National Park Service proposed a national recreation area along the Current and nearby Eleven Point River, where local people had also fought dams. The park service then wrote another report, recommended an Ozark Rivers national monument, and held hearings at which Dowling testified that in 1957 the Missouri chapter of the Nature Conservancy had "introduced the idea of 'national rivers' as a designation appropriate to the Current River." [5] This is perhaps the first official reference to "national rivers."

Ted Swem, director of park service planning, said, "We hoped that the Current River proposal would be prototypical, and that we could come forth with other river proposals." [6] In 1959 the park service studied Montana's Missouri River below Fort Benton, but the river protection plan was shelved because of infighting among federal agencies. For Maine's Allagash, the park service proposed a national recreation area, but this was vetoed by the state, which feared federal controls. The Suwannee in Florida and Georgia was also studied.

Within the Interior Department, resource planners John Kauffmann and Stanford Young thought that a whole set of rivers should be protected. Swem recalled, "After studying the Current, the Allagash, and the Missouri, we began talking about the possibility of a system of rivers." In addition to Craighead and Dowling, citizen advocates for river protection were Sigurd Olson in Minnesota, whom Stewart Udall called one of the "great philosophers" of wild rivers; Joe Penfold of the Izaak Walton League; Bud Jordahl in Wisconsin; and Leonard Hall in Missouri. Swem said, "I can't say that any one person had the idea. There were many people in different roles, and they were all crucial."

FROM DAMMING RIVERS TO SAVING THEM

To thwart President Eisenhower's policies against federal projects, the Senate formed a Select Committee on National Water Resources. The committee planned to retaliate with policies of its own and with new dam proposals that would end the impasse and move on with development. Ted Schad, director of the committee's staff, had served in a fascinating variety of jobs. As a Bureau of Reclamation budget director he had justified Echo Park and other dams, but at the same time he had also served as a volunteer representing a Seattle climbing and hiking group on a Department of the Interior advisory committee. There he met Howard Zahniser of the Wilderness Society. "Zahniser convinced me that Echo Park should not be built," Schad recalled in 1983. After transferring to the Bureau of the Budget, Schad wrote Eisenhower's rivers and harbors veto messages.

At one of Ted Schad's Senate select committee field hearings in 1959, the Craighead brothers called for a system of federally protected rivers. They urged that the newly formed Outdoor Recreation Resources Review Commission begin a system of river evaluation. The Fish and Wildlife Service in the Interior Department reported to the select committee that some rivers are most valuable if left unaltered,[7] and in 1960 interior officials wrote to the Committee on Interior and Insular Affairs: "There still remain in various sections of the country natural free-flowing streams whose integrity might be preserved in the face of the water-control onslaught if conscientious planning to this end were applied."

Armed with these recommendations, Schad proposed in the Senate select committee's report "that certain streams be preserved in their free-flowing condition because their natural scenic, scientific, aesthetic, and recreational values outweigh their value for water development and control purposes now and in the future."[8] Examples were listed: the Allagash, Current, and Eleven Point, and the Rogue in Oregon. Some senators on the select committee may not even have noticed Schad's wild river recommendation—it was one of many in the report. The committee adopted the report without discussion of the river protection idea, and this became the government's first major proposal for a national rivers system.

Through the late 1950s, debates had been held about wilderness and how much of it was needed, leading to broader questions about recreation that no one could answer. So the Outdoor Recreation Resources Review

Commission was created to prepare the nation's first thorough study of recreation needs. Arthur Davis, one of the study report's authors, said, "Water was one of the building blocks for recreation. 'Scenic river' was not a brand new term, and in the water area it was a parallel to the wilderness idea." [9] The commission issued *Outdoor Recreation for America,* stating, "Certain rivers of unusual scientific, esthetic, and recreation value should be allowed to remain in their free-flowing state and natural setting without man-made alterations." [10]

By 1961 Craighead's idea of classifying and protecting rivers had matured, and Dowling's idea of national rivers gained support. The Current River would be saved, and a growing collection of river proposals was incorporated into government reports. Interior Department planners, enthusiastic about river protection, waited only for a secretary who was ready to act.

THE SECRETARY WITH TWO VIEWS

"As a congressman in the 1960s I was prodam," Stewart Udall said in 1983. "I voted for the upper Colorado project that flooded Glen Canyon. I instinctively identified my values more with the Sierra Club than with dam building, except that I was from Arizona, and so you had to be for water. You couldn't go to Congress and be against dams." [11]

On a field trip, rarely allowed by interior committee chairman Wayne Aspinall, Udall and his family were one of the last groups to float through Glen Canyon. "I got off the river with very mixed feelings. I didn't feel guilt stricken, but I kept saying to myself that we hadn't done a very good job in the West of achieving balance. In deciding where to put dams we had made mistakes. So I began to have doubts."

In 1961 President Kennedy appointed Udall secretary of the interior. "Suddenly I had the national responsibility, and that put on my shoulders the burden of thinking for the nation and not just for Arizona, which is what a congressman would do when it comes to water. My thinking gradually changed in the early sixties at the same time that I was testifying for dams."

Udall personified the upheaval happening in water development philosophy. He had supported dams that were the epitome of river destruction and that rallied conservationists to the cause of river protection. But with the help of people who were working to save their rivers, by experiencing these waterways personally from a canoe or a raft, and with a statesman's regard for his job, Udall saw the need for balance and preservation. This man stood uniquely as a river developer and a river saver both, bearing the complications and compromises inherent in the holding of two opposite views at once.

> Three major things happened during my first year. Senator Muskie got a little floatplane and we went up to canoe the Allagash. He was anxious to leave the river alone, and it was threatened by the Rankin Rapids Dam. So the Allagash was identified as one of the finest wild rivers in the eastern part of the country, and the fact that people in Maine wanted to save it left an impression on me, particularly when I saw it, when I canoed it. I had never been canoeing really; we didn't have that many rivers in Arizona. Senator Muskie knew that Maine couldn't afford to buy land, yet the state wanted to do the job themselves, so we matched their funds with federal funds. We preserved a river for about $3 million.

Udall, unequivocally a man of the desert, saw something new, something worth saving in the soggy bogs feeding this wild river of the far eastern, far northern United States.

"Then later that summer we were looking at new parks and seashores. It was an explosive period for that, and I made it a policy to go out and see the places in order to throw the spotlight on the proposals." On a Current River canoe trip Udall met George Hartzog, whom he later appointed director of the National Park Service.

> We were all enthused about making the Current a national park, but since we were really preserving the river, we called it the national scenic riverways.
>
> The third thing was even more of a catalyst. There was a big fight over an Idaho dam called Bruce's Eddy, now called Dworshak, on the Clearwater. The conservationists opposing it came to me and wanted me to help in the fight. I got involved, and it dramatized for me the flaws and misconceptions in the dam-building philosophy of the New Deal. The values were changing, and if that dam were considered in 1964 it never would have been authorized. So for me, this is where the kernel of the idea for the wild and scenic river bill came from.

Udall sought an amendment banning additional Clearwater dams. This failed, but the concept would be resurrected for nothing less than an entire system of rivers.

In *The Quiet Crisis,* Udall articulated his new view of river protection:

> Generations to follow will judge us by our success in preserving in their natural state certain rivers having superior outdoor recreation values. The Allagash of Maine, the Suwannee of Florida, the Rogue of Oregon, the Salmon of Idaho, the Buffalo of Arkansas, and the Ozark Mountain rivers in the State of Missouri are some of the waterways that should be kept as clean, wild rivers — a part of a rich outdoor heritage.

After Udall boated on the Allagash and Current, Senator Gaylord Nelson of Wisconsin invited him to canoe the Saint Croix, and Bob Harrigan, a canoeist who had pioneered many runs in the Appalachians, guided him on the Potomac and Shenandoah.

"Big things under Kennedy were the national seashores, Canyonlands National Park, and the Ozark rivers, but the wilderness bill was the landmark legislation. As it came closer to law, my thinking began to turn more toward rivers legislation that would complement and be another kind of wilderness bill, and we started studies in interior." Udall asked Frank Craighead, who worked for the Fish and Wildlife Service, to prepare a paper on river classification. Udall acted on the key recommendation of the Outdoor Recreation Resources Review Commission by creating the Bureau of Outdoor Recreation, and he wrote to Orville Freeman, secretary of the Department of Agriculture, to organize a wild and scenic rivers study team. In 1964 planners led by Stanford Young collected a list of 650 rivers for consideration, reduced it to 67, then announced 22 rivers for detailed field study.

New national park proposals were attacked by critics who were against "locking up" resources, so to sidestep political hazards, interior officials were receptive to innovative land protection. The naming of national recreation areas (most of the early ones surrounded large reservoirs), national seashores, lakeshores, and rivers was a way to expand the federal recreation estate without the restrictions of national park status that ignited the wrath of hunters and private landowners. Ted Swem said, "Although the national monument classification was justified for the Ozark rivers, it was obvious that the proposal would not be authorized if hunting was prohibited. So we suggested the national scenic riverways classification."

While the idea of a rivers system was being explored, the political support to protect the Current River had matured. With Udall's recommendations, President Kennedy called for Current River protection in his conservation message to the Senate Select Committee on National Water Resources in 1961. At hearings in 1963 Udall said, "It would be difficult to find an area where so much beauty and variety of natural features can be preserved by setting aside so little." Also in 1963 Gaylord Nelson introduced a bill to make the Saint Croix a national river (he had helped convince the Northern States Power Company to sell to the government seventy miles along both sides of the river where a power dam had been planned). Nelson's bill passed the Senate but stalled in the House. John Saylor and others went to work, and in 1964 the Ozark National Scenic Riverways were designated as the first national rivers, for "conserving and interpreting unique scenic and other natural values, including preservation of portions of Current River and Jacks Fork River as free-flowing streams." During the same year, the Wilderness Act passed — a law requiring that certain public lands remain without development or logging, though a loophole not yet used allows water projects if the president approves. Conservation leaders, political momentum on their side, looked to their next opportunity.

"John Craighead had left all this material on my desk," recalled Stewart Brandborg, then director of the Wilderness Society. Howard Zahniser had talked about a system of "wilderness rivers," and, Brandborg said, "The idea of wild rivers was deep in the hearts of the old Wilderness Society leaders."

Comparing wilderness preservation to rivers preservation, Stewart Udall said,

> The wilderness concept began with Aldo Leopold and other foresters back in the twenties. The Wilderness Society was formed in the thirties. They said we needed a law, and wrestled around in the fifties, and the first bill was introduced in 1957. The wilderness concept had this forty-year gestation period. With wild and scenic rivers it was just a few years. It came on strong, even though there was no national constituency. The momentum of the wilderness bill had a tide moving, and sometimes you see two waves, and you jump on the second wave and ride it in. The timing was just perfect. President Johnson's chief of domestic affairs kept saying, "Johnson wants new legislation," and I told him about the wild and scenic rivers idea and he said, "That sounds great, get it ready."

In 1964 the first wild and scenic rivers bill was called the "Wild Rivers Act," focusing on the extraordinary rivers of the West, but the bill was later broadened to include "scenic" and "recreation" rivers. President Johnson called for approval of a rivers bill in his 1965 State of the Union address:

> We will continue to conserve the water and power for tomorrow's needs with well-planned reservoirs and power dams. But the time has also come to identify and preserve free-flowing stretches of our great rivers before growth and development have made the beauty of the unspoiled waterway a memory.

Udall vividly remembered his former committee chairman's reaction:

> After Johnson's message, Wayne Aspinall walked off the floor and told a reporter that wild rivers were the craziest idea he ever heard of. He thought I was off my rocker by then on a lot of things. Since Senator Frank Church had been involved on the Clearwater, he decided to take his life into his own hands and sponsor the wild and scenic rivers bill in the Senate. He was bold; he was from Idaho, and this was controversial. He was splitting from the other side. I remember going to John Saylor — he was in complete agreement with the rivers

idea — and about Aspinall's comment Saylor said, "We'll just wear him down."

In 1965 we got the bill passed overwhelmingly in the Senate, where Senators Church and Nelson were strong supporters. That said, "The country wants wild and scenic rivers." It left Aspinall with the question, Was he going to be arbitrary and obstruct the will of the country? Then Saylor started nagging him, "Wayne, better get some hearings going or things are going to get mighty unpleasant around here."

Howard Zahniser was Saylor's personal friend, and he had stressed that the rivers idea paralleled the wilderness law but was broader because it included all types of rivers and could mobilize people nationwide. Stewart Brandborg remembered, "That's all you had to say to Saylor."

The rivers act would be one of Saylor's greatest conservation accomplishments. Others included the Wilderness Act, the defeats of the Echo Park and Grand Canyon dams, the preservation of the Current and Jacks Fork, and the saving of Hells Canyon. From Johnstown, Pennsylvania, known for devastating floods, Saylor was an anomaly — a small-town politician who was also a lifetime member of the Sierra Club. He gave sacks of home-grown potatoes as Christmas presents to friends. He was pleased to see the popularization of conservation in the late 1960s but did not subscribe to the new environmentalism. Addressing "boys and girls" on Earth Day at Penn State University in 1970, he said, "I don't buy this antigrowth idea. We need growth to pay for the environmental improvements that have to be made. You can't build a sewage treatment plant unless people have money to pay for it." A champion of new parks and traditional conservation, he was a master at congressional dealing and arm twisting in the old style.

In 1967, after carefully compromising the bill so that most water developments would not be threatened, Aspinall introduced the most complex legislation. What converted Aspinall? "He must have owed Saylor some real big favors," Stewart Brandborg said in 1983. (Aspinall received support for five dams in Colorado, three of which the Bureau of Reclamation did not even recommend, authorized in 1968 as part of the Central Arizona Project.)

The national rivers bill called for three classes of rivers: wild, scenic, and recreational. The wilderness idea of preserving the "glamor" rivers of the West was broadened, and Secretary Udall said, "Rivers should be saved in all parts of the country." National conservation groups, canoe clubs, and dam fighters packed hearings in 1968. The Saint Croix, Eleven Point, and Little Miami — all in the Midwest — received the most support. Stanford Young of the Interior Department said, "Mostly the motivation was against dams. The problems of riparian development were not yet perceived because they weren't dramatic." Testimony for the rivers bill included opposition to dams on the Eleven Point, the Saint Croix, and the Little Miami in Ohio. The Middle Fork of the Feather in California was included, though two dam sites proposed by the Richvale Irrigation District had been approved by the state.

But the federal water development agencies saw that the act stopped no dams that they really wanted. Tennessee Valley Authority chairman Aubrey J. Wagner objected to protection of the French Broad River and the Little Tennessee, including the Tellico Dam site, because "planning and construction of water control and development projects have progressed to a point which would make it inappropriate to include these streams." The spectacular Green River in Wyoming was deleted because of an irrigation dam site at Kendall. A Seattle City Light representative testified against the upper Skagit, where Copper Creek Dam was planned to flood the river's only remaining whitewater. The Tocks Island Regional Advisory Council supported Delaware protection but only above the Tocks Island Dam site. Residents stopped wild and scenic designation of Potomac tributaries in West Virginia. Landowners along the Shenandoah objected, expressing fears that would grow in the next decade. Mrs. John Locke Burns, Jr., said, "When I read these scenic and wild river bills, I am almost made to feel that no longer does the right to ownership exist." All of these river sections were deleted. The National Reclamation Association flatly opposed the bills: "The concept does not conform to the principles of multipurpose development."

The acting secretary of the army was more subtle: "The Nation can well afford to forego the development of streams of unusual natural beauty. . . . But for very few of these have studies been made which provide an adequate basis for a wise decision." Because the bill would block dam proposals on the Salmon and Middle Fork of the Clearwater, several senators, led by Len Jordan of Idaho, dissented from the interior committee and stated, "The combined runoff of the Salmon and Clearwater Rivers is greater than the total runoff of the Colorado River and the combined hydroelectric potential is greater than Grand Coulee or greater than all hydroelectric potential on the entire Colorado River." [12]

Congressman Sam Steiger from Arizona flatly said, "Under the guise of protecting scenic values, this legislation will stifle progress, inhibit economic development and incur a staggering expenditure." [13]

But Stewart Udall knew what he was doing. He said, "We had the momentum, and the dam people who didn't like it just weren't in a frame of mind to fight it. I had been pretty good to them, giving them some of the things they wanted, including dams. So I looked them in the eye and said we're going to balance things off."

A SYSTEM OF THEIR OWN

Support was strong as the conservation movement matured and the environmental movement of the 1970s approached. Robert Eastman, who became director of the rivers program said, "Back then, if you had a good idea, you could put it to work. The people were concerned about conservation. They wanted to protect natural places. Secretaries Udall and Freeman wanted to push programs, and Presidents Kennedy and Johnson were receptive. There was money to do things without having to take it out of someone else's program. Times were good and people didn't mind spending funds on parks and rivers."

Stewart Udall said, "Some people think that environmental protection began with Earth Day in 1970, but a lot of action led up to that." Although the early 1970s did see the greatest advances in fighting pollution and in governmental reform regarding the environment, the 1960s were a remarkable age for natural areas protection.

Reflecting on the parks and the new systems of wilderness, seashores, and national rivers, Ted Swem said of the 1960s, "I don't know if we'll ever have a period like that again."

Because 1968 was an election year, action on the rivers bill was delayed until many people thought it was too late. The House refused to suspend rules to allow the bill to bypass committees and go straight to the floor. The interior committee quit meeting, but Wayne Aspinall agreed to poll his members, who had dispersed across the states, and they agreed to release the bill on September 6. On September 12 the House voted 265–7 in favor of the bill. On October 2, the Senate approved and President Johnson signed the National Wild and Scenic Rivers Act, designating parts of eight rivers and identifying twenty-seven others for study and possible inclusion. The act states:

It is hereby declared to be the policy of the United States that certain selected rivers of the Nation which, with their immediate environments, possess outstandingly remarkable scenic, recreational, geologic, fish and wildlife, historic, cultural, or other similar values, shall be preserved in free-flowing condition, and that they and their immediate environments shall be protected for the benefit and enjoyment of present and future generations. The Congress declares that the established national policy of dams and other construction at appropriate sections of the rivers of the United States needs to be complemented by a policy that would preserve other selected rivers or sections thereof in their free-flowing condition to protect the water quality of such rivers and to fulfill other vital national conservation purposes.[14]

Although the bill drafted by the Interior Department had simply named one category of national river, the final version called for three classes: wild rivers are "vestiges of primitive America"; scenic rivers have "shorelines or watersheds still largely primitive and shorelines largely undeveloped but accessible in places by roads"; and recreational rivers "are readily accessible by roads" and "may have some development along their shorelines." Conservationists thought the three classes made a stronger bill, but the classes also introduced troublesome complexity. Some people thought that a "wild" river had to include dangerous whitewater. Others thought that a "recreational" river would always bring crowds of tourists and busloads of people from cities. Debates often center on the semantics of classification, diverting attention from more important questions, such as, Should the river be protected from dams or not?

The original eight "instant" rivers were the Middle Fork of the Clearwater and its tributaries the Lochsa and the Selway for 185 miles in Idaho (including the Penny Cliffs dam site); the Eleven Point for 44 miles in Missouri; the Middle Fork of the Feather for 154 miles in California; the Rio Grande for 53 miles and its tributary Red River for 4 miles in New Mexico; the Rogue for 85 miles in Oregon; the Saint Croix and tributary Namakagon for 200 miles in Wisconsin and Minnesota; the Middle Fork of the Salmon for 104 miles in Idaho; and the Wolf for 25 miles in Wisconsin.

The act prohibits dams or other federal projects that would damage the river. Shoreline protection is encouraged through local zoning, public acquisition, or management of government lands. Instead of expensive and unpopular land buying, the act encourages the use of easements — partial ownership, including development rights, thus allowing residents to stay and keep their property. Land may not be condemned if more than half of the acreage in the corridor is publicly owned, or if acquisition (including easements) would exceed 320 acres a mile — an average of one-quarter mile from each shore. In many cases, far less than this amount would be bought, but landowners along some rivers would mistakenly think that all lands one-quarter mile from the water would be acquired.

To add a river to the system, Congress first votes for a study of the river. The National Park Service or Forest Service collects information, meets with people, writes a report, receives reviews, decides if the river qualifies and how it should be classified, and recommends an agency to manage it.

After approval by the Office of Management and Budget and the president, the recommendation goes to Congress, where a vote is normally needed for designation. However, an alternate route can be followed: for state-legislated scenic rivers a governor can request the secretary of the interior for national designation, requiring an environmental impact statement but no vote by Congress. The act also calls for the Interior Department planners to help the states in protecting rivers through state systems and other alternatives.

RESCUING THE PROGRAM

As the Craigheads had envisioned thirteen years before, river supporters now had a program of their own. With a positive alternative, they could take the initiative and did not have to be "against" everything. Yet the movement had far to go. River supporters were busy with rearguard battles and could not get ahead of the dam builders enough to work for long-term preservation. At Interior Secretary Walter Hickel's direction, the Bureau of Outdoor Recreation studied controversial projects of the corps (but not of the Bureau of Reclamation) and helped to stop Salem Church Dam on Virginia's Rappahannock River, but a recommendation to make the stream a national river went nowhere.

In 1972 the rivers act was amended to add the lower Saint Croix, but otherwise the system languished. Few studies, essential for congressional action, were completed. The rivers program lacked the constituency enjoyed by the wilderness supporters, and in many ways saving rivers was more difficult. Stanford Young said, "Rivers are so much more controversial than blocks of land; many people are dependent upon the rivers." Unlike the western high country, rivers and their valleys appeal to a chorus of competing users. Bottomland timber is often the best, and roads follow floodplains. Most streams are partly bordered by private lands, and whether or not government acquisition was proposed as part of a national river proposal, residents feared condemnation. The alternative — land use control — was likewise anathema, especially if coming from the state or federal government instead of the local level. Water developers with countless schemes wanted the rivers for themselves. Because of implied water quality controls, towns upstream from potential designations joined in fighting protection. State and local governments resented federal involvement even though the act allowed states to administer rivers without federal managers.

Rivers remained a secondary concern of the national environmental groups, which were busy with wilderness, parks, wildlife, water quality, and air pollution. Michael McCloskey, executive director of the Sierra Club, said in 1981, "We're interested in saving substantial tracts of land that include rivers, but we're not enamored with the linear aspects. To us in the West, that's too confined an approach. Even John Muir didn't want strips up the streams, but the whole watershed. It's against the grain for us to be real happy with corridors. With wilderness, we get the whole package."[15]

Gaylord Nelson — environmental leader for twenty years in the Senate, where he was the initiator of Earth Day in 1970 — was chairman of the Wilderness Society in 1983. "Much of the conservation activity has revolved around the issues of public lands, not rivers," he said. "The original founders of the Wilderness Society were thinking mainly about land issues."

"The rivers have taken short shrift," said Brock Evans of the Sierra Club and now of the National Audubon Society. "The conservation groups budget their work on rivers within the category of public lands, and as a result, the rivers don't get the attention they deserve." State groups were formed, such as Ohio's Rivers Unlimited in 1972 and California's Friends of the River in 1973, but no group protected rivers nationwide or lobbied for the national system. In articles in the American Whitewater Affiliation's journal, Jerry Meral and others called for a national rivers organization.

In March 1973, thirty-three conservationists, including Mike Fremont from Ohio, Jerry Mallett from Colorado, Claude Terry from Georgia, Rafe Pomerance (later director of Friends of the Earth), Jerry Meral (founder of Friends of the River), David Foreman (founder of Earth First), and others met in Denver at the invitation of Phil LaLena of Colorado to form the American Rivers Conservation Council (ARCC). Brent Blackwelder, working for the Environmental Policy Institute, has served as chairman of the board of ARCC ever since.

"We debated about what to do," Blackwelder remembered in 1983. "Should we fight dam proposals or support scenic river designations? We decided to work for scenic river protection, but some of the most logical choices are slated for damming, and if we didn't fight the developers, there would be no scenic rivers to protect. So we've always focused on getting rivers in the system and also on stopping dams." Other goals were to see deauthorization of certain water projects, establishment of state river systems, an increase in interest rates charged for water projects, and elimination of recreation benefits justifying new dams. The Salmon River — the longest river outside Alaska with no dams — was one of few streams named for special action, though its protection would for years be an elusive goal.

Mike Fremont remembered, "Eventually we got to where we knew money was needed to kick this thing off, and Brent threw a hundred bucks down. Everybody pitched in and we had a few thousand dollars to start an operation." A director to be paid $400 a month was difficult to find, but eventually the board hired Bill Painter, who had worked on the original Environmental Teach-in at the University of Michigan in 1969.

Painter recalled the council's early days when he and Blackwelder shared a one-room office packed full of paper and ringing telephones on a side street southeast of the Capitol.

> Money was always a struggle, and I spent a lot of time learning the ropes on the Hill. I knew how to run a little ragtag outfit, but the lobbying—that I had to pick up from Brent. We got a newsletter rolling and I went to work trying to get more rivers in the national system.
>
> While I was trying to do that, Brent was in the thick of two dozen scrapes between the Environmental Policy Center and the army corps. That was before the tide was turned on bad projects—they were coming from everyplace and it was an overwhelming job—Dickey-Lincoln, Salem Church, Teton, Garrison, Tenn-Tom. I could have done nothing but help Brent on each daily political crisis, but I saw that if ARCC was to have an identity, we had to get rivers in the national system. Considering how Brent was overworked, and how important it was to fight those turkey water projects, saying no to him was about the most difficult part of the job.

The efforts of Painter and others paid off. In 1974 the Chattooga River in North Carolina, South Carolina, and Georgia was designated as a national river. In January 1975, a package of twenty-nine rivers for new studies passed Congress. Painter said,

> My biggest satisfaction was working with people out there who loved their rivers. Matt Bailey was an older guy along the North Fork of the American in California. He wanted to save that river but he didn't know what to do. Being able to help was a real good feeling. We added the river to the 1975 study act, and eventually it was designated. I didn't get out of Washington much, but I fell in love with those rivers by just looking at the pictures people sent in. Then when Congress recessed, Brent and I went on a tour. Neither of us was married or had families then. We went around the country and people showed us their streams, and there's nothing like seeing a river through the eyes of somebody who really cares about it.

In 1974 ARCC lobbied and helped to win a stronger federal flood insurance program to protect river frontage through floodplain zoning. On the last day of 1975 the Hells Canyon National Recreation Area Act was passed, adding the middle Snake and the Rapid River in Idaho to the national rivers system and deauthorizing Asotin Dam, which had been planned for lower Hells Canyon (Asotin would later be proposed by private utilities).

In Painter's four years at ARCC, the New River in North Carolina was a big project. He recalled,

> The fight against those two dams had gone on for years, and somebody had already figured out that they ought to designate the river. If I were going to pick out a river, the upper New wouldn't be the one to grab me — it's real nice, but not biologically unique or anything like that. I guess it's easy to fall prey to the big gorges, but Chuck Clusen of the Sierra Club and Brent said that this one was important, and after a while I saw why: the national rivers system was mostly made up of rivers that no one else wanted for dams, but here was a case where we had to fight water developers on their own ground. The dam was already licensed by the Federal Power Commission; national designation was the only way to save it. It seemed like a tough one to win, but the local people were organized and we went to work.

Painter developed a formula that would prove effective on other rivers:

> We helped frame the campaign so it would sell in Congress. The local people were emphasizing the river, but I began to emphasize the Appalachian cultural history and the farmers who would have to move. There were people who traced their deeds to the king of England, and I played that stuff up. We quit calling it a hydroelectric project and called it a pumped storage project — all it would do was store power. And we found out in the FPC files that there were alternate sites that would affect less land and fewer people. We ran into the argument that the river didn't qualify for the national system, but the cultural angle made it, and when the New was designated in 1976, it was a huge success. We had won a river that would otherwise have been dammed.

In 1976 the North, Middle, and South forks of Montana's Flathead were designated, including the Glacier View Dam site fought in the 1940s, the Spruce Park site fought by the Craigheads in the 1950s, and the Smoky Range site fought in the 1960s. The Obed of Tennessee was included where the Tennessee Valley Authority had studied a dam site. On the upper Missouri, where Interior Department planners had proposed national protection in the early 1960s, 149 miles were finally protected. (Except for the Suwannee, this completed protection for all of the prototype rivers that had been recommended before the National Wild and Scenic Rivers Act was passed.) Three rivers had been added through governors' requests: Ohio's Little Miami and Little Beaver, and Maine's Allagash, which had been proposed by the Interior Department as a national recreation area in 1961. By 1977, 1,655 miles on nineteen river sections were designated.

When Bill Painter became director of the Conservation Society of

Southern Vermont, Howard Brown, who had analyzed water development for the Congressional Research Service, became the second ARCC director, bringing a knowledge of water policy that was important during the Carter years.

Through the late 1970s many national river proposals in the East and Midwest were stalled by landowners fearing condemnation of their property. Eminent domain was used in some of the first designations, such as the Current and Saint Croix, but by 1976 the thrust of protection was mostly on zoning. Yet it did not matter that officials emphatically assured people that they would not be evicted; the specter of a land grab could not be erased.

People blamed national designation for increased recreation, but activity was booming on other rivers too: Pennsylvania's Youghiogheny, not in any scenic rivers system, carried 5,000 floaters in 1968 and 150,000 in 1982. Even though it was in the national system, Ohio's Little Beaver received no increase in use. In 1976 Maurice Arnold, director of the Bureau of Outdoor Recreation in the Northeast, said, "All good rivers will eventually see an increase in use, but through the rivers program, we have a chance to manage that use and avoid problems."

Although ARCC's lobbying paid dividends, the rivers system did not grow much, and a national river study required a tedious five to seven years. Reports were sometimes stalled at the Office of Management and Budget for years. In 1978 the General Accounting Office published *Federal Protection and Preservation of Wild and Scenic Rivers Is Slow and Costly,* stating, "The national system is growing slowly, and processes for adding rivers are not functioning well." [16]

Howard Brown of ARCC agreed: "The way the system has been set up to protect rivers makes it agonizingly slow, and the results are disappointing. A wilderness area or national park can go through Congress once, but wild and scenic rivers must make two trips — once for a study, then for designation. Twenty-eight rivers are protected now, but the number should be closer to a hundred." To speed protection, Brown supported incentives for state action and more emphasis on easements. [17]

Even though easements had been recommended as early as 1963, when author William H. Whyte testified for national protection of the Current, little was done. "The river managers and park superintendents always opposed easements," said Bob Eastman of the park service, "but the first thing a new superintendent looks at is a map, and he wants to see a solid block of green — to own everything and to keep the job simple. We can't afford to do that today."

Overcoming all the difficulties, San Francisco representative Phillip Burton, chairman of the House Interior and Insular Affairs Subcommittee, led passage of the National Parks and Recreation Act of 1978, one of the most comprehensive natural area preservation laws ever enacted. The act designated the section of the Delaware threatened by Tocks Island Dam and also protected the Skagit, lower Rio Grande, North Fork of the American, Pere Marquette, Missouri, and Saint Joe rivers. Both the number of rivers and the mileage in the national system increased by 40 percent, and seventeen new study rivers were named. With other sections addressing national parks, wilderness, and recreation, Burton's bill approved 144 projects in forty-four states; it was dubbed "parks barrel" by both supporters and critics, who recognized the act's resemblance to pork barrel bills that had authorized dams and canals all over the country. Reflecting on the river protection movement of the 1970s, Stewart Udall said, "The American Rivers Conservation Council has been the major, effective voice for preserving America's rivers."

REACHING FURTHER

Except for the original inventory done by interior planners under Stanford Young, the process of national river selection was largely one of political hit-and-miss. No one knew how many rivers had the qualities needed for the national system or where they were, so in 1975 the Department of the Interior's Bureau of Outdoor Recreation (changed under President Carter to the Heritage, Conservation, and Recreation Service) began a nationwide rivers inventory to provide data as a guide for recommending new national river candidates, and for other uses by agencies and citizens. A point system was devised to compare amounts of development on one river to another. After studying topographic maps, surveys, and people's comments, planners listed the rivers with the highest number of points.

Covering all states but Montana, where the governor halted work owing to fears of federal controls, Department of Interior planners found that 61,700 miles on 1,524 river sections were relatively undeveloped and met standards of the national rivers system. Not counting Alaska, this is less than 2 percent of the nation's river miles.[18]

Adding teeth to the inventory, President Carter in 1979 directed federal agencies to assess the listed rivers flowing through federal lands and to recommend either designation, further study, or other uses. A memorandum to department heads stated, "The agency is encouraged . . . to prepare legislation to designate the river as part of the Wild and Scenic Rivers

System if appropriate." The president directed agencies to avoid or mitigate adverse effects on the inventoried rivers, thus giving those streams some protection without the long congressional process of designation.

A few agencies followed the directive. The Forest Service considered the inventory when writing land management plans for each national forest. Unfortunately, the agency with perhaps the most important role — the Federal Energy Regulatory Commission (FERC) — did not consult with the National Park Service, which inherited the Heritage, Conservation, and Recreation Service's duties when it was disbanded in 1981. The Reagan administration has ignored the inventory, but it has proved useful anyway. For example, when Alabama highway planners noticed that a new road project was near a listed river, they wrote to Bern Collins of the National Park Service for guidance and special construction procedures. "The inventory is simply treated as information," said Collins, "and some agencies are finding that the rivers can be protected by choosing development alternatives."

In 1980, twenty-six Alaskan rivers were designated, adding 3,071 miles for 43 percent of the national rivers system in 1984. And after years of debate, 125 miles of the Salmon River were added to the system. Both the Alaskan and Salmon actions were pushed by President Carter and rode through Congress as part of larger land protection bills.

The last advance for rivers under Carter was the federal protection of streams already in California's state rivers system. This was important because of a dam proposed on the Middle Fork of the Eel.

To divert water south, the Army Corps of Engineers and Los Angeles had in the 1960s planned Dos Rios Dam, which would eliminate the state's largest summer steelhead run, drown the town of Covelo housing two thousand people, bury much of the Yuki Indians' reservation, and flood thirty miles of popular whitewater. A bill signed by Governor Reagan in 1972 designated northern California rivers, including the Eel, in the state scenic rivers system. This halted Dos Rios Dam but invited reconsideration in 1984. Seeking better protection for four thousand miles of the northern rivers, Governor Brown requested national river designation in 1979. Federal designation makes it more difficult for the powerful southern California and San Joaquin Valley political bloc — a state majority — to rescind protection, and it means better management of logging on national forest river frontage, unregulated under the state's forest management law. Included in the proposal were the Smith, California's only major undammed river and one of the nation's outstanding scenic streams; the Klamath, one of the largest West Coast rivers and the world's greatest producer of steelhead trout; the Scott and Salmon, undeveloped Klamath tributaries; the Trinity, the largest Klamath tributary; and the Eel, with three forks running in a special beauty of grasslands, woodlands, and whitewater. All are vital to a multimillion-dollar fishing industry off the California coast, to Indians, and to sport anglers. Designation of 1,235 miles of streams (excluding several thousand miles of small tributaries requested by Governor Brown) was signed by Interior Secretary Cecil Andrus only nineteen hours before he left office in 1981. This single action increased the national rivers system by almost 25 percent and protected three adjacent rivers, establishing a wild and scenic rivers "region." [19]

To rescind federal protection, southern water agencies and northern timber companies sued, arguing that typescript rather than printed notices of the environmental impact statement did not meet requirements and that management plans were not in force (these were not required for other rivers). Earl Blaise, board chairman of southern California's Metropolitan Water District, said, "Even though I do not feel there is any rush to develop the Eel, I always felt the option should be there if the state needed the water."

Saying that an environmental report's review period had been one day too short, a federal judge in 1983 declared Andrus's designation invalid, but this decision was overturned in 1984 when an appeals court restored national status after finding the objections to be "insignificant" and "trivial." Meanwhile, the Metropolitan Water District of southern California lobbied for a bill to allow state legislatures to subtract rivers from the national system — support that the *Los Angeles Times* called "a desperation move that seems unlikely to get the Metropolitan Water District anything except a reputation as a bureaucracy that cares about nothing else in California as long as its customers' faucets make a splash when they are turned on." Bills to rescind state protection of the Eel have been introduced in the state assembly, where a majority of southern Californians could open the way for Dos Rios Dam if the river loses its federal protection.

The ARCC lobbied for bills to protect forty fishing rivers in 1980 and eight Oregon rivers in 1982 and for incentives for state programs in 1983, but these failed to pass. Under President Reagan and Interior Secretary James Watt, the rivers program was nearly eliminated; rivers and trails appropriations were cut from $3.6 million in 1981 to $1.67 million in 1983. The Heritage, Conservation, and Recreation Service, responsible for the program, was eliminated, with some functions being assumed by the National Park Service. Whereas previous administrations had recommended designations, Watt's directives declared the streams "eligible but not suitable" if private land was included or if developers objected. The Carter directives were mostly ignored. The FERC was encouraged to grant private permits for dams, with applications streamlined to cut "red tape."

In the Department of Agriculture, the Forest Service — usually less protective than the National Park Service — offered the only river proposals, recommending designation of eight streams for 505 miles, but the president's Office of Management and Budget cut the list to 245 miles by eliminating private land and possible dam sites. Of 165 miles studied on Michigan's Au Sable River, only 74 were recommended by the Forest Service, and only 23 miles passed the Office of Management and Budget.[20] The administration also recommended elimination of the park service's technical assistance to states and local governments striving to protect rivers, but Congress insisted on some funds to keep the program alive.

Worst of all, by 1982 the development moratorium for eleven rivers had expired, because there had been no congressional action after the five-year study period. Chris Brown, the new director of ARCC, asked for an extension of the moratorium and testified that his organization "feels strongly that the fate of these rivers should not be decided by congressional default." Most important was the Tuolumne in California, where San Francisco and irrigation districts had applied to the FERC to build five dams that would eliminate one of the nation's premier whitewater runs and a superb trout fishery. Oregon's Illinois and Colorado's Gunnison were also threatened by hydroelectric proposals. A bill to extend protection failed, leaving the FERC free to license dams.

In 1984 wilderness bills that came to a vote added five rivers to the national system: the Tuolumne, which had been one of the wildest but most imminently threatened rivers in the history of the national rivers system; the Illinois in Oregon, where a hydroelectric project had been proposed; the Owyhee in eastern Oregon; the Verde in Arizona; and twenty-three miles of the Au Sable in Michigan. Four new study rivers were also named.

In 1985 a 7.5-mile segment of the Loxahatchee River became Florida's first national wild and scenic river. But in the same year the Reagan administration recommended designation of only 173.7 out of 1,604 miles of rivers that had been studied and found eligible for the national wild and scenic rivers system. To protect rivers in the national system — never an easy job — became increasingly difficult in the 1980s, with opposition by landowners, a hydroelectric boom, and neglect or outright hostility on the part of the federal government itself. Chris Brown said, "We need to look harder at alternatives to national designation."

BEYOND THE NATIONAL SYSTEM

Although state wild and scenic rivers programs must clear some of the same political hurdles as the national system, state designations were the main alternative. A pioneer in river protection, Wisconsin outlawed power dams on the Brule River in 1905 and on the Flambeau in 1908. For scenery and recreation, the Oregon legislature denied water diversions from certain streams and waterfalls in 1915, and dams that would interfere with salmon were stopped on the Rogue River (the corps's Lost Creek Dam was later built anyway). Minnesota bought easements in 1919 to halt subdivisions along a 150-mile section of river. To save steelhead, California banned dams on the Klamath in 1924. To save salmon, Washington passed a law to prohibit dams in parts of the Columbia basin but was overruled by the Federal Power Commission during the Cowlitz River debate. In 1965 Wisconsin passed the nation's first wild and scenic rivers act to protect the Pine, Popple, and Pike rivers, and Montana designated rivers for recreational use.[21] Maine formed an Allagash Authority in 1963 to develop preservation plans and in 1966 designated the Allagash Wilderness Waterway. Ohio, Tennessee, and Maryland started scenic river systems in 1968. In 1974 North Carolina designated the New River to help stop power dams.

Some states adopted their own scenic rivers systems as alternatives to the federal program; others saw state action as a way to protect even more rivers than the federal government could ever hope to do. In 1972 the California scenic rivers law named 4,006 miles of waterway on fifty-nine streams — the largest state system. The act prohibits dams, including one planned for the Middle Fork of the Eel, and in spite of heavy influence by the timber industry, it restricts riverfront logging on nonfederal lands. The Minnesota system requires riverfront zoning by local governments following state standards. By talking to each landowner, planners built political support and avoided the opposition that undercut programs in other states. One of these was Maryland, where state land use regulations along the upper Youghiogheny were met by hostile mountain residents who retaliated by blocking access, threatening fishermen, and shooting at kayakers who launched from a bridge pier. Rarely were rivers designated when a dam was planned, but Pennsylvania stopped a utility's pumped storage project by naming Stony Creek a state river.

By 1983, thirty states had wild and scenic river systems or had designated

individual rivers totaling 269 waterways for 13,674 miles. Most programs
are in the East, protection varying from a toothless list to a ban on dams and
a requirement for local zoning.[22] In 1983 Stewart Udall said, "Within about
four years of the federal act, many states had passed their own rivers bills,
and nothing pleased me more. Today the states don't have wilderness acts,
but they do have wild and scenic rivers acts."

Governor Joseph Brennan of Maine won the 1983 River Conservation
of the Year Award from ARCC after he issued an executive order protecting 1,500 miles on sixteen rivers. The designation prohibiting state support
of dams came after a National Park Service study that identified the most
valuable streams. Included are the nation's only ten stretches of river with a
natural population of Atlantic salmon. The order denied approval of two
hydroelectric projects but allowed approval of an important site on the
West Branch of the Penobscot.

To avoid antigovernment feelings, alternatives to even the state programs are sometimes sought. Along Montana's Blackfoot River, residents
had an inherent bias against federal protection, so a coalition was formed
among ranchers, timber companies (Champion International and two
ranchers own 75 percent of the frontage), county planners, the state, Trout
Unlimited, and citizens, aided by the federal Bureau of Outdoor Recreation. Landowners allowed recreation on their property, and state agencies
maintained the sites. To save open space, the Nature Conservancy bought
$20,000 worth of easements where land acquisition would have cost $15
million. The program does not prohibit dams that were once proposed.

Formed in 1973 by the Maine legislature, the Saco River Corridor Commission regulates land use in a 1,000-foot-wide strip along the river. Most
construction is banned on the hundred-year floodplain, buildings are located 100 feet back from the water, and standards are set for logging within
250 feet. With representatives from each of twenty communities, the commission avoids antistate sentiment yet is more stable and capable than local
government. In Minnesota, eight counties formed the Mississippi Headwaters Board to protect 466 miles of river.

State and local protection has been effective where national designation
was not wanted, but to stop federal water projects, to prohibit federal
permits for private hydroelectric dams, and to save rivers on federal land,
national designation is still needed.

WINNING AND LOSING

By the end of 1985, sixty-six major rivers, including a total of 170 named
rivers and tributaries, were in the national wild and scenic rivers system of

7,250 miles. Twelve of the rivers were administered by states. Ninety-two rivers had been named for study, and fifty-five studies had been completed. Nineteen of these rivers were designated, and thirteen were recommended but not acted on.

Similar in some ways to the wild and scenic rivers, another official designation—"national river"—was established by Congress for the Buffalo River in Arkansas and the New River Gorge in West Virginia (the Current and Jacks Fork in Missouri were the first streams to be called national rivers). Stanford Young of the National Park Service wrote that the national rivers are "elongated national parks," where the government acquires wide corridors of land. A national recreation area on the Big South Fork of the Cumberland in Kentucky protects the river through a unique arrangement: After the Devil's Jump Dam proposal was defeated, the river was designated in 1974 in a rivers and harbors bill, which normally authorizes only dams and developments. The Army Corps of Engineers bought land and built recreation facilities, which were later turned over to the park service.

In 1983 Stewart Udall said that he was "very pleased" with the wild and scenic rivers system. "We really didn't know how successful the program would be." John Craighead said, "I never expected it to grow so much."

Not everyone is satisfied. In 1981 David Sumner wrote in *Sierra* that the national system "consists of token remnants rather than a true system." [23] With about seven thousand miles protected, the system is not in even near the same league as the national parks. Even the national wildlife refuge system has 772 units.

"I don't think the rivers program ever really came into its own," said Bob Eastman, retired from the Interior Department in 1983. "It was overshadowed in the early years by the wilderness program and was troubled in later years by political problems and budget cuts."

Stanford Young, also retired in 1983, said, "I predict that the national rivers system will have its ups and downs but that in time it will grow just as the national parks system, wilderness system, and wildlife refuge system have grown. The river protection concept is important to too many people to be denied. Money will be found to get the job done once the river constituency gets its act together. It's merely a matter of time."

The system may grow on federal lands, where hundreds of outstanding rivers are vulnerable to hydroelectric proposals, and on rivers near the people, since water quality has improved in some streams. In the early 1980s, new organizations, including the American Wilderness Alliance and the National Organization for River Sports, worked to save rivers.

The ARCC—still a small organization—grew as a leader of the river movement. The group lobbied for new legislation to aid local and state programs through federal loans for open space acquisition and to protect state-designated rivers from hydroelectric dams licensed by the FERC. Working on the Gauley River, the ARCC helped to organize a local group in West Virginia, and it fought a corps hydroelectric proposal to divert water from three miles of one of the most challenging whitewater runs in the country.

Even though the prospects for large new dams by the federal government subsided, other threats increased. By monitoring hydropower permit requests in 1983, ARCC found nine applications that would affect national rivers in Washington and California. In violation of the wild and scenic rivers act, the FERC issued a permit for a dam on the federally designated Suiattle River in Washington. The ARCC appealed.

In Alaska, the state senate unanimously passed a resolution in 1983 asking Congress to delete Birch and Beaver creeks from the national system so miners could dredge gold. Legislation was introduced to rescind federal protection for the Rio Grande in Texas, raising questions of long-term security for national rivers. One act of Congress designated them, and another can delete them. Would the national system be simply a savings account where rivers are banked for future development? "Not if people keep supporting the rivers," said Chris Brown. "The real challenge is to get the message out to people about these rivers. People take them for granted. We're sitting on a mountain of opportunity, but if we don't mobilize support for some of the rivers soon, they'll be lost to hydroelectric dams and other developments."

Conservationists hope that there will always be new designations of national parks and wilderness areas, but there is not likely to be another expansion of parks like that of the 1960s, and wilderness protection may also peak as the agencies and Congress try to resolve RARE II (Roadless Area Review and Evaluation)—a government effort to "round out" the wilderness system. Groups that have concentrated on these two programs may turn more of their attention to the rivers system, which for years has stood in the wings. It is the frontier program, and much remains to be done. It has the necessary political flexibility, and if properly presented in new ways, it may overcome the resistance to federal involvement and to the "locking up" of resources. It can appeal to a broad constituency, including landowners and urban open space users. Also, if river groups such as the American Rivers Conservation Council combine more effectively with fishermen, who in the past were often the backbone of rivers protection, a new, powerful effort could speed action. Rivers could be the major natural area protection program in the years to come.[24]

The national wild and scenic rivers system had gone partway toward establishing the balance of federal water management, but only 0.2 percent of the nation's streams were protected — about three and a half yards per mile — and the threats to even those did not go away. River conservationists had fought individual dams from Hetch Hetchy to the Stanislaus. Although the national wild and scenic rivers system added a positive alternative to dams, it was still limited to individual streams, the saving of each requiring a major campaign. To save rivers on a larger scale, the basic politics and policies for destroying them had to be changed.

CHAPTER SEVEN

Politics and Problems of Water Development

The people who worked to save rivers were motivated by special places, but what they encountered was an acquisitive brand of politics known as pork barrel. The name dates from the Old South, where planters served up barrels of salted pork as bonuses to slaves, who rushed to get as much as they could. By 1879 the term *pork barrel* was used by congressmen to refer to public works projects that were not really needed. The rule became "You vote for my project and I'll vote for yours," and the mutual bond delivered billions of tax dollars to local districts with little regard for efficiency except in terms of reelection. It is what Senator Daniel Patrick Moynihan called "a chaotic and idiosyncratic system of economic and resource development, producing a random array of benefits more responsive to the vagaries of seniority in the U.S. Congress than anything else." [1]

Votes on one water project are not only swapped indiscriminately for votes on another, they are also used as currency to buy votes on altogether different issues. President Kennedy signed the Arkansas River Barge Canal bill for Senator Robert Kerr's vote on a tax bill, and President Carter traded his approval of Tellico Dam for a Panama Canal treaty.

Senator William Proxmire explained why water projects are so vulnerable to the pork barrel process: "The question that's always raised against incumbents is: 'What have you done? You haven't *done* anything.' One thing you can point to that people can understand, see, touch, feel, is a public works project. Labor likes it, management likes it, it may even be named after you. Only the taxpayers pay for it — but the taxpayers in your district pay only a tiny fraction." [2] For many congressmen, especially from

SELECTED EVENTS IN CHAPTER 7

1914   Reclamation law allowed twenty years to pay back irrigation costs.

1926   Reclamation law allowed forty years to pay back irrigation costs.

1934   Wildlife Coordination Act passed.

1936   Flood Control Act required calculation of cost-benefit ratios.

1939   Reclamation law allowed ten years with no repayment for irrigation costs.

1944   Flood Control Act authorized drainage projects.

1950   Uniform guidelines established for cost-benefit ratios.

1961   Benefits allowed for dilution of pollution.

1962   Senate Document 97 set new guidelines for cost-benefit ratios.

1965   Water Resources Council formed.

1972   Benefits for dilution of pollution disallowed.
Texas Water Plan proposed.
Buffalo Creek Dam collapsed.
National Dam Inspection Act passed.

1973   National Water Commission called for cost sharing and controls on floodplain development.
Principles and standards for water projects established.
Montana Water Use Act passed.

1974   General Accounting Office study critical of cost-benefit ratio calculations.
Railroads and conservationists sued against Lock and Dam 26.

1976   Lawsuit delayed Tennessee-Tombigbee Canal construction.
National Wildlife Federation sued to stop Russell Dam.

1977   Tacoa Falls Dam failed.
President Carter called for dam inspections.
National Audubon Society sued to stop Garrison Diversion.

1978   Public Utility Regulatory Policies Act created incentives for hydropower.
Yellowstone River water allocated to in-stream uses.

1980   User fees for barges started.
Arizona passed groundwater management law.

1981   General Accounting Office study critical of subsidies included in water projects.

1982   Reclamation Reform Act passed.
Utility companies challenged "avoided cost" requirements.

1983   Bucks County residents rejected Delaware River diversion.
Payment in Kind program subsidized large farms.

the South and the West, water projects have clocked more mileage toward power and prestige than any pursuit of long-range solutions to people's problems.

During election year of each congressional session, two kinds of water development bills are normally passed: an authorization bill to initially approve projects, and an appropriation bill to pass out the money. Army Corps of Engineers activities are authorized through omnibus rivers and harbors bills approving many projects at once. Bureau of Reclamation projects are often passed singly, but some "projects" include a dozen or more dams. If enough projects are stacked into one bill, none of the congressmen benefiting are likely to vote against it, and with the threat of retaliation, criticism from other congressmen is scarce.

The direct beneficiaries are often an undemocratic few. In Oregon, 80 percent of the flood control benefits from Applegate Dam went to speculators owning undeveloped floodplains that appreciated at taxpayer expense. In Colorado, the Fruitland Mesa Project would have cost $1.2 million for each of sixty-nine farms. Barge companies, whose freight is 60 percent oil and coal products, enjoy locks, dams, and canals that were built at no cost to them while railroads and trucks paid at least a part of their own way. To bankers, a new dam means that old mortgages will be paid off after people are forced to abandon their homes, and new mortgages will be financed at higher rates. To western farmers, reclamation projects mean paying $3.50 an acre-foot for water that costs the government $80 an acre-foot to produce. These are the people who lobby for the projects and contribute to politicians who will push the votes and paperwork through. As water policy analyst Gilbert White more tactfully stated, "National efficiency usually has been mixed with local aspiration in promoting new projects." [3]

Not everybody agrees with the negative overtones the name *pork barrel* gives to the politics of water projects. Congressman Jim Wright wrote, "The term is both inappropriate and misleading. The connotation it conjures of slimy manipulation and backstage connivery — or the impression that the water developments authorized in these measures are really somehow unneeded — simply does not square with the facts." Even Stewart Udall wrote, "To call such projects 'pork barrel,' as they have so often and inappropriately been termed, is not only misleading — it is downright deceit." [4] Many agree that projects are needed, but water management professionals call for case-by-case study based on uniform guidelines, not on politicians' logrolling.

Political watchers say that the "iron triangle" is what makes many of the water projects possible. At one corner are the agencies: the Bureau of

Reclamation, the Army Corps of Engineers, and a few others. Congress is at the second corner, and local promoters are at the third. Although a project can be conceived at any corner, most start with the local promoters. Those who will benefit organize support, brass-band the idea, sell it to the newspaper editor, and meet with their congressman. Votes and contributions are explicit. The congressman requests a study by the corps or bureau, or sometimes he goes straight to lawmakers with an authorization amendment. All three corners of the triangle need each other: if the corps has no projects, it has no work, so corps officials meet with local business leaders and encourage them to become political. Ultimately, part of the contract for building the dam, or part of the wealth that it creates, will likely be funneled back to the congressman's campaign. To stop a water project, river supporters must break in and control one or more of the three corners.

The projects do not necessarily go where they are needed: they go to the districts of certain influential politicians. Several chairmen of public works and appropriations committees are essential to the delivery of projects, because these men call meetings, schedule hearings, draft proposals, select staff, and push a dam through or hold it up. They have been incorrigible spenders for their districts. The two senior members of the Senate Appropriations Subcommittee on Public Works received the highest and second-highest amount of corps spending in 1976, chairman John Stennis from Mississippi luring sixteen times the median level to his state. The top five states in corps spending (Mississippi, Washington, Missouri, Kentucky, and Louisiana) received 46 percent of the corps budget in 1976, and all but one of these states were represented on the subcommittee.[5]

Votes may depend on congressmen bringing home federal dollars, but why not federal largesse for hospitals and schools? Arthur Davis, who worked for the Bureau of the Budget in the Eisenhower years, said in 1983, "If the money is going to be given away, give it for something worthwhile. But there were few choices about what to give to the West. Back in the fifties it didn't need the other facilities, so it was given water projects." Likewise, eastern flood control dams had front-page appeal, and the momentum to build continued long after critical needs had been met.

In *Under the Influence,* Congressman Jim Weaver was quoted: "You know, in the old days, in the New Deal, a dam was the hope. It was! The dam sites were then worth something. You could produce power and some other things, and there was the hope of jobs. Now these people, these old pork-barreling congressmen, their minds were made up in the thirties when people were desperate, you've got to remember that. And so they're *still* for that dam, even if it's absolutely valueless."

"The water development agencies want to stay in business," said Brent Blackwelder of the Environmental Policy Institute, "and that means funding for the status quo." Without new laws, new expertise, and new commitments, the corps can not rebuild city water lines, construct sewage treatment plants, repair bridges, fill potholes, or renovate mass transit.

One way to control pork barrel is to require approval of full funding at a project's outset instead of authorizing year-by-year allowances. The difference in figures is often in multiples of ten. Other reformers called for states and beneficiaries to pay greater shares of the costs, the theory being that anybody who has to pay will discriminate between the good and the worthless. In 1983 the National Taxpayers' Union lobbied to squeeze out uneconomic projects with a balanced-budget amendment that would stop Congress from spending more than it receives. Congressman Robert Edgar advocated a capital outlay budget that would make dams and canals compete with schools and hospitals for federal dollars.

COLLECTING THE FACTS AND JUGGLING THE NUMBERS

Water projects are governed by the pork barrel system and also by a somewhat economic approach that started with the Flood Control Act of 1936, which required that benefits "to whomsoever they accrue" exceed costs. To determine if some people will gain more than everybody will pay, facts are collected. The first uniform guidelines for calculating benefits and costs were in the 1950 "Green Book," revised in 1952 by the Bureau of the Budget. In 1962 Senate Document 97 offered new guidelines. In 1965 the Water Resources Council was created as a cabinet-level group to coordinate water development, and in 1973 it issued "principles and standards" as new benefit-cost criteria.[6] Cases such as Tellico Dam showed that politics — not professional water management — is what finally counts, but in an era of growing accountability lawmakers found it difficult to run roughshod over tough benefit-cost analysis.

So instead of opposing only individual projects, the people fighting dams in the 1970s turned increasingly to economics. Though benefit-cost analysis was intended to eliminate political debate, the analysis itself led to endless argument, and in 1976 the Congressional Research Service stated, "Probably the most frequently voiced criticism of benefit-cost analysis is that because of its singular economic criterion it ignores environmental and other effects which cannot be monetarily quantified." In *Strategies of American Water Management,* Gilbert White wrote, "The ecological view was at a disadvantage in having little evidence to put up against the more confident engineering predictions of practical outcomes in water flow, power production, or visitor days at recreation sites." Dissatisfied that the emphasis was always on plans while ignoring performance, White sought study of water projects after they were built to see if they did what the builders claimed they would do.

Americans are committed to numbers — the census is a national event, bank books are consulted daily, and calculators are built pocket-size — but the economic justification for spending billions of taxpayer dollars was ludicrous, even in the narrow context that excluded social and environmental effects. Of 380 projects studied by Senator William Proxmire's office, 220 were found not to be justified by normal business standards. The senator said, "I have consistently found that projects with an alleged benefit-cost ratio of less than two-to-one provide returns less than their cost." [7] Even accepting the Army Corps of Engineers' figures, Proxmire stated that of 178 major projects studied, 83 had cost overruns of 100 percent or more.

Resource economist Robert Haveman at the University of Wisconsin studied one hundred benefit-cost ratios of the corps and estimated that only 25 percent would survive rigorous analysis and that half of these would not be cost-effective if environmental damages were counted.

A General Accounting Office (GAO) survey in 1974 found nineteen instances in which benefit-cost calculations were incorrect or unsubstantiated, the errors favoring construction in all cases but one.[8] For Lost Creek Dam on the Rogue River, the corps counted hypothetical hydroelectric benefits that might be added in the future. Fishing use to be eliminated by the dam was not deducted from recreation benefits, and irrigation benefits were claimed though the irrigation facilities were to be built in a different project. Overstatement of benefits totaled nearly $50 million, equaling 40 percent of costs, and corrections would expose the dam as unfeasible. For Pattonville Lake on Missouri's Grand River, $1.1 million were claimed for agricultural production, but the Department of Agriculture estimated a $1 million cost due to inundation of land.

Audits of forty-four corps projects were prepared by the accounting firm of Price, Waterhouse and Company, which found that the amounts of money charged for water were decreased, creating more demand for it. Repayment periods for reimbursable costs were extended beyond the legal fifty years. In 1981 the GAO reported that the corps used fifteen-year-old cost information to set 1980 water prices for the Willamette River Basin Project.[9]

"Area redevelopment" is tallied as a project benefit, sometimes meaning that active farms are condemned and then resold to the highest bidder. New dams are touted for the jobs they create, the costs of labor being turned around as an employment "benefit." However, when engineer Bruce Hannon and economist Roger Bezdek at the University of Illinois studied employment from five government programs, they found that corps construction yielded the fewest jobs — national health insurance, social security, sewage plants, tax relief, and mass transit brought more jobs per dollar spent.[10]

The discretion of cost-benefit ratios can begin with something as basic as population. For Stonewall Jackson Dam on the West Fork River in West Virginia, the corps projected that the populations of Weston and Clarksburg would grow 173 percent and 91 percent, respectively, in the next fifty years, though the Department of Labor expected only a 9.6 percent increase for the towns in the next thirty years.

Recreation benefits — popular especially in the 1960s — have padded projects' appeal. The corps claimed that recreation at Grove Reservoir in Kansas would exceed that of Yellowstone National Park. Logan Dam, proposed for Ohio's Clear Creek, was intended for flood control, but to justify it the corps claimed 76 percent of the benefits for recreation. Meramec Park Dam in Missouri would have flooded a popular recreation river, a state park, a wildlife management area, and Onondaga Cave, which attracts several hundred thousand people a year. Half of the recreation benefits justifying the dam were for "sightseeing" by people who would do nothing but look at the corps's work.

Benefits for diluting pollution were allowed in 1961. They accounted for 40 percent of the justification of Gathright Dam in Virginia, most of the dilution serving a Westvaco paper mill. Dilution claims were disallowed in 1972, but because Stonewall Jackson Dam was authorized earlier, the corps still credited 36 percent of the benefits to dilution, a claim not valid anyway because ten sewage treatment plants had been built since the corps collected its data. Water quality improves below some dams, but below others it is ruined. In 1981 tens of thousands of fish were killed below Conowingo Dam on the Susquehanna River because of low oxygen levels.

Benefits and costs are calculated for one hundred years, and interest is charged on the cost. Anyone who has bought a home knows that even at low interest rates, interest through the life of the mortgage can be larger than the principal. By manipulating the interest rate, projects can be made to appear more or less economic. During the 1950s the corps used a 2.5 percent rate. After 1968 Congress required a rate of about 5 percent — still far below the cost of borrowing money. In 1973 the Water Resources Council's principles and standards set a rate adjusted to that of fifty-year bonds, which was 6 7/8 percent that year. But the new rates did not apply to already authorized projects, and the sponsors basked in a refuge from real-world economics. Only about half of these projects would have had adequate benefit-cost ratios at the new rates.[11]

To determine the value of proposed hydroelectric dams, the corps compares the difference between the cost of the project and the cost of the cheapest alternative. For Dickey-Lincoln dams in Maine, an interest rate of 8 3/4 percent was used to calculate the cost of oil-fired power, which was then compared to the cost of the dams; the dams, however, had been assigned a lower interest rate. At the proposed Oakley Dam in Illinois, the corps charged a higher rate for alternate water supplies because they would be locally sponsored and more risky. Manipulations of interest rates bolstered many projects' failing bills of economic health.

Another question of costs is, Who pays? As a "nonreimbursable" cost, the government pays for large flood control reservoirs. For levees, channelization, and small dams, the government pays for construction but not land acquisition, operation, or maintenance. Local governments pay for a part of municipal water supplies as a "reimbursable" cost. For Bureau of Reclamation projects, the irrigators are supposed to pay back construction, operation, and maintenance costs, but no interest. Hydroelectric costs are reimbursed from power sales. Navigation costs were all paid by the government until 1980, when a tax was levied on fuel for towboats using the projects. Federal agencies are to collect interest payments from municipal and industrial water buyers, but according to a 1981 GAO study, the rates do not always reflect government costs. Titled *Reforming Interest Provisions in Federal Water Laws Could Save Millions,* the study report stated that "on four projects of 100 reviewed, GAO calculated more than $667 million in taxpayer-provided interest subsidies. The total amount of interest subsidies for all Federal water projects is in the billions of dollars."

Cost sharing by the states has been proposed many times. In 1973 the prestigious National Water Commission stated, "Cost sharing requirements would be effective in eliminating political pressures from a group seeking a project for no other reason than that they expect it to be paid for by the federal treasury."

President Carter proposed that states pay 10 percent of costs, but Colorado governor Richard Lamm and author Michael McCarthy wrote in *The Angry West,* "To saddle the West with costs never anticipated and never agreed upon is a serious enough matter. . . . A sudden shift to 25 percent front end state financing would mean, simply, no projects — at least for the forseeable future." President Reagan proposed even larger shares to be paid by the states, and in 1980 the GAO found that without legal changes, the Bureau of Reclamation and the Soil Conservation Service "have the legal authority to require non-Federal entities to share a larger percent of project costs." [12]

Beyond economic considerations affecting all kinds of projects, challenges grew against four of the main purposes of water development: flood control, hydroelectric power, navigation, and irrigation.

SPECULATION ON THE FLOODPLAIN

Whereas original authorizations in the 1930s called for federal dams to meet national needs, practice soon established that any flood control was a "national" need. Concerning a better definition, Luna Leopold and Thomas Maddock wrote in *The Flood Control Controversy*, "The truth of the matter is that no one wants such a definition. . . . What is wanted at local levels is a program that will permit unhindered development of the flood plain through federally conducted works." The policy of protecting existing development, no matter how provincial, expanded further to the support of real estate speculation and new construction along the rivers.

The 1966 Task Force on Federal Flood Control Policy noted that in the 1940s only 10 percent of the corps's flood control benefits came from protecting future floodplain development, but in the 1960s more than 40 percent of the benefits were attributed to development that was only a gleam in realtors' eyes. In 1965 the Bureau of the Budget questioned the policy of claiming up to 50 percent of benefits from nonexistent development.[13] Two-thirds of Days Creek Dam's benefits in Oregon were for future development. Opponents to Gillham Dam on Arkansas's Cassatot River pointed out that 74 percent of the original benefits were for flood control, but no significant development existed for forty-nine miles below the dam. Federal judge G. Thomas Eisele accused the corps of "circular reasoning." The dam would make possible new development that would justify the dam. A realtor estimated that Red River Dam in Kentucky would cause floodplain property to jump in value from $750 to $6,000 an acre.[14] River conservationists maintained that with only 5 percent of the nation's land being floodplain, there were other places to build and no need to subsidize river-bottom speculators.

The proposed Lincoln and Oakley reservoirs showed another problem: they would flood more farmland than they would protect. Hillsdale Dam in

Kansas would flood fourteen thousand acres to protect seven thousand. In 1974 the Department of Agriculture wrote that more than three hundred thousand acres of farmland were lost per year under reservoirs.[15]

Levees and channelization were criticized for aggravating flood hazards above and below the projects. In *Science* magazine, Charles Belt, Jr., wrote that Mississippi floods in 1972 crested at record heights in St. Louis even though the volume of water was only that of a thirty-year flood. Levees and wing dams forced a smaller amount of water to rise higher.[16]

The Flood Control Act of 1944 authorized major drainage projects as a part of flood control, and one hundred million acres were drained.[17] The wetlands no longer absorbed flood waters, and faster runoff caused erosion. A 90 percent reduction in fish was found in channelized waters of North Carolina, and the streams still have not recovered.[18] Ninety miles of Florida's Kissimmee River were straightened to fifty-two miles, resulting in a loss of 95 percent of the river's wildlife habitat and the ecological and hydrologic destruction of Lake Okeechobee, affecting much of southern Florida.

In spite of $15 billion spent for flood control by 1982, damages continued to climb ($3.4 billion in 1975), and 90 percent of disaster relief was for flood damage. Critics argued that nothing was as certain as death and floods and that flood control projects lull people into a false sense of security: levees in Wilkes-Barre, Pennsylvania, were overtopped in 1972, forcing 80,000 people from their homes, and in South Dakota, Pactola Reservoir had been built only fourteen miles above Rapid City, but when fourteen inches of rain fell below the dam, a flood killed 236 people. The Task Force on Federal Flood Control Policy in 1966 and the National Water Commission in 1973 stated that by avoiding new floodplain construction, people could avoid flood damage without more channelization and dams.[19]

WHO OWNS THE POWER OF THE RIVER?

Whereas much attention is given to the power produced at dams, it also requires power to build dams. Auburn Dam would use the equivalent of about twelve million barrels of oil, and if built in the mid-1980s it would owe an energy debt until 2016. Economists at the University of Illinois studied the energy use of six major federal programs and found corps projects to be the most consumptive, far exceeding expenditures for health, railroads, mass transit, water treatment, and education. Because dams are often far from cities, 10 percent or more of the electricity is lost in transmission.

Small hydroelectric development, defined by the Department of Energy as fifteen megawatts or less, has been backed as a soft-path approach to new energy. The Public Utilities Regulatory Policies Act of 1978 (PURPA) requires that utility companies buy electric power from producers at alternative sources such as hydroelectric dams and windmills and that the utilities pay the same rate as they pay for their costliest source of power (usually oil). The 1978 law was interpreted by the Federal Energy Regulatory Commission (FERC) to include power not only from existing dams but also from new dams. A boom in applications to build small dams has resulted.

Provided enough water is left in the stream for fish and the ecosystem, environmental effects from small hydroelectric projects may be slight. But as the kilowatts add up, so do the impacts. By 1983 in California alone, sixty-two new projects had been proposed for rivers eligible for the national wild and scenic rivers system. Two thousand miles of streams in the Sierra Nevada would be affected if the FERC approved all pending applications. The Sierra Club's Russell Shay said, "Proposals are being made for new dams and diversions . . . with potentially devastating effects on fisheries, wildlife, wilderness, recreation and water quality. Even though they are small projects, the building of any large proportion of them would drastically alter the face of the West." Fish and Game biologist Phil Pister commented on the diversion of Sierra Nevada streams: "It comes down to the logic that it's awfully hard to go fishing or grow trees in a pipe." [20]

In the remote Salmon River basin of Idaho, sixty-three hydroelectric projects were proposed. Even though the dams would be on tributaries, they could block the flow of nutrients, starve bottom life, and deplete fish numbers farther downstream. The Nez Perce Indians, Idaho Wildlife Federation, and others appealed and asked for an environmental review of the cumulative rather than the isolated effects of the dams. [21]

In 1980 a Bureau of Reclamation booklet stated, "The Bureau of Reclamation is researching and developing the potential of hydroelectric power in the West. Some new reservoir sites can and will be developed. However, there is considerable additional capacity at existing dams and facilities. Even without building new dams, hydroelectric production can be greatly increased." [22]

Side effects of repairing or adding turbines to existing dams can likewise be great. Diversion of water sometimes leaves a dry streambed, and releases at a power plant may alternate from a trickle when water is being stored to a small flood when power is generated. Hundreds of proposals in New England called for new generation at existing dams. The American Rivers Conservation Council reported that half of the renovations would involve diversions through penstocks or long pipes, sometimes dewatering streams for a thousand feet. On the Colorado River, new turbines at Glen Canyon Dam caused erratically high flows, eroding Grand Canyon beaches.

The Army Corps of Engineers reported that, nationwide, 641 large hydropower dams were feasible. Important proposals were pending on the Tuolumne in California, the West Branch Penobscot and Kennebec in Maine, the Snake below Hells Canyon, and the Gauley and Blackwater in West Virginia.

"In the sixties it looked like we were going to save a lot of streams," said Stanford Young, leader of the first national rivers study. "Then came the rush for hydro dams. Now it looks like it will be tougher to keep rivers free, and we'll have to fight for places we thought we had already saved."

Preliminary permits to study dam sites are often granted by the FERC without concern for power needs or environmental questions. People can hire a lawyer and intervene, hoping to reverse a federal decision, but they are usually unsuccessful because the permit allows only a feasibility study. When a construction license is later requested, people can intervene again, but by then, millions of dollars might have been spent by the developer. So it is difficult to fight the preliminary permit because the data are not collected, and difficult to fight a final permit because the sponsor is so committed. Since 1935, the FERC has approved nine hundred hydropower applications. In 1983 FERC commissioner Georgiana Sheldon said, "Since license applications for new projects contain many special conditions to provide for environmental protection, it has not been necessary for the commission to deny any license applications for environmental reasons." The FERC has denied several.

Among FERC reviewing agencies, only the Fish and Wildlife Service regularly comments on applications, and it is swamped with work. The FERC is supposed to consider the overall public interest and deny a permit if nonpower values are more important, but the agency has nearly always viewed its role as promoting maximum development. River basin plans, which the commission is directed to follow, do not exist for many rivers, and where they do, the plans often parrot old development proposals. Citizen appeals through Congress and the administration can influence the FERC, and some dam fights, such as those at New River and Hells Canyon, were won when Congress passed laws superceding FERC licenses.

State-required permits can also control new dams. "In California, it's the state that's holding the lid on," said Greg Thomas of the Natural Resources Defense Council in 1982. But California's concern faded with the passing of the Brown administration. Water quality permits, often administered by the states, are sometimes needed for dams and may stop projects that the FERC would otherwise approve.

In 1982 utility companies challenged the legal requirement that utilities must buy power from small hydroelectric developers, leaving the feasibility of some projects in doubt. Appeals are pending, but regardless, hydroelectric power will remain a reason to dam rivers. Chris Brown of ARCC said, "Through helter-skelter hydro development we may see a great setback in the river conservation work of the last twenty years."

TAXPAYERS PUSH BARGES

Belching smoke as they churned on the Ohio and Mississippi, the riverboats of Mark Twain's day made commerce possible through the heartland, and the pilot — wise to the ways of the currents — was a national hero. Those boats are gone, the slap of paddle wheels replaced by the drone of diesel engines, and the rivers that the early pilots knew are also gone. Now twenty-six thousand miles of river are channelized or dammed for barges.

Until 1980, all construction, operation, and maintenance for river navigation was done by the government at a subsidy of more than $400 million a year,[23] giving barge companies an advantage over railroads, which paid for their own tracks and even paid taxes on their rights of way.

The lower Mississippi, Ohio, Monongahela, and some other rivers warranted the federal investment, but new barge routes seem like the stream Mark Twain described in *The Guilded Age*: "Goose Run, if deepened, and widened, and straightened, and made a little longer, would be one of the greatest rivers in our western country."

In the 1950s "Kirwan's ditch," named after Congressman Michael Kirwan, was proposed to canalize the Beaver and Mahoning rivers between Pittsburgh and Lake Erie. The $1-billion project was never built.[24] The Cross Florida Barge Canal was also stopped, but opponents were not successful with Lock and Dam 26 or with the Tennessee-Tombigbee Waterway.

At Alton, Illinois, the corps planned in the late 1970s to replace Lock and Dam 26 with two 1,200-foot-long locks, deepening the draft from 9 to 12 feet at a cost of $400 million. Environmental groups against the expansion found support from the railroads, which funded the opposition (this unlikely alliance also fought the Tennessee-Tombigbee Waterway and coal slurry pipelines in Montana). In 1974 conservationists, twenty-one rail-roads, and a taxpayers group sued because the corps was acting only on a 1909 authorization for maintenance and emergency repairs (70 percent of the Ohio River's locks had already been enlarged to an unauthorized size).[25]

The groups argued that Lock and Dam 26 was the first step in dredging a deeper channel 670 miles to Minneapolis, which would cost $10 billion and wreak ecological havoc on the river and three hundred thousand acres of state and federal wildlife and recreation lands. Twenty-nine dams already covered riffles above St. Louis, and additional wing dams, built out from the shore to direct the flow to midstream, caused silting and partial filling of the river between the dams, smothering two hundred square miles of rich backwaters. (On sections of the Missouri River, bank and channel work has caused the loss of 50 percent of the river's surface area.) The deeper channel and the dumping of dredged silt and gravel would aggravate problems, and barge traffic would churn more sediments and destroy the bottom life, basic to the food chain.

While the corps stated that only Lock and Dam 26 was planned, Assist-ant Interior Secretary Nathaniel Reed said, "When you notice a camel's nose poking through your tent flap, you are wise to conclude that out there is a whole camel, rear-end and all." Federal judge Charles Richey found the corps's contention "unworthy of belief."[26] Thus delayed, the corps went to Congress for authorization, and the focus of the debate shifted to proposals that the barge companies pay for improvements.

Presidents Franklin Roosevelt, Eisenhower, Kennedy, Johnson, and Nixon all had proposed that barge companies pay part of the costs of locks and dams. Supporters of user fees argued that navigation benefits are not shared widely enough to warrant taxpayers' investments. For Kirwan's ditch, the corps had calculated a benefit-cost ratio of 2.5 – 1, but an Arthur D. Little study commissioned by the army found that savings to shippers were fourteen times greater than to the public. Economist Robert Have-man found a return of forty-four cents on the dollar from the Illinois River Canal.[27] Barry Allen at Ramapo College in New Jersey found that among fifty-two dredging projects for barges, only 17 percent showed positive ratios.

Barge promoters cited that on a ton-mile basis, moving freight by barge is the most energy-efficient way. But a 1974 study by Anthony Sebald at the University of Illinois found that because of the meandering of rivers, barges travel four miles to trains' three, and that the barge promoters' rail data covered the entire country, including climbs over the Rocky Mountains, where barges do not go. Sebald concluded that railroads are more energy efficient than barges by 10 to 23 percent. A U.S. Department of Commerce and Department of Transportation study of Lock and Dam 26 indicated that if barge operators paid fees, more traffic would shift to railroads.[28]

The enlarged lock and dam was authorized anyway, but with it Congress required the first user fees for barges. A Department of Transportation study had suggested a thirty-four- to thirty-eight-cent tax per gallon on towboat fuel. Congress agreed on four cents a gallon starting in 1980, increasing to ten cents in 1985, to be used for new construction. This was 6 percent of projected construction costs for the next five years and included nothing for operation and maintenance.

THE COSTLIEST DITCH OF THEM ALL

The Tennessee-Tombigbee Waterway in Alabama and Mississippi is the exemplar of federal spending for canals. Through the influence of southern congressmen, the project was authorized in 1946, even though the corps recommended against it. The 232-mile-long canal will cost about $4 billion — America's most expensive water project ever. To link the Tennessee River to the Gulf of Mexico required a twenty-seven-mile-long cut through mountains, five dams, and two and one-half times the excavation of the Panama Canal. Once a biological treasure, 217 miles of the Tombigbee River were dredged. The canal will affect 115 species of fish and 51 species of mussels; 7 of which were considered for the endangered species list. The joining of the two rivers will serve not only barges but also a parasitic lamprey and the nuisance water milfoil, which are expected to migrate through the locks. Fifty-one valleys next to the canal are dumps for dredged soil, yet a 1974 corps brochure claimed that "greater attraction will be provided for waterfowl from the Mississippi and Atlantic flyways." The canal will cut 800 miles off the route of barges — 70 percent of which are expected to carry coal, though the GAO reported that coal supposedly to be floated down the canal from Tennessee exceeds the recoverable reserves in the area to be served.[29] Two hundred and fifty families were relocated.

Costs for disposal, grading, and revegetation of soil were not counted in the 1976 benefit-cost ratio, which barely slipped through at 1.1 – 1. Several companies listed as future shippers on the canal had no intention of using it.[30] By one estimate published in the *New York Times*, railroads would lose $70 million a year. A *Times* editorial, "The Engineering of Deceit," stated that beneficiaries included a power plant that was to get coal in amounts it could not burn.[31]

In 1971 an Environmental Defense Fund lawsuit delayed the project, and in 1976 the fund, a railroad, and other groups charged that the waterway, authorized for a 170-foot width, was being dug 300 feet wide. The court delayed construction while opposition grew.[32]

In the budget-cutting 1980s, the Tenn-Tom price tag was a miasma to supporters, who won their appropriations by only two votes in the Senate and ten in the House. Brent Blackwelder credits the approval to the political leverage of John Stennis, ranking Democrat on the Senate Armed Services Committee; Jamie Whitten, chairman of the House Appropriations Committee; and Tom Bevill, chairman of the House Appropriations Subcommittee on Public Works—all from Mississippi or Alabama.

Other navigation projects accused of being costly and damaging included the Arkansas River Canal to float barges 516 miles from the Mississippi to Catoosa, Oklahoma. On the Ohio River, less turnover of water in expanded impoundments caused pollution; the Environmental Protection Agency estimated a 30 percent loss in waste assimilation capacity at Markland Dam near Cincinnati. Ohio River farmlands and roads were eroded after the larger dams were built, but courts found the corps not responsible. On Texas's 550-mile-long Trinity River, proposed channelization would cut off 180 meanders, shrinking the route to 335 miles at a 1977 cost of $2 billion. Wallsville Barrier Dam—one of three impoundments—would eliminate twelve thousand acres of estuary, but the canal was twice defeated in referendums. Some navigation projects were built at exorbitant costs and scarcely used; in the mid-1970s half of the federal operation and maintenance costs for navigation went to rivers carrying only 3 percent of the freight.[33]

While new projects received bonus appropriations, old locks such as those on Pennsylvania's Monongahela River deteriorated. In 1983 the corps's National Waterways Study stated that $5.2 to $12 billion may be needed by 2003 for navigation; the largest problem is aging locks. The corps planned to spend $7.5 billion on canals from 1983 to 1988. Now that most feasible flood control dams have been built, maintenance for navigation, which in 1824 was the corps's first role with rivers, returned as the agency's main job.

RE-CLAIMING NOTHING

With the Reclamation Act of 1902, Congress intended that irrigators repay the government for the irrigation projects, and Bureau of Reclamation brochures still claim that 80 percent of costs are reimbursed by water users:

"The Reclamation program has been and continues to be one of the soundest investments possible. . . . " But in 1981 the GAO reviewed six bureau projects and found that each provided a subsidy of more than 92 percent, some at 97 percent, and concluded, "The original rationale for building the Federal projects and increasing the subsidy was based on early 20th century goals for the settlement of the West and for regional development. Those goals have been reached and the projects should now be reevaluated in the light of current economic and social conditions." The office explained, "Irrigators are receiving a large subsidy because much of the money allocated for constructing the irrigation facilities is scheduled to be repaid by someone other than the beneficiaries." Farmers pay 5 to 10 percent of the cost of much of the irrigation water, consumers of electricity pay 33 percent, and the taxpayer pays the rest.[34]

The bureau does not base water charges on the government's cost, but on the "ability to pay." Contracts under this clause sell water at $3.50 an acre-foot. The GAO reported that the government's cost of providing the water is $54 to $130 an acre-foot. In the Fryingpan-Arkansas Project, diverting water through the Continental Divide from the Fryingpan River to the Arkansas River, the bureau estimated that the Colorado farmers could pay $.27 an acre-foot, but GAO found the ability to be $14.91. In the Pollock-Herreid Project in South Dakota, $3.10 an acre-foot is paid for water costing $130 to deliver. The GAO stated that farmers can pay from three to fifty times more than they are charged.

Hydroelectric and irrigation purposes are intertwined. A Bureau of Reclamation dam was proposed in the 1960s for Montana's Big Hole River, where $14 million of costs were nonreimbursable for uses such as flood control, $8 million would be paid by irrigators, and the remaining $63 million would be paid by power sales generated elsewhere at Missouri River dams. A 1962 audit, however, showed that the power revenues for the Missouri dams were nearly $2 million short of paying interest on the Missouri projects alone, not counting the debt that the Big Hole Dam would amass. With no other funds coming in, taxpayers would be saddled with irrigation costs. The dam has not been built.[35]

Army Corps of Engineers dams were criticized for low interest rates, but with bureau projects, farmers pay no interest at all, and even at rates far below market value the interest on a fifty-year project exceeds capital costs. The GAO stated, "Repayments for irrigation are presented to the Congress as full repayment. Since no interest is charged, however, these payments actually cover less than 10 percent of the Federal government's actual cost."

Congress first required reimbursement for water projects in ten years. Irrigators could not do this, so the law was changed in 1914 to twenty years, in 1926 to forty years, and in 1939 to allow ten years with no payback after project completion. Operation and maintenance costs are supposed to be reimbursed, but farmers at the corps's Lucky Peak Reservoir in Idaho and industries at reclamation's Glendo Reservoir in Wyoming were not charged.

Until Carter's presidency, contracts for sale of water ran forty years with no increases to reflect rising operations costs. For the Bonneville Unit of the Central Utah Project, an Interior Department audit reported that a 1965 repayment agreement precludes government recovery of about $198 million that should have been reimbursed. In 1981 an Interior Department audit of the Central Valley Project — the Bureau of Reclamation's largest — revealed $79,000 a day in losses. Unless hydroelectric rates are raised, the project will be a financial basket case facing an $8.8-billion deficit by 2038 — the intended break-even year. In 1983 Robert Broadbent, commissioner of reclamation, blamed the Central Valley Project deficit on old contracts: "We need to have new contracts to raise the price of water. But you have to remember that about 98 percent of these are contracts for long-term water. The Reclamation Reform Act of 1982 attempts to do something about that. It says that in four and a half years all people will enter into new contracts to pay at least full operation and maintenance charges." But, the commissioner added, "I'm sure those people are going to litigate. They say it's unconstitutional; you can't take away a contract right. The court will have to decide who's right. I don't know if it will stand up in court. Someone's got to keep their word." About the Central Valley Project deficit Broadbent said, "It'll come out of the taxpayer — the general appropriations."

On the question of subsidies Broadbent said, "The benefits of reclamation far exceed the costs. Look at Hoover Dam. The $10 billion has been spent, and today on reclamation farmland we produce about 10 percent of the cash food and fiber products of the country. We spend more on the subway system here in Washington than on reclamation.[36]

The way many westerners see it, the subsidies are needed for farmers to stay in business. Richard Lamm and Michael McCarthy wrote, "If the West's half-finished projects are abandoned and if Washington's 'no-new starts' mandate continues to hold, sooner or later it will cripple the farmers. No farmer can afford to pay $100 an acre foot. No farmer can bid with Exxon." [37] They argued that Army Corps of Engineers' projects "generally are completely non-reimbursable." In reference to proposed pricing changes, they argued that even though authorized water projects would total more than $30 billion of additional spending, the rules of the game should not be changed halfway through.

Former congressional budget office director Alice Rivlin said,

> These subsidies encourage wasteful use of water in regions that may no longer need subsidized development. They also distort farmers' decisions about which crops to grow. . . . Market gluts can occur, driving the market values of those commodities downward, in turn prompting the government to raise values artificially by means of price supports. . . . Under current policy, the federal government will invest roughly $3.8 billion from 1983 through 1987 in irrigation facilities. Of this amount, roughly $75 million would be recovered with charges now in place.

In 1983 the government's "Payment in Kind" (PIK) program gave surplus crops to farmers so they would not grow more crops. The GAO surveyed farms and found that cotton growers in California received the largest PIK subsidies, followed by California rice growers — two of the most water-intensive crops, already heavily subsidized by the Bureau of Reclamation. Twenty-one irrigated cotton farms received free crops worth $27 million in 1983. Seven farms each received crops valued at more than $2 million, despite the Agricultural Act of 1949, which states that one farmer should receive a maximum of $50,000 worth of surpluses.[38]

The subsidies, interest payments, and deficits have much to do with river protection. Unless the water is sold cheaply enough for farmers to buy, the bureau cannot "justify" the building of more dams. Even at bargain rates, some water cannot be sold; the GAO reported that federal reservoirs hold fifteen million acre-feet that is uncontracted for, some of it for many years.

A FRONTIER NO MORE

Some crops, needing a certain climate, can be grown only through irrigation in California and the Southwest, but other crops were grown elsewhere before the federal government subsidized irrigation. After 1950, eastern and southern farmers went out of business as crop production shifted. Through the twenty years following World War II, cotton acreage dropped by one-third in the South but increased 300 percent on lands watered by the Bureau of Reclamation. Fruit and nut acreage fell 50 percent in the north but grew 237 percent on reclamation lands. Bean acreage dropped by 449,000 acres across the country while it doubled on farms served by reclamation. Charles Howe and William Easter of Resources for the Future wrote, "Reclamation has probably replaced 5 to 18 million acres elsewhere" and that perhaps 180,000 farm workers lost their jobs in nonwestern regions.[39] Rain-soaked fields in Louisiana were abandoned while California farmers flooded drylands for rice. Grown close to seaports, much of this heavily subsidized crop is exported to Korea. Old animosities between the eastern and western United States may be renewed.

Reclamation advocates at the turn of the century had faced easterners' criticism, but Congressman Oscar Underwood of Alabama argued, "These lands are being opened to all the people, whether they be residents of the East, South, or West. The farm boys of the East want farms where they can . . . build homes without being driven into the already overcrowded cities to seek employment." Historian Frederick Jackson Turner called the struggle of West versus East one of "democracy against privileged classes." [40]

But at a 1966 conference of the American Society of Civil Engineers, Pennsylvania's environmental resources secretary Maurice Goddard said that the East

> is handed the crumbs and the cake goes west. It seems just plain ridiculous to us to keep placing eastern farm land in the "Soil Bank" while continuing to bring additional marginal western lands into production through subsidized water development. Why not bring eastern land, where the people are and where the rainfall is plentiful, back into production?

Commissioner of Reclamation Floyd Dominy answered, "Let me deny emphatically that there is an East-West conflict." Then he proceeded to stress the need to fund his program: "Important schemes will be required that will dwarf any of those in existence today. But this is a challenge that must be met if growth and development of these United States are to continue." [41]

This novel version of civil war intensified when New York City faced default and Mayor Ed Koch compared his city's needs to those of corporate farmers in California and to realtors in Arizona and Texas: "We're still fighting the old formulas that give most of the money for water projects to the South and the arid West." [42]

In 1976 the *National Journal* reported, "Federal tax and spending policies were causing a massive flow of wealth from the Northeast and Midwest to the fast growing southern and western regions of the nation . . . and eroded the tax bases of many state and local governments in the East and Midwest." From 1950 to 1976, the Northeast received slightly more than 6 percent of the national water resources funds spent by the corps and the bureau, while the West received more than 48 percent and the South 28 percent. For municipal and industrial supplies, the corps spent only $34.2 million in the New England and North Atlantic regions, compared to $214.3 million in the Southwest. All Bureau of Reclamation funds are spent on the West.

The desert notwithstanding, water costing $2 in Utah costs up to $13 in Pennsylvania, and people in Boston pay four times the Phoenix rate. The Central Arizona Project will receive more water development money than the sixteen states from Minnesota to Maine, but 70 percent of the crops grown in Arizona—including cotton, which is one of the largest consumers of water—have been classified as surplus and eligible for price supports.

Why didn't eastern politicians object to paying for projects that hurt their constituents? Gaylord Nelson answered,

> When I went on the interior committee in 1963 I was the only member from east of the Mississippi, and I wasn't from very far east of it. The committees are controlled by the beneficiaries, and the political lifeblood of western politicians is water. All the westerners become experts; if you find one who isn't, he's an accident and he won't be there for long. An eastern congressman can't get up on the floor and talk intelligently against them, and who wants to look stupid? So you have the prowater experts on one side and ignorance and lack of interest on the other side.[43]

In 1977 President Carter said, "The current pattern of water project distribution is contributing to the federal dollar drain out of the heavily populated Northeast where economic stimulus is needed."[44]

In 1983 Brent Blackwelder said, "Now that the West is settled and developed, water users should pay their way." Eastern tax dollars were redistributed to the frontier to lure settlers, but in the 1980s the Northeast and Midwest reeled from economic recession, and their urban water systems decayed for lack of funds to repair them.

FROM FAMILY FARMS TO CORPORATE CONGLOMERATES

Thomas Jefferson said, "The small landowners are the most precious part of the state,"[45] and on their behalf Congress, in passing the Newlands Reclamation Act in 1902, recognized that western agriculture would have to be subsidized. Yet lawmakers and Theodore Roosevelt were determined that reclamation would serve family farmers, not speculators like those who had corrupted irrigation planning to that date. Roosevelt said, "The money is being spent to build up the little man of the West so that no big man from East or West can come in to get a monopoly in the water or land." In 1905 F. H. Newell, active in drafting the reclamation law, said, "The object of the Reclamation Act is not so much to irrigate the land as it is to make homes."

Guarding against tax dollars feeding the fortunes of big businesses, the act required that a farmer buying government-supplied water own no more than 160 acres. In 1916 this was interpreted to mean 320 acres for a husband and wife and eventually 640 acres for a family of four, which could farm 1,280 acres if they also leased land. To get the water, farmers had to live on their farms, but in 1910 it was ruled that owners could live within fifty miles, and in 1916 the residency rule was required only of the initial applicant.[46] Even these diluted requirements were ignored, large areas such as California's Imperial Valley were excepted, and owners found loopholes as simple as deeding lands to business partners.

In 1924 a committee of special advisors on reclamation reported, "The Government reclamation program had in a measure failed to accomplish the human and economic purposes for which it was created."[47] In 1978 the Department of the Interior estimated that corporations — not family farmers — collected $150 million in irrigation subsidies in California alone. In one area farms averaged 2,200 acres,[48] though the Department of Agriculture found that the efficient size for a one-man farm in California was 200 to 400 acres.

About 145,000 farms used Bureau of Reclamation water in the 1970s, 96 percent meeting the acreage provision. Owners of "excess" lands (more than allowed under the "160 acre" limitation) included J. G. Boswell Co., with 133,228 acres; Southern Pacific Land Co. (Southern Pacific Railroad), with 106,680; and Tenneco West, Inc., with 64,941. In 1977, 1.3 million acres of excess land were held by 5,288 owners, 85 percent of them in California and Arizona. An Interior Department study indicated that less than 1 percent of the irrigators controlled 20 percent of lands served by reclamation. In the Central Valley of California the subsidy was worth $1,000 an acre, and in the Westlands District the subsidy was worth about $3.4 million for a typical 2,200-acre farm.

To reform the reclamation act, Congressman George Miller of northern California championed the cause of small farmers and water reformers. In 1981, calling water contracts for the southern Central Valley of California "an almost perfect example of socialism for the rich," he sponsored a bill to eliminate the "ability to pay" discount and to charge at least 2 percent interest. Miller said, "The Administration has correctly criticized many federal programs which have grown uncontrollable at great cost to the taxpayer. Irrigation is an example where the subsidies just grew and grew, and now we find billions of dollars in taxpayers' money used to subsidize some of the wealthiest agricultural interests in this country." Agribusiness lobbied heavily for continued subsidies.[49]

The National Farmers Union stated that if the excess lands were cut to tracts of 320 acres, 4,012 farmers would have new opportunities, and if the excess acreage were cut to the average farm size of 105 acres (in 1977), excess lands would serve 12,226 families. Family farm supporters with National Land for People supported a bill limiting eligibility for reclamation water to 640 acres.

The Reclamation Reform Act of 1982 raised the acreage limit from 160 acres for an individual to 960 for a family and granted unlimited leasing. People or corporations holding excess acreage may still receive federal water but will pay interest of 7.5 percent for water used on the excess acres. Residency requirements were repealed, and water conservation plans were required.

The new law gave large agribusiness most of what they wanted. The restrictions against nonfamily farmers are gone. The National Wildlife Federation's Edward Osann said, "Without the stipulations that reclamation have a social purpose by benefiting family farmers, the justification for the subsidy is gone." Only 1 percent of America's farms and 2 percent of the farmland are served by the bureau. With its 90 percent subsidies, the program does not pay its way. It never did.

WATER MINING

Groundwater is inseparably tied to rivers; 30 percent of streamflow comes from underground sources. The abuse of groundwater means the eventual abuse of rivers when dams are built to replace exhausted groundwater supplies. The federal Water Resources Council estimated that 33,000 trillion to 59,000 trillion gallons of water lie underground—fifty years of surface runoff. About half the population drinks from wells numbering in the millions, but 68 percent of all groundwater withdrawn is for irrigation. Of all irrigation supplies, 35 percent are from groundwater. In California, 48 percent of all water used was from underground—more groundwater than was used in all eastern regions combined.

To overdraft is to pump out more water than seeps in, and this happens at a nationwide rate of twenty-one billion gallons a day.[50] In the Central Valley of California, soils have compacted where water was overdrafted, and lands have subsided as much as thirty feet. With less water, farmers drill wells deeper, and energy costs climb. During California's drought in1977, twenty-eight thousand new wells were drilled. Eventually wells go deep enough to draw salt water that intrudes from deep formations or from the ocean in regions such as New York's Long Island and Texas's Gulf Coast.

Critically overdrafted, the Ogallala aquifer, on the plains from Nebraska south to Texas, supplies drinking water for two million people and irrigates ten million acres. The annual pumping of more water than flows in the Colorado River causes a three-foot-per-year drop in the aquifer's water level, which has been lowered a total of seven hundred feet in some places. Farms near Lubbock, Texas, have been abandoned in what could be a preview of the future; Texas A & M University reported that irrigation in the Texas Panhandle will begin a severe decline by 1985 if no water is imported from other regions.[51] On average, the Ogallala has forty years of life left if the pumping continues, and without the groundwater, the region may return to dry wheat fields, grazing lands, or forage for wildlife.

At a 1972 cost of $20 billion, the Texas Water Plan was proposed to import water from the Mississippi River, but other states were not enthusiastic. The governor of Arkansas sent the governor of Texas a jar of water and a note: "This is all you're going to get." Packed with problems, including those of damming Texas rivers, the plan was defeated by a coalition of environmentalists and schoolteachers (because the proposed funds would otherwise go to education).[52]

Arizonans overdraft 2.2 billion acre-feet a year — 46 percent of their total consumption — and the water table drops as much as twenty feet a year while developers, miners, and farmers race each other to the bottom of the well.[53] Some farmers are retiring because of declining water tables; as energy costs escalate, fewer can afford to pump. To gain water rights, the city of Tucson bought twelve thousand acres from farmers, and mining companies bought another eight thousand acres. Arizona will see continued urban growth but less farming, which now consumes 89 percent of the water but produces only 3 percent of the personal income.

The overdraft is one of the main reasons for the Central Arizona Project (CAP), designed to pump Colorado River water to the Phoenix and Tucson areas at a cost of $1.6 billion. Although the system was designed to carry 1.2 million acre-feet, only 500,000 acre-feet would have been available in 1990, decreasing to 284,000 acre-feet by 2030 because of additional withdrawals from new projects in Colorado and Utah. A centerpiece of the CAP was to have been Orme Dam, which was fought by Yavapai Indians. Charleston Dam on the San Pedro River would have flooded nesting sites of five pairs of endangered gray hawks. Hooker Dam on New Mexico's Gila River would have flooded six miles into the nation's first designated wilderness area, set aside in 1924 through the work of Aldo Leopold. The four dams and canals would evaporate 10 percent of the water—enough for a city of five hundred thousand. Also authorized under the CAP, but not for Arizonans' use, were five dams in Colorado: Dolores, Animas-LaPlata, Dallas Creek, San Miguel, and West Divide. These were added at the insistence of Congressman Wayne Aspinall. Some of the dams had less than a 1–1 benefit-cost ratio, and all became controversial in the 1970s. Only Dolores and Dallas Creek were recommended by the Bureau of Reclamation and scheduled for completion. Under the combined attacks of Indians, taxpayer groups, and environmentalists, the Arizona dams were deferred and the bureau sought alternatives.

Arizona is among the top ten states in per capita water consumption, and even with the Colorado River supplies, groundwater overdraft will likely be reduced by only two-thirds. Conservation of water could do much more to cut the overdraft, but as former Tucson city council member Barbara L. Weymann said, "People have brought their old environments with them here and they resent being told they're in the middle of the desert." [54]

In 1977 Arizona formed a Groundwater Management Study Commission, which recommended strict controls. Facing the threat of fewer water projects during the Carter administration, the state passed one of the nation's best groundwater management laws in 1980, requiring conservation of water. Other groundwater regulations had been adopted by Minnesota in 1937 and in Florida in 1957. In California's Central Valley, however, where groundwater is overdrawn at a rate of 1.5 million acre-feet a year, anybody can drill any number of wells and pump without regard for the loss of a neighbor's well and without consideration of the public costs of diverting rivers to replace the depleted underground supplies. New dams are the agricultural industry's answer to disappearing groundwater.

Underground pollution by toxic wastes was the most publicized environmental problem of the early 1980s. Thousands of water supplies were eliminated. The California State Health Department reported that 35 percent of the wells in the Central Valley were polluted with the pesticide DBCP. The Environmental Protection Agency estimated that three-fourths of the chemical waste dumps were leaking and that a hundred million Americans might be threatened by contaminated groundwater.

Even if the government strengthened programs to stop the dumping and the leaking of dangerous wastes, much damage would still be permanent. The pollution of underground water may cause a reversal of the trend to favor wells over rivers as a water source. Though the rivers have been polluted in the past, some are improving, whereas ruined groundwater supplies will remain ruined for an unknown number of generations. Stopping the pollution of surface water was an important national goal in the early 1970s, but the concern has suffered from budget cuts since then. Groundwater pollution may make cleaning up the rivers more important than ever.

LEAVING THE WATER IN

The threats to rivers include more than dams, channelization, and pollution. Diversions have ruined thousands of stream miles. Fish, wildlife, recreation, hydropower, and navigation are in-stream uses that suffer, the worst case being a dry riverbed. Other problems are warm water, silt, salt, algae, and pesticides and herbicides from returned irrigation water.

In the mid-1800s, some people recognized in-stream flow problems below dams. Catskill Falls, painted by Thomas Cole, had become a tourist attraction, but visitor George Curtis wrote, "In fact, if your romantic nerves can stand the steady truth, the Catskill Falls is *turned on* to accommodate poets and parties of pleasure." For twenty-five cents, a boy opened a sluice to let the water fall.[55] Modern plans to "mitigate" the loss of canoeing and rafting runs are just as contrived: to replace the Stanislaus whitewater, the corps proposed to dynamite channels and add boulders to another section of the river. Most boaters did not support the proposal, and it was dropped.

One of the first Bureau of Reclamation dams was built in 1906 on the Truckee River below Lake Tahoe, cutting the flow in half, eliminating world-record cutthroat trout, and shrinking the Paiute Indians' Pyramid Lake in Nevada. The lake level dropped eighty feet, and the Indians lost much of their livelihood.[56] The cui-ui, a fish found only in Pyramid Lake, is a living fossil but likely to become extinct as 9.8 billion gallons of water are diverted yearly for irrigation.

Below dams, rivers are affected by artificial releases, which sometimes improve the flow, as when water is added during dry months, but which often cause damage. Many hydroelectric dams release radically fluctuating amounts of water; irrigation and water supply dams may release only an anemic trickle.

How much in-stream flow is needed? An amount called Q 7-10 is often required, meaning that diversions may not cause a stream to drop below the amount of water in the lowest seven-day period likely to occur each ten years. Yet this minimum flow is only one element of in-stream needs and is often barely enough to keep the streambed wet. Seasonal variation is needed, the right temperatures are important, and even floods are essential to a stream's health.

In 1979 the Water Resources Council published estimates of the percentages of streamflows needed by fish and wildlife, ranging between 60 percent and 88 percent of a river's flow.[57] Most conflicts about in-stream uses are in the West, where vast quantities are withdrawn for irrigation.

A project with extreme problems is the Garrison Diversion, where the Bureau of Reclamation would channel Missouri River water across the plains and return polluted runoff to Canada's Souris River and the Red River of the North, thereby incidentally connecting the Mississippi basin with Hudson Bay. For irrigation of 250,000 acres in North Dakota, Garrison's canals and other facilities would take 220,000 acres out of agricultural production. Twelve national wildlife refuges would be damaged, including one that was started to mitigate losses that occurred when the Missouri was dammed. Sixty thousand acres of marshes and wetlands — already drained at the rate of 300,000 acres a year nationwide — would be destroyed. Waterfowl losses in North Dakota — which produces more waterfowl than any state but Alaska — were projected at 350,000 a year (original benefit-cost ratios were negative until "benefits" for wildlife were added). Fewer than a thousand farms would benefit at $800,000 each, leading Senator William Proxmire to call the project "sheer, unadulterated pork." The Canadian government protested and requested a moratorium on construction. The National Audubon Society sued in 1977 and delayed work.[58] After considering halting the project, the Carter administration approved a smaller version not affecting Canada. The Reagan administration proceeded with the plan, but in 1984 Congress required further studies before additional construction is approved.

Because of a Mexican treaty guaranteeing in-stream flows for Mexican irrigation, the United States is building the world's largest desalting plant to improve the lower Colorado River, which Mexicans cannot fully use because of ten million tons of salt a year. The $365-million plant is paid for by taxpayers, even though half of the salt is caused by upstream water projects that divert flows for irrigators[59] — when fields are flooded, salts in the soil dissolve in the water, which then flows back into the river.

Even the water quality in reservoirs can be harmed by new dams. Russell Dam on the Savannah River of Georgia and South Carolina was fought because of outstanding wildlife, fishery, and canoeing values, but construction nevertheless began in the late 1970s. The project will flood the only remaining undammed section of the upper river, where the riffles and current are needed to recharge oxygen between other reservoirs. In 1976 the National Wildlife Federation sued to stop construction. The district court ruled that dams can be point sources of pollution—a decision that may affect many dams in the future by requiring compliance with water quality regulations, but no injunction was granted for Russell.

Water for fish is the first thing sacrificed during droughts. When New York needed water in the mid-1960s, the minimum releases to the Delaware River were cut back even further. The Bureau of Reclamation diverts 80 percent of northern California's Trinity River to the south, causing an 80 percent loss of salmon and steelhead. And the bureau has planned yet more dams for northern California. As regional spokesman James Cook put it, "There are long arguments on whether fish or people will get the water, but when the nut gets tight, people are going to get the water." A Congressional Research Service study of the Missouri River stated that with minimum flows reserved for fish and wildlife, the basin will be short of water by the year 2000. Power plants, coal slurry pipelines, and oil shale processing create new demands on in-stream flows in eastern Montana and western Colorado.

On the Youghiogheny River in western Pennsylvania there has been little concern about shortages, but any more permits to withdraw water would not allow enough dilution of industrial and municipal waste. In a 1983 vote, Bucks County, Pennsylvania, residents rejected a plan to divert Delaware River water for the Limerick nuclear power plant. Sponsors of the referendum hoped to reverse decisions of the Delaware River Basin Commission to allow withdrawal of 95 million gallons of water a day.

For years, in-stream requirements were ignored in the operation of dams, but some states now require water withdrawal permits and regard in-stream flows as a "beneficial use"—a recognition reserved in earlier years mainly for irrigation. Wisconsin officials can deny a permit for a dam if it would damage aesthetic values, and in Vermont a dam can be stopped if it will hurt recreation, scenery, fish, wildlife, or the natural flow below the dam. Oregon has denied dam approvals in order to protect salmon and steelhead.

Yet some states still say that to keep cattle healthy is a beneficial use of a river, but to keep fish alive is not. Activities that need even more water, such as rafting, can rarely compete with irrigation. The high flows needed for the natural maintenance of river channels and for the formation of islands are rarely considered. States such as California that consider fish and wildlife usually regard them as less important than cities, industries, and farms.

Montana's in-stream reservation for the Yellowstone River was a path-breaking case. Headwaters of the river are in Yellowstone National Park, and upper reaches are superb trout water with spectacular scenery. In 1930 the U.S. Fish and Wildlife Service coded the Yellowstone and some other Montana streams as "blue-ribbon" trout waters—one of the first classifications given to rivers. There are no large dams on the river, and except for a diversion dam, the 670-mile-long Yellowstone would be the longest undammed river in the country outside Alaska.

In the lower basin, the Fort Union coal formation holds forty-three billion tons of strippable reserves, and with synthetic fuel potential and coal slurry pipelines, water demands could reach 2.6 million acre-feet a year, more than the river can provide while still meeting irrigation and municipal needs. Faced with coal development proposals, the state passed the Montana Water Use Act of 1973, for the first time allowing state agencies to reserve in-stream flows for fish, wildlife, and recreation. The following year the state banned further withdrawals until water was allocated. On the basis of studies of cutthroat trout on tributaries, the hydraulics creating the islands needed by Canada geese, the rising flow that triggers fish spawning, and much more, the Department of Fish and Game applied for nearly all remaining water in the river.[60]

After weeks of hearings at which coal developers attacked the Fish and Game Department's position, the Board of Natural Resources and Conservation in 1978 allocated about 62 percent of the average flow on the lower river and 76 percent in upstream reaches to in-stream uses. This was considered a success for in-stream values, and fish and game official Jim Posewitz wrote, "What we have done in our complicated way is decreed that the Yellowstone can still flow free."

Ironically, the recognition of in-stream needs may lead to even more dam proposals; water developers may treat the low-flow requirements as one more reason to store water, and the Yellowstone allocations could lead to growing pressure for Allenspur Dam near Yellowstone National Park. In 1979 Assistant Interior Secretary Robert Herbst said, "The pressure for dam building is going to grow with in-stream reservations."[61] It may be axiomatic that to protect both in-stream values on the lower ends of rivers and free-flowing reaches up above, in-stream regulations must be coupled with dam prohibitions such as the wild and scenic rivers act.

MAKING UP FOR LOSSES

To protect fish and wildlife, whether from in-stream flow reductions or from flooding by reservoirs, the Wildlife Coordination Act of 1934 was the first major law requiring that agencies consult with the Department of the

Interior's Fish and Wildlife Service. But this agency and state fish and game departments had little leverage to require adequate releases. For example, the Idaho Fish and Game Department was overruled in an attempt to save a trout fishery below a corps dam on the Boise River in the late 1950s. But through the Fish and Wildlife Service review, Interior Secretary Stewart Udall was able to stop Rampart Dam on the Yukon River, and the Interior Department has helped to stall a power company's damming of Canaan Valley in West Virginia.

To make up for fish and wildlife losses where the projects are built, federal agencies must prepare "mitigation" plans to replace whatever is to be lost. This has often meant the trading of a wild fishery for an inferior hatchery. Dam plans often exclude money for mitigation; the Bureau of Reclamation's Oahe Dam in South Dakota took 100,000 acres of river bottom, and twenty years later mitigation was still incomplete. In the South, where corps projects resulted in 1,236,045 acres of lost habitat, the Fish and Wildlife Service requested 877,078 acres of mitigation acreage — 111,300 acres were authorized, and only 33,800 acres were purchased. Although many people are not interested in these wildlife losses, other secondary effects of water development are not easily ignored.

THE ROAD TO BABYLON

Just as the Sumerians along the Tigris and Euphrates rivers were plagued with salted soil when their civilization collapsed some three thousand years ago, farmland of the American West suffers from excessive salinity. As irrigation water flows through the soil, it picks up salt and then deposits it on other fields. Many fields are underlain with impervious clay where the water is trapped; when it evaporates it leaves salts behind in growing concentrations, making it difficult for plants to take in moisture and get oxygen. Salt buildup in parts of California's Central Valley is 1.5 tons per acre annually. The Bureau of Reclamation stated that more than four hundred thousand acres are affected, and more than one million acres "may become a barren salt flat." In 1979, $31 million in farm goods were lost, and $300 million per year may be lost by the year 2000.[62]

The Bureau of Reclamation proposes to sewer the California farmland — a solution that promises yet more problems. The three-hundred-mile-long San Luis Drain would carry salty water to the San Francisco Bay at a 1979 cost of $750 million and with unknown costs of bay pollution. Treatment plants or fresh water dilution available only through more dams may be needed. Agricultural drainage including dissolved minerals, pesticides, and herbicides already pollutes the Kesterson National Wildlife Refuge in the Central Valley, where the Fish and Wildlife Service reported that up to 40 percent of hatched birds suffered birth defects, most of these dying. The water would kill most fish in two days.

Evaporation from reservoirs is another secondary effect of dams. Called "the river's storage charge" by Bureau of Reclamation officials, evaporation from Lake Mead equals seven feet off the top of the reservoir each year. Interior Secretary Cecil Andrus said, "Water projects don't create water, they move it around and sometimes lose some in the process." [63] All large reservoirs in the West evaporate eleven billion gallons daily — enough for about 40 percent of the nation's public water supply.[64] Evaporation intensifies the problems of salt, which remains behind. Water users argue that less water evaporates than would flow down the river and "waste to sea" if it were not for dams. But in the Colorado and some other basins, the flow is already evened out through normal years, and more dams would add only evaporative losses.

Other secondary debts of water projects are easier to see. After most Colorado River floods were stopped below Hoover Dam, plants grew in the riverbed at Needles, California, and silt piled up, raising the river bottom and requiring that one hundred families be moved out and that a levee be raised. Total expenses for the Colorado River Front Work and Levee System were $70 million, but the area was flooded again in 1983. Gavins Point Dam on the Missouri River caused rising groundwater to flood basements in the town of Niobrara, where six hundred people had to be moved at a government expense of $14.2 million.

SAFETY LAST

Older dams are showing wear and tear. The TVA bought Nolichucky Dam from the Tennessee Eastern Electric Power Company in 1945. Silt filled 77 percent of the reservoir, and the dam's cracked concrete required $2.5 million worth of safety improvements.[65] Budgets show increasing spending to repair dams and to correct damages that they cause. On Kentucky's Cumberland River, Wolf Creek Dam creates the largest reservoir in the East, but water seeped through the dam and required repairs costing more than the original project. Twenty-seven provisions in the 1979 omnibus water development bill were to correct problems caused by projects already built. In 1983 the corps's maintenance budget exceeded its construction budget.

In 1972 Buffalo Creek Dam, made of coal waste, collapsed and killed 125 people in West Virginia. Three hundred and fifty major dam failures have occurred in the United States, fifteen of them since 1972, most being privately owned dams. Public safety will require climbing costs for generations.

The National Dam Inspection Act of 1972 directed the Army Corps of Engineers to inspect all 50,000 large dams, 40 percent of them located where their failure would imperil life and property. No money was released until 1977, however, when President Carter, spurred by the Tacoa Falls failure, which killed thirty-nine people in Georgia, ordered the inspections. Of 9,000 dams that the corps checked in populated areas, nearly one-third were unsafe, and 130 posed imminent danger, but many of the dam owners could not be found. Much of the inspection job is left to states. In Pennsylvania, two inspectors are responsible for 3,000 dams.

Old dams are part of the "infrastructure crisis" given front-page attention in 1982 as people became aware of the backlog of crumbling roads, bridges, water mains, sewer lines, and subways. Old public works are neglected. As an assistant secretary for housing and urban development stated in *Newsweek,* "Have you ever seen a politician presiding over a ribbon-cutting for an old sewer line that was repaired?" Billions of dollars still shower new projects having nothing but political appeal.

Many scoff at the chance of sabotage or wartime destruction of dams. Yet consider what our own nation has done: In World War II, American bombers destroyed Ruhr Valley dams, as Wing Commander Guy P. Gibson wrote in the *Atlantic,* "Cars speeded along the roads in front of this great wave of water which was chasing them and going faster than they could even hope to go. . . . Until quietly and rather quickly there was no longer anything except the water. . . . The floods raced on, carrying with them as they went viaducts, railways, bridges, and everything that stood in their path." [66] In Korea, only days before peace, American planes bombed North Korean dams to damage the economy of that country.

By the mid-1970s, river conservationists and others had built a powerful case against the pork barrel politics of water development. No longer were they fighting against only Echo Park Dam as one part of the Upper Colorado Basin Storage Project, or Grand Canyon dams as one part of the Central Arizona Project; rather, they were addressing complex, deep-rooted problems: unfair subsidies, wildlife impacts, energy consumption, salinity, international needs, Indians' rights, and more. Campaigns had been won to save certain rivers, and now people had succeeded in using science and economics, in capitalizing on everyone's concern for safety, and in exposing an anachronistic political system. But could the politics of water development be changed?

CHAPTER EIGHT

A New Era

On horseback and by canoe, George Washington explored the Appalachians for possible canal routes, including the Youghiogheny, Cheat, and Casselman rivers. He believed that western settlement depended on water development. But Thomas Jefferson said, "Talk of making a canal of 350 miles through the wilderness—it is little short of madness."[1] Andrew Jackson, president in 1830, touted river development and defended the Army Corps of Engineers: "In improving the navigation of our rivers, bays, and harbors . . . this corps forms an essential reliance." Following Jackson, President Martin Van Buren thought waterway projects were unconstitutional, and in 1839 he halted them.[2]

President John Tyler put the corps back to work on the Ohio River in 1842, and about river development and the West he said, "The great importance of these subjects to posterity . . . and the security of the whole country in time of war cannot escape observation." In 1844 President James Polk stopped all of the corps's river work. Presidents Zachary Taylor and Millard Fillmore supported projects in 1848 and 1852, but Congress disagreed. Then when Congress pushed water development in 1853, President Franklin Pierce fought appropriations, but his vetoes were overridden.

In 1882 Chester A. Arthur refused to sign one of the first water development bills recognized as pork barrel. The president pointed out that each state was scrambling for federal money and that "as the bill becomes more objectionable it secures more support." Congress overrode the veto.[3]

President Theodore Roosevelt, in many ways a great conservationist,

SELECTED EVENTS IN CHAPTER 8

1830   President Jackson supported river development.

1839   President Van Buren halted water projects.

1842   President Tyler supported corps projects.

1844   President Polk stopped corps projects.

1848   President Taylor supported water projects.

1852   President Fillmore supported water projects.

1853   President Pierce fought water project appropriations.

1882   President Arthur unsuccessfully vetoed water projects.

1936   Flood Control Act passed under President Franklin Roosevelt.

1941   National Resources Planning Board formed.

1949   President Truman supported Echo Park Dam.

1955   Hoover Commission proposed water project reforms.

1956   President Eisenhower vetoed water project bills.

1960   President Kennedy supported Cross Florida Barge Canal.

1968   President Johnson signed National Wild and Scenic Rivers Act.

1973   National Water Commission proposed reforms.

1977   President Carter announced "hit list."

President Carter approved compromise water projects appropriations bill.

1978   President Carter announced new water policy.

President Carter vetoed water projects appropriations bill.

"Potholes" bill for water projects stopped by Congressman Edgar and others.

1979   President Carter approved water projects bill including Tellico Dam.

1981   President Reagan appointed James Watt as secretary of the interior. First major water projects deauthorization bill passed.

1983   Jobs bill passed with funds for water development.

approved Hetch Hetchy Dam. He created the Reclamation Service and touched off a half century of wild-river damming by calling to "make the streams . . . of the arid regions useful by irrigation works for water storage." President Woodrow Wilson also approved Hetch Hetchy.

President Harding applied no breaks to private dam development in the Northwest despite growing evidence that fisheries were being eradicated, but he opposed building a dam in Yellowstone National Park. President Herbert Hoover took steps to control water pollution and Alaskan salmon fishing, but he also expanded river navigation and championed the authorization of Hoover Dam, a milestone of river development.

Under President Franklin D. Roosevelt the greatest age of dam building began with the flood control acts of 1936 and 1937, the Works Progress Administration, the TVA, and the Columbia River dams for hydropower and jobs.

President Harry Truman supported Echo Park Dam, deriding the importance of "dinosaur bones" even though these had nothing to do with the controversy. He raised water power to a prime goal, "a subject close to my heart and vital to the future of the nation." To accelerate the damming of the Columbia he proposed a Columbia Valley Authority.[4]

President Dwight Eisenhower promoted state and federal "partnership," with the government encouraging private and state dam builders. In his first State of the Union message he said, "This combined effort will advance the development of the great river valleys of our nation and the power they can generate." While Eisenhower's policies allowed free reign to private river developers, his "partnership" was an undisguised euphemism for limited federal construction. He opposed federal water development on principle referring to the TVA as "creeping socialism." Despite his approval of Echo Park Dam, the Bureau of Reclamation's budget plummeted from $364 million in 1950 to $165 million in 1955. Eisenhower adopted a "no new starts" policy for federal projects and twice vetoed omnibus water development bills. But Ted Schad, author of the veto messages, said in 1983, "The vetoes didn't really have anything to do with the preservation of rivers." Bringing new analysis to the planning of water projects that had been hustled with a minimum of critique, Eisenhower's Bureau of the Budget set economic standards designed to cut federal spending. It was the first serious attempt to stop projects on the basis of economic criteria, which some viewed as placing New Deal development policies on the chopping block. The Eisenhower analysts' approach preceded a curious blend of environmental liberalism and fiscal conservatism that would mature in twenty years.

President John F. Kennedy was a liberal conservationist but also a New

Deal developer. He used water projects as political currency, supporting the Cross Florida Barge Canal to garner Florida votes. Although Kennedy's personal support for environmental protection focused on the seashores, he backed Interior Secretary Stewart Udall on many issues and was the first president to call for a national system of protected rivers.

President Lyndon Johnson said that "material progress is only the foundation on which we will build a richer life of mind and spirit." His rhetoric was at once prodevelopment and proconservation, but it was more than any other president had given to river preservation. The dam-building momentum slowed as the best projects were completed, the Vietnam war preempted money, and conservationists gained strength. Johnson told the Water Resources Council to raise the interest rate charged to water projects, and he ignored the Bureau of Reclamation in congressional messages that emphasized parks, rivers, and pollution control.[5] He signed the National Wild and Scenic Rivers Act, establishing the first major national program for river preservation and nailing the coffins of dam proposals on the Eleven Point, Feather, and Saint Croix rivers.

President Richard Nixon was attacked for anticonservationist views — exemplified, for instance, in his support for the Supersonic Transport — but he signed the National Environmental Policy Act, which provided unprecedented and unexpected means for the Natural Resources Defense Council, the Environmental Defense Fund, and other groups to sue and delay dam projects long enough to stop some of them politically. Nixon's characteristic of exceeding his authority benefited river protection: he halted the Cross Florida Barge Canal even though courts later ruled that he did not have the authority to do so. His controversial impoundment of funds delayed several destructive water developments, including the Central Arizona Project. But, saying, "There is too much pork in this barrel," [6] he also canceled the building of sewage treatment plants. When Nixon's staff prepared a "filthy fifty" list of project terminations, political advisors seeking cooperation from Congress convinced the president to scrap the list, and the projects went uncontested.

THE HIT LIST

Among presidents, Jimmy Carter was the greatest rivers enthusiast. Unlike the motivations of Van Buren, Polk, Pierce, Arthur, Eisenhower, and Nixon, Carter's reasons for stopping water projects were more than fiscal and political conservatism. He had canoed on the Chattooga River in Georgia. As governor, he had canoed the Flint River and halted Spewrell

Bluff Dam. Eisenhower golfed, Ford skied, and Carter paddled. On a presidential vacation in 1978 he rafted the Middle Fork of the Salmon in Idaho. Campaigning for president, he said, "I will halt the construction of unnecessary dams by the Corps of Engineers." A campaign paper stated, "Each new project must be subjected to careful study. . . . We must realize that the federal government's dam building era is coming to an end. Most beneficial projects have been built." [7] Even after New Melones Dam was completed, but before the reservoir was filled, Carter said that if Congress passed a bill granting national protection to the Stanislaus River, he would sign it.

Carter appointed Cecil Andrus secretary of the interior. As governor of Idaho, Andrus had fought the lower Hells Canyon dams. He had supported the Bureau of Reclamation's Teton Dam, then presided as governor during its impressive failure. When questioned by congressmen, Andrus said, "We are coming to the end of the dam-building era in America." [8] Guy Martin, who as Alaska's natural resources commissioner had reversed decisions to allow oil drilling in rich estuaries, was Andrus's assistant secretary in charge of the Bureau of Reclamation. Robert Herbst, responsible for one of the best state scenic river programs when he was Minnesota's commissioner of resources, became the assistant secretary for fish, wildlife, and parks, in charge of the national rivers system. Leo Eisel, a former EDF engineer and scientist, was appointed to head the Water Resources Council. With these men came an unprecedented opportunity to reform water development and to save rivers.

In February 1977, one month after his inauguration, Carter announced a "hit list" of water projects. His staff had reviewed 341 proposals and recommended that 32 be scrutinized and possibly cut. Carter then recommended deletion of $289 million for 19 projects having economic, environmental, or safety problems.

Included was California's Auburn Dam on an earthquake fault above Sacramento. Oklahoma's Lukfata Dam would cover 10,000 acres of timber for one catfish farm and the town of Idabel, population six thousand, which would receive enough water for one hundred thousand. The Cache River Basin Project would ditch two hundred miles of Arkansas's rivers and streams so that soybeans could replace 110,000 acres of wetlands and hardwood forests — the continent's largest wintering ground for mallard ducks. The Bayous Chene, Boeuf, and Black Project in the Atchafalaya River basin would dry up thousands of acres of Louisiana wetlands so that two oil rig manufacturers could assemble rigs inland and float them to the Gulf, rather than assemble them on open water.

Meramec Park Dam would be cut, and the Central Arizona Project would be modified. Parts of the Central Utah Project, designed to divert water from the Uinta Mountains to the Salt Lake City area, would be halted to save twenty-three thousand acres of land and two hundred miles of streams. The Garrison Diversion in the Dakotas would be stopped, saving the Cheyenne Lake National Wildlife Refuge and seven others, and avoiding the pollution of the James, Souris, and Red rivers, about which Canadians were enraged. Applegate Dam in Oregon would be cut, where four-fifths of the flood control benefits were for speculative development and fifty miles of salmon streams would be blocked.

Carter scrapped the Savery–Pot Hook and Fruitland Mesa projects in Colorado, each to benefit less than 100 farm families at a cost of $1 million or more per farm while adding brine to the already-salty Colorado River. And more: Narrows Dam in Colorado would provide water to the equivalent of 230 farm families, but required relocation of 216; Platte River flows would be cut by 11 percent, eliminating high spring runoff crucial to habitat of the endangered whooping crane. Thirteen of fifteen irrigation districts in the area opposed the project, and a landowners group stated, "If they took the money they wanted to spend on Narrows and put it in a trust fund, they could pay the farms that would supposedly benefit $5,000 per year, every year, forever." Carter considered stopping other projects but allowed them to proceed, including the Dolores Project, which would flood fifteen miles of river, reduce in-stream flows, add salts to the Colorado, and eliminate elk and deer herds. Who but people with the most vested of interests would not support Carter in stopping this barrel-bottom crop of projects?

Former commissioner of reclamation Ellis Armstrong called the administration's decision makers "uninformed amateurs." [9] In halting these environmental and economic boondoggles, Carter threw pork barrel politics into a ferment.

Unfortunately for the president, he had not discussed the cuts with some important congressional leaders. At the American Rivers Conservation Council's conference in 1980, Secretary Andrus said that he did not know that the list had been announced when a reporter asked him for comments. Adding to difficulties, the announcement came during the worst western drought in years.

Jimmy Carter was not playing the game the way congressmen were accustomed to play, and their reaction was vitriolic. Most congressmen beyond Missouri accused Carter of declaring "war on the West." Even environmentally conscious members such as Arizona's Morris Udall and Colorado's Gary Hart complained — projects in their states were included.

President Carter encountered a classic dilemma of Democrats engaged in river protection: party members remained philosophically committed to the New Deal ideal of income redistribution, and they remained politically dependent on the beneficiaries of federal water projects. Age-old party solidarity recognized water projects as sacred cows of a sort, and members who split from that platform often paid a high price in lost cooperation. Where they could, the Democrats sought to represent conservation as a liberal cause that was a companion to other social causes holding no appeal for Republicans. *Where they could* is the crucial phrase. Even with an administration strongly in support of river protection, even with a Democratic Congress, even with all the advances in river protection in recent years, the reform of water development appeared to remain subservient to the powerful political support of the water development lobby.

The *Denver Post* accused Carter of "vengeful opposition" because the West did not vote for him in 1976. Colorado governor Richard Lamm called the hit list "a study in federal arrogance . . . riddled with antiwestern prejudice and wrapped in ignorance." [10] He argued that federal projects had already been built for California, and that Colorado needed its dams to use its 34 percent share of the Colorado River.

Westerners argued that the federal projects were needed so that farmers and ranchers, consuming 90 percent of the water used in the West, could stay in business. Meanwhile, farmers were amiably selling their water to energy companies: for the Intermountain Power Project in Utah, farmers sold $10-per-acre-foot water for $1,750 an acre-foot, yielding $3 million to one rancher. Along Utah's Sevier River, 375 farmers sold their water to an electric utility for $79 million, and for oil shale development, Colorado farmers sold water for $2,300 an acre-foot. [11]

In *The Angry West,* Governor Lamm and Michael McCarthy maintained that farmers could not afford to pay for water without the subsidy:

> Westerners know, as nonwesterners do not, that drought tends to be cyclical, settling in perhaps twice a decade, then staying and searing and suffocating everything it touches for several seasons. Though westerners know their history, know the cycles, they remain at the mercy of drought. All they can do to survive is dam, impound, and protect every foot when times are good and hold it until times are bad. There is no fallback. And there are few alternatives.

In an open letter to Congress, Carter wrote, "I am aware of your concerns and I sympathize with them, but I cannot meet my commitment to balance the budget unless the Congress and I can cooperate in reducing unnecessary spending." [12]

In March 1977, the Senate approved a bill requiring the president to spend money for all but one of the nineteen projects. After public hearings that drew thousands of witnesses, the administration added more projects to be cut, but the House passed a bill funding all but one of Carter's deletions and stocking the dam builders with twelve new projects. In April the president revised his proposal: eighteen projects were to be dropped entirely, and another five were to be modified. Carter said, "In the arid West and across the entire nation, we must begin to recognize that water is not free — it is a precious resource. As with our energy problem, the cornerstone of future water policy should be wise management and conservation." [13]

A House amendment that supported Carter by killing all nineteen projects won 194 votes — enough to sustain a veto — but congressional leaders convinced Carter to go along with a compromise that cut only nine projects. So this battle between Carter and Congress appeared to be a draw. In August 1977 Carter signed an appropriations bill funding half of the hit list, approving Applegate Dam, the Atchafalaya channel, the Cache River channel, Columbia Dam in Tennessee, Hilldale Lake in Kansas, Richard B. Russell Dam in South Carolina, Tallahala Creek in Mississippi, and Bayou Bodcau in Louisiana. The Sierra Club's Brock Evans said that Carter's signing was not a "compromise" but a "betrayal."

Critical but optimistic, Brent Blackwelder said, "The Carter hit list generated lots of press. All the major papers did a series on water. CBS had TV programs. Even though there were a lot of media problems with the cuts being seen as a 'war on the West,' the issues of pork barrel finally reached the public." But battling symptoms was not enough for victory. The site-by-site attack was disappointing, and seeing futility in this approach, the Carter administration turned toward long-term reform.

REWRITING THE COOKBOOK

Carter next proposed to change the rationale that had justified bad projects. In June 1978 he announced a new water policy with four main objectives: to improve planning so that projects are economically and environmentally sound; to conserve water and reduce demand; to foster state planning and cooperation; and to increase attention to environmental quality.

Not surprisingly, projects had received straight A's when reviewed by the agencies that built them. The Carter policies therefore sent plans to the Water Resources Council for an independent review. The council would revise the principles and standards used in project justification and, by escaping the influence of the "iron triangle," would strike to the heart of the pork barrel process. For the first time, the government was to weigh environmental and economic objectives equally.

For every proposed dam or channel, the sponsoring agency was required to write a nonstructural plan. A limit was put on flood control benefits to undeveloped lands. States would pay 10 percent of hydroelectric and water supply costs and 5 percent for navigation, flood control, and "area redevelopment." Water conservation was required for sewage treatment grants, Housing and Urban Development programs, and new federal buildings. Reform of irrigation was weak but included technical assistance to farmers and water contracts with price revisions every five years instead of every forty. (Under the old contracts, irrigators never had to pay for the increasing costs of operations and maintenance during the forty-year period.) Fifty percent funding for state water management plans was proposed. New water projects were to provide in-stream flows for fish, wildlife, recreation, aesthetics, and water quality.

The policy reforms were mostly ineffective on projects already begun, leading one water lobbyist to say, "Even if you talk about no new authorizations, you've got fifty years of authorized projects out there waiting to be built. All this 'no new projects' stuff is as phony as a three-dollar bill. What the development agencies say is, 'call us in fifty years and then we'll apply the new policies.' " The reforms did not touch some projects in the thicket of controversy, but the new policies were a turnaround never before attempted, and in support, twenty-four conservation groups formed the Coalition for Water Project Review. "Profiles in Pork," weekly press releases sent out by coordinator Edward Osann of the National Wildlife Federation, alerted the press to upcoming votes. The effort paid off: Congress's press gallery was packed during important votes. Pork barrel was at least getting exposure.

The Carter reforms were the most progressive step ever taken toward water development reform; but would they last? Franklin Roosevelt's National Resources Planning Board, established in 1941 to review corps projects, disapproved only 76 of 426 requests, but Congress still authorized 62 of the rejected projects. Then the board was disbanded. The 1955 Hoover commission report was mostly ignored. The National Water Commission's 1973 report recommended dozens of changes and served as a springboard for groups like the Environmental Policy Center to push for reforms, but few resulted. Yet one indication that Carter's policies might endure came from two of the development agencies themselves: the corps and the Soil Conservation Service were each able to propose about twelve projects under the new rules. The Bureau of Reclamation, however, justified only one project.

The new water policies were meant to redirect water development, but the belief in the unlimited does not die easily. House majority leader Jim Wright of Texas said, "If [Carter] wants to pick a fight, here's the place to pick one."

FROM PORK BARREL TO POTHOLES

Reflecting on his 1977 compromise approving nine hit-list projects, Carter said, "If I had it to do over again, I would have vetoed it." Another chance came in 1978.

Water appropriations bills would have reinstated six of the nine projects dropped in the 1977 compromise, added 2,300 jobs for dam-building agencies, and authorized fifty-three new construction starts. For one dam failing to meet benefit-cost criteria, a bill simply declared, "Congress hereby finds that the benefits . . . exceed the costs." Congress planned to kill funding for the Water Resources Council, and it authorized three dozen projects not even studied by the corps. For the Trinity River Canal in Texas the appropriation bill recognized "national economic development benefits" as well as "net regional benefits," which New Mexico senator Pete Domenici criticized as benefits "stolen from another area of the country."

The *Washington Post* reported, "With this largesse touching every state and many congressional districts — in an election year when goodies for the home folks count for something — little criticism is heard on Capitol Hill." [14] Only two of forty-four House Public Works Committee members spoke against the spending of $3.4 billion for water projects: David Bonoir of Michigan and Robert Edgar of Pennsylvania. Howard Jarvis, who had promoted California's tax-cutting Proposition 13 in 1978, called the bill "the big-tax, big-government, big-spending, big-waste bill of the year." On October 7 Jarvis sponsored a full-page advertisement in the *Washington Post*: "Congress: You must be kidding! Any politician who supports this bill now must have his head in the sand." But it passed.

President Carter vetoed the bill on October 5, 1978, calling it "inflationary . . . wasteful . . . and absolutely unacceptable." The veto held, with 190 House members supporting Carter, many of them freshmen who rode to office on post-Watergate reform tickets.

Congressman Butler Derrick of South Carolina, who had unsuccessfully fought Russell Dam on the Savannah River, addressed a group of river activists and said, "Five years ago you just didn't mess with anybody's water projects. That has changed. You're going to see projects looked at much more closely. That is the main thing that was accomplished with the veto."

Congress responded with an appropriation bill that deleted six of the nine projects that Carter objected to, cut eleven new projects, and dropped the 2,300 new jobs. Perhaps sensing that this was a reasonable compromise, Carter approved, but still to come was the water projects authorization bill — a separate measure — and with it a whirlwind of political maneuvering.

Just before dawn on one of the final days of the session, Senator Mike Gravel called up a bill to name a Shreveport, Louisiana, federal building after Congressman Joe Waggonner. Knowing that the water developers would try to slip their bill through, Brent Blackwelder and other conservationists had talked to Senators Proxmire, Leahy, and Abourezk, who agreed to watch for trouble, and now Abourezk asked Gravel, "Can we inquire what that thick stack of paper is?" It was a thirty-five-page amendment to the Shreveport bill authorizing new water projects costing $1 billion. That stopped Gravel, but in midafternoon, Pennsylvania congressman Allen Ertel talked to senators and had the Emergency Highway and Transportation Repair Act of 1978 released and passed by the Senate. The bill originally provided federal aid to patch potholes, but that language had been taken out and 158 water projects inserted under the pothole title. Wanting a levee for Harrisburg in his home district, Ertel asked the House Speaker to suspend rules and vote on the bill, but Congressman Robert Edgar objected. When pressed, Ertel admitted, "This is the pothole bill, but they took out the potholes and put in the water projects." Ertel pushed for a vote as time ran out, but an objection was heard regarding a quorum. Congressmen Edgar, Siberling, and others buttonholed colleagues and asked them to ignore the quorum call. Two hundred and sixty-five members did not answer, and the bill died.[15]

Beneath the parliamentary shenanigans, it was a historic moment. This was the first Congress in twenty years that did not pass a biennial authorization bill for water projects. Pork barrel had finally collapsed as environmental lobbyists, congressional reform, the Carter policies, and fiscal conservatism brought the process down. The irony most encouraging to environmentalists was that whereas the omnibus bill for dams failed, an omnibus bill for wild rivers and parks passed.

But the gains of 1978 were short-lived. In September 1979 Carter signed the $10.6-billion Energy and Water Development Act, authorizing nine projects outside the budget and without army corps review, stopping funds for the Water Resources Council, and budgeting Arcadia and McGee Creek dams in Oklahoma with no water conservation planning. In its most celebrated abuse of the new water policies, the law waived the Endangered Species Act and "all other laws" for the completion of Tellico Dam. Majority leader Jim Wright had told the president that a veto "would just add fuel to the fire" and guarantee hostility from Congress. The Tellico approval brought river conservationists' greatest disappointment in Carter, but congressmen had attached Tellico riders to other bills, requiring vetos of forthcoming laws if Carter insisted on halting the dam.

Another disappointment was the Interior Department's approval of cheap irrigation contracts in Westlands, the Bureau of Reclamation's largest district in California. Cecil Andrus no longer prophesied the "end of the dam-building era" but said, "Water construction projects will continue in the West. We just want to make sure they are good, safe projects."

Presidential directives supported the wild and scenic rivers system in 1979, but Carter also approved record budgets for water development: a 29 percent increase for the Bureau of Reclamation in fiscal year 1980 and a 15 percent gain for the corps to a record budget of $3,060,400,000, though inflation eroded the amount to a real level that was lower than during some earlier years. Brent Blackwelder said, "We expected some massive cuts this year; instead we got increases. The problem with the president is that after every gain he retreats."

In October 1980, Carter approved $4 billion for water projects, including Yatesville and Orme dams. When funding was eliminated for Water Resources Council project reviews, the president said that he would work to reinstate the council's role the next year. One month later Ronald Reagan was elected.

REAGAN AND WATT

President Reagan won on a platform to cut government size, influence, and spending — promises not conducive to wasteful water projects. William Gianelli, director of the California Department of Water Resources when it developed ambitious plans to dam northern California rivers, was chosen as assistant secretary of the army, responsible for the corps. For secretary of the interior, Reagan named James Watt, president of the Mountain States Legal Foundation, representing corporations involved in resource development in the Rockies. Watt had said, "I fear that our states may be ravaged as a result of the actions of the environmentalists — the greatest threat to the ecology of the West." He asked if the environmentalists' real motive was "to weaken America." To a *Wall Street Journal* reporter he explained, "My responsibility is to follow the Scriptures, which call upon us to occupy the land until Jesus returns." [16] Watt said that he was "bored" on the second day of a raft trip through the Grand Canyon.

Contradicting rhetoric to cut the budget, Watt declared of water development, "We are committed to new projects," and called for western governors to submit proposals. The wild and scenic rivers program was sliced to the bone, and rivers that would have been recommended even under Nixon or Ford were found "eligible but not suitable."

Allowing for inflation, water projects had faced a tightening economic noose since the mid-1970s. In 1982 Reagan's water development budget cut $230 million from the Carter proposal but was still the highest water development budget ever when other domestic programs were eliminated. The Bureau of Reclamation received about $1 billion — 23 percent greater than the year before — a larger percentage increase than the much-debated growth in defense. After a $4-billion water development budget in 1983, the president's request for 1984 cut 7 percent.

James Watt used water projects — solidly backed in the West — to leverage his less popular development proposals. Ed Osann said, "Many in the West don't agree with what Watt's doing to expand mining, oil drilling, and gas exploration, but they can't press him too hard because he has to sign for the next water project." In his first year as secretary of the interior, Watt was repeatedly called to Congress and grilled about public lands giveaways, but after the secretary warned that sessions on the Hill were interfering with his approval of dams and canals, including the Central Arizona Project, congressmen backed off.

In 1983 a jobs bill to ease unemployment was passed, earmarking $545 million for water development. As unemployment reached 20 percent in Pittsburgh, Detroit, and even Oregon, one of the highest-funded job generators under the Bureau of Reclamation's allowance was for the Central Arizona Project, serving the suburbanization of Phoenix.

Under Watt, Robert Broadbent became commissioner of reclamation. He had practiced pharmacy in Boulder City, Nevada, for twenty-five years and served as a county commissioner. In a 1983 interview, the commissioner cited the Reclamation Reform Act as the focus of his work. The 1982 law requires water conservation planning, but the commissioner denied any new priority for the bureau's Irrigation Management Service, which advises farmers about how to save water. In 1980 the service consisted of only two full-time employees out of a 1,200-person bureau staff in California.

When asked if the era of water development was past, the commissioner

said, "The budget is going up substantially. There are a lot of water resource problems that have to be answered and you can't answer them all
with conservation. Five new starts are being considered right now." But the
poor economy and Reagan's record federal deficit prevented authorization
of costly dams and canals. To simply finish projects such as the bureau's
Garrison Diversion and the corps's Tennessee-Tombigbee Waterway
would dominate construction budgets for the rest of the century.

Reagan, a self-proclaimed "sagebrush rebel," was able to propose even
more cost sharing than Carter had done, but without incurring the wrath of
the western bloc. Reagan asked for user fees to recover all expenses for
navigation, hydropower, and water supply. Thirty-five percent cost sharing
was proposed for flood control and irrigation. As a result, new projects
were stalled during the Reagan years with effectiveness equal to or greater
than during Carter's term. Secretary of the Army William Gianelli, who
supported cost sharing and also front-end funding of projects instead of
yearly appropriations, sounded strangely like Cecil Andrus when he said,
"Water project construction as we knew it in the past is not going to be that
way in the future."[17] Interior Secretary Watt, however, did not support the
cost-sharing formulas. Instead, he called for a "case-by-case" determination, with himself in charge.

Congress did not approve Reagan's user-fee proposal and planned to
spend in the usual pork barrel fashion. The *Washington Post* reported in
January 1982, "Throughout this painful budget-cutting process . . .
more than 300 water projects emerged almost unscathed, including several
that Reagan had targeted for extinction." Pushing for approval of Willow
Creek Dam for flood control in Heppner, Oregon, population 1,500,
Chairman Mark Hatfield of the Senate Appropriations Committee said, "I
have to confess to you, that's just raw political power. . . . They'd petition
to have me hanged at high noon if I didn't do anything about Willow
Creek."[18] But in a precedent-setting case, Congress required 20 percent
cost sharing for the Central Arizona Project's irrigation distribution system.

As chairman of the Water Resources Council, James Watt saw that all
funding for the council was stopped. The principles and standards that had
been so tediously developed for economic respectability were rescinded by
Watt "to reduce the burden on agencies in complying with detailed and
legally binding rules." The standards were replaced with unenforceable
"guidelines" administered under Watt. Without the principles and standards, agencies were openly invited to tamper with project justifications.
Nonstructural alternatives no longer needed to be considered. The environmental quality goal was dropped from its dual position with economic
development.

Defending the principles and standards, a National Wildlife Federation spokesman said, "We don't recall this administration having come into office on a platform of making life easier for federal bureaucrats, particularly those like the federal dam builders with a penchant for spending money by the billions." About Watt's "guidelines" editors of the *Sacramento Bee* wrote, "If building inefficient water projects is not in the public's interest, then neither are these vague and incomplete project guidelines that make construction of inefficient projects more likely."

Commissioner Broadbent said that the Water Resources Council was

just another layer of government that you didn't need. The new guidelines will allow us to consider a lot of things as justifications to build a project and to meet water quality standards. It will be easier to show a balanced justification. Personally, I feel the Water Resources Council was a bureaucratic nightmare. Government is tough enough already. Somewhere the buck stops and you have to make a decision, and the Water Resources Council was another review board that could never make up its mind on anything. The independent review is the Office of Management and Budget's job. The ultimate review agency is Congress.[19]

The council had represented the one serious effort to break control of water projects by the iron triangle of the construction agencies, Congress, and local promoters, and that effort was now abandoned. Watt's successor, William Clark, called for a repeal of some Reclamation Reform Act requirements regarding payments for irrigation water, and postponed consideration of increases in cost sharing.

Nevertheless — even though many of the Carter reforms failed and the Reagan administration rescinded environmental protection measures — the times had changed. Some new congressmen did not share the old boosterism for any dam on any river, and some were bright enough and determined enough to attack the politics that had needlessly destroyed so much.

CHANGING THE POLITICS

Bob Edgar gained an appreciation for rivers when he and his father hiked and fished, but growing up near Philadelphia he also saw what needed to be changed. "You could almost walk on the water, the pollution was so bad," he said in a 1983 interview. Edgar was ordained as a Methodist minister and served as Drexel University's chaplin. Then he decided to run for Congress. A Democrat had not been elected in his district since before the Civil War, but Republicans squabbled among themselves and Edgar won. At age thirty he went to Washington, in the Watergate reform class of 1974 that would change the pork barrel system. "My constituents did not elect me to come down here to continue business-as-usual supporting lopsided priorities," Edgar said, just hinting at what he would do.

Gaining a seat on the House Public Works Subcommittee on Water Resources, Edgar opposed wasteful water projects so efficiently that he was removed from the subcommittee by its leadership. He later reclaimed his seat.

Edgar stopped the "potholes repair" bill that meant $1 billion for water projects but nothing for potholes. He forced debate on another water development bill by threatening to call up 184 amendments, each exposing a congressman's pet boondoggle. About new authorizations Edgar said something basic to common sense but radical to pork barrel politics: "The criteria for all of these projects ought to be on their merit."

In June 1979 Edgar addressed Congress about a proposed dam: "The more I learn about the Stonewall Jackson project, the angrier I become. Angry at the Corps for abusing the system of benefit-cost analysis that is supposed to screen water projects. Angry at various bureaucracies for allowing the project to muddle along without serious review. And finally, angry at the Congress for its failure to stand up to the politics of pork." For this view he enjoys few favors from colleagues. Congressman Harley Staggers from West Virginia, where the proposed project was located, said, "What right has a minister from Philadelphia to question a project in my district?" After Edgar spoke on the floor of the House, Don Young from Alaska recommended a Pinocchio award for the member who sticks his nose the farthest into another member's affairs.

William Proxmire had been the leader in opposing pork barrel of all kinds, but Edgar could claim that role for water projects. Brent Blackwelder said, "He is one of the few people in Congress who seeks to ascertain the public interest. Then he pursues it. He saw public works as a disaster and he took it on, not to be dissuaded by the abuse heaped on him."

"I've attempted to bring attention to important problems by opposing all omnibus bills," Edgar said after having stopped three successive water project bills during a six-year period.

> We need to rap the backs of the heads of Jamie Whitten and Tom Bevill and others. We're holding both good and bad projects hostage until we get a better water policy, one based on the environment, one that spends money wisely. In the past we've spent lots of money on new projects and some of them are very bad. We've built many projects without local investment. We don't rehabilitate and maintain older structures and waterways, and we ignore nonstructural

alternatives. We need to correct problems of toxic wastes, declining aquifers, diversions of water, and projects creating unfair economic advantages to some people. How ridiculous it is to work three shifts a day on a bad project like the Tennessee-Tombigbee Waterway that costs more than the money being spent on renewable energy. This administration [Reagan's] is not proenvironment. If we don't alter that, we could be in serious trouble as a society.

Edgar proposed a four-part reorientation of water development: "If we're going to build new projects, we need local cost sharing, nonstructural alternatives, a national policy recognizing the value of water and rivers, and assurance that environmental improvement will result. Until then, I'll be holding up new project starts."

In 1980 the lobbyists against destructive water projects included the American Tax Reduction Movement, the National Taxpayers Union, Common Cause, Americans for Democratic Action, and, an old ally, the League of Women Voters. Supported by this union of very liberal and very conservative causes, President Reagan in 1981 signed the first bill ever to deauthorize a group of water developments by cutting eight projects costing $2.5 billion, including Dickey-Lincoln dams in Maine, Meramec Park Dam in Missouri, Helm and Lincoln dams in Illinois, and Big Blue and Clifty Creek dams in Indiana. A bill to charge the taxpayer for Bureau of Reclamation safety improvements was defeated in 1982 by environmentalists and taxpayer groups who argued that direct beneficiaries should pay their share of the safety costs. With new optimism, Brent Blackwelder said, "Our system of government allows people to influence the process. If people understand the process they can make a difference."

Another water lobbyist said, "It used to be that the appropriations members would gain fifty-five out of sixty votes in the committee and then go with that kind of strength to the floor and say, 'Come on, come on,' like Mohammed Ali, and everyone would be scared. Now we've broken the old system and made it okay to vote against pork." More than vote: in 1983 Congressman Silvio Conte, a Massachusetts Republican, wore a pig's mask in the House cloakroom and grunted on the floor of Congress to make his point.

Bob Teeters, chief of interagency coordination for the corps, said, "The political support for development has diminished since the sixties. Now it's the exception — not the rule — when a congressman will go around wanting to spend lots of money." The corps itself had also changed, employing four hundred people to work on environmental issues.

A logjam of water projects piled up behind Edgar's political blockade. Corps division engineers had cleared 160 projects, and the chief of engineers had approved 60 — all of them candidates for an omnibus bill. Yet Bob Teeters said, "The era of big water projects has come to an end. After the drought of 1977, there was no mass movement to build new dams the way there was after the eastern drought of the sixties. The best projects have been built, and the times have changed."

Bob Edgar said, "I'm an optimist. I think we can turn the pork barrel process around. There is more concern than there used to be. If a congressman supports projects that are wasteful now, he is criticized. I get strong endorsements from local newspapers, and help from the taxpayer groups." In 1982 Edgar won reelection by 11,000 votes (two years earlier his margin had been 1,200), despite the political pundits' predictions of defeat. "Congressmen who want new projects were beginning to ask, 'How can we accommodate the Bob Edgars of this world?' They want to come to some resolution so that we can get the Army Corps of Engineers back in business."

Edgar cautioned, "Pork barrel development could come back unless laws are improved so that our use of water and money is more resourceful. The army corps will be there, long into the future, nibbling at edges, anxious to get projects moving."

Edgar served as chairman of the 213-member Northeast-Midwest Congressional Coalition in the House, which reported that the South and West received 82 percent of the corps's dollars, compared to 17.9 percent in the Northeast and Midwest, where 45 percent of the people live. Edgar said,

All of the Bureau of Reclamation dollars go to the West. The Central Arizona Project will spend $600 million on municipal and industrial water supply, while federal agencies are not allowed to help fund single-purpose water supply projects in the Northeast, where repairs are desperately needed. My goal is to see a higher priority on maintenance and rehabilitation. The bridges, sewers, and water systems — the basic building blocks that hold the country together — are old. If we don't renew them, society will be more and more distressed. We cannot continue with new megastructures without taking care of the old ones.

With the same concerns, Senators Daniel Patrick Moynihan of New York and Pete Domenici of New Mexico introduced a water resources policy and development bill calling for development funds on the basis of population and land area rather than on logrolling, which is now the case. Their bill requires 25 percent cost sharing by the states and puts water conservation "on an equal footing with structural, capital-intensive solutions."

In 1984 a bill was passed appropriating $3.8 billion to the corps and bureau, but no new construction starts were approved, and for the eighth year in a row no new corps projects were authorized.

Bob Edgar said, "We need to realize that water is a national treasure. It is the next big crisis after energy. We need new goals for water development, and an administration that implements water policy with protection and with love and care for the resource. We need to raise public awareness of water and our resources."

CHAPTER NINE

Needs and Alternatives

River conservationists mobilized support for special places, they built powerful arguments based on science and economics, and they capitalized on other movements for political reform. But success would have ended if the real needs for water development could not have been met without more dams and canals. So after exposing faults in the procedures that were used to "justify" water projects, river protection groups built a case for meeting needs without the destruction and waste so prevalent in the past.

SUPPLY AND DEMAND

Before discussing the alternatives to big water projects, it is important to know how much water we really have, how much we use, and how much we will demand in the future. Only with this information can planners effectively prepare for water projects or for alternatives to the traditional solutions of dams and canals.

About 97 percent of the earth's water is in the oceans, 2.2 percent in the ice caps, and 0.3 percent too deep underground to pump out — leaving less than 0.5 percent available to people. Canada and Russia each has about 20 percent of the freshwater. The United States has 4 percent, with runoff highest in the Northwest and lowest in the Southwest and the Great Basin of Nevada and Utah.[1]

If all the freshwater in the country were divided up, each person would get 6,000 gallons a day. The United States Geological Survey (USGS) estimated that 450 billion gallons a day were withdrawn for all uses in 1980, with fresh surface water accounting for 65 percent, fresh groundwater for 20 percent, and saline water for 15 percent.[2] The East and the West withdrew roughly equal amounts, but 91 percent of the irrigation water was used in the West, where only 30 percent of the rain and snow fall, and the majority of water for homes, industry, and energy was used in the East. Per person, westerners used twice the water of easterners — three times, if water for hydroelectricity is counted.[3]

In 50,000 reservoirs of 50 acre-feet or more, 450 million acre-feet are stored (one acre-foot equals 325,851 gallons or 43,560 cubic feet). More than 1.8 million small reservoirs and ponds store another 10 million acre-feet.

In medieval times, one person used an estimated 3 to 5 gallons of water per day (gpd); in the nineteenth century, 10 to 15 gpd. In 1980 the Water Resources Council (WRC) reported that in the United States an average of 118 gpd were used per person in homes and businesses — more than in any other nation. Withdrawals for all uses averaged 2,000 gpd per person, ranging from 19,000 in Idaho to 180 in Rhode Island. Californians withdrew twice the water of either of the next-largest users, Florida and Texas.[4] While the United States population increased 44 percent between 1950 and 1975, water use more than doubled. From 1975 to 1980, use climbed 8 percent, compared to 12 percent for the previous five years. The slower rate was credited to economic decline, droughts, restrictions on water use, and recycling.

Whereas most withdrawals are later returned (although sometimes unrecognizably altered) to a stream, consumptive use occurs when water is withdrawn and not returned, usually because of evaporation. About 100 billion gpd were consumed in 1980. In the East, 8 percent of freshwater withdrawals were consumed; in the West, 41 percent.[5]

Public water systems serving 81 percent of the people in seventeen thousand towns and cities used 8.5 percent of nationwide withdrawals and 6.9 percent of the water that was consumed, 66 percent coming from surface supplies (rivers and reservoirs). Manufacturing used 17 percent of the withdrawals and accounted for 7.7 percent of the consumption. Energy production took 26.3 percent of withdrawals and 1.3 percent of consumption, mostly for the cooling of power plants.[6]

For irrigation, 170 million acre-feet were withdrawn in 1980 to water fifty-eight million acres, an increase of 7 percent since 1975. Irrigation took 47 percent of withdrawals and 81 percent of consumption. Withdrawals were expected to decline slightly owing to overdraft in the Southwest as well as to improved efficiency; however, more than half of the irrigation water was consumed, and consumption was expected to increase. Sixty percent of the irrigation water came from surface supplies. California used 25 percent of all irrigation water—more than the next-highest irrigation users (Idaho and Colorado) combined.[7]

Hydropower plants withdrew by far the greatest amount of water, using 2.7 times the average annual runoff of the nation, but nearly all of this was quickly returned to streams after turning turbines. In 1980, hydroelectric capacity was up 17 percent from 1975,[8] accounting for 12 percent of America's electricity.

A person needs only five to six pints of water a day, but amounts used in agriculture and manufacturing are enormous. To produce one pound of beef can require 4,000 gallons of water. One pound of cotton requires 3,100 gallons, a pound of rice, 500. For a gallon of milk, 932 gallons of water are used; for an egg, 120 gallons.[9] About 40 percent of all water used in California is for livestock. This includes irrigated pasture, which in terms of total acreage uses more water than any other crop. Alfalfa ranks second, and cotton, third. Crops requiring the most water per acre are rice, using 8 acre-feet a year; pasture, using 5.2; alfalfa, using 4.9; and cotton, using 4. A medium-sized paper mill uses enough water for a city of a million, and a coal liquification plant producing fifty thousand barrels of oil a day would use the water of 100,000 people.[10] Aluminum production, which requires twelve times the energy needed for iron, is often dependent on hydroelectricity, one large plant using the energy of a 179,000-person city.[11]

THE COMING YEARS

How much water do people need? Water Resources Council projections called for withdrawals to decrease to 306.4 billion gpd by the year 2000, the cut being due to recycling and conservation, most importantly in manufacturing, expected to decrease from 60.9 billion gpd in 1975 to 29.1 billion gpd in 2000 because of recycling encouraged by water quality laws. But consumption for all water uses was expected to increase 27 percent by the year 2000.

Even though population growth has slowed from a fertility rate of 3.7 to 2.0, population will increase, possibly peaking at 250 million in the year 2015; some of the regions now growing new houses the fastest grew only sagebrush a few years ago. People move to the Southwest, where, insulated by sprinklers, they pretend that the desert does not exist. They bring their watered lawns and car washes, and they add swimming pools and air conditioners. The population of Phoenix increased 30 percent between 1970 and 1980; the Salt Lake City area, 37.2 percent; Albuquerque, 34.5

percent; and Austin, 36 percent. In the Denver area, one hundred immigrants arrive every day.[12]

The WRC projected water deficits by the year 2000 in 17 of 106 subregions, mainly in the Southwest and Midwest. Shortages already exist in the Rio Grande and lower Colorado basins, where water is made scarce by agricultural control. Increased energy development in dry regions will aggravate shortages; in 1974 the Interior Department reported that energy development on the Rockies' west slope could require 25 percent of the upper Colorado River's flow. The Western States' Water Council estimated that new energy projects in eleven states would require 2.3 million acre-feet a year by 1990 (these great expectations for an energy boom have since faded). Boston, New York, Washington, and other cities will face rationing if a major drought occurs. In-stream flows for fish, wildlife, and recreation are inadequate throughout much of the West. Groundwater overdraft is severe on the plains from Nebraska to Texas, in central Arizona, and in the Central Valley of California. Although pollution makes surface water unusable, especially in the Northeast, Midwest, and Great Lake states, toxic and hazardous wastes that ruin groundwater may force a greater dependence on rivers.

Even though dams reduce floods in thousands of communities, support for flood control continues. Because of uncontrolled lowland development, the WRC expects flood damage to increase to $4.3 billion a year by 2000. Barge use on navigable rivers will continue, though it will probably decrease on the old industrial waterways of the East. Hydroelectric generation is the main reason for dam proposals in the 1980s. The Federal Energy Regulatory Commission estimated that production of about 66,000 megawatts can be increased to 113,000.[13] New hydroelectric proposals threaten some of the finest rivers.

The coming years could bring hundreds of new power dams and diversions from basins of plenty, such as the Susquehanna, Great Lakes, and Columbia, to thirsty cities and desert farms. The economic, social, and environmental costs could dwarf those of the past because the best sites are already developed. With a recurrence of the mid-1960s drought in the Northeast or the 1977 drought in the West, when twenty-nine states were eligible for disaster relief because there had been no rain, there may be renewed pressure to build dams and divert rivers. Farmers will fight for the status quo, which requires new projects so that irrigation in places such as southern California can remain "surplus" and available to large corporations at a fraction of the real cost. Indian tribes will claim water under the Winters Doctrine and use sources that other people planned to take. Energy developers will wield political power to get the water they want. Water developers compete among themselves, but on one point they have been united: they want more dams.

In the late 1960s the Susquehanna River Basin Study reported, "The abundant water in the Susquehanna Basin is being looked to by communities outside the drainage area as a supply source for the future." In the 1960s the California Water Plan called for dams on the Klamath, Trinity, Eel, and other northern rivers, and the Bureau of Reclamation's Pacific Southwest Water Plan recommended Grand Canyon dams, the connection of northern California rivers to Lake Mead, and the study of diversions from the Northwest. The Colorado River is drained dry and ends as an intermittent stream in Mexico, yet more water is scheduled to be taken by Arizona and upper-basin states. The time of reckoning has been put off so far, but someday Colorado River allocations must be reduced, or more water will have to be taken from other basins through cloud seeding or diversions. In 1983 — a flood year — Commissioner of Reclamation Robert Broadbent had no proposed solution to the overappropriation. Concerning a future crisis he said, "It's not going to happen for a number of years. The reservoirs are full. The wet cycle we're in now could last." [14]

The North American Water and Power Alliance (NAWAPA), a private group with headquarters in southern California, proposed dams in Alaska, Canada, and the Rockies, including a reservoir five hundred miles long and a colossal scheme with tunnels, canals, and lifts to shunt water to thirty-three states. Congressman Jim Wright wrote,

> This dream is, admittedly, both grandiose and visionary. However, the nation was built by visionaries. There have been some disturbing indications in recent years that we may have lost some of our capacity for dreaming and acting in those areas concerning our survival upon this earth. We must recapture that capability. . . . NAWAPA has an almost limitless potential if we possess the courage and the foresight to grasp it. [15]

Wright was Congress's majority leader in 1985.

Should we divert wild rivers for Sun Belt growth while ignoring other ways to avoid shortages? President Carter said, "We must face the prospect of changing our basic ways of living. This change will either be made on our own initiative in a planned and rational way, or forced on us with chaos and suffering by the inexorable laws of nature." To give up the search for new dams was once thought to mean locking up the desert cities, inflating food costs beyond family budgets, and surrendering to the next flood. Some people, including President Reagan, argue that cutting back on the use of water and energy lowers the standard of living, but others maintain that the standard of living would be lowered more if the Grand Canyon were dammed or the Columbia sucked south to Texas. How can needs be met without losing too much in the process of watering crops, turning turbines, or pushing barges?

THE OTHER FUTURE

In *Strategies of American Water Management,* Gilbert White pointed out that multiple use — embraced in river development since the 1930s — has not been accompanied by multiple means; instead of looking at different solutions to a water problem, the development agencies saw only more dams. Alternatives were ignored because contractors and engineers pushed for controversial construction, projects were proffered as panaceas in the wake of flood disasters, few precedents existed for alternatives, the large-dams-versus-small-dams argument preempted discussion of important issues, and, most important, no agency held the responsibility for address-ing whole problems.[16] White and others argued that nonstructural solutions — ones not requiring a dam or a channel — may be cheaper, more effective, faster to build, reversible, and less destructive. Senate Document 97 of 1969 called for consideration of nonstructural alternatives, but it resulted in little action.

People turned to the technological fix to delay reform, but following recent droughts, boosters of development attracted fewer followers. Some talked of Auburn and Tocks Island dams, but many people were resigned to the fact that the big projects were too costly and that alternatives were within reach. In 1977 Amory Lovins wrote that "soft path technologies" for energy development are "not vague, mushy, speculative, or ephemeral, but rather flexible, resilient, sustainable, and benign," and public accept-ance of this idea helped to prepare the way for alternatives in water devel-opment.

Growing evidence shows that most water needs can be met without costly and destructive new projects. Alternatives are available. Brent Black-welder wrote, "The best way to dispel the suspicion that conservationists want to return the country to the Stone Age by opposing water resource development projects is to consider some of the superb alternatives we have proposed to traditional dam building, canal digging and stream channeliza-tion."

KEEPING DRY

Nonstructural supporters argued that we have done enough to keep floods away from people. People should also stay away from floods. House Document 89-465 of August 1966 stated, "Flood damages result from acts of men. Those who occupy the flood plain should be responsible for the results of their action." Locating new development above the floodplain is the key nonstructural solution. Through zoning, municipalities can minimize construction on lands expected to flood once every hundred years. Farms, yards, parks, and other kinds of open space can be encouraged.

The Tennessee Valley Authority helped local governments to manage floodplains, and by 1964, 38 of 150 communities had adopted land use regulations.[17] But such management was the exception, and few other communities restricted development. In 1966 President Johnson issued an executive order that the Army Corps of Engineers encourage proper land use on the floodplain. Seeking to reduce disaster relief, Congress passed the Federal Flood Insurance Program in 1968, offering subsidized flood insurance to residents in municipalities with floodplain regulations. Even with this incentive, however, few communities zoned land or required flood proofing of new buildings. During America's most damaging flood, caused by Hurricane Agnes in 1972, only two residents in heavily hit Wilkes-Barre, Pennsylvania, were insured. Congress strengthened the program in 1973, denying federally guaranteed mortgages unless buildings are insured, thus requiring floodplain regulations for most real estate sales. Though the standards and enforcement were weak and do not eliminate riverfront construction, the program forced thousands of municipalities to regulate development. Nearly half of the money paid to flood victims is a subsidy, but program supporters argue that this is better than the giveaway of disaster relief. In several states, including Wisconsin, zoning is effective because mandatory state standards exist.

The government can buy the floodplain instead of buying upstream areas for reservoirs. Citizen or planning agencies proposed greenbelts for the Sangamon River in Illinois and the Current in Missouri. Along Tennessee's Duck River, acquisition of key parcels of the floodplain would be much cheaper than buying the reservoir area and building the dam. In opposing LaFarge Dam on the Kickapoo River, Senator Gaylord Nelson supported relocation and park development because the $50-million dam would protect property assessed at only $25 million. Some redevelopment programs have moved buildings to higher ground, as in Rapid City, South Dakota.

In a case in which the University of Washington's Office of Environmental Mediation brought opposing groups together to compromise, Washington's Middle Fork of the Snoqualmie was saved. Instead of damming some of the most spectacular river scenery in America, zoning was adopted, levees were proposed, and a North Fork dam was studied.

As an alternative to channelization of small streams, George Palmiter of Montpelier, Ohio, perfected techniques that use only chain saws and hand tools to make strategic changes that cause floodwaters to "clean out" the stream. At one-tenth the cost of bulldozer channelization, the Palmiter method was found to work better and require less maintenance,[18] all without environmental damage. Hired by local governments and landowners, Palmiter and his son are now exporting their process throughout the Midwest.

In urban areas, local flooding has been reduced by means of porous pavement on parking lots, dry wells that absorb runoff, and ponds for storm water. Warning systems by county governments and evacuation plans by industries have cut losses.

Local governments often ignored nonstructural flood control because they would have to pay for it, whereas the army corps builds dams at no local expense. Then the Water Resources Development Act of 1974 authorized cost sharing for some nonstructural solutions and required federal agencies to consider these alternatives. On the South Fork of the Platte near Denver, the corps found that it would be cheaper to buy the floodplain than to channelize. A similar project at Indian Bend Wash in Arizona received a distinguished engineering award from the American Society of Civil Engineers. Along the Charles River above Boston, the corps bought wetlands to avoid the increased runoff from urbanization, and flood damage has been reduced by an estimated $17 million a year. But the Office of Management and Budget blocked most nonstructural programs, which in 1982 accounted for only $15 million in a $3.5-billion water development budget.

HARMLESS POWER

Energy became the issue of the 1970s, each source of power promising more trouble than the last. Faced with political barricades on Arabian oil, the Trans-Alaska Pipeline, Three Mile Island, strip mining and acid rain from coal, and oil shale devastation, hydropower looked harmless to many. Then studies by Amory Lovins and the Ford Foundation showed that rivers do not need to be dammed for electricity. In *Soft Energy Paths,* Lovins documented the potential for stretching existing supplies and for benign sources such as the sun and wind. A Ford Foundation study concluded that "it could well be technically and economically feasible to achieve stability in energy consumption while continuing economic growth." The Council on Environmental Quality stated that conservation and soft paths can meet most new energy needs by the year 2000, and the Joint Economics Committee of Congress reported that energy conservation requires only one-fifth the costs of new generation.

To save energy means to save rivers from hydroelectric dams. In central Arizona, where Grand Canyon dams were proposed for hydropower, air conditioners accounted for up to one-third of energy consumed during hot months.[19] In the hydropower-dependent Northwest, a Skidmore, Owings, and Merrill study found that the average home could be made about 50 percent more efficient in electrical use.[20] The California Resources Agency found that the New Melones Dam would yield only one-sixteenth the amount of energy that would be saved if Californians properly inflated their tires, one-thirteenth the energy saved if they slowed down to 55 miles per hour, and one-eleventh the energy saved if they tuned their car engines.[21]

In the 1980s, people are verifying that we may be able to avoid all of the worst energy development options, including new dams. Americans reduced energy consumption by 2.2 percent in 1981.

Most new hydroelectric dams are for peaking power, generating electricity only a few hours a day. "Peaking demands are the easiest kind to alleviate," said Laura King, energy specialist for the Natural Resources Defense Council. Sacramento had intended to buy power from new dams proposed on the North Fork of the Stanislaus, but instead it launched a peak-load management program: on hot afternoons the power company transmits a signal to devices wired to air conditioners, shutting them down for ten minutes and, if done every hour, cutting demands by one-sixth. Additional savings can result through higher rates at peak hours, the rescheduling of industrial processes, and nighttime pumping of irrigation and city water supplies. Tests in three California cities indicated that management can reduce peak needs by 10 to 20 percent.

Hydroelectricity can be produced without destroying more streams. The Ohio River is continuously dammed for 981 miles. Hydraulically it is comparable to the Rhône of France, but hydroelectrically it is not; the Rhône generates 3,000 megawatts, the Ohio 180. Generators on this industrialized waterway would raise few objections.

Today only 3 percent of the major dams in the United States are used for hydropower. However, studies undertaken by the Army Corps of Engineers indicate that 5,162 existing small dams could yield 5,691 megawatts, equal to six nuclear power plants. Although even small generators at existing dams can dry up riverbeds if diversions are built, at many sites the impacts would be small. Municipal water lines and irrigation canals are a harmless source of power. In 1979, a 550-kilowatt generator was built on an irrigation canal in the San Joaquin Valley of California. The project's engineering firm estimated that 2,000 megawatts were available from similar sites in California.

MULTIPLE MEANS

Instead of new barge canals, Congressman Robert Edgar and others maintained that we should take better care of the locks and dams already built. Whereas the Tennessee-Tombigbee Waterway will duplicate a route to the Gulf of Mexico, existing locks and dams on the Ohio, Monongahela, and Mississippi grow obsolete. The Environmental Policy Center called for rehabilitation of railroads, since the tracks already exist.

Recreation may be the easiest of all needs to meet without dams. Just use the rivers. River recreation boomed through the 1970s, while flatwater recreation did not, yet the country has only sixty-six major protected national rivers, compared to fifty thousand large reservoirs. River parks were developed as alternatives to dams along the Delaware, Current, Buffalo, and Big South Fork of the Cumberland. In 1980 the WRC ranked the preservation of free-flowing streams as a high recreation priority in 73 of 106 subregions; protecting floodplains and wetlands was another priority — more flatwater was not even mentioned as a need.

Like dams, forests hold rainfall and release it slowly to streams, resulting in less flooding after heavy storms and in higher flows during droughts. Hydrologist Norman Curtis found that a forest of mature maple trees stored twelve inches of rain during a daylong storm, whereas open land held only three and one-half inches. Instead of dams, watershed management was New York's alternative in 1885 when the Adirondack Forest Preserve, including twenty thousand miles of streams, was created to preserve forests for protection of Hudson River supplies to the Erie Canal and New York City. The Weeks Act of 1911 called for federal acquisition of eastern national forests to protect navigable streams.[22]

Less irrigation may be needed if productive land could be saved in the rainy East, Midwest, and South, where three million acres of farms are urbanized each year. Different crops consuming less water can be grown in drylands. Grading equipment guided by lasers can level fields precisely to avoid excess flooding of low spots. Desalting plants using reverse osmosis to clean agricultural wastewater can make it usable again. The California

Department of Water Resources estimated that treatment costs for reused water averaged $150 an acre-foot, compared to $175 to $245 for new dams.

STRETCHING WHAT WE HAVE

Conservation of water can save vast amounts and stretch supplies far into the future. In traditional western irrigation, conservation means controlling the flow of water; water is "conserved" if it is impounded. But to most people, conserving water means using less. Cutting demands in half can effectively double the supply of water.

Because agriculture uses 81 percent of water consumed, most conservation plans begin here. The Soil Conservation Service reported that farm irrigation efficiency is only 53 percent.[23] In 1976 the GAO found that half the irrigation water was wasted and that efficiency reached only 44 percent on farms supplied by the Bureau of Reclamation. The office reported, "Irrigation practices have not changed appreciably in the past three decades even though irrigation science and technology have made substantial advances." The California Department of Water Resources found a typical loss of 25 percent between reservoir and farm, and the USGS reported that unlined and uncovered canals lose 16 percent of their water.

Spray irrigation requires far less water than is used in the prevalent open ditch systems (sometimes one-sixth the amount), and drip irrigation, where hoses drip water slowly at the plants' roots, requires even less. Spray systems, however, need more energy for pumping, and many crops cannot be served by drip systems, which are expensive to install. Reducing the amount of water can sometimes increase crop yields: in Israel 9.5 tons of melons were grown with spray irrigation, 17 tons with drip systems.[24] The Bureau of Reclamation's Irrigation Management Service offered advice that increased crop yields 16 percent while cutting water use 15 percent. Other advantages of using less water are reduced fertilizer needs and fewer drainage problems. Funding for irrigation efficiency is less than 1 percent of the water resources money spent by the departments of interior and agriculture. In one year, the Irrigation Management Service helped farmers holding only 2 percent of California's irrigated lands.[25]

Some conservation measures will be adopted only after laws are reformed. Under the use-it-or-lose-it doctrine of the West, a farmer who curbs waste may forgo his right to the water in future years. But most reform will happen through simple economics. When the government stops subsidizing waste, farmers will respond. Higher prices for water will encourage conservation. Some figures indicate that increasing irrigation supplies through conservation will require one-tenth the cost of new dams.

Through a plan originally proposed by the Environmental Defense Fund, the Metropolitan Water District of Southern California may finance conservation facilities for the Imperial Irrigation District in exchange for the water that would be saved. This could yield about four hundred thousand acre-feet of Colorado River supplies—enough for two million people—for much less than new dams would cost.

Manufacturing and energy consume the second-largest volume of water. Now, because of the Clean Water Act, industries are recycling supplies. A Kaiser steel plant at Fontana, California, uses about 3 percent of the water that an average plant uses. Through recirculation, a steel plant in Maine cut use to one-tenth its earlier amount.[26]

The USGS estimated waste from public water systems at 20 percent. A Rand study stated that New York City could save 150 million gallons per day (gpd) if it only repaired leaks in water mains. In Boston, where only a third of the system's water reaches the taps, repairs in 260 miles of pipes reduced leakage to 2 percent.[27] By eliminating illegal fire hydrant use and cutting other waste, Philadelphia reduced peak demand by 200 million gpd.

In six large cities and many smaller ones, residential water is not metered, and flat-rate customers use up to two times the normal amount. A Rand study estimated that metering would save about 200 million gpd in New York. The Environmental Protection Agency estimated that metering saves 20 to 30 percent.

Most water suppliers encourage waste by charging less money per gallon from bulk users, but during a drought, officials in Marin County, California, changed their rate structure to reward conservation. After a reasonable monthly amount of water was used, the rate jumped from $1.22 to $10 per 100 cubic feet. With other methods, this reduced use by 75 percent. Montgomery County, Maryland, reduced withdrawals by charging large users more. Tucson, Arizona, cut use 30 percent through a 17 percent rate increase along with public education and forty thousand home kits for the retrofitting of plumbing fixtures.[28]

Reduced consumption also means sewage treatment savings. The New England Interstate Water Pollution Control Commission estimated that water conservation can cut sewer construction costs 5 percent or more and can add twenty years to the life of sewers and treatment plants.[29]

Although conservation can extend supplies in the Southwest, population growth will probably require that farmlands be retired so that the irrigation water can go to cities instead. Tucson has already bought farmers' water rights. Will this be enough, or will controls on migration someday be needed to limit population in arid lands? Arizona congressman John Rhodes said, "People from the congested East and elsewhere are attracted to Arizona. There is no way Arizona could keep them out, even if it wanted to. Americans have a right to live wherever they want." [30] Regulations will not stop people from moving, but the costs of water may. Elimination of subsidies would discourage new industry, energy development, and agriculture, leaving fewer reasons for people to move to the desert.

Even though it accounts for less than 10 percent of water withdrawals, home use of water is the only kind individuals can easily reduce. Forty-five percent of home water is for the toilet, 30 percent for baths and showers. In dry areas, outdoor watering takes 44 percent of domestic supplies.

The California Department of Water Resources found that saving water can lower home utility bills by $200 a year, most of the savings resulting from reduced hot water. Shower fixtures that increase pressure can save 15 percent of water used; toilet dams that displace some of the water in the tank can save 20 percent. Water use can be cut by 55 percent in new houses and 43 percent in existing ones. [31]

Outdoors, careful sprinkling and less water consumptive plant species can lead to water savings of up to 60 percent. New plumbing fixtures costing only $12 per house can save 38 to 68 percent of domestic water. The benefits outweigh costs by at least 19–1—a claim that can be made for no dam. New technology can further increase savings. Dual water systems that separate and recirculate gray water, such as laundry waste, allow normal living on spartan supplies.

Due to rising costs and public consciousness, electric use decreased in the early 1980s, and the same could happen with our use of water. The evidence shows that people can save water and still live efficiently and comfortably. Brent Blackwelder said, "There are two aspects to conservation: efficiency and change in lifestyle. I believe in both, but efficiency alone can solve shortages for a long time. Europeans use much less water than we do, and no one accuses them of being backward or of having a Third World standard of living."

Bob Teeters of the Army Corps of Engineers said, "Water conservation is the significant reform that is persisting from the Carter administration." Being a management rather than a construction program, conservation costs less than new dams but creates more employment. The Department of Agriculture estimated that nearly eighty thousand jobs could be required to develop conservation potential in California alone.

Addiction to the obsolete will be abandoned slowly; as Mark Twain wrote, "Habit is habit, and not to be flung out of the window by any man, but coaxed downstairs one step at a time." But changes can be made; there is no need to rely on the dam-it-up approach that has dominated water development through most of our nation's history. Will the changes come soon enough? Even with the movement to save rivers, the national rivers system, the beginnings of political reform, and the knowledge of alternatives, many more rivers could be lost.

STILL ENDANGERED

Despite river protection and the changing politics, hundreds of federal water projects remain authorized and hundreds of private ones are proposed. (See the appendixes for a list of threatened rivers and a narrative about some of the most important projects.) While some people say that the age of big dam building is over, congressional bills could revive Grand Canyon dams and the Cross Florida Barge Canal. The Bureau of Reclamation seeks nonfederal financing for Auburn Dam. Local congressmen, still steadfast for development, block deauthorization of dams on Wisconsin's Kickapoo River and Indiana's Wildcat Creek. With the first months of drought Philadelphians once again praise the Tocks Island proposal, and each new flood revives a clamor for Keating Dam on the West Branch of the Susquehanna. If history is a guide, consider New Melones Dam. The army corps labeled it "semideauthorized" during the Eisenhower era — which was similar to the Reagan years in terms of water development. As soon as the politics changed, New Melones was built. Dozens of proposals, now shelved, could be dusted off again.

A modern Gold Rush for hydroelectric dams seemed to be imminent in the early 1980s. Large projects born during the 1973 oil embargo and small ones capitalizing on incentives of the Public Utility Regulatory Policies Act of 1978 were proposed in all river and mountain regions. In 1982 a drop in oil prices eased the dam-building pressure, but some analysts predict climbing prices again.

Cost sharing of government dams is regarded by economists, environmentalists, and conservatives as a way to rein the flow of federal dollars, under the theory that states now welcoming federal largesse will reconsider before throwing their own money away. But some state governments see dams as worth the cost. California has spent many millions on water development. Alaska intends to spend oil revenues building Susitna River dams, Wyoming plans water projects for more energy development, and Utah believes dams to be essential for growth.

The specter of water shortage remains. Through conservation, supplies can be stretched unexpectedly far, yet the drive for new development does not die. With southern California losing its extra Colorado River allotment, and with court rulings that could restrict Los Angeles's pumping of water from Owens Valley, a plan to bend northern California's rivers to the south might be resurrected. A day of reckoning approaches when southwesterners using the Colorado River must change their ways or take water from the Northwest. And in this long-term future, suppose people emigrate toward the water instead of toward today's target of sunshine? Will the Northwest house the Phoenix of the future? Will the people in Oregon, so opposed to sending their water south, rather have Los Angeles in their lap? Will the Salmon of Idaho — the longest undammed river outside Alaska — be ripe for hydroelectric development? And will people's return to the rainy East bring the damming of the last wild rivers scattered like rare jewels between high green ridges of the Appalachians?

CHAPTER TEN

The Last Wealth

To destroy a dam and turn a river free, a ceremony was held in northern Idaho. Governor Cecil Andrus detonated an explosion that fatally cracked the Washington Water Power Dam, and six miles of the Clearwater River ran free once more.[1] And on California's Mad River, Sweesey Dam, built in 1938, was blasted away in 1970. Through the concrete ruins the river reclaims its channel, and Chinook salmon now spawn upstream from the dam's wreckage. All over the country small dams have given way to renewed flows of the rivers. In Minnesota alone, a thousand dams have been washed out or destroyed (fifteen hundred remain).[2]

In his pathbreaking book about the salmon, Anthony Netboy wrote, "If society in its wisdom some day decides that food and game fishes are more valuable to the nation than electricity (which can be generated elsewhere), some of the territory once inhabited by the salmon and steelhead will be returned to them."[3]

More dams will be destroyed, and long before they are gone, thousands will be useless or worse. In 1971 Gilbert White wrote, "Few who contemplate the bleak inaction of a railroad station which 50 years before was bustling with traffic . . . can escape at least a fleeting question as to whether the noble dams now being planned for 50 to 100 years ahead may not be similarly obsolete before those horizons are reached."[4]

Many dams are unsafe, such as the ones at Johnstown, Pennsylvania, and Buffalo Creek, West Virginia, that burst and killed thousands of people. Nationwide, 350 major dam failures have occurred, most of them at privately owned sites.[5] In Pennsylvania alone, 151 dams are unsafe, including yet another one near Johnstown.

To avoid disasters, money must be spent. Built in 1914, Coon Rapids Dam on the Mississippi was sold to the Hennepin County Park Reserve District by the Northern States Power Company, which donated $800,000 for repairs, but the county's cost was $2.4 million. That is one small example. What will be the costs of safety below large dams?

In 1983 the Bureau of Reclamation reported that forty-four of its dams needed repairs. Water seeps in ominous dark patches through the concrete face of Shasta Dam — the 560-foot-high centerpiece of the Central Valley Project in California — and landslides plague the abutment of Trinity Dam. In a *Sacramento Bee* interview, the bureau's David Prosser said, "Until recently, we never had to deal with a question like how much longer could a dam safely stand before we had to do something to it. . . . We haven't thought things like a dam's life to be applicable." [6]

"We're trying to get away from the idea that old means unsafe," said Bob Teeters of the Army Corps of Engineers. "With proper maintenance, dams can be safe forever." [7]

Whether or not dams are maintained, every reservoir is filling with silt washed in by the river from up above. All of those flooded canyons and valleys, from John Muir's Hetch Hetchy to Mark Dubois's Stanislaus, are doomed to encasement in mud. At Lake Austin in Texas, silt decreased storage capacity by 96 percent in thirteen years. Mud in the corps's Fishtrap Dam in Kentucky was expected to reduce flood control capacity in ten years. [8] Little Pine Creek Dam in Pennsylvania was silt-filled in only thirty years. Government hydrologists say that Lake Powell will be full of silt in three hundred years or less, and many people think that this "gem of the Colorado" will be a brown quagmire in only a century. Federal reservoirs are designed with space for silt accumulation during the expected one-hundred-year life of the project, but what happens after that? "I don't think anybody has bothered to think about it," Bob Teeters said. "There are more pressing problems. Obsolescence of locks, for example, is a bigger concern."

In 1983 Stewart Udall said, "Glen Canyon is probably the most beautiful man-made lake in the world, but it's going to fill up with silt in a hundred years, and what is the judgment of posterity then? That's the real down side of the big dams — the rivers are not renewable." Flowing water is symbolic of renewable resources, but the damming of a river is the ultimate in the consumption of land.

Someday the reservoirs will be "dry" dams — mud flats with a river winding through, then spilling over the aged dam. And in time, the dams themselves will be worn by the river and washed away. As Henry David

Thoreau wrote of a hydropower dam built in 1847, "Perchance after a thousand years . . . nature will have leveled the Bellerica Dam, and the Lowell factories, and the Grass-ground [Concord] River will run clear again."

The blasting of the dam on Idaho's Clearwater River was a ceremony marking a new day for a revitalized river. And it may signify a coming age when people will recognize the uselessness of some dams and quicken the earth's process of destroying them.

For eighty years the attitude has been that we can bring in all the water we want simply by invoking enough technology and money. This belief had a religious fervor and approached the patriotic in moving people to act. That era is over, however, killed in part by costs but also accompanied by the undercurrent of a new religion that recognizes the importance of the natural world and of a new patriotism that sees the rivers as a part of America that is worth keeping.

Dams are with us for generations to come, but the National Water Commission reported in 1973 that the Bureau of Reclamation had nearly exhausted new justifiable projects. As deputy director of water resources for California, Jerry Meral wrote that the building of more dams is not attractive because the better sites are developed, in-stream needs are recognized, economic and environmental damage is too great, people want to keep water where it is instead of exporting it, and government funding will not keep up with costs. President Carter and Interior Secretary Andrus declared that the age of big dam building was over, and from the opposite political pole, President Reagan's commissioner of reclamation Robert Broadbent said, "I don't know that there are any major dams left except Auburn."

Bob Teeters of the army corps said, "It's my prediction that in five or ten years, water projects will be approved like parks used to be — one at a time. The irony is that now we have omnibus parks bills that designate many parks at once."

Unconvinced that the dam-building era is over, Utah governor Scott Matheson said in 1979, "By no means have we exhausted the need to develop water." [9] Just as the forties and fifties were the era for flood control dams, the eighties are the era for hydropower. And crises that arise overnight can jar resource policies from one extreme to another: Dickey-Lincoln dams on the St. John River in Maine had been nearly forgotten when the oil embargo of 1973 set the dam builders in motion. Politics in faraway Arabia almost resulted in the building of those two dams, and other crises could reactivate old threats on many rivers. When will the next push for

dams be? Maybe when eastern cities that have not patched leaks face
another drought, or when the Sun Belt civilization sprawls to its thirsty
limits of growth. River conservationists may find that in stopping federal
dams in the 1970s, they have simply opened the sites for corporate powers
to preempt public water for single-purpose projects like hydropower and
oil shale development. If lasting protection is not agreed on, old proposals
could be reactivated. Look at the past: the corps called New Melones Dam
"semideauthorized," then they built it. Is this the twilight to an era of
bulldozing, or will the powerful interests that profit so greatly by controlling the flow of water simply wait for new opportunities?

Despite the uncertainties, Brent Blackwelder looks beyond the dam-
and-canal-stopping work and sees new goals: groundwater management,
water conservation, and, perhaps most important, preventing disastrous
dams in other countries.

Much has been written about High Aswan Dam on Egypt's Nile. The
dam created hydropower and irrigation benefits, but it also caused the loss
of beneficial flooding and made farmers dependent on petroleum-based
fertilizers. It caused erosion and salinization of the rich Nile Delta, the
infection of millions of people with blood flukes that thrive because of the
reservoir, the leaking of one-third of the water through the bedrock, and
the devastation of Mediterranean fisheries.[10] Similar environmental, public
health, and economic catastrophes plague undeveloped countries around
the globe. One hundred thousand people will be forced from homes by a
reservoir in the Ivory Coast.[11] Thirty major dams are under construction in
India. One proposal in that country would relocate 1.4 million people.
Tehri Dam, sixth largest in the world, was planned for a life of only forty
years and may silt up more rapidly. On tributaries of the Amazon, Brazil
plans a series of dams that would flood an area the size of Montana. In the
Philippines, leaders of antidam forces were murdered, but the Chico
Project was finally stopped.

Funding for dams in undeveloped countries comes from the United
States and United States–supported organizations such as the World Bank.
The Army Corps of Engineers, Bureau of Reclamation, and American
corporations boast of their roles in exporting American dam-building technology.

Indians in Alberta are fighting hydroelectric projects on the Slave River.
At the 1983 conference of the American Rivers Conservation Council,
Chief Clifford Freeman said, "When they kill the environment, they will kill
us, because we are a part of it. The dam is just for money. After these dams,
there will be nothing left but suicides and alcohol problems. We can't allow

a government that's supposed to be ours to do this. We will fight with our lives against this, because if we don't fight, we will be giving our lives anyway."

In Tasmania, the fight over Gordon-below-Franklin Dam became the largest conservation issue in Australian history: two thousand demonstrators who blocked bulldozers were arrested in 1983, and fifteen thousand people demonstrated in Melbourne. An election brought proriver leaders to office, halting the dam.[12]

In northern Norway, one hundred hydroelectric dams have been built, but a proposal on the Alta River — the last large undammed stream — was fought by the native Sami, or Laplanders. After many appeals that their land and culture be spared, one thousand people staged a sit-down, some chained to rocks in midwinter arctic conditions. After six weeks, a police force of six hundred removed the demonstrators. The dams are being built.

A Soviet Union plan to divert the Yenisei and Ob rivers for irrigation would greatly reduce the freshwater entering the Arctic Ocean, possibly altering the ocean's salinity balance, the ice cap, and the world climate.[13]

Development proposals are rampant in many countries, but in the United States a new view is emerging with regard to rivers and dams. We are learning how to use our rivers without consuming them — to meet needs while leaving rivers the way they are.

The need for legal protection of waterways in wild and scenic rivers systems may seem less urgent now that many dam proposals have been stopped, but with less pressure to develop, long-term protection for rivers may now be possible where it was not possible before. The wild and scenic rivers systems could be the major natural areas program of the future, especially if the well-rounded constituency of river conservationists, established environmental groups, fishermen, landowners, and people along urban rivers join together.

Brent Blackwelder said, "If we don't have reforms and new policies on all aspects of water development, it will be like past years when we were playing defense all the time." It is those reforms that conservationists, a few congressmen such as Bob Edgar, and others work for today.

Is it too much to ask, too much to work for, too much to expect, that the special rivers — the best natural places and homelands — can be saved so that people can be saved from the killing boredom, the stifling artificiality, the loneliness of life without wild creatures, the dread of a world so lopsidedly controlled by the institutions dedicated to making money? There is a new attitude about rivers, but to make the change permanent will require the energy of all those affected by the loss of special river places: park and wilderness enthusiasts, anglers, landowners, naturalists and ecologists, river runners, people who just like rivers, and those who find a metaphysical and spiritual power in the free-flowing water.

To save rivers demands the enthusiasm of John Muir, the forethought of John Craighead, the prose of Wallace Stegner, the dedication of Mark Dubois, the calculations of Jerry Meral, the organization of Brent Blackwelder, the drive of David Brower, the public attention of William O. Douglas and Richard Chamberlain, the old political style of John Saylor, and the new style of Bob Edgar. No tactics are outdated, and none can be ignored. Personal explorations, conversations with friends, articles and press releases, river trips for politicians, letters to congressmen, lobbyists in Washington, coalitions of everyone affected by the changes, demonstrations, direct action, campaigning and voting — all are needed. All may be needed forever, because, even at our best, we save rivers only for a while. Then they need saving again.

River conservationists have grown into positions of influence, arguing that there are many kinds of values in the free-flowing rivers. By 1985 the opposition to dams and other destructive projects had matured through eighty years, involving many people, regions, and motives, all building toward greater awareness of rivers. The national and state wild and scenic rivers systems have been started. Water policy reforms have begun, and the politics of pork barrel have been shaken. Yet the threats to rivers will increase again as resources become more scarce and as new pressures grow to squeeze the last wealth from the rivers that remain.

Sources

Much of the information in *Endangered Rivers and the Conservation Movement* was taken from printed sources. Many sources are identified within the text itself and are not repeated here. In the source notes I have mainly cited sources that are readily available. Dozens of government documents were also used, including reports by the Army Corps of Engineers printed each year for every state, project reports by the corps, state and annual reports by the Bureau of Reclamation, many brochures by the federal dam-building agencies, environmental impact statements, testimony from hearings, wild and scenic river studies, and General Accounting Office reports. Most of these are not cited in the notes but can be found in large libraries or through the public information staffs of the agencies.

Following numbered notes to the chapters, other sources relevant to topics treated in a given chapter are listed.

Hundreds of magazines, bulletins, and newsletters were also consulted. Dealing specifically with water and the environment are *American Forests* by the American Forestry Association, *American Rivers* by the American Rivers Conservation Council, *Audubon* by the National Audubon Society, *Headwaters* by Friends of the River, *National Parks* by the National Parks and Conservation Association, *National Wildlife* by the National Wildlife Federation, *Not Man Apart* by Friends of the Earth, *Outdoor America* by the Izaak Walton League, *Sierra* by the Sierra Club, *Trout* by Trout Unlimited, *Trends* by the National Park Service, *Water Spectrum* by the Army Corps of Engineers, and *Wilderness* by the Wilderness Society. Some of these are available in large libraries; old issues of some publications may be found only at the organizations' headquarters. Other magazines included *Atlantic, Canoe, Collier's, Conservationist, Forbes, GEO, Harper's, National Geographic, Newsweek, Outdoor Life, Plateau, Sports Afield, Time, U.S. News and World Report,* and *Western Wildlands.* Major newspapers consulted include the *New York Times, Washington Post, Los Angeles Times,* and *Sacramento Bee.* The files of the American Rivers Conservation Council and the Environmental Policy Center were especially helpful. Files of the Army Corps of Engineers and National Park Service were also used.

I also drew heavily from more than a hundred interviews and from visits during the last five years to most of the rivers in the book. Interviews are listed after other sources.

CHAPTER 2   A DELICATE BALANCE

1. Marie Morisawa, *Streams: Their Dynamics and Morphology* (New York: McGraw-Hill, 1968).

2. William H. Amos, *The Infinite River* (New York: Ballantine, 1970).

3. H. B. N. Hynes, *The Ecology of Running Waters* (Toronto: University of Toronto Press, 1970).

4. Charles M. Clusen, ed., *Engineering a Victory for Our Environment* (San Francisco: Sierra Club, 1973).

5. Oral Bullard, *Crisis on the Columbia* (Portland, Oreg.: Touchstone Press, 1968).

6. Army Corps of Engineers, *The Corps Cares About Fish* (Seattle: The Corps, North Pacific Division, 1982). Brochure.

7. Anthony Netboy, *The Salmon: Their Fight for Survival* (Boston: Houghton Mifflin, 1974).

8. Bruce Brown, *Mountain in the Clouds* (New York: Simon & Schuster, 1982).

9. Paul Bodin, *Are California's North Coast Rivers Really "Wasting Away to Sea"?* (Arcata, Calif.: Northcoast Environmental Center, 1982). Booklet.

10. Tim Palmer, *Youghiogheny: Appalachian River* (Pittsburgh, Pa.: University of Pittsburgh Press, 1984).

11. Department of the Interior, Bureau of Outdoor Recreation, *Outdoor Recreation: A Legacy for America* (Washington, D.C.: The Department, 1973).

OTHER SOURCES

Collins, Robert O., and Nash, Roderick. *The Big Drops*. San Francisco: Sierra Club Books, 1978.

Dunne, Thomas, and Leopold, Luna B. *Water in Environmental Planning*. San Francisco: W. H. Freeman, 1978.

Editors of Outdoor World. *Rivers of North America*. Waukesha, Wis.: Outdoor World, 1973.

Helfman, Elizabeth. *Rivers and Watersheds in America's Future*. New York: David McKay, 1965.

Hoyt, W. G., and Langbein, Walter B. *Floods*. Princeton: Princeton University Press, 1955.

Russell, Richard J. *River Plains and Sea Coasts*. Berkeley and Los Angeles: University of California Press, 1967.

Thomas, Bill. *American Rivers: A Natural History*. New York: Norton, 1978.

U.S. Forest Service, North Central Experiment Station. *Proceedings: River Recreation Management and Research Symposium*. St. Paul, Minn.: The Service, 1977.

White, Gilbert, ed. *Environmental Effects of Complex River Development*. Boulder, Colo.: Westview Press, 1977.

CHAPTER 3   CHANGING THE FLOW OF WATER

1. Gilbert White, *Strategies of American Water Management* (Ann Arbor: University of Michigan Press, 1971), 1.

2. Michael Robinson, *Water for the West* (Chicago: Public Works Historical Society, 1979), 2.

3. Albert N. Williams, *Water and Power* (New York: Duell, Sloan & Pearce, 1951), 10.

4. Norman Smith, *A History of Dams* (London: Peter Davies, 1971), 146.

5. Ibid., 145.

6. John M. Kauffmann, *Flow East* (New York: McGraw-Hill, 1973).

7. Anthony Netboy, *The Salmon: Their Fight for Survival* (Boston: Houghton Mifflin, 1974), 182.

8. Paul Shepard, *Man in the Landscape* (New York: Knopf, 1967), 141.

9. Daniel Boorstin, *The Americans: The Democratic Experience* (New York: Random House, 1973).

10. Ibid.

11. Barry Allen and Mina Hamilton Haefele, *In Defense of Rivers* (Delaware Valley Conservation Association, 1976), 115. Available from the American Rivers Conservation Council.

12. Western Writers of America, *Water Trails West* (New York: Avon, 1978).

13. Henry Nash Smith, *Virgin Land* (New York: Vintage Books, 1950), 181.

14. Pacific Northwest River Basins Commission, *Roll on Columbia* (Vancouver, Wash.: The Commission, about 1980). Brochure.

15. John Boslough, "Rationing a River," *Science* 81 (June 1981): 26.

16. Robinson, *Water for the West*.

17. Smith, *Virgin Land*, 209.

18. Robinson, *Water for the West*, 12.

19. Wallace Stegner and Page Stegner, *American Places* (New York: Greenwich House, 1983), 14.

20. Fred Powledge, *Water* (New York: Farrar, Straus & Giroux, 1982), 279.

21. Charles R. Goldman and James McEvoy III, *Environmental Quality and Water Development* (San Francisco: W. H. Freeman, 1973), 43.

22. Robinson, *Water for the West*, 9.

23. W. Turrentine Jackson and Stephen D. Mikesell, *The Stanislaus River Drainage Basin and the New Melones Dam* (Davis, Calif.: California Water Resources Center, University of California, June 1979).

24. Raymond F. Dasmann, *The Destruction of California* (New York: Collier Books, 1966).

25. Army Corps of Engineers, *Historical Highlights of the Army Corps of Engineers* (Washington, D.C.: The Corps, 1973). Brochure.

26. Army Corps of Engineers, *The Headwaters District,* by Leland Johnson, (Pittsburgh, Pa.: The Corps, about 1979).

27. Beatrice Hort Holmes, *History of Federal Water Resources Programs and Policies, 1961–70* (Washington, D.C.: U.S. Department of Agriculture, 1979), 6.

28. Arthur Morgan, *Dams and Other Disasters* (Boston: Porter Sargent, 1971), 311.

29. Army Corps of Engineers, Youghiogheny River files, Army Corps of Engineers office, Pittsburgh, Pa.

30. Robert H. Haveman, *Water Resources Investment and the Public Interest* (Nashville, Tenn.: Vanderbilt University Press, 1965).

31. Thomas Y. Canby, "Water: Our Most Precious Resource," *National Geographic,* August 1980.

32. Bureau of Reclamation, *Hydropower* (Washington, D.C.: The Bureau, about 1980). Brochure.

33. Smith, *A History of Dams,* 59.

34. *Scholastic,* March 25, 1940.

35. Natural Resources Defense Council, newsletter, January 1978.

36. Federal Energy Regulatory Commission, *Water Power* (Washington, D.C.: The Commission, about 1980). Brochure.

37. "Water for Peace," *Department of State Bulletin,* September 26, 1966, 456–57.

38. Roy Gordon, "Engineering for the People: 200 Years of Army Public Works," *Military Engineer,* May/June 1976, 180–85.

39. Bureau of Reclamation, *Reclamation* (Washington, D.C.: The Bureau, 1975). Brochure.

40. Ibid.

41. Robinson, *Water for the West.*

42. William E. Warne, *The Bureau of Reclamation* (New York: Praeger, 1973).

43. Boslough, "Rationing A River," 26.

44. White, *Strategies of American Water Management.*

45. Peter Wiley and Robert Gottlieb, *Empires in the Sun* (New York: Avon, 1982), 88.

46. Holmes, *History of Federal Water Resources,* 53.

47. Kathleen K. Wiegner, "The Water Crisis: It's Almost Here," *Forbes,* August 20, 1979.

48. Bureau of Reclamation, *Reclamation.*

49. David F. Salisbury, "Water Fights: The West Goes to Court," *Christian Science Monitor,* March 1, 1979, 12–13.

50. Department of the Interior, Office of Audit and Investigation, *Review of the Central Valley Project, Bureau of Reclamation* (Washington, D.C.: The Department, January 1978).

51. Department of the Interior, press release, October 9, 1981.

52. Bureau of Reclamation, *Reclamation.*

53. Department of the Interior, Geological Survey, *Estimated Use of Water in the United States in 1980* (Alexandria, Va.: The Survey, 1983).

54. Frank Graham, Jr., *Man's Dominion: The Story of Conservation in America* (New York: M. Evans, 1971), 245.

55. Frank E. Smith, *The Politics of Conservation* (New York: Pantheon, 1966), 206.

56. Elmo Richardson, *Dams, Parks and Politics* (Lexington: University Press of Kentucky, 1973), 14.

57. Fred Powledge, "Can TVA Change Its Spots?" *Audubon,* March 1983, 61–75.

58. Powledge, *Water,* 84.

59. Luna B. Leopold and Thomas Maddock, *The Flood Control Controversy* (New York: Ronald Press, 1954), 88.

60. Thomas Y. Canby, "Water: Our Most Precious Resource," *National Geographic,* August 1980.

61. "The Browning of America," *Newsweek,* February 23, 1981, 26.

62. Larry Kohl, "Quebec's Northern Dynamo," *National Geographic,* March 1982.

63. Robinson, *Water for the West,* 83.

64. Arthur Maass, *Muddy Waters: The Army Engineers and the Nation's Rivers* (Cambridge: Harvard University Press, 1951), 214.

65. White, *Strategies of American Water Management.*

66. Samuel Hays, *Conservation and the Gospel of Efficiency* (New York: Atheneum, 1959), 114.

67. Holmes, *History of Federal Water Resources,* 62.

68. Goldman and McEvoy, *Environmental Quality and Water Development,* 56.

69. Richard D. Lamm and Michael McCarthy, *The Angry West* (Boston: Houghton Mifflin, 1982), 168.

70. "By a Damsite," *Time,* June 19, 1944, 79–80.

71. Canby, "Water."

72. Army Corps of Engineers, *National Waterways Study* (Washington, D.C.: The Corps, July 1981).

OTHER SOURCES

Chandler, William U. *The Myth of TVA.* Cambridge, Mass.: Ballinger, 1984.

Cullen, Allan H. *Rivers in Harness: The Story of Dams.* Philadelphia: Chilton Books, 1962.

Davis, Kenneth S. *River on the Rampage.* New York: Doubleday, 1953.

Degan, James P. "The Desert Shall Rejoice and Be Made to Blossom as the Rose." *The Living Wilderness,* Summer 1982.

Fradkin, Philip L. *A River No More.* New York: Knopf, 1981.

Hart, Henry C. *The Dark Missouri.* Madison: University of Wisconsin Press, 1957.

Kahrl, William L., ed. *California Water Atlas.* Los Altos, Calif.: William Kaufmann (dist.); Sacramento: Governor's Office of Planning and Research, 1979.

Owen, Marguerite. *The Tennessee Valley Authority.* New York: Praeger, 1973.

Stegner, Wallace. *Beyond the Hundredth Meridian.* Boston: Houghton Mifflin, 1953.

CHAPTER 4   THE BEGINNINGS OF RIVER
PROTECTION

1. Charles R. Goldman and James McEvoy III, *Environmental Quality and Water Development* (San Francisco: W. H. Freeman, 1973), 81.

2. James Mitchell Clarke, *The Life and Adventures of John Muir* (San Francisco: Sierra Club Books, 1979), 306.

3. Ibid., 304.

4. Frank Graham, Jr., *Man's Dominion: The Story of Conservation in America* (New York: M. Evans, 1971), 166.

5. Goldman and McEvoy, *Environmental Quality and Water Development,* 53.

6. Samuel Hays, interview with author, April 1979.

7. Frederick Haynes Newell, *Water Resources: Present and Future Uses* (New Haven: Yale University Press, 1920), 148.

8. Goldman and McEvoy, *Environmental Quality and Water Development,* 80.

9. Judson King, *The Conservation Fight: From Theodore Roosevelt to the Tennessee Valley Authority* (Washington, D.C.: Public Affairs Press, 1959), 17.

10. Ibid., 19.

11. Ibid, 14.

12. Department of the Interior, *Outdoor Recreation Action,* Spring 1977.

13. National Parks Association, newsletter, September 30, 1920.

14. Ibid., October 1923.

15. Edward James, ed., *Dictionary of American Biography* (New York: Scribner's, 1973).

16. National Parks Association, newsletter, June 1, 1920.

17. Ibid., December 1921.

18. "The Browning of America," *Newsweek,* February 23, 1981, 26.

19. George Laycock, *The Diligent Destroyers* (Garden City, N.Y.: Doubleday, 1970), 33.

20. Bruce Brown, *Mountain in the Clouds* (New York: Simon & Schuster, 1982) 95.

21. Army Corps of Engineers, *The U.S. Army Corps of Engineers and the Environmental Community: A History to 1969,* by Michael Robinson (Washington, D.C.: The Corps, 1982. Draft.

22. Ibid.

23. Marguerite Owen, *The Tennessee Valley Authority* (New York: Praeger, 1973), 91.

24. W. V. Howard, *Authority in TVA Land* (Kansas City, Mo.: Frank Glenn, 1948) 94.

25. Elmer T. Peterson, *Big-Dam Foolishness* (New York: Devin-Adair, 1954), 103.

26. Goldman and McEvoy, *Environmental Quality and Water Development,* 55.

27. Peterson, *Big-Dam Foolishness,* 62.

28. Paul Friggins, "The Battle of the Blue," *Farm Journal,* April 1953, 51.

29. Henry C. Hart, *The Dark Missouri* (Madison: University of Wisconsin Press, 1957), 147.

30. Martin Heuvelmans, *The River Killers* (Harrisburg, Pa.: Stackpole Books, 1974).

31. E. T. Scoyen, "Kilowatts in the Wilderness," *Sierra Club Bulletin* 37 (1952): 75–84.

32. Elmo Richardson, *Dams, Parks and Politics* (Lexington: University Press of Kentucky, 1973), 9.

33. National Parks Association, *National Parks,* October 1948.

34. Ibid.

35. *The Living Wilderness,* Summer 1948.

36. Richardson, *Dams, Parks and Politics,* 119.

37. Ibid, 123.

38. Ted Schad, interview with author, April 1983.

39. Richardson, *Dams, Parks and Politics,* 123.

40. Ibid, 66.

41. Frank Graham, Jr., "Dave Brower: Last of the Optimists?" *Audubon,* November 1982.

42. Peter Wiley and Robert Gottlieb, *Empires in the Sun* (New York: Avon, 1982), 288.

43. Paul Brooks, *Speaking for Nature* (San Francisco: Sierra Club Books, 1980), 250.

44. Bernard DeVoto, "Shall We Let Them Ruin Our National Parks?" *Saturday Evening Post,* July 22, 1950, 44.

45. Ibid., "The Easy Chair," *Harper's,* March 1954, 10–11; September 1954, 10–11; May 1955, 9.

46. "Are You for or Against the Echo Park Dam?" *Collier's,* February 1955.

47. Richardson, *Dams, Parks and Politics,* 139.

48. Wiley and Gottlieb, *Empires in the Sun,* 43.

49. Raymond Moley, "Pork, Unlimited," *Newsweek,* May 9, 1955, 108.

50. Brooks, *Speaking for Nature,* 250.

51. Roderick Nash, *Wilderness and the American Mind* (New Haven: Yale University Press, 1967), 213.

52. Richardson, *Dams, Parks and Politics,* 68.

53. Nash, *Wilderness and the American Mind,* 215.

54. Philip L. Fradkin, *A River No More* (New York: Knopf, 1981), 193.

55. *Congressional Record,* 84th Cong. 1st sess., vol. 101 (April 19, 1955), 4657.

56. John McPhee, *Encounters with the Archdruid* (New York: Farrar, Straus & Giroux, 1971), 165.

57. Brown, *Mountain in the Clouds,* 97.

58. A. Dan Tarlock, "Preservation of Scenic Rivers," *Kentucky Law Journal,* 1967, 762.

59. Alvin M. Josephy, Jr., "Cornplanter, Can You Swim?" *American Heritage,* December 1968, 4–9.

60. Arthur E. Morgan, *Dams and Other Disasters* (Boston: Porter Sargent, 1971), 321.

61. Ibid., 48.

62. John M. Kauffmann, *Flow East* (New York: McGraw-Hill, 1973).

63. Eliot Porter, *The Place No One Knew* (San Francisco: Sierra Club Books, 1963), 34.

64. *Congressional Record,* 85th Cong. 2d sess., February 29, 1956, 3619–21.

65. François Leydet, *Time and the River Flowing* (San Francisco: Sierra Club, 1964), 127.

66. Martin Litton, interview with author, April 1983.

67. Richard Leonard, interview with author, August 1984.

68. Verne Huser, "Rainbow in the Rock," *American Forests,* February 1974, 42.

69. Fradkin, *A River No More,* 197.

70. Leydet, *Time and the River Flowing,* 112.

71. Department of the Interior, Geological Survey, *Water Yield and Reservoir Storage in the United States,* Circular 409, by Walter B. Langbein (Washington, D.C.: The Department, 1959).

72. Leydet, *Time and the River Flowing,* 129.

73. Editorial, *Sierra Club Bulletin,* March 1965.

74. Leydet, *Time and the River Flowing,* 112.

75. Stewart Udall, interview with author, April 1983.

76. William K. Wyant, *Westward in Eden* (Berkeley and Los Angeles: University of California Press, 1982), 347.

77. Laycock, *The Diligent Destroyers,* 63.

78. Paul Brooks, *The Pursuit of Wilderness* (Boston: Houghton Mifflin, 1971), 82.

79. S. H. Spurr, "Rampart Dam: A Costly Gamble," *Audubon,* May/June 1966, 173.

80. *Pine Bluff Commercial,* February 13, 1972.

81. *Ozark Society Journal,* Autumn 1982.

OTHER SOURCES

Everhart, William C. *The National Park Service.* New York: Praeger, 1972.

Frank, Bernard, and Netboy, Anthony. *Water, Land, and People.* New York: Knopf, 1950.

Krutch, Joseph Wood. "Dam the Grand Canyon?" *Audubon,* September 1966.

League of Women Voters. *The Big Water Fight.* Brattleboro, Vt.: Stephen Green Press, 1966.

Moreell, Ben. *Our Nation's Water Resources: Policies and Politics.* Chicago: University of Chicago Law School, 1956.

Seaborg, Eric. "The Battle for Hetch Hetchy." *Sierra,* Nov./Dec. 1981, 61–65. (This and *Wilderness and the American Mind* by Roderick Nash are excellent sources regarding Hetch Hetchy.)

Stegner, Wallace, ed. *This Is Dinosaur: Echo Park Country and Its Magic Rivers.* New York: Knopf, 1955.

Udall, Stewart. *The Quiet Crisis.* New York: Avon, 1963.

"The Upper Hudson: Time for Decision." *Conservationist,* December 1968, 2–5.

INTERVIEWS

Harold Alexander, Arkansas Fish and Game Department

Frank Bell, canoeist, North Carolina

Bill Chandler, Environmental Policy Institute

Arthur Davis, Bureau of the Budget

Samuel Hays, professor of history, University of Pittsburgh

Richard Leonard, Sierra Club

Martin Litton, river outfitter

Jerry Meral, deputy director, California Department of Water Resources

Ted Schad, Bureau of Reclamation and other agencies

Elsie Spurgeon, resident, Confluence, Pa.

Claude Terry, river outfitter

Stewart Udall, secretary of the interior

John Varley, Fish and Wildlife Service, Yellowstone National Park

Edgar Wayburn, Sierra Club

CHAPTER 5   THE MOVEMENT TO SAVE RIVERS

1. Army Corps of Engineers, *The U.S. Army Corps of Engineers and the Environmental Community, 1969–1980,* by Jeffrey Stine (Washington, D.C.: The Corps, 1982). Draft.

2. "A Lawyer Answers the Technocrats," *Trial,* August/September 1969, 14.

3. Don G. Cullimore, "The Cassatot River . . . Another Legal Milestone," *American Forests,* May 1971, 8.

4. Beatrice Hort Holmes, *History of Federal Water Resources Programs and Policies, 1961–70* (Washington, D.C.: U.S. Department of Agriculture, 1979), 114.

5. "The Cross-Florida Boondoggle," *Enfo: A Publication of the Florida Conservation Foundation,* June 1974.

6. Bob Teeters, interview with author, March 1983.

7. Eugene H. Methvin, "The Fight to Save the Flint," *Reader's Digest,* August 1974.

8. Governor Jimmy Carter, *Statement on Spewrell Bluff Dam* (Atlanta: The Governor's Office, October 1, 1973).

9. Bruce Hannon and Julie Cannon, "The Corps Out-Engineered," *Sierra Club Bulletin,* August 1969.

10. Army Corps of Engineers, *The Corps and the Environmental Community.*

11. Chuck Hoffman, interview with author, March 1983.

12. "The GAO Released Its Long-awaited Report on the Proposed Red River Dam," *National Parks,* November 1975, 25.

13. "Fish v. Dams," *Time,* February 17, 1958, 88–89.

14. Brock Evans, "Success at Hells Canyon," *Sierra,* April 1976.

15. Brock Evans, interview with author, April 1983.

16. Verne Huser, "Will Hells Canyon Be Sold Down the River?" *American Forests,* June 1972, 12.

17. Evans, "Success at Hells Canyon."

18. Michael McCloskey; interview with author, March 1981.

19. Thomas Schoenbaum, *The New River Controversy* (Winston-Salem, N.C.: J. F. Blair), 1979.

20. Holmes, *History of Federal Water Resources,* 66.

21. Will Morgan, *The Effect of Federal Water Projects on Cultural Resources* (Washington, D.C.: Environmental Policy Institute, September 1977).

22. Harold A. Feiveson, Frank W. Sinden, and Robert H. Socolow, eds., *Boundaries of Analysis: An Inquiry into the Tocks Island Dam Controversy* (Cambridge, Mass.: Ballinger, 1976).

23. Pete duPont, "The Tocks Island Dam Fight," *Sierra,* July 1972, 13.

24. Peter Wiley and Robert Gottlieb, *Empires in the Sun* (New York: Avon, 1982), 179.

25. "The Indian Water Wars," *Newsweek,* June 13, 1983, 80–82.

26. House Committee on Government Operations, *Teton Dam Disaster:* H.R. 94-1167, 94th Cong., 2d sess., September 23, 1976.

27. Thomas Dunne and Luna B. Leopold, *Water in Environmental Planning* (San Francisco: W. H. Freeman, 1978), 410.

28. "Auburn Dam: Earthquake Hazards Imperil $1-Billion Project," *Science,* August 1977.

29. Tim Palmer, "The Auburn Dam Debate," *Sacramento,* April 1981, 46–53.

30. Michael Catino, interview with author, January 1981.

31. Robert Broadbent, interview with author, March 1983.

32. William O. Douglas, *A Wilderness Bill of Rights* (Boston: Little, Brown, 1965).

33. Elizabeth Kaplan, "Carter Signs Tellico Dam Bill: Snail Darter to Join Dinosaurs," *Not Man Apart,* November 1979.

34. National Indian Youth Council, "Tellico Dam," *Before Columbus,* December 1, 1979.

35. Peter Matthiessen, "My Turn," *Newsweek,* December 17, 1979.

36. "Troubled Waters," *Country Journal,* April 1978, 88.

37. Robert Cahn, "The Triumph of Wrong," *Audubon,* November 1979, 12.

38. Zygmunt Plater, interview with author, April 1983.

39. Stewart Udall, interview with author, March 1983.

40. Richard Saltonstall, "The Case for a Wild River," *Country Journal,* July 1975.

41. Joel Garreau, *The Nine Nations of North America* (New York: Avon, 1982), 22.

42. Tim Palmer, *Stanislaus: The Struggle for a River* (Berkeley and Los Angeles: University of California Press, 1982).

43. Craig Wright, "The Tuolumne River: A Question of Balance," *Headwaters,* September 1983. Friends of the River newsletter.

44. *Los Angeles Times,* December 14, 1982.

45. Anne W. Simon, *The Thin Edge* (New York: Avon, 1978), 160.

OTHER SOURCES

Brooks, Paul. *The Pursuit of Wilderness.* Boston: Houghton Mifflin, 1971.

"Decision on the Snake." *Time,* April 1, 1966, 79–80.

Drew, Elizabeth. "Dam Outrage: The Story of the Army Engineers." *Atlantic,* April 1970, 51–62.

Environmental Policy Center. *Disasters in Water Development*. Washington, D.C.:
    The Center, 1976.
"The Gillham Dam Project on the Cassatot River Is Back on the Tracks." *Audubon,*
    July 1972, 100.
Laycock, George. *The Diligent Destroyers*. Garden City, N.Y.: Doubleday, 1970.
Mager, Russ. "Wilderness and the Living Middle Snake." *The Living Wilderness,*
    Autumn 1969.
Miller, James Nathan. "Bitter Battle of the Waterways." *Reader's Digest,* Sep-
    tember 1977, 83.
Norton, Boyd. *Snake Wilderness*. San Francisco: Sierra Club Books, 1972.
Rubin, Hal. "The Political Aftershocks of Carter's Auburn Dam Decision." *Califor-
    nia Journal,* May 1977.
"Too Many Dam Failures." *Literary Digest,* July 9, 1921.
Trueblood, Ted. "Must the Salmon River Die?" *Field and Stream,* October 1960,
    10.
U.S. Council on Environmental Quality. *The Delaware River Basin*. Washington,
    D.C.: The Council, 1975.

INTERVIEWS

Barry Allen, Coalition to Save the Delaware
John Amodio, Tuolumne River Preservation Trust
Betty Andrews, Friends of the River
Tom Arnold, New England Rivers Center
Brent Blackwelder, Environmental Policy Institute
Robert Broadbent, commissioner of reclamation, Sacramento, Calif.
Howard Brown, American Rivers Conservation Council
Marjorie Carr, Florida Defenders of the Environment
Michael Catino, Bureau of Reclamation, Sacramento, Calif.
Kevin Clark, Bureau of Land Management, Folsom, Calif.
David Conrad, Friends of the Earth
Mark Dubois, Friends of the River
Brock Evans, National Audubon Society
Alexander Gaguine, Friends of the River
Tom Graff, Environmental Defense Fund
Chuck Hoffman, River Conservation Fund
Huey Johnson, secretary, the Resources Agency, Calif.
Dick Linford, river outfitter
Martin Litton, river outfitter
Billy Martin, Bureau of Reclamation, Sacramento, Calif.
Michael McCloskey, Sierra Club
Jerry Meral, California Department of Water Resources
Bill Painter, American Rivers Conservation Council

Guy Phillips, California Assembly Office of Research
Zygmunt Plater, lawyer, Boston, Mass.
Mike Quick, National Park Service, Delaware Water Gap
Bob Teeters, Army Corps of Engineers
Greg Thomas, Natural Resources Defense Council

CHAPTER 6 NATIONAL RIVERS

1. John Craighead, interview with author, February 1983.
2. Ibid. "Wild River," *Montana Wildlife,* June 1957.
3. Ibid. "Wild Rivers," *Naturalist,* Autumn 1965.
4. Paul Bruce Dowling, interview with author, February 1983.
5. Senate Subcommittee on Public Lands, Committee on Interior and Insular Affairs, *The Ozark Rivers Hearings,* 88th Cong., 1st sess. April 8 and 9, May 13, 1963.
6. Ted Swem, interview with author, March 1983.
7. Department of the Interior, *National Wild and Scenic Rivers Study Team to the Secretaries of the Interior and Agriculture,* by Stanford Young (Washington, D.C.: The Department, 1964). Draft.
8. Senate Select Committee on National Water Resources, *Senate Report 29,* 87th Cong. 1st sess. 1961.
9. Arthur Davis; interview with author, February 1983.
10. Outdoor Recreation Resources Review Commission, *Outdoor Recreation for America* (Washington, D.C.: The Commission, January 1962).
11. Stewart Udall; interview with author, March 1983.
12. Senate Committee on Interior and Insular Affairs, *Report 792,* 89th Cong. 1st sess., September 28, 1965.
13. House Committee on Interior and Insular Affairs, *Report 1623,* 90th Cong. 2d sess., July 3, 1968.
14. Congress, *Wild and Scenic Rivers Act As Amended Through P.L. 95–625,* Washington, D.C., November 10, 1978.
15. Michael McCloskey, interview with author, March 1983.
16. Comptroller General, *Federal Protection and Preservation of Wild and Scenic Rivers Is Slow and Costly* (Washington, D.C.: General Accounting Office, May 22, 1978).
17. John Viehman, "Advocate for the Rivers: A Conversation with Howard Brown," *Canoe,* June 1981, 20.
18. Department of the Interior, National Park Service, *Nationwide Rivers Inventory* (Washington, D.C.: The Park Service, 1979).
19. Tim Palmer, "The North Coast National Rivers," *American Forests,* August 1981, 30.
20. Christopher N. Brown, "River Conservation in the 1980s," *Western Wildlands,* Summer 1983, 26.
21. Department of the Interior, National Park Service, "Stream Protection in the United States," by Stanford Young (Seattle: The Park Service, April 1982). Unpublished report.

22. River Conservation Fund, *America's Rivers: An Assessment of State River Conservation Programs,* by Robert C. Hoffman and Keith Fletcher (Washington, D.C.: The Fund, 1984).

23. David Sumner, "Rivers Running Free." *Sierra,* September 1981, 41.

24. Tim Palmer, "A Time For Rivers," *Wilderness,* September 1984.

OTHER SOURCES

A Citizen's Guide to River Conservation. Washington, D.C.: The Conservation Foundation, 1984.

The River Conservation Fund. *Flowing Free.* Washington, D.C.: The Fund, 1977.

U.S. Department of the Interior. *National Wild and Scenic Rivers System: Guidelines for Eligibility, Classification, and Management of River Areas.* Washington, D.C.: The Department, revised September 1980.

U.S. Department of the Interior. Bureau of Outdoor Recreation. "Wild and Scenic Rivers." *Outdoor Recreation Action,* Spring 1977.

Utter, Jack G., and Schultz, John D., eds. *A Handbook on the Wild and Scenic Rivers Act.* Missoula: University of Montana School of Forestry, 1976.

INTERVIEWS

Maurice Arnold, Bureau of Outdoor Recreation

Brent Blackwelder, American Rivers Conservation Council

Cliff Blake, National Forest Service

Stewart Brandborg, the Wilderness Society

Christopher Brown, American Rivers Conservation Council

Howard Brown, American Rivers Conservation Council

Al Buck, Bureau of Outdoor Recreation

Don Christensen, Bureau of Outdoor Recreation

Bern Collins, National Park Service

John Craighead, wildlife biologist, Missoula, Mont.

Dale Crane, staff, House Interior and Insular Affairs Committee

Arthur Davis, Outdoor Recreation Resources Review Commission

Paul Bruce Dowling, the America the Beautiful Fund

Bob Eastman, National Park Service

Glen Eugster, National Park Service

Brock Evans, Sierra Club and National Audubon Society

Roger Fickes, Pennsylvania Department of Environmental Resources

Dave Foreman, Earth First

Mike Fremont, Rivers Unlimited, Ohio

Maurice Goddard, Pennsylvania Department of Environmental Resources

John Haubert, National Park Service

Chuck Hoffman, the River Conservation Fund

Jim Huddleston, Bureau of Outdoor Recreation
John Kauffmann, National Park Service
Loren Kreck, Columbia Falls, Mont.
Tom Lennon, National Forest Service
Deen Lundeen, National Forest Service
Michael McCloskey, Sierra Club
Bob McCullough, Trout Unlimited
Jerry Meral, Planning and Conservation League, Calif.
Pat Munoz, American Rivers Conservation Council
Gaylord Nelson, Senate and the Wilderness Society
Bill Painter, American Rivers Conservation Council
Pat Porchot, Bureau of Outdoor Recreation
Bob Potter, Oregon State Scenic Rivers Program
John Saylor, House of Representatives
Ted Schad, staff, Select Senate Committee on National Water Resources
Larry Stevens, Outdoor Recreation Resources Review Commission
Ted Swem, National Park Service
Stewart Udall, secretary of the interior
Grant Werschkull, Smith River Alliance
Stanford Young, National Park Service

CHAPTER 7 POLITICS AND PROBLEMS OF WATER DEVELOPMENT

1. Daniel Patrick Moynihan, press release, March 5, 1981.

2. Elizabeth Drew, "Dam Outrage: The Story of the Army Engineers," *Atlantic,* April 1970, 51–62.

3. Gilbert White, *Strategies of American Water Management* (Ann Arbor: University of Michigan Press, 1971), 25.

4. Jim Wright, *The Coming Water Famine* (New York: Coward-McCann, 1966).

5. William Ashworth, *Under the Influence* (New York: Hawthorn/Dutton, 1981), 84.

6. Library of Congress, Congressional Research Service, *United States Army Corps of Engineers Background Paper* (Washington, D.C.: The Service, January 8, 1974).

7. George Laycock, *The Diligent Destroyers,* (Garden City, N.Y.: Doubleday, 1970), 123.

8. Comptroller General, *Improvements Needed in Making Benefit-Cost Analysis for Federal Water Resource Projects* (Washington, D.C.: General Accounting Office, September 7, 1973).

9. Ibid., *Changes in Federal Water Projects Repayment Policies Can Reduce Federal Costs* (Washington, D.C.: General Accounting Office, September 7, 1981).

10. Bruce Hannon and Roger Bezdek, "Few Jobs Created by Dams," *Engineering Issues, Journal of Professional Activities,* September 1973, 521–31.

11. Library of Congress, *Army Corps of Engineers Background Paper*.

12. Comptroller General, *Congressional Guidance Needed on Federal Cost Share of Water Resources Projects When Project Benefits Are Not Widespread* (Washington, D.C.: General Accounting Office, November 13, 1980).

13. White, *Strategies of American Water Management*, 50.

14. A. Marsh, "Daniel Boone's Wilderness May Be Tamed by a Lake," *Smithsonian*, September 1975, 56–62.

15. Council on Environmental Quality, *Loss of Agricultural Land*, by Roger Blobaum, for the Citizens Advisory Committee (Washington, D.C.: The Council, 1974).

16. C. B. Belt, Jr., "The 1973 Flood and Man's Constriction of the Mississippi River," *Science*, August 1975.

17. Thomas Y. Canby, "Water: Our Most Precious Resource," *National Geographic*, August 1980.

18. Laurence Pringle, *Wild River* (Philadelphia: Lippincott, 1975).

19. National Water Commission, *Water Policies for the Future* (Port Washington, N.Y.: Water Information Center, 1973).

20. Tim Palmer, "What Price 'Free' Energy?" *Sierra*, July 1983.

21. Phillip Johnson, "Will Small Dams Create Big Problems?" *National Wildlife*, October 1981, 18.

22. Bureau of Reclamation, *Hydropower* (Washington, D.C.: The Bureau, about 1980). Brochure.

23. Lee Lane, "Waterway User Charges," *Sierra Club Bulletin*, May 1977.

24. Gene Marine, *America the Raped* (New York: Avon, 1969).

25. James Nathan Miller, "Big Dam Decision at Alton," *Reader's Digest*, February 1976.

26. Ibid.

27. Environmental Policy Center, *Benefit Claims of the Water Development Agencies* (Washington, D.C.: The Center, June 1976). Booklet.

28. Department of Transportation, *Inland Waterways Users Taxes and Charges* (Washington, D.C.: The Department, February 1982).

29. Environmental Policy Center, *Disasters in Water Development* (Washington, D.C.: The Center, 1976).

30. James Nathan Miller, "Trickery on the Tenn-Tom," *Reader's Digest*, September 1978.

31. "The Engineering of Deceit," *New York Times*, December 14, 1978.

32. Paul Gibson, "Boondoggle," *Forbes*, March 1, 1976.

33. Lane, "Waterway User Charges."

34. Comptroller General, *Federal Charges for Irrigation Projects Reviewed Do Not Cover Costs* (Washington, D.C.: General Accounting Office, March 13, 1981).

35. George Laycock, "Dam the Big Hole," *Field and Stream*, May 1967, 12.

36. Robert Broadbent, interview with author, March 1983.

37. Richard D. Lamm and Michael McCarthy, *The Angry West*, (Boston: Houghton Mifflin, 1982), 195.

38. John Johnson, "Big Farms Harvest U.S. Crop Payments," *Sacramento Bee*, November 3, 1983, A24.

39. Richard L. Berkman and W. Kip Viscusi, *Damming the West* (New York: Grossman, 1973).

40. Henry Nash Smith, *Virgin Land* (New York: Vintage Books, 1950), 299.

41. "The East-West Water Conflict," *American City,* August 1966, 37.

42. Fred Powledge, *Water* (New York: Farrar, Straus & Giroux, 1982), 193.

43. Gaylord Nelson, interview with author, March 1983.

44. Peter Wiley and Robert Gottlieb, *Empires in the Sun* (New York: Avon, 1982), 61.

45. Smith, *Virgin Land,* 144.

46. Michael Robinson, *Water for the West* (Chicago: Public Works Historical Society, 1979), 100.

47. Ibid., 44.

48. Powledge, *Water,* 113.

49. "A Bumper Crop of Subsidies," *Newsweek,* July 25, 1983, 60.

50. "The Browning of America," *Newsweek,* February 23, 1981, 26.

51. Department of Agriculture, Soil Conservation Service, *America's Soil and Water: Conditions and Trends* (Washington, D.C.: The Service, 1980).

52. John Graves, *The Water Hustlers* (San Francisco: Sierra Club, 1971).

53. William Wyant, *Westward in Eden* (Berkeley and Los Angeles: University of California Press, 1982), 345.

54. Rice Odell, *Environmental Awakening* (Cambridge, Mass.: Ballinger, 1980), 76.

55. Paul Shepard, *Man in the Landscape* (New York: Knopf, 1967), 149.

56. "The Indian Water Wars," *Newsweek,* June 13, 1983, 80–82.

57. Water Resources Council, *The Nation's Water Resources* (Washington, D.C.: The Council, 1978).

58. Jon R. Luoma, "Water: Grass-roots Opposition Stymies Garrison Diversion," *Audubon,* March 1982, 114.

59. John Boslough, "Rationing a River," *Science 81,* June 1981.

60. Hank Fisher, "Montana's Yellowstone River: Who Gets the Water?" *Sierra,* July 1978.

61. Robert Herbst, interview with author, March 1979.

62. Brad Knickerbocker, "Salt Where Crops Should Be," *Christian Science Monitor,* June 21, 1979, 12–13.

63. Odell, *Environmental Awakening,* 81.

64. Water Resources Information Center, *Water Atlas of the U.S.* (Port Washington, N.Y.: The Center, 1973), plate 81.

65. Rice Odell, "Silt, Cracks, Floods, and Other Dam Foolishness," *Audubon,* September 1975.

66. Guy P. Gibson, "Cracking the German Dams," *Atlantic,* December 1943, 45–50.

OTHER SOURCES

Ashworth, William. *Nor Any Drop to Drink.* New York: Summit Books, 1982.

Eckstein, Otto. *Water-Resource Development: The Economics of Project Evaluation.* Cambridge: Harvard University Press, 1965.

Ferejohn, John A. *Pork Barrel Politics.* Stanford, Calif.: Stanford University Press, 1974.

Gernerd, Kurt A. "Protection of Instream Flows." *Water Spectrum*, Spring 1982.

"The Homestead Act Hits Home." *Time*, October 17, 1977, 20.

Johnson, Rich. *The Central Arizona Project*. Tucson: University of Arizona Press, 1977.

McCaull, Julian. "Dams of Pork." Environment, January 1975.

Miller, James Nathan. "Needed: A Bill of Rights for Our Rivers." *Reader's Digest*, July 1971.

Mishan, E. J. *Cost-Benefit Analysis*. New York: Praeger, 1976.

Moss, Frank E. *The Water Crisis*. New York: Praeger, 1967.

Schwinden, Ted. "Water of the Yellowstone." *Montana Outdoors*, May 1978.

Sheridan, David. "The Overwatered West: Overdrawn at the Well." *Environment*, March 1981.

Turner, Frederick. "Sumerian Implications." *Wilderness*, Summer 1982.

INTERVIEWS

Brent Blackwelder, Environmental Policy Center

Robert Broadbent, commissioner of reclamation

Christopher Brown, American Rivers Conservation Council

James Cook, Bureau of Reclamation, Sacramento, Calif.

Ronald Corso, Federal Energy Regulatory Commission

Arthur Davis, Bureau of the Budget

Quenton Edson, Federal Energy Regulatory Commission

Robert Herbst, assistant secretary of the interior

Gaylord Nelson, Senate

Edward Osann, National Wildlife Federation

James Posewitz, Montana Fish and Game Department

Ronald Robie, California State Water Resources Control Board

Richard Roos-Collins, Friends of the River

Russell Shay, Sierra Club

Jeffrey Stine, historian under contract with the Army Corps of Engineers, Washington, D.C.

Don Sundeen, Fish and Wildlife Service, Portland, Oreg.

David Weiman, lobbyist, Washington, D.C.

Frank Welsch, Phoenix, Ariz.

Stanford Young, National Park Service

CHAPTER 8   A NEW ERA

1. Western Writers of America, *Water Trails West*, (New York: Avon, 1978), x.

2. U.S. Army Corps of Engineers, *The Headwaters District*, by Leland Johnson (Pittsburgh, Pa.: The Corps, about 1979), 77.

3. George Laycock, *The Diligent Destroyers* (Garden City, N.Y.: Doubleday, 1970), 200.

4. Elmo Richardson, *Dams, Parks and Politics* (Lexington: University Press of Kentucky, 1973).

5. Beatrice Hort Holmes, *History of Federal Water Resources Programs and Policies, 1961–70,* (Washington, D.C.: U.S. Department of Agriculture, 1979), 142.

6. Peter Wiley and Robert Gottlieb, *Empires in the Sun* (New York: Avon, 1982), 52.

7. The Conservation Foundation, newsletter, December 1976.

8. Arthur Magida, "Renovating the Bureaucracy," *Environmental Action,* October 1977, 3.

9. Philip L. Fradkin, *A River No More* (New York: Knopf, 1981), 9.

10. Richard Lamm and Michael McCarthy, *The Angry West,* (Boston: Houghton Mifflin, 1982), 188.

11. Ibid., 37.

12. William Ashworth, *Under the Influence* (New York: Hawthorn/Dutton, 1981), 165.

13. Fradkin, *A River No More,* 11.

14. Ward Sinclair, *Washington Post,* August 29, 1978.

15. *Washington Post,* October 23, 1978.

16. Fred Powledge, *Water* (New York: Farrar, Straus & Giroux, 1982), 248.

17. John Johnson, *Sacramento Bee,* July 13, 1983, A28.

18. *Washington Post,* January 25, 1982.

19. Robert Broadbent, interview with author, March 1983.

OTHER SOURCES

Hubbard, Henry. "Carter Versus Congress: Another Showdown Over Water." *National Wildlife,* April 1979.

INTERVIEWS

Brent Blackwelder, Environmental Policy Institute
Robert Broadbent, commissioner of reclamation
Robert Edgar, House of Representatives
Guy Martin, assistant secretary of the interior
Edward Osann, National Wildlife Federation
Ted Schad, Bureau of the Budget
Bob Teeters, Army Corps of Engineers

CHAPTER 9   NEEDS AND ALTERNATIVES

1. Department of Agriculture, Soil Conservation Service, *America's Soil and Water: Conditions and Trends* (Washington, D.C.: The Service, 1980).

2. Water Resources Council, *The Nation's Water Resources, 1975–2000,* vol. 1, *Summary* (Washington, D.C.: The Council, 1979).

3. Fred Powledge, *Water* (New York: Farrar, Straus & Giroux, 1982), 37.

4. Department of the Interior, Geological Survey, *Estimated Use of Water in the United States in 1980,* Circular 1001 (Alexandria, Va.: The Survey, 1983).

5. Ibid.

6. Water Resources Council, *The Nation's Water Resources.*

7. Department of the Interior, Geological Survey, *Estimated Use of Water in the United States.*

8. Ibid.

9. "The Browning of America," *Newsweek,* February 23, 1981, 26.

10. Ibid.

11. Natural Resources Defense Council, newsletter, January 1978.

12. John Naisbitt, *Megatrends* (New York: Warner Books, 1984).

13. Water Resources Council, *The Nation's Water Resources.*

14. Robert Broadbent, interview with author, March 1983.

15. Jim Wright, *The Coming Water Famine* (New York: Coward-McCann, 1966).

16. Gilbert White, *Strategies of American Water Management* (Ann Arbor: University of Michigan Press, 1971), 46.

17. Beatrice Hort Holmes, *History of Federal Water Resources Programs and Policies, 1961–70* (Washington, D.C.: U.S. Department of Agriculture, 1979), 27.

18. "Muddy Water," *Wall Street Journal,* September 13, 1982.

19. Philip L. Fradkin, *A River No More* (New York: Knopf, 1981), 201.

20. Natural Resources Defense Council, newsletter, January 1978.

21. Tim Palmer, *Stanislaus: The Struggle for a River* (Berkeley and Los Angeles: University of California Press, 1982).

22. Robert Rienow and Leona Train Rienow, *Moment in the Sun,* (New York: Ballantine, 1967), 76.

23. Department of Agriculture, Soil Conservation Service, *America's Soil and Water.*

24. "The Browning of America," 26.

25. Tim Palmer, *Stanislaus,* 155.

26. Environmental Policy Institute, *Survey of Water Conservation Programs in the Fifty States,* by Brent Blackwelder and Peter Carlson (Washington, D.C.: The Institute, 1982).

27. Ibid.

28. Ibid.

29. Ibid.

30. Rice Odell, *Environmental Awakening* (Cambridge, Mass.: Ballinger, 1980), 86.

31. Environmental Policy Institute, *Survey of Water Conservation Programs in the Fifty States.*

OTHER SOURCES

California. Department of Water Resources. *Water Conservation in California.* Bulletin 198. Sacramento: The Department, 1976.

Gibbons, John, and Chandler, William. *Energy: The Conservation Revolution.* New York: Plenum Press, 1981.

Lovins, Amory. *Soft Energy Paths: Toward A Durable Peace.* San Francisco: Friends of the Earth, 1977.

McGhee, Ronnie, Reardon, Mary, and Shulman, Arleen, eds. *Readings in Water Conservation.* Washington, D.C.: National Association of Counties Research, about 1976.

U.S. Environmental Protection Agency. Office of Water Program Operations. *Proceedings, National Conference on Water Conservation and Municipal Wastewater Flow Reduction.* Washington, D.C.: The Agency, August 1979.

U.S. Water Resources Council. *Floodplain Management Guidelines.* Washington, D.C.: The Council, February 10, 1978.

"Watering a Continent." *Newsweek,* February 22, 1965, 53.

INTERVIEWS

Brent Blackwelder, Environmental Policy Institute

Robert Broadbent, commissioner of reclamation

Verne Huser, Office of Environmental Mediation, University of Washington

Laura King, Natural Resources Defense Council

Jonas Minton, California Department of Water Resources

George Palmiter, Channelization Consultant, Montpelier, Ohio

Bob Teeters, Army Corps of Engineers

CHAPTER 10   THE LAST WEALTH

1. Charles M. Clusen, ed., *Engineering a Victory for Our Environment* (San Francisco: Sierra Club, 1973), 5.

2. Thomas F. Waters, *Streams and Rivers of Minnesota* (Minneapolis: University of Minnesota Press, 1977), 329.

3. Anthony Netboy, *The Salmon: Their Fight for Survival* (Boston: Houghton Mifflin, 1974), 310.

4. Gilbert White, *Strategies of American Water Management* (Ann Arbor: University of Michigan Press, 1971), 84.

5. Rice Odell, "Silt, Cracks, Floods, and Other Dam Foolishness," *Audubon,* September 1975.

6. Jeff Raimundo, "Dam-Safety Bill Faces Key Test Despite U.S. Public Inattention," *Sacramento Bee,* September 18, 1983, A4.

7. Bob Teeters, interview with author, March 1983.

8. Odell, "Silt, Cracks, Floods, and Other Dam Foolishness."

9. Kathleen K. Wiegner, "The Water Crisis: It's Almost Here," *Forbes,* August 20, 1979.

10. Claire Sterling, "Super Dams: The Perils of Progress," *Reader's Digest,* July 1972.

11. Ibid.

12. William Steffen, "Furor over the Franklin," *Sierra,* September 1984, 45–49.

13. Fred Powledge, *Water* (New York: Farrar, Straus & Giroux, 1984), 276.

INTERVIEWS

Brent Blackwelder, Environmental Policy Institute
Robert Broadbent, commissioner of reclamation
Clifford Freeman, Chief, Driftpile, Alberta, Canada
Bob Teeters, Army Corps of Engineers
Stewart Udall, secretary of the interior
Philip Williams, hydrologist, San Francisco, Calif.

ENDANGERED RIVERS
INTERVIEWS

Brent Blackwelder, Environmental Policy Center
Roy Breuklander, rancher, Valentine, Nebr.
David Brown, Ocoee River Council
Peter Carlson, Environmental Policy Center
Clarence Davis, Northern Lights Power Company
Nancy Duhnkrack, Portland, Oreg.
Frank Fly, Duck River, Tenn.
Charles Fryling, Louisiana State University
Chuck Hoffman, the River Conservation Fund
Verne Huser, river outfitter, Seattle, Wash.
Nancy Jack, Kansas City, Kans.
Doris Kaplan, Denver Water Board
Mike McCarty, outfitter, Gauley River, West Virginia
Pat Munoz, American Rivers Conservation Council
Sandy Neily, outfitter, Greenville, Maine
Bob Pierce, Portland, Oreg.
Jim Posewitz, Montana Fish and Game Department
John Reed, Army Corps of Engineers, Pittsburgh, Pa.
Dick Shaffer, Bureau of Reclamation, Denver, Colo.
Ben Skerrett, Lafayette, La.
Bob Weaver, Trout Unlimited, Denver, Colo.
John Welch, Army Corps of Engineers, Seattle, Wash.
Brad Welton, Friends of the River
Connie Wick, Lafayette, Ind.
Chuck Williams, White Salmon, Wash.

Endangered Rivers

Hundreds of rivers remain endangered. In this section seventeen of the most important river controversies of the 1980s are described, listed in alphabetical order by state. Following this section is a list with condensed information about rivers where development is proposed or was proposed in the past and could be reintroduced.

ALASKA

SUSITNA RIVER

In size and cost, a Susitna River dam would dwarf any other in America. The Alaska Power Authority—an arm of state government—proposed a project originally planned by the Army Corps of Engineers but dropped by that agency in the 1970s. Watana Dam would rise 885 feet, blocking twenty-eight miles through a wilderness canyon carrying runoff from the Alaska Range. At a 1982 cost of $3.6 billion, the dam would produce 1,620 megawatts, which the Fairbanks Environmental Center contends is three times the amount usable by Alaska. Devil's Canyon Dam would cost $1.5 billion. The state legislature appropriated $25.6 million for design.

The Susitna Fault runs through the area, and the dams would cripple the migration of caribou, flood a moose range, destroy salmon habitat, and mar a $15-million commercial fishery. The Watana site lies fifty miles from the nearest road in a potential Bureau of Land Management wilderness area. Whitewater experts prize the Susitna canyon as one of the most challenging big-water runs in the world with enormous waves and hydraulics powerful beyond comparison.

In a surprise move, the Federal Energy Regulatory Commission in 1984 released an environmental impact statement that called for study of cheaper, alternative sources of energy.

CALIFORNIA

NORTH FORK OF THE STANISLAUS

The Stanislaus's North Fork begins in the Sierra north of Yosemite, wraps around high meadows, and carves a white granite canyon. Though middle elevations, fir, cedar, and ponderosa pine crowd rapids and green pools luring trout fishermen, campers, and expert paddlers.

For hydroelectric power, the Calaveras County Water District proposed to build three North Fork dams, one dam on nearby Beaver Creek, two powerhouses, and a tunnel to deliver water to another reservoir. An average of 560,000 megawatt hours a year would be generated, 0.3 percent of California's electric energy demand. The district planned to use the earnings to build additional dams for water supply to encourage rural development. In a county election, a vote to approve $350 million of construction bonds lost, but the dam promoters returned with an advertising campaign including the slogan "Save Our River," and won in the next election.

Friends of the River, the Sierra Club, and local landowners argued that the FERC should not issue permits. Gabbot Meadow and Highland Creek — prime fawning grounds in a national forest — would be flooded. Five miles of exquisite granite canyon below the existing Utica Reservoir would be buried. In upper sections of the river, increased releases would drown riparian habitat. For lower sections the federal Fish and Wildlife Service stated that 50 cubic feet per second (cfs) were needed, but the state Fish and Game Department agreed to 16.5 cfs. Clark Flat, a popular meadow with archaeological sites along the Stanislaus River just above New Melones Reservoir, would be used for roads, powerlines, and a powerhouse. Nobody knew the impacts of the full project because the future water supply dams were not addressed in the environmental statement.

Friends of the River attorney Brad Welton said, "The compromises have been made. Fourteen existing dams in the Stanislaus basin are enough. We've lost most of our good California streams, and if a line is not drawn somewhere, we'll have nothing but chains of reservoirs on all our rivers." Friends of the River supported an alternate plan that would not bury Gabbot Meadow or the wild canyon, and would not cause extreme high and low flows. Water district engineers calculated 20 percent less cost but 20 percent less energy and ruled out the alternative.

The conservationists' appeal of the FERC construction license was denied in 1983, and construction of support facilities began in 1985. Other hydroelectric dams are proposed for the Sierra's Kern, Kings, Merced, Mokelumne, and Cosumnes rivers.

COLORADO

DOLORES RIVER

From the San Juan Mountains, the Dolores River winds for 250 miles through Colorado canyons and foothills, ending in Utah as a large tributary to the Colorado River. Two-thousand-foot-deep canyons include Slickrock, known for its similarity to the Colorado's Glen Canyon. Indian pictographs, unspoiled desert, wildlife, and rapids make a 97-mile reach a favorite rafting run, and a boatable section without dams continues for a rare length of 160 miles. President Carter recommended national river status for 140 miles but Congress did not act.

As one of five Colorado dams authorized with the Central Arizona Project in 1968, McPhee was built below the town of Dolores on a canoeing section eleven miles upstream from the popular whitewater. Diversions will lower the river's flow, limiting rafting. A minimum flow of twenty cubic feet per second below the dam is less than one-third of the amount required by the Colorado Division of Wildlife. The Environmental Protection Agency questioned the ability of local farmers to pay for the costly irrigation water, but construction continued, and the Bureau of Reclamation began filling the reservoir in 1984. The Environmental Policy Institute still hoped for in-stream flow reservations, and neither the irrigators nor the state has agreed to pay for a water delivery system whose costs have doubled since repayment was negotiated.

PINEY RIVER

Only sixty miles from Denver, the Piney River rushes as an alpine stream from the western side of the Continental Divide in the Gore Range. The Denver Water Board planned to divert the Piney, Gore Creek, and other trout streams near Vail through a tunnel to the Denver area, which houses half the state's people. Supported by environmentalists strangely allied with energy developers who wanted to use the water in western Colorado, the Eagle's Nest Wilderness was designated in 1976, halting part of the water board's plans.

With or without wilderness restrictions, the board owns water rights to Piney and other streams, and a spokesperson said, "It's just a matter of how to get the water over." With a presidential exception allowed for water developments in wilderness areas, the project could still be built, but this was fought by the American Wilderness Alliance. Diversions below the wilderness area could be taken, but would require pumping and would also take water from excellent stretches of wild river.

Before diverting the west-slope water, Denver planned to build the Foothills Project—a dam and water treatment plant on the South Fork of the Platte near the city. Because this would give Denver the storage and treatment capacity for the new diversions, Trout Unlimited opposed the dam, director Bob Weaver saying that Foothills "is only a small component of a much larger project." In 1978 the Environmental Protection Agency stated that the added water will encourage further suburbanization resulting in air pollution around Denver, and opposed federal permits for Foothills, making this one of few cases in which a dam was delayed because of secondary effects on air quality.

Environmentalists argued that a 50-foot-high Foothills Dam instead of the proposed 243-foot dam would meet the region's needs, and that supplies could be stretched through conservation. But the Foothills Project is being built, and the Piney and other west-slope streams may be the next to be dammed and diverted.

INDIANA
WILDCAT CREEK

Quiet pools and riffles draw canoeists, fishermen, and hikers to gorges of Indiana's Wildcat Creek, running thirty-six miles through farms, forests, and villages. East of

Lafayette, the corps proposed a 126-foot-high dam to flood 9,500 acres and eleven miles of Wildcat Creek at a 1982 cost of $200 million. The project was justified for recreation and flood control in the Wabash valley, but the dam would reduce high water by only inches. More than 18,000 acres—most of it farmland—would be taken and five hundred families moved. Instead, the Wildcat Creek Federation proposed floodplain management and recreational use along the creek. Due to rising costs and opposition, the governor withdrew support in 1976. In 1981 the dam was to be deauthorized in a bill backed by Congressman Floyd Fithian from the reservoir area, but the congressman from downstream towns objected, and Lafayette Dam remains authorized.

LOUISIANA

ATCHAFALAYA RIVER

The Atchafalaya River is the country's largest distributary—the opposite of a tributary—carrying part of the Mississippi River (which carries 40 percent of the country's runoff) through an ancestral channel 110 miles to the Gulf of Mexico. The Army Corps of Engineers diverts Mississippi floodwater to the Atchafalaya to avoid overtopping New Orleans's levees. The river includes the country's largest hardwood swamp, fifteen miles wide, with three hundred species of nesting birds, including the southern bald eagle and the endangered ivory-billed woodpecker, sixty-five species of amphibians and reptiles, and ninety species of fish, crawfish, crabs, and shrimp.

Dredging and levees dried up 30 percent of the wetlands. Plans called for more dredging and completion of 449 miles of levees costing $2.37 billion, one-fifth of it already spent. A deeper channel would cause floodwater to move faster and wetlands to be drained for farms and industry. Opponents led by Charles Fryling and others argued that the swamp was more valuable for its wildlife, and that sediment from the dredging would destroy the ecosystem.

A compromise was reached in 1981 by conservationists, the corps, the governor, and landowners. The corps developed a path-breaking nonstructural proposal: further dredging would be limited; 450,000 acres of easements to save wetlands would be bought; 40,000 acres would be donated by Dow Chemical Company; and another 48,000 would be bought by the government for $50 million. Federal funding, however, was needed for 90 percent of the costs, and without it, support for the dredging could resume.

MAINE

WEST BRANCH OF THE PENOBSCOT RIVER

From headwaters at the Quebec border, the West Branch of the Penobscot cuts through wild gorges and spruce-fir forests for 220 miles. Great Northern Paper Company proposed a 120-foot-high dam at Big Ambejackmockamus Falls ("Big A") to supply a pulp mill with 233 million kilowatt-hours of electricity a year. The dam would flood three miles of landlocked salmon habitat and New England's most exciting whitewater, where ten thousand people rafted in 1981. The Penobscot Indian Nation and every major conservation group in Maine fought the dam. A development moratorium for a national river study expired in 1980, and Great Northern planned to apply for a FERC construction license in 1985. American Rivers Conservation Council director Chris Brown said that the Penobscot was probably "the most important threatened river of 1985."

MONTANA
KOOTENAI RIVER

In western Montana the Kootenai River flows over one of the last major northwestern waterfalls unaffected by a hydroelectric project. In 1976 the FERC issued a permit for the Northern Lights Power Company to study a proposal for a thirty-foot-high dam and a 3.5-mile-long reservoir above the falls. Up to 97 percent of the river's flow would be diverted around the falls to produce an average of 500 million kilowatt-hours of electricity a year. The cooperative stated that hydroelectricity could be provided at one-fifth the cost of nuclear or coal power.

The Save the Kootenai Association, fishermen, and the Cabinet Mountain Resources Group opposed the dam because it would flood China Rapids, a popular fishing area, and the lands acquired as bighorn sheep range to replace habitat that was flooded when the corps built Libby Dam upstream. The Confederated Salish and Kootenai Tribes and the Kootenai Tribe of Idaho called the falls a ceremonial place and "a vision quest site of deep religious significance." They argued that construction would violate the American Indian Religious Freedom Act by denying access to a religious site.

In 1984 the FERC found that the project would probably result in a surplus of power at the expense of "unique values associated with the Falls," and that the dam would infringe upon religious beliefs and practices protected by the First Amendment, for which the case may be an important precedent. Long-term protection of the river is uncertain.

YELLOWSTONE RIVER

Allenspur Dam was first planned in 1902 when St. Louis investors wanted to build the project privately. In 1944 the Army Corps of Engineers' Pick plan for the Missouri basin recommended the dam. The river was included in the Department of the Interior's proposals for national wild and scenic rivers in 1963, but during the same year the Bureau of Reclamation recommended Allenspur. Interior dropped the national river proposal.

In 1973 the Bureau of Reclamation again proposed Allenspur to store 1.5 million acre-feet of water a year for coal development and other uses. The 380-foot-high dam would flood 32,000 acres, mostly ranchland in Paradise Valley, and thirty-one miles of river at a gap between the Absaroka and Gallatin ranges just downstream from Yellowstone National Park. The river is among the best trout fisheries in the country, and offers some of the finest mountain scenery of any canoeable river. In 1974 the Montana legislature passed a resolution asking the secretary of the interior to recommend that Allenspur not be built, but two months later the Bureau of Reclamation listed the site as "Federal recommended."

In a landmark case of water allocation, the state reserved more than half of the

Yellowstone flow for in-stream uses so that downriver withdrawals for coal processing will not destroy the ecosystem. While protecting the lower river, this could lead to new support for Allenspur when developers seek makeup water for the amount that they withdraw. The dam would be prohibited by national river status, but this was fought by ranchers.

NEBRASKA

NIOBRARA RIVER

Described by a University of Nebraska ecologist as the "biological crossroads of the Midwest," the Niobrara River runs the length of Nebraska as one of the least affected and most scenic rivers on the plains. Offering cool relief from summer heat, the river is paddled by twenty thousand canoeists a year. The Nature Conservancy's largest preserve lies along a twenty-mile stretch of river where endangered whooping cranes and bald eagles stop during migration. Fossils of sixteen species previously unknown were found near the river, and two hundred archaeological sites remain unexplored.

In 1972 Norden Dam was authorized as part of the Bureau of Reclamation's O'Neill Project to flood 20 miles of river, including part of the Nature Conservancy's preserve, and to divert water 362 miles to 77,000 acres of farmland, half of it already irrigated by groundwater and only 12 percent of it classified as highly suitable for irrigation. About 30,000 acres would be consumed by reservoirs and ditches. Much of the water would be used to grow corn—already under price supports because too much is produced.

Congressman Douglas Bereuter of Nebraska stated, "I will take whatever legitimate action is necessary to see that the O'Neill project—as presently conceived—is never built." Studies by his office and by others showed that the bureau's investment of $335 million would be four times greater than the value of the land to be served, and that reauthorization was needed before construction could begin. The Environmental Policy Center reported that the project would cost more than $1 million per farm served. To frustrate the bureau's land acquisition and to raise money, landowners sold deeds to properties of one square yard in size, each requiring a separate condemnation. In 1982 the House voted to halt the O'Neill Project, but funding was later restored. In 1983 funding was stopped while the Bureau of Reclamation began evaluation of a nondam alternative prepared by the Nature Conservancy.

TENNESSEE

DUCK RIVER

Popular for fishing and canoeing, the Duck River runs for 268 miles past farms, caves, tributary waterfalls, Indian sites, and the habitat of endangered species. The Tennessee Valley Authority proposed the eighty-foot-high Columbia Dam to impound 56 river miles at a 1982 cost of $214 million. Flood control would benefit forty-three houses and 3,000 acres of farmland, whereas the reservoir would displace 255 families from 31,800 acres, two-thirds of it farmland. Water supply accounted for 15 percent of the justification, but the Tennessee Department of

Public Health reported that phosphate and shallow water would cause the growth of blue-green algae and render water unfit to drink. Geological Survey data indicated that all five towns to receive the water have adequate sources. The reservoir would flood 12,600 acres but two and a half times that amount would be bought by the TVA, the extra land slated for industrial development to yield 39 percent of project benefits after forcing residents to move. The TVA claimed that the dam would help fish and wildlife, but the state Department of Fish and Game fought the project because it would destroy 24,000 acres of habitat. Recreation accounted for 23 percent of the benefits, but nine reservoirs are within 50 miles.

In 1977 President Carter's water project screening committee reported that the project had a benefit-cost ratio of only 0.8 – 1. The dam was on the president's hit list, but was removed. In 1980 the House Committee on Government Operations reported that Columbia Dam "is perhaps the best example of how difficult it is to stop, or even modify, a water project once it has started. It is a record of arrogance, bad faith and broken promises by a powerful agency [the TVA] and weakness and political accommodation by a less powerful one [the Fish and Wildlife Service]." The committee noted that a TVA staff report showed that every benefit of the dam could be achieved by a nondam alternative at one-quarter of the cost. One-third of the land was bought by 1982 when appeals from the Environmental Defense Fund, the Tennessee Scenic Rivers Association, and other groups temporarily stopped construction and TVA tried to comply with the Endangered Species Act by transplanting mussels.

OCOEE RIVER

Through the Appalachians in Georgia and Tennessee, the Ocoee River runs for 95 miles. In 1913 a 4.6-mile-long diversion was built for hydroelectric power, but when the rotted wooden flume was abandoned in 1976, water again plunged down the riverbed, where kayakers, rafters, and canoeists discovered excellent whitewater. In 1982, ninety thousand paddlers traveled this section, making it the nation's third most floated whitewater (behind the Youghiogheny in Pennsylvania and the Nantahala in North Carolina) and one of the first waterways reclaimed from a diversion.

In 1979 the Tennessee Valley Authority approved plans to reconstruct the flume for $26 million. The agency maintained that the project's 135 million kilowatt-hours a year would be enough for nine thousand homes, but the riverbed would be left nearly dry, and the Tennessee Department of Tourist Development stated that whitewater paddling generated $3 million a year and employed 150 workers.

The TVA offered to release water for recreation on eighty-two days a year if boaters would pay $270,000 annually to cover power losses, but one-fourth of the days would be from October to May. River supporters compared their case to the Tennessee-Tombigbee Waterway, where diversions will cause an annual loss of $1.5 million at TVA power plants, but barge operators will not be charged.

Funded by rafting outfitters, the Ocoee River Council hired David Brown as a full-time director to organize river support. Under a state law that calls for no degradation of resources of regional and national significance, the state commissioner of public health advised TVA in 1981 to submit a permit application for the diversion, but the TVA refused and sued the state over the requirement. Another court decision is pending that could require recreational releases without charge. In 1984 Congressman John Duncan led passage of a funding measure that would reimburse TVA and allow 117 days of river recreation per season, but unresolved was the question of who will pay for the power that is foregone.

UTAH
UINTA MOUNTAIN RIVERS

The Bureau of Reclamation's Central Utah Project (CUP) is designed to divert water from the Uinta Mountains to central Utah and the Salt Lake City area through the building of ten reservoirs and the enlargement of two others. These would allow Utah to use much of its 23 percent share of the upper Colorado. The Whiterocks River, Strawberry River, Rock Creek, and others would be dammed, causing destruction of two hundred miles of streams, 28,000 acres of marshes, and scores of beaver ponds. The Environmental Protection Agency estimated that $800,000 in annual salinity damages would be caused by diverting 300,000 acre-feet from the Colorado River basin.

Facing criticism about costs, and seeing urban growth, the bureau redesigned the project to stress municipal supply. Ute Indians, who had agreed to the diversion of streams in exchange for the construction of their own irrigation system, threatened to withdraw their support in 1979 because their dams and canals—last on the list—may not be built.

The Carter administration recommended changes but the project enjoyed Utah's unified support. A Farm Bureau representative said, "It would be extremely shortsighted for us to leave our mountain streams to run wild. . . ." To gain Congressman Gunn McKay's vote for missile sitings in Utah, President Carter dropped his objections, and the plans continued, but Assistant Interior Secretary Guy Martin warned Utah residents that CUP water may be the most expensive the bureau has ever developed. Citizens may yet reject the project when they vote on a water supply repayment contract.

WASHINGTON
WHITE SALMON RIVER

Beginning on the glacial slopes of Mount Adams, the White Salmon River flows for thirty-five miles to the Columbia. A chasm in volcanic rock runs for ten miles, and lower sections of the river are popular among paddlers and fishermen.

The FERC granted a permit for the Kickitat County Public Utility District to study hydroelectric dams, and it proposed a six-dam plan for 810 million kilowatt-hours of electricity a year. A storage reservoir would flood elk habitat and marshland at Trout Lake, and five hydroelectric dams would block the vertical-sided gorge.

Eighty percent of the electricity would be sold outside the district. A utility spokesman said that the study was a "protective device" against other utilities preempting the river, and added, "If we didn't get the federal permit, Seattle City Light probably would."

Friends of the White Salmon fought the dams, and fearing loss of irrigation rights, sixty farmers signed a petition against the project. Other residents expressed concerns about safety because the area is riddled with lava caves. The Fish and Wildlife Service recommended the razing of a small dam at the lower end of the river to restore steelhead and salmon, but only if the new dams are not built. In 1983 the power company's permit expired and was not renewed, but without scenic river designation or restoration of the salmon fishery, the dams could be proposed again.

WEST VIRGINIA
BLACKWATER RIVER

The Blackwater River begins in Canaan Valley, the largest muskeg bog in the Appalachians. At three thousand feet above sea level, the basin creates a frost pocket housing ice age plant communities, some of West Virginia's best native trout fishery, and one-third of the state's wetlands. The Department of the Interior designated the valley a national natural landmark, the National Park Service found the Blackwater eligible for wild and scenic river status, and the Fish and Wildlife Service recommended acquisition of the valley as a wildlife refuge in 1978.

But the Allegheny Power System had proposed the Davis Project with a seventy-five-foot-high dam to flood 7,000 acres of Canaan, ten miles of the Blackwater, and forty-three miles of tributaries and beaver ponds. One million kilowatts would be produced at a 1982 cost of $500 million. Three million dollars a year would be paid in utility taxes to Tucker County. Power company officials stated that the project is needed in the next decade; however, a federal interagency team reported in 1980 that alternatives were available. Dam opponents called the project wasteful: for pumped storage, water would be lifted by pumps using coal-fired power to a 620-acre upper reservoir during nonpeak hours, then dropped to make electricity when needed, the entire process consuming much more energy than it generates.

The Federal Power Commission issued a license for the project in 1977. One lawsuit by the Sierra Club, West Virginia, and the Department of the Interior, and another lawsuit regarding a permit denial by the Army Corps of Engineers, which opposes the project, have delayed construction in a case that could go to the Supreme Court. A plan proposed by West Virginia would allow the dams provided another 13,000 acres of wildlife habitat are donated by the utility to the government.

GAULEY RIVER

A twenty-six-mile-long section of the Gauley River is the zenith of eastern rafting trips and one of the favorite runs of expert paddlers nationwide. Truck-sized boulders decorate the undeveloped gorge with one hundred rapids. In 1981 more than five thousand people from as far away as California and Europe paddled here.

Above the whitewater section, Summersville Dam flooded 13.7 miles of river in 1965. A new hydroelectric proposal by the corps called for a higher reservoir that would drown 2 more miles above the dam, and a diversion that would nearly dry up the river below the dam. The project would generate an average of 400,000 mega-watt-hours of peaking power daily—enough for twenty-six thousand homes if it were consistently available as base load. The American Rivers Conservation Council argued that the power was not needed because demand was declining and because the Allegheny Power System — the most likely customer — was developing other projects. A corps study indicated a 35.7 percent surplus in regional capacity. The project would eliminate some of the largest rapids, and even below the diversion, the power plant might not release water when paddlers are able to run the river. After completing a wild and scenic river study, the National Park Service found the Gauley eligible as a national wild river (only two designated "wild" rivers are in the East), and called the Gauley "one of the most outstanding whitewater rivers in the United States," but the three-mile reach would be ineligible if diverted.

With opposition by ARCC, river outfitters, and residents from nearby towns, the local congressman, Bob Wise, fought the corps's plan. Fearing controls on commercial river trips, outfitters also opposed national river status, but without it, the hydroelectric project could be reintroduced.

WISCONSIN

KICKAPOO RIVER

Through hills and farmland of southern Wisconsin, the Kickapoo River runs ninety-five miles, a favorite of fishermen and canoeists. For flood control in five small towns, LaFarge Dam was planned by the corps to rise 103 feet and impound twelve miles of the river and 1,780 acres at a 1980 cost of $68.8 million.

Construction began in 1971, but after studies at the University of Wisconsin showed that the project would be uneconomic, that flood protection would be incomplete, and that the reservoir would be polluted, Governor Patrick Lucey withdrew support. Work was halted in 1978, making this one of few projects to be stopped after construction had begun. As an alternative to the dam, the town of Soldiers Grove relocated its business district from the floodplain after receiving a $900,000 Housing and Urban Development grant. In 1982 the corps stated that the project was in "standby status," and Governor Dreyfus urged dam construction. Congressional and local support grew for a dry dam that would be empty except during floods. Senator William Proxmire supported relocation of additional floodprone buildings but the local congressman blocked deauthorization of the dam.

Endangered Rivers List

Many sites listed are currently threatened; others involve past proposals that could be reintroduced. For more information, see the index or write to the American Rivers Conservation Council, 801 Pennsylvania Av. SE, Washington, D.C. 20003.

ABBREVIATIONS

ACE	Army Corps of Engineers
auth	authorized
BR	Bureau of Reclamation
Co	company
const	construction
Corp	corporation
Cr	Creek
Dist	District
fl con	flood control
FERC	Federal Energy Regulatory Commission
govt	government
irrig	irrigation
nav	navigation
nwsrs	national wild and scenic rivers system
prelim	preliminary
Proj	Project
rec	recreation
res	reservoir
TVA	Tennessee Valley Authority
ws	water supply

RIVER	PROJECT	PROJECT SPONSOR	PROJECT PURPOSE	STATUS	NOTES
ALABAMA					
Coosa	Coosa River	ACE	nav	in planning	
Tombigbee	Tennessee-Tombigbee Waterway	ACE	nav	under const	see Chapter 7
ALASKA					
Susitna	Watana & Devil's Canyon dams	Alaska Power Authority	power	in planning	see Endangered Rivers
ARIZONA					
Colorado	Glen Canyon power increase	BR	power	deferred	would erode Grand Canyon beaches
Gila	Buttes Dam	BR	ws, irrig	auth, alternatives being studied	
San Pedro	Charlston Dam	BR	irrig	auth, deferred	
Verde	Orme Dam	BR	ws, fl con, irrig	auth, alternatives planned	see Chapter 7
CALIFORNIA					
American	Auburn Dam	BR	irrig, multipurpose	const halted, reauth required	see Chapter 5
American South Fork	Lower SOFAR	El Dorado Irrig Dist	power	study temporarily stopped by state law	4th most popular whitewater in the nation

River	Dam/Project	Developer	Purpose	Status	Notes
American South Fork, Silver Fork, Alder Cr, Webber Cr	Upper SOFAR	El Dorado Irrig Dist	power	final approval pending	agreements were made with rafting groups for water releases
Cosumnes	Nashville Dam	irrig districts	power	in planning	
Fall River	6 dams	local govt and private developers	power	FERC prelim permit issued	would affect 3rd highest waterfall outside Alaska, and a national river tributary
Hardscrabble Cr	3 dams	Cal Nickel Co	ws for mining	in planning	1st dams in Smith River basin
Kings River	Rodgers Crossing Dam	Kings River Conservation District	power, fl con	in planning	outstanding white-water run
McCloud	McCloud River dams	City of Santa Clara	power	FERC permit requested	trout fishery, rec river
Mad River	Butler Valley Dam	ACE	ws, fl con	deferred	voted down in local referendum
Merced River	El Portal Dam	private developer	power	FERC permit pending	would flood to Yosemite Park
Merced, South Fork	South Fork Merced	Merced Irrig Dist	power	deferred	would flood to boundary of Yosemite Park, affect wildlife in the park
Mokelumne	Upper Mokelumne 3 dams	East Bay Municipal Utility Dist	power	deferred	popular canoeing run

RIVER	PROJECT	PROJECT SPONSOR	PROJECT PURPOSE	STATUS	NOTES
Santa Margarita	dams	BR	ws	proposed	would flood 20 miles of stream in San Diego County
Stanislaus, North Fork	North Fork dams	Calaveras Co Water Dist	power	final FERC license issued	see Endangered Rivers
Stanislaus, South Fork	Bell Meadow	Tuolumne Co Irrig Dist	power	in study	wilderness area
Tuolumne, South Fork	South Fork Project	Modesto and Turlock Irrig Districts, San Francisco	power	prelim FERC permit issued	site is just outside Yosemite National Park
Yuba	Marysville Dam	ACE	multipurpose	inactive	
Yuba, South Fork	Miners Tunnel Project	private developer	power	prelim FERC permit issued	state park would be affected
COLORADO					
Animas	Animas–La Plata	BR	irrig, ws	awaiting const funds	scenic mountain river
Cache La Poudre	Grey Mt dams	cities of Fort Collins & Greeley	power, ws, irrig	in planning	national study river, bill introduced for nwsrs
Colorado	Una Dam	private developers	power	in study	
Dolores	McPhee Dam	BR	irrig	res being filled	see Endangered Rivers

River	Dam	Developer	Purpose	Status	Notes
Elk River	Hinman Park Dam	Colorado Public Service Co	ws for coal	in study	study river for nwsrs
Gunnison	2 dams	Colorado-Ute Power Co	power	prelim FERC permit issued	
Gunnison	Cedar Flats Dam	coal companies	ws for coal mining	inactive	
Gunnison	Dominguez Dam	BR	ws for energy development, irrig	in planning	desert canyon
Gunnison	South Fork Dam	City of Delta	ws for energy development	deferred	study river for nwsrs
Little Snake	Savery–Pot Hook	BR	irrig	auth, awaiting funding	was on President Carter's hit list
Piney River, Eagle Cr, Gore Cr	west-slope diversions	Denver Water Board	ws	water rights bought	see Endangered Rivers
Platte, South Fork	Foothills Dam	Denver Water Board	ws	const planned	see Endangered Rivers
Platte, South Fork	Narrows Dam	BR	irrig	deferred	see Chapter 8
Platte, South Fork	Two Forks Dam	BR	irrig, ws	deferred	scenic river near Denver
San Miguel	Saltado Dam	BR	irrig	auth, deferred	scenic foothills river elk habitat, was on Carter's hit list
Soap Cr	Fruitland Mesa	BR	irrig	deferred	was on Carter's hit list
Uncompahgre	Ridgway Dam, Dallas Cr Proj	BR	irrig	const planned	was on Carter's hit list

RIVER	PROJECT	PROJECT SPONSOR	PROJECT PURPOSE	STATUS	NOTES
Yampa	Cross Mountain Dam, Juniper Dam	Colorado River Water Conservation Dist, Colorado-Ute Electric Assn	power	FERC license pending	last large Colorado River tributary that remains free flowing
CONNECTICUT					
Farmington, West Branch	Farmington Dam	Hartford Metropolitan Dist Commission	ws	deferred	defeated in local referendum
FLORIDA					
Apalachicola	channel, Blountstown Dam	ACE	nav	channel auth, deferred	wildlife, commercial fishery
Oklawaha	Cross Florida Barge Canal	ACE	nav	auth, inactive	see Chapter 5
GEORGIA					
Flint	Spewrell Bluff Dam	ACE	multipurpose	auth, inactive	see Chapter 5
Savannah	Russell Dam	ACE	power, multipurpose	const completed	see Chapter 7
IDAHO					
Challis Cr	Challis Cr Dam	BR	irrig	inactive, listed as proposed in 1970	

River	Project	Developer	Purpose	Status	Comments
Henrys Fork of the Snake	3 dams	private developers	power	prelim FERC permits issued	would dam or divert Upper and Lower Mesa Falls, Malad Gorge
Payette, Middle Fork & South Fork	Garden Valley Dam	BR	irrig	deferred, listed as auth or proposed in 1970	scenic ranching valley
Payette, North Fork	North Fork dams	Idaho Power Co	power	deferred until 1991	Class V rapids spectacular canyon, in 1980 Idaho Power Co was denied a rate increase needed to build the dams
Payette, South Fork	South Fork dams	Idaho Power Co	power	inactive	
Snake	Asotin Dam	power companies	power	in study	just below Hells Canyon, study river for the nwsrs
Snake	Swan Falls Dam	BR	irrig	deferred, listed as auth or proposed in 1970	wildlife
Snake	Wiley & Dike dams	Idaho Power Co	power	PUC authority granted, FERC permit denied	impacts on sturgeon
Teton	Teton Dam	BR	multipurpose	reconst in study	see Chapter 5
ILLINOIS Sangamon	Oakley Dam	ACE	multipurpose	auth, inactive	see Chapter 5

RIVER	PROJECT	PROJECT SPONSOR	PROJECT PURPOSE	STATUS	NOTES
INDIANA					
Big Walnut Cr	Big Walnut Dam	ACE	rec, fl con	auth, inactive	unique vegetation
Flatrock	Downeyville Lake	ACE	rec, fl con	auth, inactive	
Wabash	Wabash Canal	ACE	nav	in study	
Wildcat Cr	Lafayette Dam	ACE	rec, fl con	auth, inactive	see Endangered Rivers
KANSAS					
Soldier Cr	Grove Dam	ACE	multipurpose	auth	farmland
KENTUCKY					
Blaine Cr	Yatesville Dam	ACE	rec	const planned	massive natural stone arch
Cumberland	Celina Dam	ACE	multipurpose	inactive	
Licking	Falmouth Dam	ACE	multipurpose	in planning	farmland, small town
LOUISIANA					
Atchafalaya	channel	ACE	fl con	alternative proposed but not funded	see Endangered Rivers
Red	channel	ACE	nav	under const	wetlands and wildlife
MAINE					
Kennebec	Kennebec Gorge Dam	Central Maine Power Co	power	deferred	wild gorge and whitewater

River	Dam	Agency	Purpose	Status	Values
Penobscot, West Branch	Big Ambejackmockamas Dam	Great Northern Paper Co	power	FERC license pending	see Endangered Rivers
MARYLAND St. Mary's	St. Mary's Dam	Soil Conservation Service	rec	const delayed by lawsuit	wetlands, wildlife
MINNESOTA Kettle	Kettle River Dam	utilities	power	in planning	scenic river, canoeing and fishing
Red Lake River	Crookston Dam	ACE	multipurpose	proposed	2,000 acres of wildlife habitat
Roseau	channel	ACE	fl con, drainage	deferred	national wildlife refuge
Wild Rice	Twin Valley Lake	ACE	rec	deferred	wildlife habitat
MONTANA Big Hole	Reichle Dam	BR	irrig	deferred, listed as auth or proposed in 1970	excellent trout fishery, ranches
Blackfoot	McNamara's Landing, Ninemile Prairie dams	ACE	power	inactive	scenic river, local protection programs
Clark Fork	Quartz Cr Dam	ACE	power	deferred	large undeveloped river
Flathead	Buffalo Rapids #2 Dam, other sites	ACE and Confederated Salish and Kootenai Tribes	power	in study	rapids, wildlife, Indian reservation

RIVER	PROJECT	PROJECT SPONSOR	PROJECT PURPOSE	STATUS	NOTES
Kootenai	Kootenai Falls Dam	Northern Lights Power Co	power	prelim FERC permit issued	see Endangered Rivers
Kootenai	Libby Reregulation Dam	ACE	power	awaiting const funds	trout fishery, wildlife
Yellowstone	Allenspur Dam	BR	ws for coal	deferred	see Endangered Rivers
NEBRASKA					
Calamus	Calamus Dam	BR	irrig	listed as auth or proposed in 1970	
Niobrara	Norden Dam	BR	irrig	in study	see Endangered Rivers
Platte	Nebraska Midstate	BR	irrig	auth	migratory bird site
NEW HAMPSHIRE					
Androscoggin	Pentock Dam diversion	private	power	FERC license pending	85% would be diverted from a canoeing and fishing reach
Connecticut	Sumner Falls Dam	town of Windsor, Vt.	power	FERC license pending	kayaking reach
Pemigewasset	Livermore Falls Dam	private	power	FERC permit being appealed	one of three rivers on East Coast selected for salmon restoration

State / River	Project	Developer	Purpose	Status	Comments
NEW MEXICO					
Gila	Hooker Dam	BR	irrig	auth, alternatives being studied	nation's first designated wilderness area
Pecos	Los Esteros Dam	ACE	multipurpose	under const	
NEW YORK					
Black	Hawkinsville Dam	Black River Regulating Dist	power	in planning	600 families would have to relocate, good fishery
	Lower Black River Dam	Brownsville Paper Co.	power	in planning	canyon, rafting reach
Moose	Moose River diversion	Long Lake Energy Corp	power	prelim FERC permit issued	would dewater scenic and recreation reach
St. Lawrence	winter navigation	ACE	nav	waiting auth	would open seaway in winter, require dredging
NORTH CAROLINA					
Neuce	Falls Dam	city of Raleigh	ws	const completed	undeveloped river near city
NORTH DAKOTA					
James River, Red River of the North, others	Garrison Diversion	BR	irrig	const underway, parts delayed	see Chapter 7

RIVER	PROJECT	PROJECT SPONSOR	PROJECT PURPOSE	STATUS	NOTES
OHIO					
Clear Cr	Clear Cr Dam	ACE	fl con	in planning	undeveloped valley
OREGON					
Calapooia	Callapooia Dam	ACE	multipurpose	inactive	small scenic river
Elk Creek	Elk Cr Dam	ACE	fl con, rec	auth	see Chapter 7, may cause turbidity in Rogue River
Grande Ronde	Grande Ronde Dam	Boise-Cascade Corp	power	prelim FERC permit issued	fishing, rafting, ranches
Klamath	Salt Caves Dam	city of Klamath Falls	power	in planning	scenic river, state park
Santiam, South Fork	Cascadia Dam	ACE	fl con	auth, inactive	
Umpqua, South Fork	Days Dam	ACE	fl con, irrig	auth, inactive	150 families would be moved, salmon & steelhead
Wallawa	Wallawa River Dam	Boise-Cascade Corp	power	prelim FERC permit issued	scenic river
PENNSYLVANIA					
Clarion	St. Petersburg Dam	ACE	power, multipurpose	inactive	part of Cook Forest State Park
Delaware	Tocks Island Dam	ACE	rec, ws, multipurpose	auth, inactive	see Chapter 5

Susquehanna, West Branch	Keating Dam	ACE	multipurpose	unauth, inactive	one of the wildest gorges in state
SOUTH CAROLINA					
Saluda	Saluda Dam	SC Electric & Gas Co	power	prelim FERC permit issued, but proj found uneconomical	historic sites, urban recreation
TENNESSEE					
Duck	Columbia Dam	TVA	multipurpose	awaiting const funds	see Endangered Rivers
Ocoee	Ocoee No. 2 Flume	TVA	power	const completed	see Endangered Rivers
TEXAS					
Big Sandy	Big Sandy Dam	BR	ws	in study	small plains river
Navasota	Navasota Dam	ACE	multipurpose	auth	
Sulphur	Cooper Dam	ACE	fl con, ws	auth, delayed	
Trinity	Trinity River Canal, Wallisville Dam, Tennessee Colony Dam, Lakeview Dam	ACE	power	const deferred	

RIVER	PROJECT	PROJECT SPONSOR	PROJECT PURPOSE	STATUS	NOTES
UTAH					
Strawberry, Whiterocks, Rock Cr, others	Central Utah Proj	BR	irrig, ws	auth, awaiting const funds	see Chapter 7, appendix
White	Hells Hole Canyon Dam	oil shale companies	ws for oil shale	in study	canoeing
VERMONT					
West	Ball Mountain Diversion	towns in West River basin	power	prelim FERC permit issued	whitewater and fishing stream to be dewatered
VIRGINIA					
Back Creek	Bath Dam	Virginia Electric & Power Co	power	prelim FERC permit issued, proj deferred	scenic stream
Calfpasture	Marble Valley Dam	Virginia Electric & Power Co	power	FERC license withdrawn	scenic stream
Cowpasture	Griffith Dam	ACE	multipurpose	unauth, inactive	scenic, canoeing
Craig Cr	Hipes Dam	ACE	multipurpose	unauth, inactive	scenic stream
Rappahannock	Salem Church Dam	ACE	multipurpose	inactive	farms, whitewater, historic sites

River	Dam	Developer	Purpose	Status	Comments
Staunton	Cub Cr Dam, in Randolph Proj totaling 11 dams	Southside Electric Power Cooperative	power	prelim FERC permit issued, state legislation passed against project	homes, farms, historic buildings, fishery
WASHINGTON					
Columbia	Ben Franklin Dam	ACE	nav, power	inactive	50 miles, last reach of free-flowing Columbia
Skagit	Cooper Cr Dam	Seattle City Light	power	prelim FERC permit issued, proj deferred	last Skagit whitewater, salmon habitat
Skagit & Big Beaver Creek	High Ross Dam	Seattle City Light	power	FERC license issued but proj deferred	wilderness, virgin cedar, Canada objects
Snoqualmie, Middle Fork	Middle Fork Dam	ACE	fl con, multipurpose	inactive	proposal dropped in lieu of North Fork Dam
Snoqualmie North Fork	North Fork Dam	ACE, city of Bellevue	ws, fl con	in study	
Sultan	Sultan River diversion	Snohomish Power & Utility Dist	power	FERC permit pending	dewater 12 miles of river, Class V rapids
White Salmon	White Salmon Hydroelectric	Klickitat County Public Utility Dist	power	prelim FERC permit expired	see Endangered Rivers

RIVER	PROJECT	PROJECT SPONSOR	PROJECT PURPOSE	STATUS	NOTES
WEST VIRGINIA					
Blackwater	Davis Hydroelectric	Allegheny Power System	power	FERC license appealed	see Endangered Rivers
Cheat	Rowlesburg Dam	ACE	ws, multipurpose	inactive	farms, canoeing
Gauley	Gauley River diversion	ACE	power	in study	see Endangered Rivers
New	Bluestone Dam addition, Pipestem Cr Dam, Bull Falls Dam, others	ACE	power	inactive	proposals would flood New River or tributaries
West Fork	Stonewall Jackson Dam	ACE	multipurpose	auth, awaiting const funds	1,050 residents
WISCONSIN					
Kickapoo	LaFarge Dam	ACE	fl con	const started, now inactive	see Endangered Rivers
WYOMING					
Clarks Fork	Clarks Fork Dam	Shoshone–Heart Mountain Irrig Dist	irrig	in study	recommended for nwsrs, one of most spectacular wilderness canyons in America

| Green | Kendall Dam | BR | irrig | inactive | scenic Rocky Mountain river, Kendall Warm Springs, endangered fish |
| Laramie | Grayrocks Dam | Missouri Basin Electric Power Cooperative | ws for power plant | in study | whooping crane sites on North Fork Platte River endangered |

The National Wild and Scenic Rivers System

The following list includes all rivers and tributaries in the national wild and scenic rivers system as of 1985. The names of tributaries are followed by the names of the major wild and scenic river in parentheses. Many of the rivers are administered by federal agencies, including the National Park Service (NPS), the Forest Service (FS), the Bureau of Land Management (BLM), and the Fish and Wildlife Service (FWS); some are administered by state resource agencies.

Several other rivers, including the Current, Jacks Fork, Buffalo, and New River Gorge, have been designated "national rivers" and are not a part of the national wild and scenic rivers system.

RIVER	STATE	MILEAGE	ADMINISTRATION
Alagnak	Alaska	56	NPS
Alatna	Alaska	83	NPS
Albert Johnson Creek (Aniakchak)	Alaska	9	NPS
Allagash	Maine	95	Maine
American	Calif.	23	Calif.
American, North Fork	Calif.	38	BLM, FS
Aniakchak	Alaska	33	NPS
Aniakchak	Alaska	14	NPS
Andreafsky	Alaska	125	FWS
Andreafsky, East Fork	Alaska	137	FWS
Au Sable	Mich.	23	FS
Beaver Creek	Alaska	135	BLM
Birch Creek	Alaska	130	BLM
Bonanza Creek (Charley)	Alaska	11	NPS

RIVER	STATE	MILEAGE	ADMINISTRATION
Cascade (Skagit)	Wash.	21	FS
Cascade, South Fork (Skagit)	Wash.	1	FS
Chilikodrotna	Alaska	12	NPS
Champion Creek (Forty-Mile)	Alaska	29	BLM
Charley	Alaska	104	NPS
Charley (unnamed tributary)	Alaska	22	NPS
Chattooga	N.C., S.C., Ga.	50	FS
Chattooga, West Fork	Ga.	7	FS
Clear Creek (Obed)	Tenn.	18	NPS
Clearwater, Middle Fork	Idaho	22	FS
Copper Creek (Charley)	Alaska	28	NPS
Crescent Creek (Charley)	Alaska	31	NPS
Daddys Creek (Obed)	Tenn.	2	NPS
Delaware	Pa, N.Y., N.J.	110	NPS
Delta	Alaska	59	BLM
Derwent Creek (Charley)	Alaska	17	NPS
Eel	Calif.	157	Calif.
Eel, North Fork	Calif.	34	Calif.
Eel, Middle Fork	Calif.	54	Calif.
Eel, South Fork	Calif.	101	Calif.
Eleven Point	Mo.	44	FS
Emory (Obed)	Tenn.	1	NPS
Feather, Middle Fork	Calif.	93	FS
Flat-Orthmer Creek (Charley)	Alaska	20	NPS
Flathead, North Fork	Mont.	58	NPS, FS
Flathead, Middle Fork	Mont.	101	NPS, FS
Flathead, South Fork	Mont.	60	FS
Forty-Mile	Alaska	40	BLM
Forty-Mile, Dennison Fork	Alaska	19	BLM
Forty-Mile, Dennison Fork, West Fork	Alaska	13	BLM
Forty-Mile, Middle Fork	Alaska	42	BLM
Forty-Mile, North Fork	Alaska	58	BLM
Forty-Mile, South Fork	Alaska	28	BLM
Forty-Mile, Mosquete Fork	Alaska	38	BLM
Forty-Mile, Walker Fork	Alaska	12	BLM

RIVER	STATE	MILEAGE	ADMINISTRATION
Franklin Creek (Forty-Mile)	Alaska	6	BLM
Gulkana	Alaska	46	BLM
Gulkana, Middle Fork	Alaska	27	BLM
Gulkana, West Fork	Alaska	79	BLM
Hidden Creek (Aniakchak)	Alaska	7	NPS
Hosford Creek (Charley)	Alaska	14	NPS
Hutchison Creek (Forty-Mile)	Alaska	19	BLM
Illinois	Oreg.	50	FS
Ivishak	Alaska	80	FWS
John	Alaska	52	NPS
Joseph Creek (Forty-Mile)	Alaska	23	BLM
Klamath	Calif.	190	Calif.
Kobuk	Alaska	110	NPS
Koyukuk, North Fork	Alaska	102	NPS
Little Beaver	Ohio	33	Ohio
Little Miami	Ohio	94	Ohio
Lochsa (Clearwater, Middle Fork)	Idaho	69	FS
Logging Cabin Creek (Forty-Mile)	Alaska	17	BLM
Loxahatchee	Fla.	7.5	Fla.
Missouri	Mont., Nebr., S.Dak.	149(Mont.) 59(Nebr., S.Dak.)	BLM, NPS
Morane Creek (Charley)	Alaska	4	NPS
Mystery Creek (Aniakchak)	Alaska	6	NPS
Mulchatna	Alaska	24	NPS
Namekagon (Saint Croix)	Wis.	97	NPS
New (Trinity)	Calif.	21	Calif.
New	N.C.	26	NPS
Noatak	Alaska	330	NPS
Nonvianuk (Alagnak)	Alaska	11	NPS
Napoleon Creek (Forty-Mile)	Alaska	7	BLM
Nowitna	Alaska	225	FWS
Obed	Tenn.	24	NPS
O'Brien Creek (Forty-Mile)	Alaska	27	BLM
Owyhee	Oreg.	112	BLM
Pere Marquette	Mich.	66	FS
Rapid	Idaho	24	FS
Red (Rio Grande)	N.Mex.	4	BLM

RIVER	STATE	MILEAGE	ADMINISTRATION
Rio Grande	N.Mex., Tex.	49(N.Mex.) 191(Tex.)	BLM, NPS
Rogue	Oreg.	84	BLM, FS
Saint Croix	Wis., Minn.	155	NPS, Wis., Minn.
Saint Joe	Idaho	73	FS
Salmon	Alaska	70	NPS
Salmon (Klamath)	Calif.	20	Calif.
Salmon, North Fork (Klamath)	Calif.	26	Calif.
Salmon	Idaho	125	FS
Salmon, Middle Fork	Idaho	104	FS
Sauk (Skagit)	Wash.	43	FS
Sauk, North Fork (Skagit)	Wash.	8	FS
Scott (Klamath)	Calif.	24	Calif.
Selway (Clearwater, Middle Fork)	Idaho	94	FS
Selawik	Alaska	160	FWS
Sheenjek	Alaska	160	FWS
Skagit	Wash.	58	FS
Smith	Calif.	16	Calif.
Smith, South Siskiyou Fork	Calif.	5	Calif.
Smith, Middle Fork	Calif.	32	Calif.
Smith, South Fork	Calif.	38	Calif.
Smith, North Fork	Calif.	13	Calif.
Smith, Siskiyou Fork	Calif.	8	Calif.
Smith (38 smaller tributaries*)	Calif.	217	Calif.
Snake	Idaho and Oreg.	67	FS
Suiattle (Skagit)	Wash.	27	FS
Tinayguk	Alaska	44	NPS
Tlikakila	Alaska	51	NPS
Trinity	Calif.	111	Calif.

* Also included are the following thirty-eight smaller tributaries in the Smith River system: Bear Creek, Buck Creek, Bummer Lake Creek, Canthook Creek, Coon Creek, Craigs Creek, Diamond Creek, North Fork Diamond Creek, Dominie Creek, Eight Mile Creek, Goose Creek, East Fork Goose Creek, Gordon Creek, Griffin Creek, High Plateau Creek, Hurdy-Gurdy Creek, Jones Creek, Kelly Creek, Knopki Creek, Little Mill Creek, Mill Creek, East Fork Mill Creek, Lower West Branch Mill Creek, Monkey Creek, Muzzleloader Creek, Myrtle Creek, Packsaddle Creek, Patrick Creek, East Fork Patrick Creek, West Fork Patrick Creek, Quartz Creek, Rock Creek, Rowdy Creek, Savoy Creek, Shelly Creek, Prescott Fork Smith River, Still Creek, and Williams Creek.

RIVER	STATE	MILEAGE	ADMINISTRATION
Trinity, Middle Fork	Calif.	15	Calif.
Trinity, South Fork	Calif.	56	Calif.
Tuolumne	Calif.	83	FS
Uhler Creek (Forty-Mile)	Alaska	8	BLM
Unalukleet	Alaska	66	BLM
Van Duzen (Eel)	Calif.	48	Calif.
Verde	Ariz.	39	FS
Wade Creek (Forty-Mile)	Alaska	10	BLM
Wind	Alaska	140	FWS
Wolf	Wis.	25	NPS
Wooley Creek (Klamath)	Calif.	8	Calif.
		7,223	

Organizations Involved in River Protection

The following is a selected list. Dozens of state and local groups are organized for river protection. The American Rivers Conservation Council is the best source for current addresses for these groups.

American Rivers Conservation Council
801 Pennsylvania Ave. SE
Washington, D.C. 20003

Environmental Policy Institute
218 D Street SE
Washington, D.C. 20003

Sierra Club
730 Polk Street
San Francisco, Calif. 94109

Trout Unlimited
501 Church Street NE
Vienna, Va. 22180

National Organization for River Sports
Box 6847, 314 N. 20th Street
Colorado Springs, Colo. 80904

National Wildlife Federation
1412 16th Street NW
Washington, D.C. 20036

The Wilderness Society
1901 Pennsylvania Ave. NW
Washington, D.C. 20006

Friends of the River
Building C, Fort Mason Center
San Francisco, Calif. 94123
   (for California and the Southwest)

New England Rivers Center
3 Joy Street
Boston, Mass. 02108
   (for New England)

Index

291